Patterns of Reflection

A Reader

Sixth Edition

Dorothy U. Seyler

Northern Virginia Community College

PEARSON
Longman

New York San Francisco Boston
London Toronto Sydney Tokyo Singapore Madrid
Mexico City Munich Paris Cape Town Hong Kong Montreal

Senior Sponsoring Editor: Virginia L. Blanford
Executive Marketing Manager: Megan Galvin-Fak
Production Manager: Denise Phillip
Project Coordination, Text Design, and Electronic Page Makeup: Electronic
    Publishing Services Inc., NYC
Cover Designer/Manager: Wendy Ann Fredericks
Cover Art: Harrison, Lowell Birge (1854–1929), Moonlight over the River.
    Musee d'Orsay, Paris, France. Photo by Gerard Blot. Réunion des Musées
    Nationaux/Art Resource, NY
Manufacturing Buyer: Roy Pickering
Printer and Binder: R.R. Donnelley & Sons
Cover Printer: Phoenix Color Corporation

Library of Congress Cataloging-in-Publication Data

Patterns of reflection : a reader / [compiled by] Dorothy U. Seyler.-- 6th ed.
    p. cm.
  Includes bibliographical references and index.
  ISBN 0-321-35563-6
  1. College readers. 2. English language--Rhetoric--Problems, exercises, etc.
  3. Report writing--Problems, exercises, etc. I. Seyler, Dorothy U.
  PE1417.P396 2007
  808'.0427--dc22

                                    2005032677

Please visit us at www.ablongman.com

ISBN 0-321-35563-6

1 2 3 4 5 6 7 8 9 10—DOH—09 08 07 06

It is not enough to have a good mind.
The main thing is to use it well.

René Descartes

I like to find
What's not found
at once, but lies
within something of another nature
in repose, distinct.

Denise Levertov

Contents

Preface   **xiii**

1. On Reading and Writing   1

The Challenges and Rewards of Writing   1
Good Reasons for Reading   2
Guidelines for Active Reading   4
Guided Reading: *Ellen Goodman*, "Learning
    to Brake for Butterflies"   8
Writing Focus: Using Summary, Analysis,
    and Synthesis   11
Getting Started   16
Richard Wilbur, "The Writer"   16
Gail Godwin, "The Watcher at the Gates"   18
Terry McMillan, "On Reading and Becoming
    a Writer"   22
Kurt Vonnegut, "How to Write with Style"   28
Gretel Ehrlich, "Santa Rosa Island, 1998"
    (Journal)   33
Communicating with Instructors and Peers: In
    Person and Online   38
Making Connections   39
Topics for Writing   40

2. Using Narration: Growing Up, Growing Wiser   42

When to Use Narration   42
How to Use Narration   43

Writing Focus: Preparing Your Essay
for Readers 44
Getting Started: Reflections on
Growing Up or Growing Wiser 45
Santha Rama Rau, "By Any Other Name" 46
N. Scott Momaday, "The End of My Childhood" 53
Luis J. Rodriguez, "Always Running" 56
Gaye Wagner, "Death of an Officer" 60
Barbara Kingsolver, "How Mr. Dewey Decimal
Saved My Life" 68
Meredith F. Small, "Captivated" 72
Making Connections 76
Topics for Writing 77
A Checklist for Narration Essays 79

3. Using Description: Reflecting on People and Places 80

When to Use Description 80
How to Use Descriptive Details 81
Writing Focus: It's All About Words 83
Getting Started: Reflections on a Painting 84
Francisco de Goya y Lucientes, *The Third of May,
1808;* Edgar Degas, *The Dance Class;* Vincent Van
Gogh, *The Night Café;* Pablo Picasso, *Three
Dancers;* Salvador Dali, *The Persistence of
Memory,* Georgia O'Keeffe, *Jack-in-the-Pulpit*
Tracy Kidder, "Mrs. Zajac" 84
Amy Tan, "Lost Lives of Women" 89
Pat Mora, "Remembering Lobo" 93
Diane Ackerman, "Let It Snow!" 98
Lance Morrow, "Africa" 102
Jonathan Schell, "Ground Zero" 109
Student Essay—Description: Alexa Skandar,
"Time's Trophy" 113

Making Connections 116
Topics for Writing 117
A Checklist for Description Essays 119

4. **Using Comparison and Contrast:
   Ways of Learning** **121**

When to Use Comparison and Contrast 121
How to Use Comparison and Contrast 122
Writing Focus: Coherence Is Crucial 124
Getting Started: Reflecting on Expectations
   of College 125
Nancy Masterson Sakamoto, "Conversational
   Ballgames" 126
E. B. White, "Education" 131
Brent Staples, "What Adolescents Miss When We
   Let Them Grow Up in Cyberspace" 135
Judith Viorst, "Boys and Girls: Anatomy
   and Destiny" 139
Amanda Ripley, "Who Says a Woman Can't Be
   Einstein" 146
Colbert I. King, "Surveying the Damage on
   Campus USA" 154
Linda Pastan, "Marks" 157
Student Essay—Contrast: Denisse M. Bonilla,
   "The Faded Stain" 159
Making Connections 164
Topics for Writing 165
A Checklist for Comparison and
   Contrast Essays 166

5. **Explaining and Illustrating:
   Examining Media Images** **168**

When to Use Examples 168

How to Use Examples   169
Writing Focus: Vary Your Sentences   170
Getting Started: Thinking About
   Advertising   172
Four Ads: Fila, Got Milk?, Council for
   Biotechnology Information, Expedia.com   173
Jack McGarvey, "To Be or Not to Be as Defined
   by TV"   177
Gloria Steinem, "Sex, Lies, and Advertising"   185
Stephanie Mencimer, "Violent Femmes"   191
Vincent P. Bzdek, "More Powerful Than . . . Ever:
   On-Screen and Off, Superheroes Are a Force
   to Reckon With"   199
Suzanne Fields, "Bad Raps: Music Rebels
   Revel in Their Thug Life"   207
Dave Barry, "Call Hating"   211
Student Essay—Using Examples: Michael King,
   "Rap's Refusal of Injustice"   214
Making Connections   219
Topics for Writing   220
A Checklist for Essays Using Examples 222

6.   Using Process Analysis: How We Work and Play   224

When to Use Process Analysis   224
How to Use Process Analysis   225
Writing Focus: Punctuating Properly   226
Getting Started: Reflections on Your
   Favorite Game   228
John P. Aigner, "Putting Your Job Interview
   into Rehearsal"   228
Suzette H. Elgin, "Improving Your Body
   Language Skills"   234
Caroline Hwang, "How to Turn No Into Yes!"   244
Gail Saltz, "How to Get Unstuck Now!"   250

Carol Krucoff, "Restoring Recess" 255
Ernest Hemingway, "Camping Out" 259
Making Connections 264
Topics for Writing 265
A Checklist for Process Essays 267

7. Using Division and Classification: Examining Human Connections— and Misconnections   268

When to Use Division and Classification 268
How to Use Division and Classification 269
Writing Focus: Words to Live Without! 271
Getting Started: Classifying Recent Reading
    or Viewing 272
Russell Baker, "The Plot Against People" 272
Judith Martin, "The Roles of Manners" 275
Franklin E. Zimring, "Hot Boxes for
    Ex-Smokers" 282
Curt Suplee, "The Science and Secrets
    of Personal Space" 287
Stephanie Ericsson, "The Ways We Lie" 293
Ralph Whitehead, Jr., "Class Acts: America's
    Changing Middle Class" 303
Student Essay—Division and Classification:
    Garrett Berger, "Buying Time" 310
Making Connections 317
Topics for Writing 318
A Checklist for Division and Classification
    Essays 320

8. Using Definition: Understanding Ideas and Values   322

When to Use Definition 322
How to Develop an Extended Definition 323

Writing Focus: Using Metaphors, Avoiding
  Clichés   324
Getting Started: Reflections on E. B. White's
  Ideas of Democracy   325
Margaret Mead and Rhoda Metraux,
  "On Friendship"   326
John Ciardi, "Is Everybody Happy?"   332
Robert Keith Miller, "Discrimination
  Is a Virtue"   337
William Lutz, "Doubts About Doublespeak"   341
Andrew Vachss, "The Difference Between 'Sick'
  and 'Evil'"   347
David Hackett Fischer, "Freedom's Not Just
  Another Word"   353
Alastair Reid, "Curiosity"   358
Student Essay—Definition: Laura Mullins,
  "Paragon or Parasite?"   361
Making Connections   365
Topics for Writing   366
A Checklist for Definition Essays   367

9. Using Causal Analysis: Examining Family and Community Issues   369

When to Use Causal Analysis   369
How to Use Causal Analysis   370
Writing Focus: References to Authors, Works,
  and the Words of Others   372
Getting Started: Reflections on Why You Are
  in College   374
Amitai Etzioni, "Duty: The Forgotten Virtue"   374
Keith Ablow, "When Parents Are Toxic to
  Children"   380
Linda J. Waite, "Social Science Finds: 'Marriage
  Matters'"   386

Judith D. Auerbach, "The Overlooked Victims of
AIDS"   397
Stephanie Coontz, "Not Much Sense in Those
Census Stories"   400
David Ropeik, "What Really Scares Us?"   406
Langston Hughes, "Dream Deferred"   411
Making Connections   412
Topics for Writing   413
A Checklist for Causal Analysis Essays   414

10.   Using Argument and Persuasion: Preserving a Safe and Sane World   **416**

The Characteristics of Argument   416
How to Use Argument and Persuasion   418
Writing Focus: Logical Fallacies   420
Getting Started: Reflections on the
Challenges Facing Ourselves,
Our Society, Our World   423
Molly Ivins, "Ban the Things. Ban
Them All."   423
Ned Andrews, "Why Guns Matter"   427
Linda J. Collier, "Adult Crime,
Adult Time"   430
Richard Cohen, "Kids Who Kill Are Still
Kids"   436
John Borneman and Laurie Kain Hart, "An Elastic
Institution"   439
Michael Kinsley, "Abolish Marriage"   444
Andrew Sullivan, "The Case for Compromise on
Abortion"   448
Laura W. Murphy, "No Safer and Less Free"   451
Robert Kuttner, "Try National ID Card—You
Might Like It"   454

Student Essay—Refutation: David M. Ouellette,
"Blame It on the Media and Other Ways to
Dress a Wolf in Sheep's Clothing"   457
Making Connections   460
Topics for Writing   461
A Checklist for Argument Essays   463

11.   Works for Further Reading and Analysis   464

Elizabeth Cady Stanton, "Declaration of
Sentiments"   464
Kate Chopin, "The Story of an Hour"   467
Amy Lowell, "Taxi"   471
Richard Rodriguez, "Border Hazards: An
Obsession to Become Unhealthy"   472
Suzanne Britt, "Neat People vs. Sloppy
People"   475
Lisa Mundy, "A Date to Remember"   478

Glossary   483

Credits   489

Index   494

▇▇ Preface

What This Book Is About

Patterns of Reflection provides engaging selections on personal, social, and political concerns and issues, selections that also demonstrate varied uses of the major rhetorical strategies or patterns. The organizing of chapters by both rhetorical patterns and topics makes *Patterns of Reflection* a special text, both a practical guide to the various writing structures and purposes students will use in their college writing and a study of themes generating lively class discussions and personal reflections.

Patterns of Reflection asks students in its opening chapter to think about the challenges and rewards of reading and writing, both in an honest and helpful introduction and in four essays on issues such as writing anxiety, journal writing, and style. Each of the subsequent chapters illustrates one specific pattern or purpose, beginning with those strategies students are most comfortable with and then progressing to the more demanding ones: narration, description, comparison and contrast, explaining and illustrating, process analysis, division and classification, definition, causal analysis, and, finally, argument and persuasion. At the same time, each chapter's thematic core allows students to begin by reflecting on what is closest to them—their childhood, the people and places they know, the learning process—and then move beyond their immediate lives to their society—the media, working and playing, interpersonal relations, values, and social issues—and then to reflect on how they want to live as individuals, as members of a group, and as part of an interdependent environment.

Within the two broad organizational patterns are diverse works appealing to readers of varied backgrounds and interests. Instructors can skip some chapters and order others to meet their needs; students will have their favorite selections at the same time that they can be reminded of how much we all share as individuals who must grow up, learn, and prepare for work. Each chapter gains further diversity by:

- Essays of varied length
- A mix of essays, op-ed columns, and excerpts from longer works
- The addition of a poem, short story, or visual
- The inclusion of six annotated student essays.

Patterns of Reflection is indeed a rich storehouse of opportunity.

Although the selections are important, this is not just an anthology. It is a text, providing many aids to learning. Each chapter begins with a clear explanation of the strategy that includes specific guidelines for writing. Then students are encouraged to "get started" by engaging in some reflecting and/or writing activity useful as a preparation for reading, as a class activity, or as a basis for journal writing. Following each reading are vocabulary exercises and questions that guide students from understanding to analyzing to responding to their reading. After all of the selections in each chapter comes "Making Connections," a section that helps students stretch their minds beyond one reading. These topics can be used for discussion, research, writing, or all three. Following "Making Connections" are topics for writing based on the chapter's readings and designed to provide practice in the chapter's rhetorical strategy. Finally, students will find a helpful checklist for writing that is a specific guide to each chapter's strategy.

What's New in the Sixth Edition

This sixth edition offers some changes and additions that both instructors and students will appreciate. They include:

- Twenty new readings out of the 72 total.

- The greatest number of new works in Chapter 10 on argument, to keep that chapter updated with current issues. Most chapters have at least two new readings.
- One new piece of art in the collection of six color reproductions in Chapter 3.
- One new advertisement in the collection of four in Chapter 5.
- A total of six annotated student essays, including the new one in Chapter 5, offering a response to one of the professional essays in that chapter.
- Two questions preceding each selection, one a reading prompt, the second now a guide to individual reflection on the selection's topic.
- In Chapter 1, new guidelines for communicating with peers and instructors.
- New questions on selections and *Making Connections* topics that encourage online searching for additional information, marked with an icon to indicate the online search.
- At the end of Chapters 2 through 10, a checklist for writing to help students prepare essays in each of the rhetorical strategies.

Acknowledgments

No book of value is written alone. I am happy to acknowledge the help of friends and colleagues in preparing this new edition. Once again I am indebted to my daughter Ruth for her always sound advice on selections. Thanks are also due, as always, to the library staff at the Annandale Campus of Northern Virginia Community College, especially to Marian Delmore and Ruth Stanton, for their help in solving my research problems.

I remain grateful to Scott Rubin, Barbara Heinssen, Tim Julet, and Eben Ludlow for their help with the early editions of *Patterns of Reflection*. I would not be writing the preface to the sixth edition if it were not for the continued support of senior vice president and publisher Joe Opiela and my new sponsoring editor, Virginia L. Blanford. I also appreciate the many fine suggestions of the following reviewers: Eric Anderson, University of Massachusetts Dartmouth; Cheryl Divine-Jonas, Columbia College; Ann Jordan, Winthrop University; Tamara Karn, Mt. San Antonio College; Terry-

Mathias, Southeastern Illinois College; and Karen Petit, Bristol Community College.

Finally, I want to give a special thank you to the students who gave me permission to use their essays. They were hardworking and thoughtful writers who should be proud of their achievements. I hope they will find the same joy that I have in reaching out to students all over the country.

DOROTHY U. SEYLER

On Reading and Writing

You have purchased your texts and are ready to begin another English course. What papers will be assigned, you wonder, perhaps somewhat nervously. And why has this text of readings been assigned? After all, writing is difficult enough; must you read, too? Let's give these questions some reflection, a good beginning for this course.

The Challenges and Rewards of Writing

Many people, of all ages, become nervous about writing; they experience what is called writing anxiety. Some are so anxious, as Gail Godwin observes in this chapter (see pp. 18–20), that they dream up all kinds of excuses to put off a writing task. If you have some anxiety about writing, you can take comfort in knowing that others share your nervousness, including professional writers who sometimes go through lengthy periods of writer's block. You can also take some comfort in recognizing the appropriateness of your feelings. When faced with a term of writing compositions, students can expect a degree of anxiety, because writing well is not easy.

Let's consider some realities of the writing process. First, writing is a skill, like dancing or riding a bike or playing tennis. You were not born knowing how to ride a bike. You had to learn, perhaps with some painful bumps and bruises to both bike and ego. To be a competent writer, you must develop your skills the same way tennis players develop a spin serve: good instruction, a strong desire to succeed, and practice, practice, practice. A second fact of writing is that some writers are more talented than others, just as Andre Agassi is a more talented tennis player than most. But Andre's ability did not come from a genie in a bottle. The best in any field make their abilities look "like magic." You need to remember, however, that they also spend years of study, self-discipline, and practice to achieve their excellence. This text cannot give you a great tennis game, but it can help you to become, with practice and commitment on your part, a competent writer.

Even for those willing to practice, learning to write well is not easy because writing is a complex skill. Topics to write about, audiences to write for, and reasons to write cannot be completely catalogued, and the ways of choosing and combining words into sentences are infinite in their variety. Still, you can, through instruction and practice in this course, develop some good strategies for planning, organizing, drafting, and revising your writing. In addition, this text will provide opportunities for thinking about issues important to all of us and worthy of exploring through writing.

If learning to write well is difficult, why bother to try to develop your skills? For a good answer to this question, ask any student over twenty-five why he or she is now in college. Many "older" students are training for a second career, but many more want to improve basic skills so that they can advance in their current careers. They will assure you, from their experience in the workplace, that all language skills are essential: reading, speaking, listening, and writing. More immediate and personal goals for writing well can also be noted:

- The more you develop your awareness of the writing process, the better a reader you will become. You will understand, from your own experience, how writers select and organize material to achieve their purpose.
- The more confident a writer you become, the more efficiently you will handle written assignments in your other college courses.
- Since writing is an act of discovery, the more you write, the more you will learn about who you are and what matters to you. After all, how accurately do you see your parents, your friends, your campus? Writing will sharpen your vision of the world around you and your understanding of the world inside you.

Good Reasons for Reading

Good writers make good readers. It is also true that reading well improves writing. The strong connection between reading and writing skills explains why students in reading courses are asked to write and students in writing courses are asked to read. Here are three specific uses of reading in a composition course.

Reading for Models

At times students are assigned readings to illustrate a type of writing: the personal essay, the book review, the scholarly report. Or, the readings may illustrate a strategy or purpose in writing: description, illustration, argument. Chapters 2 through 10 in this text contain readings grouped by a dominant writing pattern or purpose. If you are assigned Tracy Kidder's description of Mrs. Zajac and then asked to write a descriptive essay of someone you know, you have been asked to use Kidder's essay as a model for your assignment.

Readings can also be studied as models of effective writing. They can illustrate clever openings, the use of transitions, varied sentence patterns, and effective metaphors. Read, then, not just for what the work says but for what kind of writing it represents and for what writing techniques it illustrates. Questions on strategies and style following each reading will guide your study of the work's special merits. Remember: In the broadest sense, reading contributes to language development. You learned your first language by imitating the speech you heard around you. Imitate the readings in this text to improve your writing skills.

Reading for Information and Insight

You may also be asked to read for information: for facts, for new ideas, for startling analyses. Even when you are reading for models, you will have the chance to explore many subjects, some new to you. Reading, as syndicated columnist Robert Samuelson has observed, "allows you to explore new places, new ideas and new emotions." In this text when you read, you can travel with Lance Morrow to Africa, understand with Linda Waite the ways that marriage improves people's lives, and contemplate with John Ciardi the meaning of happiness. When preparing reading assignments, be sure to think about the questions asking for your reactions. Approach each reading assignment as an opportunity to grow in knowledge, understanding, and imagination.

Reading for Writing

One of the interesting effects of reading is that it produces writing, more works to read and react to in a never-ending chain reaction. A columnist writes about assault weapons. A reader responds with a letter to the editor opposing the banning of such guns. A student, to complete an argument assignment, writes a refutation of the letter. At times writing assignments in this course may call for a response to reading. You may be asked to summarize an essay, analyze a writer's use of details, or contrast writers' differing views on a subject. When writing about reading, you will need to show both skill in writing and understanding of the reading, a challenging task.

Guidelines for Active Reading

When first looking over library materials or texts for courses, you are wise to begin by skimming to see how the material is put together and what, in general, it is about. But, once you become engaged in a particular work that you need to know well, accuracy—not speed—is your goal. You can improve your reading skills by becoming an active, engaged reader who follows a clear reading strategy. A good reading strategy calls for the following preparation, reading, and responding steps.

Prepare

1. *Prepare to become a part of the writer's audience.* Not all writers write with each one of us in mind. Some writers prepare scholarly reports for other specialists. Some scholars, such as Linda Waite (see page 386), present the results of research to a more generally educated audience. Writers of the past wrote for readers in their time, readers who may be expected to know their times or other works with which you may be unfamiliar. So, prepare yourself to join the writer's audience by learning as much as you can about each of the following:

   - the writer
   - the time in which the work was written
   - the kind of work it is (a textbook chapter, a newspaper editorial, a personal narrative)
   - the writer's anticipated audience.

For writings in this book, you will be aided in this step by introductory notes. Be sure to study them. *Never start to read words on a page without first knowing what you are reading!*

2. *Prepare to read with an open mind.* Good readers seek new knowledge and ideas. They do not "rewrite" a work to suit themselves. Keep in mind that not all who write will share your views or express themselves as you do. Read what is on the page, giving the writer a fair chance to develop ideas, giving yourself the thoughtful reflection needed to understand those ideas. Remember: You are in a college course to learn, not to be entertained. So, stick to the task of reading with understanding, not complaining that you didn't "like" this work or that the assignment was "boring." If the reading is difficult for you, look up words or references you do not know and be prepared to read a second time to really learn the material.

3. *Prepare by prereading.* To be prepared to read with understanding, you need to skim the selection to see what kind of work you are about to read (#1 above), to get some idea of the author's subject, and to start thinking about what you already know on that topic. Follow these steps:

- Read all introductory or biographical notes.
- Consider the title. What clues in the title reveal the work's subject and perhaps the writer's approach to or attitude about that subject?
- Read the opening paragraph and then skim the rest of the work, noting in particular any subheadings and/or graphics.
- Ask yourself: "What do I already know about this subject?" and "What do I expect to learn—and what will I need to know—from reading this work?"
- From your prereading, raise two or three questions about the subject that you hope to find answers to by reading the work.

Read Actively

4. *Read with concentration.* Your goal is understanding, not completing an assignment as quickly as possible, so read as slowly as necessary to achieve comprehension. Maintain concentration. Avoid reading a page and then gazing out the window or getting a snack. You will have to go back to the beginning to really know what you have read if you keep

interrupting the reading process. Read an entire essay, story, poem, or chapter at one time.

5. *Use strategies for understanding words and references.* Reading a work containing words you do not know is like trying to play tennis with some of the strings missing from your racket. When you come to a word you do not know, begin by studying the sentence in which it appears. You may be able to guess the word's meaning from its context. If context clues do not help, study the parts that make up the word. Many words are combinations of words or word parts that appear in other words that you do know. For example, take the word *autobiography.* This is made up of *auto*, a root meaning "self" (*auto*mobile), *bio*, a root meaning "life" (*bio*logy), and *graph*, a root meaning "writing" (auto*graph*). You can understand many longer words if you think about their parts. Often these strategies will allow you to keep reading. But, be sure to look up words that you cannot figure out. You should also use a dictionary or encyclopedia to learn about writers an author refers to. Understanding references to people, places, and other written works is essential for full comprehension.

6. *Be alert to the use of figurative language and other writing strategies.* Figures of speech such as metaphors, irony, and understatement help shape a writer's tone and convey a writer's attitude toward his or her topic. Use the Glossary if necessary to check the definitions of these terms.

7. *Annotate or make notes as you read.* Studies have demonstrated that students who *annotate* (underline key passages and make notes in the margin) their texts get higher grades than those who do not annotate. So, to be a successful student, develop the habit of reading with pen in hand. As you read, underline key sentences such as each paragraph's topic sentence and the writer's thesis, if stated. When you look up a definition or reference, write what you learn in the margin so that you can reread that section with understanding. When you underline a writer's thesis, note in the margin that this is the main idea. When you see a series of examples or a list, label it as examples (exs) or list and then number each one in the

margin. If you read that there are *three* reasons for this or *four* ways of doing that, be sure to find all three or all four in the passage and label each one. Put a question mark next to a difficult passage—and then ask about it in class. Pay attention to transition words and phrases; these are designed to show you how the parts of the work fit together. Become engaged with the text, as illustrated by the sample annotation in Figure 1.

8. *As you read and annotate, think about the writer's primary purpose in writing and the structures or strategies being used.* Keep in mind the strategies examined in Chapters 2 through 10 and identify the primary strategy that gives the work its structure and/or purpose. Consider, as well, if the writer's

---

Johnson?
Descartes?

"I write, therefore I am," wrote Samuel Johnson, altering Descartes' famous dictum: "I think, therefore I am."   1

Thesis—
advan-
tages
of journal
writing

When writing in my journal, I feel keenly alive and somehow get a glimpse of what Johnson meant.   2

My journal is a storehouse, a treasury for everything in my daily life: the stories I hear, the people I meet, the quotations I like, and even the subtle signs and symbols I encounter that speak to me indirectly. Unless I capture these things in writing, I lose them.   3   ①

All writers are such collectors, whether they keep a journal or not; they see life clearly, a vision we only recognize when reading their books. Thoreau exemplifies the best in journal writing— his celebrated *Walden* grew out of his journal entries.   4

Thoreau—
example
of journal
writer

By writing in my own journal, I often make discoveries. I see connections and conclusions that otherwise would not appear obvious to me. I become a craftsman, like a potter or a carpenter who makes a vase or a wooden stoop out of parts. Writing is a source of pleasure when it involves such invention and creation.   5   ②

interesting
simile

meaning?

I want to work on my writing, too, hone it into clear, readable prose, and where better to practice my writing than in my journal. Writing, I'm told, is a skill and improves with practice. I secretly harbor this hope. So my journal becomes the arena where I do battle with the written word.   6   ③

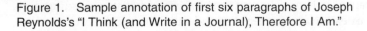

Figure 1.   Sample annotation of first six paragraphs of Joseph Reynolds's "I Think (and Write in a Journal), Therefore I Am."

primary purpose is to share feelings and experiences, to inform readers, or to argue for a claim. However, also keep in mind that writers can—and usually do—mix strategies and may have more than one purpose. For example, a writer using a contrast pattern can develop the points of contrast by providing examples.

9. *Keep a reading journal.* You may want to develop the habit of writing regularly in a journal. A reading journal records your responses to reading assignments but is more informal and personal than class notes. Keeping a journal gives you the chance to list impressions and feelings in addition to ideas that you may use in your next paper. Develop the habit of writing regularly and often. Chances are that both your reading and writing skills will improve.

Respond

10. *Review your reading.* To aid memory, review your reading immediately and then periodically. After finishing an assignment in this text, you can review by answering the questions following each selection. Then, look over your annotations and your reading journal shortly before class discussion of the assigned selection. *Warning: When you are called on, the instructor does not want to hear that you read the selection but cannot remember enough to answer the question!*

11. *Reflect.* In addition to reviewing to check comprehension, reflect on your reading and connect it to other parts of the course and other parts of your life. Remember that reading is not "drill." It is one of the most important ways that we gain new knowledge and new insights into ourselves and our world.

Guided Reading

Read the following article (published August 27, 1994), practicing all the guidelines for active reading. Remember to prepare, to read actively, and then to respond to your reading. Use the questions to the right of the article to guide your reading and thinking. Add your own annotations as well.

Learning to Brake for Butterflies

ELLEN GOODMAN

Ellen Goodman has been a syndicated columnist since 1976. Her columns have appeared in over 250 newspapers, and she has won a Pulitzer Prize for distinguished commentary. Although Goodman has written many thoughtful columns during her career, among her most memorable are those written from her summer home in Maine, reminding us of our need to slow down and reconnect to the natural world.

Casco Bay, Maine—I arrive here coasting on the fumes of high-octane anxiety. The split-second timing of my daily life has adhered to my mood like a watch strapped to a wrist. 1

1. Where has the author gone? What has she tried to accomplish? Has she succeeded?

Behind me is a deadline met by the skin of my teeth. A plane was late. A gas tank was empty. A boat was missed. 2

The carry-on baggage of my workaday life has accompanied me onto the island. An L. L. Bean bag full of work, a fax machine, a laptop with a modem. I have all sorts of attachments to the great news machine that feeds me its fast-food through the electronic stomach tube. 3

Fully equipped this way, I tell myself that I can get an extra week away. And so I spend that week wondering why I cannot get away. 4

For days I perform the magic trick unique to my species. My head and my body are in two different places. 5

Like some computer-generated animation, my body is on an island where the most important news is the weather report. My head is on the mainland of issues, ideas, policies. My body is dressed in shorts, T-shirt, baseball cap. My mind is in a suit, pantyhose, heels. 6

I am split across the great divide between this place and the other. Neither here nor there. The 7 desk chair is full, the hammock empty. On the road, I am able to see the brown-eyed Susans and Queen Anne's lace only in my peripheral vision. My focus remains elsewhere.

2. Why can't the author see the flowers?

8   I feel like a creature of the modern world who has learned to live much—too much—of the time on fast-forward and to pretend that it is a natural rhythm.

9   What would Charlie Chaplin make of these Modern Times? Our impatience when the computer or the ATM machine "slows" down, or when the plane is late? The way many of us have to do two things at once, to ratchet up our productivity, that buzzword of the era, as if life were an assembly line?

10   In some recess of this modern times mind-set, I thought I could be on vacation and at work. Instead, these two masters wrangle for custody over me and I learned that there are two things you cannot do at once: something and nothing.

3. What is Goodman's subject? Taking a vacation? Something else?

11   But finally, this morning, walking down the country road at a distracted, aerobic, urban speed, I brake for butterflies.

12   I am aware suddenly of four monarchs in full orange and black robes at their regal work. They have claimed a weedy plot of milkweeds as their territory.

13   As I stand absolutely still, these four become eight and then 12. My eye slowly adjusts to monarchs the way it adjusts to the dark or the way you can gradually see blueberries on a green bush.

4. What is the effect on Goodman of standing in the midst of the butterflies?

14   There are 20 butterflies harvesting a plot no bigger than my desk. Here are 30 in a space smaller than my office. The flock, the herd, has followed its summer taste buds onto my island the way native tribes once came here for the clams. They leave as suddenly as summer people.

15   The monarchs allow me, a commoner, to stand among them in the milkweeds while they work. I feel foolishly and deliciously like some small-

time anthropologist, some down-home Jane Goodall,[1] pleased to be accepted by the fluttering royals.

I am permitted to watch from inches away. For half a minute, one monarch chooses my baseball cap as his throne. For half an hour I am not an intruder but part of the native landscape.   16

I remember now the lines of poetry I read in the icy dead of last winter. After watching two mockingbirds, spinning and tossing "the white ribbons of their songs into the air," Mary Oliver wrote, "I had nothing/better to do/than listen./I mean this/seriously."   17

Such moments are rare in our world of Rapid Eye Moments. We have been taught to hurry, to scan instead of read, to surf instead of watch.   18

5. What does the experience teach Goodman? What is her thesis? What does she want readers to understand?

We can go from zero to 100 miles an hour in seconds—but only by leaving the natural world in the dust.   19

We pride ourselves on speed—and forget that time goes by fast enough. The trick is to slow down long enough to listen, smell, touch, look, live.   20

At long last, the faxes and phones and ties all disconnect. And for a summer afternoon, surrounded by monarchs, I know this: I have nothing better to do than watch. I mean this seriously.   21

6. Are many of us living much as the author does? Is this a problem in your view? Reflect on her ideas.

WRITING FOCUS:
USING SUMMARY, ANALYSIS, AND SYNTHESIS

You will have many occasions, in your composition class, in other classes, and in the workplace, to write using summary, analysis, and synthesis. The book review, for example, combines all three.

---

[1]Famous for her observations of chimpanzees in Africa—Ed.

Summary

Whether it is paragraph length or a few pages, a *summary* is a condensed, nonevaluative restatement of a writer's main ideas.

To prepare a good summary, read carefully and then follow these guidelines for writing:

1. Maintain a direct, objective style without using overly simplistic sentences.
2. Begin with the author's thesis and then present additional key points.
3. Exclude all specific examples, illustrations, or background sections. However, you may want to indicate the kinds of evidence or methods of development used.
4. Combine main ideas into fewer sentences than were used in the original article or book.
5. Select precise, accurate verbs (*asserts, argues, concludes*) rather than vague verbs (*says, talks about*) that provide only a list of ideas. Pay attention to word choice to avoid such judging words as: "Jones then develops the *silly* idea that . . ."

With these guidelines in mind, read the following summary of Ellen Goodman's "Learning to Brake for Butterflies" (pp. 9–11) and consider why it needs revision.

Summary #1

In "Learning to Brake for Butterflies," Ellen Goodman tells us that she has come to Maine but was late. She says that she is divided between her work and vacation. She continues to be impatient that the plane was late. Then she walks fast and sees some butterflies. She stops to watch them. Goodman quotes lines from Mary Oliver's poem and says she really doesn't have anything better to do than to watch the butterflies.

We can agree that the writer of this summary has read Goodman's essay, but we can also assert that the summary lacks focus and may even be misleading. The writer has gone through the essay, picked out some ideas, and strung them together. One result is no clear statement of Goodman's main idea. Another is that the ending of the summary misrepresents Goodman's thesis. Now read the second summary and be able to explain why it is a better summary.

Summary #2

In "Learning to Brake for Butterflies," Ellen Goodman describes heading for a Maine vacation while taking along her laptop and unfinished work. She hopes to have a longer vacation by taking some work with her, but finds that she cannot both work and be on vacation. As she goes for a walk, she finds herself walking with a fast, purposeful stride until she comes upon a large number of Monarch butterflies. She stands quietly among them, watching them feed on some milkweeds. She understands the value of slowing down and disconnecting from work to look and listen to and reconnect to the natural world.

Analysis

You will find chapters on process analysis and causal analysis in this text. The process of comparison (or contrast) is also analysis. To establish some guidelines for writing analysis, let's consider one paragraph in an essay that analyzes a writer's style.

Suppose your thesis is that the writer uses connotative words, clever metaphors, and ironic understatement to convey her attitude. You will need a paragraph on each element of style: word choice, metaphors, irony, and understatement. Follow these guidelines for each paragraph.

1. Have a *topic sentence* that conveys the paragraph's subject and ties the paragraph to the essay's thesis.
2. Quote or paraphrase to present *examples* of the element of style, at least three examples taken from throughout the work.
3. *Explain* how the examples support the paragraph's topic sentence and hence your thesis. This is your analysis, the "glue" that holds the paragraph together and makes your point.
4. Use the correct tense. Analyze style in the *present tense*.

Here is one paragraph from student Alan Peterson's style analysis of an essay by Ellen Goodman.

Sample Analysis

Perhaps the most prevalent element of style present in Goodman's article, and a dominant characteristic of her essay style, is her use of metaphors. From the opening sentences through to the end, this article is full of metaphors. Keeping with the general focus of the piece (the essay appeared on Thanksgiving day), many of the metaphors liken food to family. Her references include "a cornucopia of family," "chicken-sized households" and "a turkey-sized family," people who "feast on the sounds as well as the tastes," and voices that "add relish to a story." She imparts that a politician can use the word "family" like "gravy poured over the entire plate." Going to the airport to pick up members of these disjointed American families has become "a holiday ritual as common as pumpkin pie." Goodman draws parallels between the process of "choosing" people to be with us and the simple ritual of passing seconds at the table. Indeed, the essay's mood emphasizes the comparison of and inextricable bond between food and family.

Synthesis

There are many reasons for drawing on two or more sources to develop your own piece of writing, and there is more than one way to acknowledge sources to readers. But what you must do, whether with a formal pattern of documentation or informally including details of author and title in your essay, is *always* let readers know where ideas and information not original with you have been found. Follow these general guidelines for creating synthesis.

1. Have a clear topic sentence in each paragraph. Material from sources is used to support an idea; it is not just "filler."
2. Combine information/ideas from several sources. If you devote each paragraph to only one source, you are writing a series of summaries. You are not synthesizing.
3. Put most of the borrowed material in your own words. When necessary, use brief quotations.

4. Make the sources of your borrowed material absolutely clear throughout. Use introductory tags; guide your reader through the material.
5. Explain and discuss the material. Do not just dump material from sources on your reader. The result is a list, not a synthesis.

The following paragraph, part of a documented report on theories of dinosaur warm-bloodedness, illustrates one student's command of synthesis. (The essay concludes with a "works cited" page that includes the sources cited after the paragraph.)

Sample Synthesis

The body weight of a dinosaur provides one of the arguments supporting the assertion that some dinosaurs were endotherms. Don Lessem reports that one reason for paleontologists' change of thinking arose in 1964 from Dr. John Ostrom's discovery of *Deinonchyus*, "terrible claw," in central Montana (43). Christopher Lampton argues that since *Deinonchyus* had large claws on its feet and was only as tall as a human, it must have been endothermic to remain active enough to flee from larger predators and to attack its own prey with its terrible claw (90). Lampton quotes Ostrom in further support of *Deinonchyus's* endothermy: "'It does not surprise us to see a hawk slash with its talons. . . . Reptiles are just not capable of such intricate maneuvers, such delicate balance'" (88–89). Lampton concludes that *Deinonchyus* could not have been cold-blooded and still remain an aggressive predator that actively hunted by slashing with the claws on its feet (89). The evidence suggests that at least this one dinosaur was warm-blooded.

Works Cited

Lampton, Christopher. <u>New Theories on Dinosaurs</u>. New York: Watts, 1989.

Lessem, Don. <u>Dinosaurs Rediscovered: New Findings Which Are Revolutionizing Dinosaur Science</u>. New York: Simon, 1992.

Getting Started

Read the following poem by Richard Wilbur; it is not a difficult poem to read, I promise! Enjoy his images and metaphors as you picture the scene he re-creates. Then think about what Wilbur has to say about the writing process. Use these questions to guide your reading and thinking:

1. What is his daughter doing in her room? Why are there silences in between the periods of typing?
2. Five stanzas are about a bird trapped in his daughter's room. What does this story have to do with his daughter's current activity?
3. What does he wish for his daughter? Why, at the end of the poem, does he wish her the same thing—but harder?
4. What would you say is the basic meaning or point of the poem?
5. Why has this poem been included in this chapter?

Did you like this poem? If so, do you think you can use it as a useful reminder or as a guide through this writing course? If not, why not? You may want to answer these questions in a journal entry or have answers ready for class discussion.

The Writer

RICHARD WILBUR

Born in New York City, Richard Wilbur attended Amherst College and fought in World War II. He then taught at several colleges, including Harvard and Smith. He has published poetry, literary criticism, and children's books. His books have led to two Pulitzer Prizes and a National Book Award. The following poem is from his collection *The Mind Reader* (1971).

In her room at the prow of the house
Where light breaks, and the windows are tossed with linden,
My daughter is writing a story.

I pause in the stairwell, hearing
From her shut door a commotion of typewriter-keys   5
Like a chain hauled over a gunwale.*

Young as she is, the stuff
Of her life is a great cargo, and some of it heavy:
I wish her a lucky passage.

But now it is she who pauses,
As if to reject my thought and its easy figure.
A stillness greatens, in which

The whole house seems to be thinking,   10
And then she is at it again with a bunched clamor
Of strokes, and again is silent.

I remember the dazed starling
Which was trapped in that very room, two years ago;
How we stole in, lifted a sash   15

And retreated, not to affright it,
And how for a helpless hour, through the crack of the door,
We watched the sleek, wild, dark

And iridescent creature
Batter against the brilliance, drop like a glove   20
To the hard floor, or the desk-top,

And wait then, humped and bloody,
For the wits to try it again; and how our spirits
Rose when, suddenly sure,

It lifted off from a chair-back,   25
Beating a smooth course for the right window
And clearing the sill of the world.

It is always a matter, my darling.
Of life or death, as I had forgotten. I wish
What I wished you before, but harder.   30

*Upper edge of the side of a boat, pronounced gŭn'əl—Ed.

The Watcher at the Gates

GAIL GODWIN

With degrees from the Universities of North Carolina and Iowa, Gail Godwin began her career as a journalist and English instructor before becoming primarily a fiction writer. She has published a collection of short stories and several novels, including her 1982 best-seller *A Woman and Two Daughters.* In the following essay, published in 1977 in the *New York Times Book Review,* Godwin examines the sources of writer's block and offers some solutions to the problem.

Questions to Guide Your Reading and Reflection
  1. What two unpleasant traits do most "Watchers" have?
  2. What advice do you have for students who have trouble getting started on a writing assignment?

---

1   I first realized I was not the only writer who had a restraining critic who lived inside me and sapped the juice from green inspirations when I was leafing through Freud's *Interpretation of Dreams* a few years ago. Ironically, it was my "inner critic" who had sent me to Freud. I was writing a novel, and my heroine was in the middle of a dream, and then I lost faith in my own invention and rushed to "an authority" to check whether she could have such a dream. In the chapter on dream interpretation, I came upon the following passage that has helped me free myself, in some measure, from my critic and has led to many pleasant and interesting exchanges with other writers.

2   Freud quotes Schiller, who is writing a letter to a friend. The friend complains of his lack of creative power. Schiller replies with an allegory. He says it is not good if the intellect examines too closely the ideas pouring in at the gates. "In isolation, an idea may be quite insignificant, and venturesome in the extreme, but it may acquire importance from an idea which follows it. . . . In the case of a creative mind, it seems to me, the intellect has withdrawn its watchers from the gates, and the ideas rush in pell-mell,

and only then does it review and inspect the multitude. You are ashamed or afraid of the momentary and passing madness which is found in all real creators, the longer or shorter duration of which distinguishes the thinking artist from the dreamer . . . you reject too soon and discriminate too severely."

So that's what I had: a Watcher at the Gates. I decided to get   3
to know him better. I discussed him with other writers, who told me some of the quirks and habits of their Watchers, each of whom was as individual as his host, and all of whom seemed passionately dedicated to one goal: rejecting too soon and discriminating too severely.

It is amazing the lengths a Watcher will go to keep you from   4
pursuing the flow of your imagination. Watchers are notorious pencil sharpeners, ribbon changers, plant waterers, home repairers and abhorrers of messy rooms or messy pages. They are compulsive looker-uppers. They are superstitious scaredy-cats. They cultivate self-important eccentricities they think are suitable for "writers." And they'd rather die (and kill your inspiration with them) than risk making a fool of themselves.

My Watcher has a wasteful penchant for 20-pound bond   5
paper above and below the carbon of the first draft. "What's the good of writing out a whole page," he whispers begrudgingly, "if you just have to write it over again later? Get it perfect the first time!" My Watcher adores stopping in the middle of a morning's work to drive down to the library to check on the name of a flower or a World War II battle or a line of metaphysical poetry. "You can't possibly go on till you've got this right" he admonishes. I go and get the car keys.

Other Watchers have informed their writers that: 6

"Whenever you get a really good sentence you should stop   7
in the middle of it and go on tomorrow. Otherwise you might run dry."

"Don't try and continue with your book till your dental   8
appointment is over. When you're worried about your teeth, you can't think about art."

Another Watcher makes his owner pin his finished pages to   9
a clothesline and read them through binoculars "to see how they look from a distance." Countless other Watchers demand "bribes" for taking the day off: lethal doses of caffeine, alcoholic doses of Scotch or vodka or wine.

10   There are various ways to outsmart, pacify or coexist with your Watcher. Here are some I have tried, or my writer friends have tried, with success:

11   Look for situations when he's likely to be off guard. Write too fast for him in an unexpected place, at an unexpected time. (Virginia Woolf captured the "diamonds in the dustheap" by writing at a "rapid haphazard gallop" in her diary.) Write when very tired. Write in purple ink on the back of a Master Charge statement. Write whatever comes into your mind while the kettle is boiling and make the steam whistle your deadline. (Deadlines are a great way to outdistance the Watcher.)

12   Disguise what you are writing. If your Watcher refuses to let you get on with your story or novel, write a "letter" instead, telling your "correspondent" what you are going to write in your story or next chapter. Dash off a "review" of your own unfinished opus. It will stand up like a bully to your Watcher the next time he throws more obstacles in your path. If you write yourself a good one.

13   Get to know your Watcher. He's yours. Do a drawing of him (or her). Pin it to the wall of your study and turn it gently to the wall when necessary. Let your Watcher feel needed. Watchers are excellent critics after inspiration has been captured; they are dependable, sharp-eyed readers of things already set down. Keep your Watcher in shape and he'll have less time to keep you from shaping. If he's really ruining your whole working day sit down, as Jung did with his personal demons, and write him a letter. On a very bad day I once wrote my Watcher a letter. "Dear Watcher," I wrote, "What is it you're so afraid I'll do?" Then I held his pen for him, and he replied instantly with a candor that has kept me from truly despising him.

14   "Fail," he wrote back.

Expanding Vocabulary

   1. In her essay Godwin refers to four people and one work. She does not identify them because she expects her readers to know them. Find the people and book and identify each one in a sentence. Use your dictionary or a biographical dictionary in your library or online.
   2. Match each word in column A with its definition in column B. When in doubt, first find the word in the essay and look for con-

text clues to aid your understanding of the word's meaning. Then, if necessary, use your dictionary to complete the matching exercise. The number in parentheses is the number of the paragraph in which the word appears.

Column A	*Column B*
restraining (1)	note differences
sapped (1)	those who strongly dislike
allegory (2)	deadly
duration (2)	liking
discriminate (2)	holding back
severely (2)	symbolic story
notorious (4)	work
abhorrers (4)	frankness
eccentricities (4)	weakened or cut off
penchant (5)	calm down
begrudgingly (5)	reluctantly
admonishes (5)	length of time in an activity
lethal (9)	famous in a negative way
pacify (10)	warns
opus (12)	seriously or harshly
candor (13)	oddities

Understanding Content

1. Where did Godwin find the idea of a Watcher at the Gates?
2. What are some of the tricks Watchers use to keep us from writing?
3. What do Watchers fear? Why do many writers have a Watcher at the Gates problem?
4. What are some ways writers can outsmart their Watchers?

Drawing Inferences about Thesis and Purpose

1. What is a Watcher at the Gates? That is, what problem does the Watcher stand for?
2. What is Godwin's primary purpose in writing? To develop the idea of the Watcher? To offer some understanding of writing anxiety? To explain ways to get rid of writing anxiety?

Analyzing Strategies and Style

1. What strategy does Godwin use when she calls a restraining critic a Watcher at the Gates and suggests that writers get to know him or her? What is effective about this strategy, this approach to her subject?

2. Godwin opens with a metaphor: "sapped the juice from green inspirations." Explain the metaphor.
3. Godwin's piece is a good example of a personal essay. On the basis of your study of this essay, list the characteristics of a personal essay.

Thinking Critically

1. Follow Godwin's suggestion about getting to know your Watcher. Begin by drawing, as best you can, a picture of your Watcher. Then write a brief description of this person or thing.
2. What are some of your favorite excuses for avoiding writing? Now pretend that you are Gail Godwin; how might she tell you to get around these excuses and go on to write?

On Reading and Becoming a Writer

TERRY MCMILLAN

Terry McMillan has published several novels, including *Waiting to Exhale* (1992), *How Stella Got Her Groove Back* (1996), and *The Interruption of Everything* (2005). An instructor in writing at the University of Arizona, McMillan has also edited *Five for Five: The Films of Spike Lee* (1991) and *Breaking Ice: An Anthology of Contemporary African-American Fiction* (1990). The following excerpt, from the introduction to *Breaking Ice*, recounts McMillan's exciting discovery of black writers and her development as a writer.

Questions to Guide Your Reading and Reflection

1. What did McMillan learn from her college course in African-American literature?
2. What advice do you have for someone who wants to be a writer?

1   As a child, I didn't know that African-American people wrote books. I grew up in a small town in northern Michigan, where the only books I came across were the Bible and required reading for school. I did not read for pleasure, and it wasn't until I was sixteen when I got a job shelving books at the pub-

lic library that I got lost in a book. It was a biography of Louisa May Alcott. I was excited because I had not really read about poor white folks before; her father was so eccentric and idealistic that at the time I just thought he was crazy. I related to Louisa because she had to help support her family at a young age, which was what I was doing at the library.

Then one day I went to put a book away, and saw James 2 Baldwin's face staring up at me. "Who in the world is this?" I wondered. I remember feeling embarrassed and did not read his book because I was too afraid. I couldn't imagine that he'd have anything better or different to say than Thomas Mann, Henry Thoreau, Ralph Waldo Emerson, Nathaniel Hawthorne, Ernest Hemingway, William Faulkner, etc. and a horde of other mostly white male writers that I'd been introduced to in Literature 101 in high school. I mean, not only had there not been any African-American authors included in any of those textbooks, but I'd never been given a clue that if we did have anything important to say that somebody would actually publish it. Needless to say, I was not just naïve, but had not yet acquired an ounce of black pride. I never once questioned why there were no representative works by us in any of those textbooks. After all, I had never heard of any African-American writers, and no one I knew hardly read *any* books.

And then things changed. 3

It wasn't until after Malcolm X had been assassinated that I 4 found out who he was. I know I should be embarrassed about this, but I'm not. I read Alex Haley's biography of him and it literally changed my life. First and foremost, I realized that there was no reason to be ashamed of being black, that it was ridiculous. That we had a history, and much to be proud of. I began to notice how we had actually been treated as less than human; began to see our strength as a people whereas I'd only been made aware of our inferiorities. I started thinking about my role in the world and not just on my street. I started *thinking*. Thinking about things I'd never thought about before, and the thinking turned into questions. But I had more questions than answers.

So I went to college. When I looked through the catalog and 5 saw a class called Afro-American Literature, I signed up and couldn't wait for the first day of class. Did *we* really have enough writers to warrant an entire class? I remember the textbook was called *Dark Symphony: Negro Literature in America* because I still have it. I couldn't believe the rush I felt over and over once I discovered Countee Cullen, Langston Hughes, Ann Petry, Zora Neale Hurston, Ralph Ellison, Jean Toomer, Richard Wright, and rediscovered and read James Baldwin, to name just a few. I'm surprised I didn't need glasses by the end of the semester. My world opened up. I accumulated and gained a totally new insight about, and perception of, our lives as "black" people, as if I had been an outsider and was finally let in. To discover that our lives held as much significance and importance as our white counterparts was more than gratifying, it was exhilarating. Not only had we lived diverse, interesting, provocative, and relentless lives, but during, through, and as a result of all these painful experiences, some folks had taken the time to write it down.

6   Not once, throughout my entire four years as an undergraduate, did it occur to me that I might one day *be* a writer. I mean, these folks had genuine knowledge and insight. They also had a fascination with the truth. They had something to write about. Their work was bold, not flamboyant. They learned how to exploit the language so that readers would be affected by what they said and how they said it. And they had talent.

7   I never considered myself to be in possession of much of the above, and yet when I was twenty years old, the first man I fell in love with broke my heart. I was so devastated and felt so helpless that my reaction manifested itself in a poem. I did not sit down and say, "I'm going to write a poem about this." It was more like magic. I didn't even know I was writing a poem until I had written it. Afterward, I felt lighter, as if something had happened to lessen the pain. And when I read this "thing" I was shocked because I didn't know where the words came from. I was scared, to say the least, about what I had just experienced, because I didn't understand what had happened.

8   For the next few days, I read that poem over and over in disbelief because *I* had written it. One day, a colleague saw it lying on the kitchen table and read it. I was embarrassed and shocked when he said he liked it, then went on to tell me that he had just started a black literary magazine at the college and he wanted to publish it. Publish it! He was serious and it found its way onto a typeset page. Seeing my name in print excited me. And

from that point on, if a leaf moved on a tree, I wrote a poem about it. If a crack in the sidewalk glistened, surely there was a poem in that. Some of these verbose things actually got published in various campus newspapers that were obviously desperate to fill up space. I did not call myself a poet; I told people I wrote poems.

Years passed. 9

Those poems started turning into sentences and I started get- 10
ting nervous. What the hell did I think I was doing? Writing these little go-nowhere vignettes. All these beginnings. And who did I think I was, trying to tell a story? And who cared? Even though I had no idea what I was doing, all I knew was that I was beginning to realize that a lot of things mattered to me, things disturbed me, things that I couldn't change. Writing became an outlet for my dissatisfactions, distaste, and my way of trying to make sense of what I saw happening around me. It was my way of trying to fix what I thought was broken. It later became the only way to explore personally what I didn't understand. The problem, however, was that I was writing more about ideas than people. Everything was so "large," and eventually I had to find a common denominator. I ended up asking myself what I really cared about: it was people, and particularly African-American people.

The whole idea of taking myself seriously as a writer was ter- 11
rifying. I didn't know any writers. Didn't know how you knew if you "had" it or not. Didn't know if I was or would ever be good enough. I didn't know how you went about the business of writing, and besides, I sincerely wanted to make a decent living. (I had read the horror stories of how so few writers were able to live off of their writing alone, many having lived like bohemians.) At first, I thought being a social worker was the right thing to do, since I was bent on saving the world (I was an idealistic twenty-two years old), but when I found out I couldn't do it that way, I had to figure out another way to make an impact on folks. A positive impact. I ended up majoring in journalism because writing was "easy" for me, but it didn't take long for me to learn that I did not like answering the "who, what, when, where, and why" of anything. I then—upon the urging of my mother and friends who had graduated and gotten "normal" jobs—decided to try something that would still allow me to "express myself" but was relatively safer, though

still risky: I went to film school. Of course what was inherent in my quest to find my "spot" in the world was this whole notion of affecting people on some grand scale. Malcolm and Martin caused me to think like this. Writing for me, as it's turned out, is philanthropy. It didn't take years for me to realize the impact that other writers' work had had on me, and if I was going to write, I did not want to write inconsequential, mediocre stories that didn't conjure up or arouse much in a reader. So I had to start by exciting myself and paying special attention to what I cared about, what mattered to me.

12   Film school didn't work out. Besides, I never could stop writing, which ultimately forced me to stop fighting it. It took even longer to realize that writing was not something you aspired to, it was something you did because you had to. . . .

13   I've been teaching writing on the university level now for three years, and much to my dismay, rarely have I ever had an African-American student. I wish there were more ways to encourage young people to give writing a shot. Many of them still seem to be intimidated by the English language, and think of writing as "hard"—as in Composition 101–hard. So many of them are set on "making it" (solely in material terms) that we find many of our students majoring in the "guaranteed" professions: the biological sciences, law, engineering, business, etc. If I can make an appeal to those who will read this anthology, I would like to say this to them: If for whatever reason you do not derive a genuine sense of excitement or satisfaction from your chosen field, if you are majoring in these disciplines because of a parent's insistence, if you are dissatisfied with the world to any extent and find yourself "secretly" jotting it down whenever or wherever you can; if you don't understand why people (yourself included) do the things that they do and it plagues you like an itch—consider taking a fiction writing course. Find out if there are African-American writing groups or *any* workshops that are available in your area. Then write. Read as much "serious" fiction as you can—and not just African-American authors. Then, keep writing. "Push it," says Annie Dillard. "Examine all things intensely and relentlessly. Probe and search . . . do not leave it, do not course over it, as if it were understood, but instead follow it down until you see it in the mystery of its own specificity and strength."

14   Persist.

Expanding Vocabulary

Determine the meaning of each of the following words either from its context in this essay or from studying your dictionary. Then select five of the words and use each one in a separate sentence of your own. The number in parentheses is the number of the paragraph in which the word appears.

eccentric (1)	bohemians (11)
exhilarating (5)	philanthropy (11)
provocative (5)	inconsequential (11)
flamboyant (6)	mediocre (11)
verbose (8)	conjure (11)
vignettes (10)	specificity (13)

Understanding Content

1. In what way did the author identify with Louisa May Alcott?
2. What writers was McMillan introduced to in high school? What writers were not part of her required reading?
3. How did McMillan come to write and publish her first poem? Why did she not want to call herself a poet? What seems to have been her attitude toward writers and writing?
4. What were her reasons for writing fiction? How did she narrow and focus her writing?
5. Why did she go to film school? What was the result?
6. What dismays McMillan as a college teacher? What reasons does she offer for students' not taking a fiction writing course? What advice does she give to potential African-American writers?

Drawing Inferences about Thesis and Purpose

1. What is McMillan's purpose in writing?
2. From your reading of this essay, what sort of person do you imagine McMillan to be? Describe her personality.

Analyzing Strategies and Style

1. How would you characterize the style in which this essay is written? (Style is shaped from word choice and sentence structure.) List examples of McMillan's word choice and sentence patterns that help to create the essay's style.
2. What is McMillan's tone? That is, what voice do you hear? How does she create that tone?

Thinking Critically

1. McMillan presents a list of writers in paragraph 2 and another list in paragraph 5. How many writers from the first list do you know? How many from the second list? From your own survey (or the class's as a whole), would you conclude that students today are more familiar than McMillan was with African-American authors, or has the situation not changed much?
2. McMillan believes that students think of fiction writing as "hard" in the same way that freshman composition is hard. Which course do you think would be harder for you? Why?
3. The author concludes with advice directed to the expected audience for *Breaking Ice*, African-American students, some of whom may possibly become writers. How can her advice be applied to composition writers as well as to fiction writers? Explain.

How to Write with Style

KURT VONNEGUT

Kurt Vonnegut is one of the most popular contemporary novelists. A former employee of General Electric in public relations, Vonnegut is now famous for such novels as *Cat's Cradle* (1963), *Slaughterhouse Five* (1969), and, most recently, *Timequake* (1993). The following advice on style was published by International Paper Company as one of a series of articles used as ads on the "Power of the Printed Word."

Questions to Guide Your Reading and Reflection

1. What will happen when you break rules, give new meanings to words, or try to create an avant-garde style?
2. What do yo think is the most important element in a writer's style?

1   Newspaper reporters and technical writers are trained to reveal almost nothing about themselves in their writings. This makes them freaks in the world of writers, since almost all of the other ink-stained wretches in that world reveal a lot about themselves to readers. We call these revelations, accidental and intentional, elements of style.

These revelations tell us as readers what sort of person it is 2
with whom we are spending time. Does the writer sound ignorant or informed, stupid or bright, crooked or honest, humor-
less or playful—? And on and on.

Why should you examine your writing style with the idea 3
of improving it? Do so as a mark of respect for your readers,
whatever you're writing. If you scribble your thoughts any
which way, your readers will surely feel that you care nothing
about them. They will mark you down as an egomaniac or a
chowderhead—or worse, they will stop reading you.

The most damning revelation you can make about yourself 4
is that you do not know what is interesting and what is not.
Don't you yourself like or dislike writers mainly for what they
choose to show you or make you think about? Did you ever
admire an empty-headed writer for his or her mastery of the
language? No.

So your own winning style must begin with ideas in 5
your head.

1. Find a Subject You Care About

Find a subject you care about and which you in your heart 6
feel others should care about. It is this genuine caring, and not
your games with language, which will be the most compelling
and seductive element in your style.

I am not urging you to write a novel, by the way—although 7
I would not be sorry if you wrote one, provided you genuine-
ly cared about something. A petition to the mayor about a pot-
hole in front of your house or a love letter to the girl next door
will do.

2. Do Not Ramble, Though

I won't ramble on about that. 8

3. Keep It Simple

As for your use of language: Remember that two great mas- 9
ters of language, William Shakespeare and James Joyce, wrote
sentences which were almost childlike when their subjects were
most profound. "To be or not to be?" asks Shakespeare's Hamlet.

The longest word is three letters long. Joyce, when he was frisky, could put together a sentence as intricate and as glittering as a necklace for Cleopatra, but my favorite sentence in his short story "Eveline" is this one: "She was tired." At that point in the story, no other words could break the heart of a reader as those three words do.

10   Simplicity of language is not only reputable, but perhaps even sacred. The *Bible* opens with a sentence well within the writing skills of a lively fourteen-year-old: "In the beginning God created the heaven and the earth."

4. Have the Guts to Cut

11   It may be that you, too, are capable of making necklaces for Cleopatra, so to speak. But your eloquence should be the servant of the ideas in your head. Your rule might be this: If a sentence, no matter how excellent, does not illuminate your subject in some new and useful way, scratch it out.

5. Sound Like Yourself

12   The writing style which is most natural for you is bound to echo the speech you heard when a child. English was the novelist Joseph Conrad's third language, and much that seems piquant in his use of English was no doubt colored by his first language, which was Polish. And lucky indeed is the writer who has grown up in Ireland, for the English spoken there is so amusing and musical. I myself grew up in Indianapolis, where common speech sounds like a band saw cutting galvanized tin, and employs a vocabulary as unornamental as a monkey wrench.

13   In some of the more remote hollows of Appalachia, children still grow up hearing songs and locutions of Elizabethan times. Yes, and many Americans grow up hearing a language other than English, or an English dialect a majority of Americans cannot understand.

14   All these varieties of speech are beautiful, just as the varieties of butterflies are beautiful. No matter what your first language, you should treasure it all your life. If it happens not to be standard English, and if it shows itself when you write standard English, the result is usually delightful, like a very pretty girl with one eye that is green and one that is blue.

I myself find that I trust my own writing most, and others 15
seem to trust it most, too, when I sound most like a person from
Indianapolis, which is what I am. What alternatives do I have?
The one most vehemently recommended by teachers has no
doubt been pressed on you, as well: to write like cultivated Eng-
lishmen of a century or more ago.

6. Say What You Mean to Say

I used to be exasperated by such teachers, but am no more. 16
I understand now that all those antique essays and stories with
which I was to compare my own work were not magnificent for
their datedness or foreignness, but for saying precisely what
their authors meant them to say. My teachers wished me to
write accurately, always selecting the most effective words, and
relating the words to one another unambiguously, rigidly, like
parts of a machine. The teachers did not want to turn me into
an Englishman after all. They hoped that I would become
understandable—and therefore understood. And there went
my dream of doing with words what Pablo Picasso did with
paint or what any number of jazz idols did with music. If I broke
all the rules of punctuation, had words mean whatever I wanted them to mean, and strung them together higgledy-piggledy,
I would simply not be understood. So you, too, had better avoid
Picasso-style or jazz-style writing, if you have something worth
saying and wish to be understood.

Readers want our pages to look very much like pages they 17
have seen before. Why? This is because they themselves have a
tough job to do, and they need all the help they can get from us.

7. Pity the Readers

They have to identify thousands of little marks on paper, and 18
make sense of them immediately. They have to *read*, an art so
difficult that most people don't really master it even after having studied it all through grade school and high school—twelve
long years.

So this discussion must finally acknowledge that our stylis- 19
tic options as writers are neither numerous nor glamorous, since
our readers are bound to be such imperfect artists. Our audience requires us to be sympathetic and patient teachers, even

willing to simplify and clarify—whereas we would rather soar high above the crowd, singing like nightingales.

20   That is the bad news. The good news is that we Americans are governed under a unique Constitution, which allows us to write whatever we please without fear of punishment. So the most meaningful aspect of our styles, which is what we choose to write about, is utterly unlimited.

8. For Really Detailed Advice

21   For a discussion of literary style in a narrower sense, in a more technical sense, I commend to your attention *The Elements of Style*, by William Strunk, Jr., and E. B. White (Allyn & Bacon, 2000). E. B. White is, of course, one of the most admirable literary stylists this country has so far produced.

22   You should realize, too, that no one would care how well or badly Mr. White expressed himself, if he did not have perfectly enchanting things to say.

Expanding Vocabulary

Match each word in column A with its definition in column B. When in doubt, first find the word in the essay and look for context clues to aid your understanding of the word's meaning. Then, if necessary, use your dictionary to complete the matching exercise. The number in parentheses is the number of the paragraph in which the word appears.

Column A	Column B
egomaniac (3)	having many complexly arranged parts
chowderhead (3)	moving, expressive language use
intricate (9)	iron or steel with zinc coating
reputable (10)	appealingly provocative
eloquence (11)	one who is pretty dense, like a soup
piquant (12)	
galvanized (12)	particular style of speaking
locutions (13)	angrily impatient
exasperated (16)	one who has an obsessive focus on the self
higgledy-piggledy (16)	in utter disorder
	esteemed, of good reputation

Understanding Content

1. How will readers respond to you if you "scribble your thoughts any which way"?
2. A winning style begins with what?
3. List the specific guidelines Vonnegut provides, each in a separate sentence, in your own words.
4. Explain Vonnegut's rule for cutting text.
5. Why is it best to sound like yourself?

Drawing Inferences about Thesis and Purpose

1. What is Vonnegut's purpose?
2. More than anything else, what does your style tell readers?
3. What, for Vonnegut, is the most important "element of style"?

Analyzing Strategies and Style

1. The author has little to say about his second point. What does he gain by his brevity?
2. Find some examples of clever word choice or metaphors. Explain why they are effective.

Thinking Critically

1. Which of Vonnegut's points do you think is most important for writers? Why? Which point is most important for *you* to focus on as you work on your writing? Why?
2. Vonnegut writes that simplicity is "perhaps even sacred." Explain how simple language can be called sacred. Is this a new idea for you? Does it make sense?
3. Vonnegut begins and ends emphasizing the importance of having something to say. Do you agree with him that this is the most important element of style? Why or why not?

Santa Rosa Island, 1998

GRETEL EHRLICH

A writer of poetry, fiction, and nonfiction books, Gretel Ehrlich divides her time between Wyoming and California. Among her books are *The Solace of Open Spaces* (1986), *This Cold Heaven: Seven Seasons in Greenland* (2003), and *The Future of Ice: A Journey into Cold* (2004). The following work, first published in *American Scholar* in Autumn 2001, is a portion of the journal Ehrlich kept while living and working on Santa Rosa Island. Many professional writers keep journals, perhaps in part because they are happy when writing, but also to record material that may eventually be reshaped into a published work. If your instructor assigns journal writing, you can use Ehrlich's journal as a guide.

Questions to Guide Your Reading and Reflection

1. What *kinds* of topics does Ehrlich include in her journal?
2. How might keeping a journal help you in your composition course?

---

1   For two years, I "cowboyed" on Santa Rosa Island, one of the Channel Islands off central California. Santa Rosa had been ranched by a single family for nearly a century, but after its acquisition by the National Park Service in the 1980s, a policy of phasing out all livestock, ostensibly for the protection of endangered native plants, was unnecessarily accelerated, and a century of California ranching history came to a halt.

2   August 19. Rough crossing. Stood on port side with Jesus Bracamontes, one of the vaqueros, and basked in the sun. Sometimes the boat tipped down so far we were horizontal, standing on water. A flying fish zoomed by like a piece of light, and four least terns. A seal was asleep on a raft of seaweed, like a dog sitting on top of a tree. The vaqueros are coming back to the island from their vacation back home in Mexico, a little fatter, and with eager smiles—except for Jesus, who has been on his rancho digging a well by hand, at age 72. Let's keep going, I say to him. Let's make this boat go down the coast of Mexico. His eyes brighten. Good idea. Because *mi corazon es muy malo*, I tell him. Ben, my friend and lover, has left me.

3   August 21. Yesterday a sorrel horse with a blaze was cut away from its best friend to be shipped tomorrow to the mainland, where he'll be either sold or canned. That is the fate of these animals now that the Park had ordered everything off this island. The horse whinnied all night and all morning, pacing a mile of fence line, trying to catch a glimpse of his friend, a

mare he had been born next to, grown up with, never parted from. Today his sorrow is also mine. Ben is gone.

August 22. Sunday morning. Nights and days of rawness, 4 burning, as if my whole being had been seared. Everyone has gone back to the mainland except me, the foreman, and the vaqueros. We eat beans and rice, salad and tortillas in the cookhouse. Jesus walks me home. He is so elegant, a natural horseman, a gentleman. On the way he asks me to marry him and I say no, that would not be possible, and he asks if it's because he is Mexican and I say no, it isn't that, and he asks if it's because he's so old and I say, no, not that either, and he asks if he can kiss me when we get to the ranch house and I say yes, and after, he says, "Ah, *Mamita,* I'll remember this kiss forever."

August 23. Now it is mine, this island, this loneliness, which 5 I know to be only a fiction of sorts—not the island, but the illusion that there is anything but the indestructibility of impermanence. Nevertheless, I am alone here. The wind blows. An old pine bends against the white house. When the ravens come, they come for me, black, sleek, wraithlike. Sun is hot, wind is feisty, dust softens the cliffs and erases waves. How good it would feel to be erased today.

August 25. The wind roars. Sometime in the middle of the night 6 a jet helicopter comes to pick up a fisherman whose boat went down. The old familiar sound of the thumping blade reminds me of Greenland. The clouds come in and the wind tears itself in half, rattling from the northwest and coming back on itself from the other direction, one battling the other. We are all two selves, the wild hermit and the social, sexual being seeking unity. But all is unified already, always was. That night I sat next to Stephen Hawking[1] at the concert and his breathing machine clicked in perfect contrapuntal time with the Bach fugue, and he smiled.

Today the ravens visit early. No warnings, just a casual hello. They check the yard for gifts of food or glitter—a stray diamond 7 in the grass would do. Last week a peregrine falcon took a songbird out of the air in front of my horse. The birds go, but the ghosts of this island stay: Howard the cook, who burned up in the cookhouse; the wives of cowboys who couldn't stand the wind. Jesus tells me one of them killed herself in the room where

[1]Famous contemporary physicist who has a debilitating disease and speaks through a computer—Ed.

I'm sleeping, so at night I should talk to her. Twelve sorrel horses appear from out of the wind-break and run fast past the house,
the vaqueros on horseback behind them, at full tilt, yelling.

8 Then the rain comes, a single drop blown from a hurricane
in Mexico as if to say that Ben is still a torment, a whirling dervish
that provides no calm in a day. Bill (the foreman), his wife, and
I drive to Old Ranch to check on the broodmares. We find three
mares, three live foals, and one dead one. The salt grass is green,
overlaid with wild oats like unruly hair. This is our favorite part
of the 54,000-acre island, the place where we come for solace. A
slough lined with ducks gives out to sand dunes beyond which
schooners once anchored. "This is a hell of a good place for a
horse to die," Bill mutters, implying that he'd like being buried
there as well. He just had his sixty-ninth birthday.

9 Later. How the wind slices down, how it tears across the
stomach, how everything retreats, and it fills the vacuum.

10 August 26. Fog in. Wind stopped. A horse whinnies. Twen-
ty-three horses are being shipped today to be killed on the
mainland. Jesus and I will go with them on the boat. We will
say good-bye to them there. It is an unthinkable end to horses who have been born and raised and ridden all their lives
on this island, who have given themselves to us so selflessly,
who have tried to work hard and to please us, to do what we
ask of them. "If I had my way I'd take them down to the beach
one evening and give them each a big bucket of oats and do
away with them there," Bill says. He wipes away tears from his
wind-hardened face. "The Park sons of bitches only know how
to manage by killing—first the slaughter of the deer from heli-
copters, then spraying with herbicides. My God, do they know
how many birds and bugs they've killed off? And now the
horses. They say it's because they're 'exotics.' Well, what the
hell do they think they are? They weren't born here, but they
think it's 'theirs.'"

11 September 4. Rustic joys. No one arrives. Wind blows.
Scorching hot days followed by lightning. Thunder and rain last
night, remnants from another Mexican hurricane—a *tormenta*,
Jesus says. I drink red wine and listen to Ray Charles singing
Leon Russell songs. Exquisite! I'm not out of my body; I'm so
far in that the mind cannot comment any further, and I do a
wild, barefoot, single-bodied dance on the grass, where the

ravens fence-watch my apocalyptic gaiety, at summer's end, before snowfall. Derek Walcott reminds me in a poem that "the stream's bliss / contradicts the self-importance of despair."   12

September 15. All words are thoughts. All thoughts are mistakes, the random outcome of typos. That's how a whole language could be made, and from it new thoughts would occur. So much language obfuscates. To think without language, ahhhh, that's the way. I'm more and more eager for its complete absence. Instead, I'll let the strings of peptides, cardiac cells, eye cells, do the flashing on and off. Tonight I think I'll shine a flashlight on the backs of my knees, which will tell my body to produce melatonin. Then I'll sleep and be happy.   13

September 25. Evening. The L-shaped cabin on the leeward side of the island is the only embrace I know. Look, the clouds are empty. The sun at the horizon balloons out like a red saucer, then drops. A new moon sets early, chasing the sun. Basho writes: *Kono michi ya / yuku hito nashi ni / aki no kure.* Along this road / there are no travelers / Darkness in autumn.

Expanding Vocabulary

Match each word in column A with its definition in column B. When in doubt, first find the word in the essay and look for context clues to aid your understanding of the word's meaning. Then, if necessary, use your dictionary to complete the matching exercise. The number in parentheses is the number of the paragraph in which the word appears.

Column A	*Column B*
acquisition (1)	reddish-brown horse
ostensibly (1)	ghostlike
vaqueros (2)	hollow or swamp
sorrel (3)	not lasting
impermanence (5)	dance involving fast turning
wraithlike (5)	possession
contrapuntal (6)	confuses, distorts
dervish (8)	cowboys
slough (8)	doom-filled
apocalyptic (11)	apparently, presumably
obfuscates (12)	use of contrasting but parallel musical elements

Understanding Content

1. What are some of the animals that live on Santa Rosa?
2. What is happening to them? What strategies is the Park Service using?
3. What elements of nature does Ehrlich write about the most?
4. What element of personal life does she include?

Drawing Inferences about Thesis and Purpose

1. What picture of Santa Rosa, of the natural setting, emerges from Ehrlich's details? How does she want readers to see, to feel about, this island?
2. Why might the author have decided to cowboy on Santa Rosa for two years at this time in her life? What clues support your inference?

Analyzing Strategies and Style

1. What topics are repeated to provide a kind of unity or connectedness to the journal entries?
2. What kinds of sentences does the author often use at the beginning of entries? What might writers gain by beginning a day's entry this way?

Thinking Critically

1. Ehrlich has selected these entries from her journal to create a kind of essay for publication. What parts of her experience do you think she is most interested in getting across to readers? Why?
2. Based on Ehrlich's journal, what would you conclude to be good topics for journal writing? Make a list of the various *kinds* of topics the author has included.

COMMUNICATING WITH INSTRUCTORS AND PEERS: IN PERSON AND ONLINE

During your college experience, you will be communicating with both faculty and students—in your classes, in the instructor's office, and, increasingly, electronically. Here are some suggestions for effective communication.

1. In general, err on the side of formality. Do not assume that instructors will accept a first-name relationship. Use Professor, Doctor, or Mr./Ms. until asked to do otherwise.

2. Speak politely to classmates, even when disagreeing in class discussions. Most faculty will not accept obscenities or name calling in class, in their offices, or in online discussion forums.

3. Do not write personal messages in online discussion boards. Keep your postings focused on the assignment.

4. If your college provides e-mail addresses for students, use that address when communicating with your instructors. If you use a private account, make sure that your address does not appear to be spam—or is not blocked as spam. (You may need to give up that sexy handle you chose some years ago. It will be blocked or some faculty will delete your message without reading it.)

5. You can find lists of netiquette rules online, or follow the basic ones provided here.

   a. Always use a basic letter format—a salutation, body of the message, in paragraphs if it is long, and your name at the end.

   b. Never send unsigned e-mails to faculty or classmates.

   c. Never send an e-mail without a clear subject heading.

   d. Never write in all capitals. This is the equivalent of shouting.

   e. Never write in all lowercase letters. This appears childish to many, and is difficult to read. Capitalize those "I's."

   f. Do not use a variety of symbols. Not everyone knows what they represent.

   g. Take the time to reread your message—and to use spell check—before you send it. When rereading, pay close attention to the tone of the message.

MAKING CONNECTIONS

---

1. Several writers in this chapter refer to other writers in their essays. Select a writer referred to about whom you know little and read about that writer in at least two sources. Select sources either from your library or online. (Your library will own several biographical indexes, both in paper and electronic formats. You can also "Google" your writer to see

what the Internet offers.) Prepare a short biography (that includes a list of the author's main works) for your class.

2. Alternatively, keep a journal for several days. Include in your entries your thoughts and reflections on the writer whose life you learned about.

3. Godwin, Vonnegut, and McMillan are all authors of novels. After becoming acquainted with each of these writers through their essays in this chapter, which one's novels do you most want to read? Be prepared to defend your choice. Alternatively, read a novel by the writer of your choice and prepare a two-page summary and evaluation of the novel for your class.

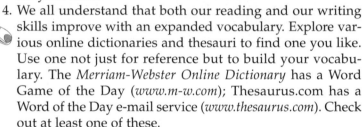

4. We all understand that both our reading and our writing skills improve with an expanded vocabulary. Explore various online dictionaries and thesauri to find one you like. Use one not just for reference but to build your vocabulary. The *Merriam-Webster Online Dictionary* has a Word Game of the Day (*www.m-w.com*); Thesaurus.com has a Word of the Day e-mail service (*www.thesaurus.com*). Check out at least one of these.

TOPICS FOR WRITING

---

1. Terry McMillan offers some insight into how she creates her literature. How do you get started on a piece of writing? How do ideas come to you? What strategies do you use? In an essay explain the ways you get started on a piece of writing. Your purpose in writing should be either to offer your strategies as a useful way to get started or to offer your approach as something to avoid because, on reflection, you have decided that your approach is not effective.

2. How have you learned to fool your "Watcher at the Gates" (see Godwin, pp. 18–20)? In an essay give your advice to anxious writers for avoiding writer's block, based on techniques that have worked for you. Think of your essay as possibly a feature article in your college paper. (Remember: If you use the term "Watcher at the Gates," give Godwin credit.)

3. What kind of reading do you enjoy most? Do you like science fiction, romance novels, the newspaper, magazines devoted to a special interest or hobby? In an essay explain why you enjoy the kind of material you usually read. Illustrate your reasons with specific examples from your reading.

4. Terry McMillan advises future writers to read as much fiction as they can. What are good reasons for reading? In an essay explain and support reasons for encouraging college students to read more.

5. This chapter's introduction offers some reasons for writing. Why should adults become competent writers? Why should an engineer, a banker, or a teacher be able to write? In an essay answer these questions. Focus either on the practical considerations of a particular job or on more philosophical reasons having to do with personal growth and discovery or general career needs. Remember to explain and illustrate each reason.

2

___Using Narration
Growing Up, Growing Wiser

"Once upon a time there lived a princess"—so the fairy tale begins. A story, or narrative, relates a series of events in time sequence. If the narrative relates events that are made up out of the writer's imagination, then the narrative is *fiction*. If the narrative relates events that have taken place, it is *nonfiction*. Nonfiction narratives are found in histories, biographies, newspaper articles, and essays that use narration as a development strategy.

In some writing, distinction between fiction and nonfiction blurs. The historical novel, for example, is fiction bound by the author's research of a particular time and place. Many feature articles in newspapers and magazines reveal the use of such story elements as conflict and point of view. Santha Rama Rau's "By Any Other Name" is a good example of nonfiction that strikes us as very much like a story.

When to Use Narration

Your instructor may ask you to write a story, a narrative account drawn, perhaps, from some incident in your life, complete with characters and dialogue. More likely, you will be asked to draw on incidents from your life to develop a narrative essay. This means that narration will be used as a technique for developing a main idea or thesis. Your purpose in writing may be to share experiences or inform readers of a different time, place, or culture, or some blending of both purposes. (In other classes, you may use narrative to answer test questions, especially in history classes.) However you see your primary purpose in writing, the incidents you select, the way you tell about them, and the reflective comments you include will add up to a statement (or strong implication) of the main point you want to make.

How to Use Narration

Purpose and Thesis

The fewer observations you make about the significance of the events you narrate, the more you need to rely on the telling of the events to carry your meaning. Rau, for example, tells her story with only the briefest of comments about the significance of one's first day at school. Gaye Wagner, on the other hand, reflects on the events she narrates, observing in paragraph 4, "With the death of a comrade, I understood that I was inside the fence." Only you can decide just how much comment you want in a given narrative essay and where those comments should be placed to greatest effect. But first, and most important, have a clear sense of purpose and thesis. An unfocused retelling of some event in your life does not become a polished essay.

When thinking about experiences you might use in a narrative essay, reflect on your purpose and subject as a way to decide on a thesis. Ask, "Why do I want to tell readers about a particular incident?" "What insights into human life do I find in the incident?" Try analyzing your experiences as potential stories shaped by a central conflict that is resolved in some way. But remember that resolution does not necessarily mean a happy ending. Often the only resolution to some experiences is a lesson, bitterly learned. Growing up seems, all too often, to be filled with such painful lessons. Fortunately, they can become the topics of good stories and essays.

Organization and Details

After selecting your topic and deciding on a tentative thesis, think about the shape of your essay. The good narrative essay does not include every stray telephone call that you received the day of the big game. Select the details that are truly significant, that will carry the meaning of the experience for readers. Make your writing vivid through the use of concrete details, but be sure that they are details that contribute to the support of your thesis.

Usually narratives are presented in chronological order, but you may want to consider beginning at the end of the event and then going back to recount the events leading up to the key moment. For example, Gaye Wagner begins with her feelings after an officer's death and then goes back in time to recount his death and funeral before going forward to tell of the event after his death that altered her thinking. Varying time sequence requires careful attention to verb tenses and transition words and phrases so that readers can follow the shifts in time. Some transition words you may need to use include *first, next, then, after, the following day (week, etc.), meanwhile, at the same time.* You will find other examples in the essays in this chapter and in Chapter 5's *Writing Focus* that lists many transition words.

Another choice you must make is the perspective or point of view from which the incident will be told. Most narrative essays are told in the first person. Some writers prefer to use the third person (he, she, they) even though they are writing about their own experiences. Another choice to make is the vantage point of the narrator or essayist. Do you want to take your reader into the event at the time it occurred in your life? That is, should you tell it as if it is occurring as you write? Or, should you select the distance of the adult voice reflecting back on a childhood experience?

Keep in mind these several issues when planning your narrative essay. We all have stories to tell, experiences worth sharing with others. The key is to shape those experiences into a composition that brings readers into our lives and makes them want to know us and understand us, and thereby to understand better what they share with us.

WRITING FOCUS:
PREPARING YOUR ESSAY FOR READERS

Your instructor has probably emphasized the writing process early in your course. You may have reviewed invention strategies, ways to state a good thesis, and tips for revising and editing drafts. These steps are important, but also important is preparing your essay to meet the expectations of readers. Here are basic guidelines that will usually work. List in the margin any variations required by your instructor.

1. Always type (keyboard) papers not written in class.
2. Double-space throughout, with 1-inch margins.
3. Use a 12-point font and a standard form of type, such as Times New Roman or Courier. Never use unusual type or a script type; these are hard to read.
4. Indent paragraphs five spaces. Do not quadruple space between paragraphs.
5. Modern Language Association style guidelines call for placing your name, the date, and course information (e.g., English 111) in the upper left of your paper. Starting at the left margin on the first line, place your name. Put the date and course information on separate lines following your name.
6. Center your title and capitalize appropriately. (Capitalize first and last words and all other words except articles, conjunctions, and prepositions of five letters or less.) Do not underline the title or put it in quotation marks. *Remember:* Every essay has a title. "Essay #1" is not an effective title. Make your title clever if you can—but not "cutesy." Clear and direct are always good goals for titles.
7. Refer to Chapter 9's *Writing Focus* (p. 372) for handling references to people and titles and for handling direct quotations.

Getting Started: Reflections on Growing Up or Growing Wiser

Think back over your growing-up years. What periods in your life, particular events, or individuals come to mind as having had an impact on you, perhaps moving you closer to adulthood, to a clearer understanding of yourself and of life? What, on reflection, was an important period in your life? What was an event that changed you in some way? Who was an influential person? Why was he or she important? Write some of your reflections on these questions in a journal entry. Keep your reflections in mind as you read the essays in this chapter, thinking as you read about ways you might use your experiences in an effective narrative essay.

By Any Other Name

SANTHA RAMA RAU

Santha Rama Rau was born in India and lived her early years there, during British colonial rule of India. She has also been educated in England and at Wellesley College in the United States. A novelist, essayist, and travel writer, Rama Rau's books include *Home to India* (1945) and *Gifts of Passage* (1961). "By Any Other Name," a recounting of her experience at a British-run school in India, was first published in 1951 in *The New Yorker*.

Questions to Guide Your Reading

1. How did the author feel when she was asked to tell the class her name? How do you know?
2. Why do we get upset when someone mispronounces our name or decides to give us a nickname?

1   At the Anglo-Indian day school in Zorinabad to which my sister and I were sent when she was eight and I was five and a half, they changed our names. On the first day of school, a hot, windless morning of a north Indian September, we stood in the headmistress's study and she said, "Now you're the *new* girls. What are your names?"

2   My sister answered for us. "I am Premila, and she"—nodding in my direction—"is Santha."

3   The headmistress had been in India, I suppose, fifteen years or so, but she still smiled her helpless inability to cope with Indian names. Her rimless half-glasses glittered, and the precarious bun on the top of her head trembled as she shook her head. "Oh, my dears, those are much too hard for me. Suppose we give you pretty English names. Wouldn't that be more jolly? Let's see, now—Pamela for you, I think." She shrugged in a baffled way at my sister. "That's as close as I can get. And for *you*," she said to me, "how about Cynthia? Isn't that nice?"

4   My sister was always less easily intimidated than I was, and while she kept a stubborn silence, I said, "Thank you," in a very tiny voice.

5   We had been sent to that school because my father, among his responsibilities as an officer of the civil service, had a tour of duty

to perform in the villages around that steamy little provincial town, where he had his headquarters at that time. He used to make his shorter inspection tours on horseback, and a week before, in the stale heat of a typically postmonsoon day, we had waved good-by to him and a little procession—an assistant, a secretary, two bearers, and the man to look after the bedding rolls and luggage. They rode away through our large garden, still bright green from the rains, and we turned back into the twilight of the house and the sound of fans whispering in every room.

Up to then, my mother had refused to send Premila to school 6 in the British-run establishments of that time, because, she used to say, "you can bury a dog's tail for seven years and it still comes out curly, and you can take a Britisher away from his home for a lifetime and he still remains insular." The examinations and degrees from entirely Indian schools were not, in those days, considered valid. In my case, the question had never come up, and probably never would have come up if Mother's extraordinary good health had not broken down. For the first time in my life, she was not able to continue the lessons she had been giving us every morning. So our Hindi books were put away, the stories of the Lord Krishna as a little boy were left in mid-air, and we were sent to the Anglo-Indian school.

That first day at school is still, when I think of it, a remark- 7 able one. At that age, if one's name is changed, one develops a curious form of dual personality. I remember having a certain detached and disbelieving concern in the actions of "Cynthia," but certainly no responsibility. Accordingly, I followed the thin, erect back of the headmistress down the veranda to my classroom feeling, at most, a passing interest in what was going to happen to me in this strange, new atmosphere of School.

The building was Indian in design, with wide verandas 8 opening onto a central courtyard, but Indian verandas are usually white-washed, with stone floors. These, in the tradition of British schools, were painted dark brown and had matting on the floors. It gave a feeling of extra intensity to the heat.

I suppose there were about a dozen Indian children in the 9 school—which contained perhaps forty children in all—and four of them were in my class. They were all sitting at the back of the room, and I went to join them. I sat next to a small, solemn girl who didn't smile at me. She had long, glossy-black braids and wore a cotton dress, but she still kept on her Indian jewelry—a gold chain around her neck, thin gold bracelets, and tiny ruby studs in her ears. Like most Indian children, she had a rim of black kohl around her eyes. The cotton dress should have looked strange, but all I could think of was that I should ask my mother if I couldn't wear a dress to school, too, instead of my Indian clothes.

10   I can't remember too much about the proceedings in class that day, except for the beginning. The teacher pointed to me and asked me to stand up. "Now, dear, tell the class your name."

11   I said nothing.

12   "Come along," she said, frowning slightly. "What's your name, dear?"

13   "I don't know," I said, finally.

14   The English children in the front of the class—there were about eight or ten of them—giggled and twisted around in their chairs to look at me. I sat down quickly and opened my eyes very wide, hoping in that way to dry them off. The little girl with the braids put out her hand and very lightly touched my arm. She still didn't smile.

15   A lot of that morning I was rather bored. I looked briefly at the children's drawings pinned to the wall, and then concentrated on a lizard clinging to the ledge of the high, barred window behind the teacher's head. Occasionally it would shoot out its long yellow tongue for a fly, and then it would rest, with its eyes closed and its belly palpitating, as though it were swallowing several times quickly. The lessons were mostly concerned with reading and writing and simple numbers—things that my mother had already taught me—and I paid very little attention. The teacher wrote on the easel black-board words like "bat" and "cat," which seemed babyish to me; only "apple" was new and incomprehensible.

16   When it was time for the lunch recess, I followed the girl with braids out onto the veranda. There the children from the other classes were assembled. I saw Premila at once and ran over to her, as she had charge of our lunchbox. The children were all opening packages and sitting down to eat sandwiches. Premila and I were the only ones who had Indian food—thin wheat chapatties, some vegetable curry, and a bottle of buttermilk. Premila thrust half of it into my hand and whispered fiercely that I should go and sit with my class, because that was what the others seemed to be doing.

The enormous black eyes of the little Indian girl from my   17
class looked at my food longingly, so I offered her some. But
she only shook her head and plowed her way solemnly
through her sandwiches.

I was very sleepy after lunch, because at home we always   18
took a siesta. It was usually a pleasant time of day, with the
bedroom darkened against the harsh afternoon sun, the drifting off into sleep with the sound of Mother's voice reading a
story in one's mind, and, finally, the shrill, fussy voice of the
ayah waking one for tea.

At school, we rested for a short time on low, folding cots on   19
the veranda, and then we were expected to play games. During the hot part of the afternoon we played indoors, and after
the shadows had begun to lengthen and the slight breeze of the
evening had come up we moved outside to the wide courtyard.

I had never really grasped the system of competitive games.   20
At home, whenever we played tag or guessing games, I was always allowed to "win"—"because," Mother used to tell Premila, "she is the youngest, and we have to allow for that." I had
often heard her say it, and it seemed quite reasonable to me, but
the result was that I had no clear idea of what "winning" meant.

When we played twos-and-threes that afternoon at school, in   21
accordance with my training, I let one of the small English boys
catch me, but was naturally rather puzzled when the other children did not return the courtesy. I ran about for what seemed like
hours without ever catching anyone, until it was time for school
to close. Much later I learned that my attitude was called "not
being a good sport," and I stopped allowing myself to be caught,
but it was not for years that I really learned the spirit of the thing.

When I saw our car come up to the school gate, I broke away   22
from my classmates and rushed toward it yelling, "Ayah!
Ayah!" It seemed like an eternity since I had seen her that
morning—a wizened, affectionate figure in her white cotton
sari, giving me dozens of urgent and useless instructions on
how to be a good girl at school. Premila followed more se-
dately, and she told me on the way home never to do that again
in front of the other children.

When we got home we went straight to Mother's high,   23
white room to have tea with her, and I immediately climbed
onto the bed and bounced gently up and down on the springs.
Mother asked how we had liked our first day in school. I was

so pleased to be home and to have left that peculiar Cynthia behind that I had nothing whatever to say about school, except to
ask what "apple" meant. But Premila told Mother about the
classes, and added that in her class they had weekly tests to see
if they had learned their lessons well.

24   I asked, "What's a test?"

25   Premila said, "You're too small to have them. You won't
have them in your class for donkey's years." She had learned
the expression that day and was using it for the first time. We
all laughed enormously at her wit. She also told Mother, in an
aside, that we should take sandwiches to school the next day.
Not, she said, that *she* minded. But they would be simpler for
me to handle.

26   That whole lovely evening I didn't think about school at all.
I sprinted barefoot across the lawns with my favorite playmate,
the cook's son, to the stream at the end of the garden. We quar-
reled in our usual way, waded in the tepid water under the
lime trees, and waited for the night to bring out the smell of the
jasmine. I listened with fascination to his stories of ghosts and
demons, until I was too frightened to cross the garden alone in
the semidarkness. The ayah found me, shouted at the cook's
son, scolded me, hurried me in to supper—it was an entirely
usual, wonderful evening.

27   It was a week later, the day of Premila's first test, that our
lives changed rather abruptly. I was sitting at the back of my
class, in my usual inattentive way, only half listening to the
teacher. I had started a rather guarded friendship with the girl
with the braids, whose name turned out to be Nalini (Nancy, in
school). The three other Indian children were already fast
friends. Even at that age it was apparent to all of us that friendship with the English or Anglo-Indian children was out of the
question. Occasionally, during the class, my new friend and I
would draw pictures and show them to each other secretly.

28   The door opened sharply and Premila marched in. At first,
the teacher smiled at her in a kindly and encouraging way and
said, "Now, you're little Cynthia's sister?"

29   Premila didn't even look at her. She stood with her feet
planted firmly apart and her shoulders rigid, and addressed
herself directly to me. "Get up," she said. "We're going home."

30   I didn't know what had happened, but I was aware that it
was a crisis of some sort. I rose obediently and started to walk
toward my sister.

"Bring your pencils and your notebook," she said. 31

I went back for them, and together we left the room. The 32
teacher started to say something just as Premila closed the
door, but we didn't wait to hear what it was.

In complete silence we left the school grounds and started to 33
walk home. Then I asked Premila what the matter was. All she
would say was "We're going home for good."

It was a very tiring walk for a child of five and a half, and I 34
dragged along behind Premila with my pencils growing sticky
in my hand. I can still remember looking at the dusty hedges,
and the tangles of thorns in the ditches by the side of the road,
smelling the faint fragrance from the eucalyptus trees and
wondering whether we would ever reach home. Occasionally
a horse-drawn tonga passed us, and the women, in their pink
or green silks, stared at Premila and me trudging along on the
side of the road. A few coolies and a line of women carrying
baskets of vegetables on their heads smiled at us. But it was
nearing the hottest time of day, and the road was almost de-
serted. I walked more and more slowly, and shouted to Premila, from time to time, "Wait for me!" with increasing
peevishness. She spoke to me only once, and that was to tell me
to carry my notebook on my head, because of the sun.

When we got to our house the ayah was just taking a tray of 35
lunch into Mother's room. She immediately started a long,
worried questioning about what are you children doing back
here at this hour of the day.

Mother looked very startled and very concerned, and asked 36
Premila what had happened.

Premila said, "We had our test today, and she made me and 37
the other Indians sit at the back of the room, with a desk between each one."

Mother said, "Why was that, darling?" 38

"She said it was because Indians cheat," Premila added. "So 39
I don't think we should go back to that school."

Mother looked very distant, and was silent a long time. At 40
last she said, "Of course not, darling." She sounded displeased.

We all shared the curry she was having for lunch, and after- 41
ward I was sent off to the beautifully familiar bedroom for my
siesta. I could hear Mother and Premila talking through the
open door.

Mother said, "Do you suppose she understood all that?" 42

Premila said, "I shouldn't think so. She's a baby." 43

44   Mother said, "Well, I hope it won't bother her."

45   Of course, they were both wrong. I understood it perfectly, and I remember it all very clearly. But I put it happily away, because it had all happened to a girl called Cynthia, and I never was really particularly interested in her.

Expanding Vocabulary

Find the meaning of each of the following words either from its context in this essay or from studying your dictionary. Then select five of the words and use each one in a separate sentence of your own. The number in parentheses is the number of the paragraph in which the word appears.

precarious (3)	ayah (18)
intimidated (4)	wizened (22)
insular (6)	sari (22)
kohl (9)	tepid (26)
palpitating (15)	tonga (34)
incomprehensible (15)	coolies (34)
chapatties (16)	peevishness (34)

Understanding Content

1. Why did Rama Rau and her sister start attending the Anglo-Indian day school? What was the author's mother's view of the British?
2. What happened to the author and her sister at the beginning of their first day?
3. What did Rama Rau have to learn about games?
4. What happened the day her sister had a test?

Drawing Inferences about Thesis and Purpose

1. What was the author's reaction to her first day of school?
2. What is the author's purpose in writing? What does she want readers to understand from her experience? Write a thesis for the essay.

Analyzing Strategies and Style

1. Look at Rama Rau's description of the headmistress (paragraph 3). What do the details tell us about the author's view of this woman?
2. What differences in cultures are revealed by the details of afternoons at school and afternoons and evenings at home?

Thinking Critically

1. What, if any, details of Indian culture are new to you? Has Rama Rau captured the Indian—and Anglo-Indian—life effectively? What details are most important in creating this glimpse of Indian culture?

2. Santha and Premila respond differently to the discrimination they experience. Do you think that one strategy is better than the other? Defend your views.

3. Should students from other cultures change their names—or the pronunciation of their names—to fit in better in U.S. schools? Why or why not?

The End of My Childhood

N. SCOTT MOMADAY

For many years an English professor at the University of Arizona, N. Scott Momaday is an artist, poet (*The Gourd Dancer*), Pulitzer Prize–winning novelist (*House Made of Dawn*), and author of a much-praised autobiography, *The Names: A Memoir,* published in 1976. Momaday, whose father was a Kiowa, explores this heritage in his memoir, capturing the American Indian's sense of harmony with the Earth. The following excerpt from *The Names* recounts Momaday's loss of childhood innocence.

Questions to Guide Your Reading

1. How is the narrative organized? What is Momaday's point of view, the perspective from which the event is presented to readers?

2. Think about your most frightening experience. How did you feel then? What do you think about it now?

1   At Jemez I came to the end of my childhood. There were no schools within easy reach. I had to go nearly thirty miles to school at Bernalillo, and one year I lived away in Albuquerque. My mother and father wanted me to have the benefit of a sound preparation for college, and so we read through many high school catalogues. After long deliberation we decided that

I should spend my last year of high school at a military academy in Virginia.

2   The day before I was to leave I went walking across the river to the red mesa, where many times before I had gone to be alone with my thoughts. And I had climbed several times to the top of the mesa and looked among the old ruins there for pottery. This time I chose to climb the north end, perhaps because I had not gone that way before and wanted to see what it was. It was a difficult climb, and when I got to the top I was spent. I lingered among the ruins for more than an hour, I judge, waiting for my strength to return. From there I could see the whole valley below, the fields, the river, and the village. It was all very beautiful, and the sight of it filled me with longing.

3   I looked for an easier way to come down, and at length I found a broad, smooth runway of rock, a shallow groove winding out like a stream. It appeared to be safe enough, and I started to follow it. There were steps along the way, a stairway, in effect. But the steps became deeper and deeper, and at last I had to drop down the length of my body and more. Still it seemed convenient to follow in the groove of rock. I was more than halfway down when I came upon a deep, funnel-shaped formation in my path. And there I had to make a decision. The slope on either side was extremely steep and forbidding, and yet I thought that I could work my way down on either side. The formation at my feet was something else. It was perhaps ten or twelve feet deep, wide at the top and narrow at the bottom, where there appeared to be a level ledge. If I could get down through the funnel to the ledge, I should be all right; surely the rest of the way down was negotiable. But I realized that there could be no turning back. Once I was down in that rocky chute I could not get up again, for the round wall which nearly encircled the space there was too high and sheer. I elected to go down into it, to try for the ledge directly below. I eased myself down the smooth, nearly vertical wall on my back, pressing my arms and legs outward against the sides. After what seemed a long time I was trapped in the rock. The ledge was no longer there below me; it had been an optical illusion. Now, in this angle of vision, there was nothing but the ground, far, far below, and jagged boulders set there like teeth. I remember that my arms were scraped and bleeding, stretched

out against the walls with all the pressure that I could exert.
When once I looked down I saw that my legs, also spread out
and pressed hard against the walls, were shaking violently. I
was in an impossible situation: I could not move in any direction, save downward in a fall, and I could not stay beyond another minute where I was. I believed then that I would die
there, and I saw with a terrible clarity the things of the valley
below. They were not the less beautiful to me. It seemed to me
that I grew suddenly very calm in view of that beloved world.
And I remember nothing else of that moment. I passed out of
my mind, and the next thing I knew I was sitting down on the
ground, very cold in the shadows, and looking up at the rock
where I had been within an eyelash of eternity. That was a
strange thing in my life, and I think of it as the end of an age. I
should never again see the world as I saw it on the other side
of that moment, in the bright reflection of time lost. There are
such reflections, and for some of them I have the names.

Expanding Vocabulary

Examine the following words in their contexts in the essay and then
write a brief definition or synonym for each one. (Do not use a dictionary; try to guess the word's meaning from its context.) The number in
parentheses is the number of the paragraph in which the word appears.

mesa (2)
negotiable (3)
chute (3)
optical illusion (3)

Understanding Content

1. What were the circumstances that led Momaday to the event
   at Jemez?
2. Momaday presents dramatic details of the incident. Where was
   he climbing? What could he see at the top of his climb? How did
   the view make him feel?
3. Why did Momaday choose to come down a different way? After
   starting down, what decision did he have to make?
4. How did that decision turn out to be critical? What situation did
   it lead to?
5. When stretched across the rocky chute, what does Momaday
   think about initially? Then what happens to him?

Drawing Inferences about Thesis and Purpose

1. Momaday says that this experience marked "the end of an age." Why? Why will he "never again see the world as I [he] saw it on the other side of that moment"? What did Momaday have to face on the rocky chute?
2. What is Momaday's thesis?

Analyzing Strategies and Style

1. Analyze Momaday's style of writing. Is his word choice mostly informal or formal, concrete or abstract? Are his sentences mostly simple or complex, short or long, straightforward or highly qualified? Do the choices seem right for the telling of this narrative? What does he gain by his choice of style?
2. Momaday uses an effective metaphor in the middle of paragraph 3: "jagged boulders set there like teeth." Explain the comparison and its emotional effect.

Thinking Critically

1. Momaday took his climb "to be alone with my [his] thoughts" before his move to a new state and school. Why is it good to take time for reflection before major changes in our lives? Do you take time for reflection, for time alone, on a regular basis? Why or why not?
2. Many people like to test themselves physically, believing that such activities build character as well as muscles. Do you enjoy some strenuous physical activity? If so, what are your reasons for the activity? What do you think you have gained?

Always Running

LUIS J. RODRIGUEZ

Luis Rodriguez (b. 1954), a poet, journalist, and community activist, grew up poor in Los Angeles, struggled with drugs and gangs, and held many odd jobs before and during his years at East Los Angeles College, Berkeley, and UCLA. He has served as a facilitator for various writing workshops and has published two books of poems, *Poems Across the Pavement* (1989) and *The Concrete River* (1991). In the following (an excerpt from Chapter 2 of Rodriguez's memoir *Always Running* [1993]), observe how the author combines descriptive details and dialogue—and uses restraint effectively.

Questions to Guide Your Reading and Reflection

    1. Why does Rodriguez begin with the "barrio" quotation? What does it contribute to the essay?

    2. What is your response to the quotation below?

"If you ain't from no barrio, then you ain't born."
                   —a 10-year-old boy from South San Gabriel

1   One evening dusk came early in South San Gabriel, with wind and cold spinning to earth. People who had been sitting on porches or on metal chairs near fold-up tables topped with cards and beer bottles collected their things to go inside. Others put on sweaters or jackets. A storm gathered beyond the trees.

2   Tino and I strolled past the stucco and wood-frame homes of the neighborhood consisting mostly of Mexicans with a sprinkling of poor white families (usually from Oklahoma, Arkansas and Texas). *Ranchera* music did battle with Country & Western songs as we continued toward the local elementary school, an oil-and-grime stained basketball under my arm.

3   We stopped in front of a chain-link fence which surrounded the school. An old brick building cast elongated shadows over a basketball court of concrete on the other side of the fence. Leaves and paper swirled in tiny tornadoes.

4   "Let's go over," Tino proposed.

5   I looked up and across the fence. A sign above us read: NO ONE ALLOWED AFTER 4:30 PM, BY ORDER OF THE LOS ANGELES COUNTY SHERIFF'S DEPARTMENT. Tino turned toward me, shrugged his shoulders and gave me a who-cares look.

6   "Help me up, man, then throw the ball over."

7   I cupped my hands and lifted Tino up while the boy scaled the fence, jumped over and landed on sneakered feet.

8   "Come on, Luis, let's go," Tino shouted from the other side.

9   I threw over the basketball, walked back a ways, then ran and jumped on the fence, only to fall back. Although we were both 10 years old, I cut a shorter shadow.

10   "Forget you, man," Tino said. "I'm going to play without you."

11   "Wait!" I yelled, while walking further back. I crouched low to the ground, then took off, jumped up and placed torn sneakers in the steel mesh. I made it over with a big thud.

12   Wiping the grass and dirt from my pants, I casually walked up to the ball on the ground, picked it up, and continued past Tino toward the courts.

13   "Hey Tino, what are you waiting for?"

14   The gusts proved no obstacle for a half-court game of B-ball, even as dark clouds smothered the sky.

15   Boy voices interspersed with ball cracking on asphalt. Tino's lanky figure seemed to float across the court, as if he had wings under his thin arms. Just then, a black-and-white squad car cruised down the street. A searchlight sprayed across the school yard. The vehicle slowed to a halt. The light shone toward the courts and caught Tino in mid-flight of a lay-up.

16   The dribbling and laughter stopped.

17   "All right, this is the sheriff's," a voice commanded. Two deputies stood by the fence, batons and flashlights in hand.

18   "Let's get out of here," Tino responded.

19   "What do you mean?" I countered. "Why don't we just stay here?"

20   "You nuts! We trespassing, man," Tino replied. "When they get a hold of us, they going to beat the crap out of us."

21   "Are you sure?"

22   "I know, believe me, I know."

23   "So where do we go?"

24   By then one of the deputies shouted back: "You boys get over here by the fence—now!"

25   But Tino dropped the ball and ran. I heard the deputies yell for Tino to stop. One of them began climbing the fence. I decided to take off too.

26   It never stopped, this running. We were constant prey, and the hunters soon became big blurs: the police, the gangs, the junkies, the dudes on Garvey Boulevard who took our money, all smudged into one. Sometimes they were teachers who jumped on us Mexicans as if we were born with a hideous stain. We were always afraid. Always running.

27   Tino and I raced toward the dark boxes called classrooms. The rooms lay there, hauntingly still without the voices of children, the commands of irate teachers or the clapping sounds of books as they were closed. The rooms were empty, forbidden places at night. We scurried around the structures toward a courtyard filled with benches next to the cafeteria building.

Tino hopped on a bench, then pulled himself over a high   28
fence. He walked a foot or two on top of it, stopped, and pro-
ceeded to climb over to the cafeteria's rooftop. I looked over
my shoulder. The deputies weren't far behind, their guns
drawn. I grabbed hold of the fence on the side of the cafeteria.
I looked up and saw Tino's perspiring face over the roof's edge,
his arm extended down toward me.

I tried to climb up, my feet dangling. But then a firm hand   29
seized a foot and pulled at it.

"They got me!" I yelled.   30

Tino looked below. A deputy spied the boy and called out: 31
"Get down here . . . you *greaser*!"

Tino straightened up and disappeared. I heard a flood of foot-   32
steps on the roof—then a crash. Soon an awful calm covered us.

"Tino!" I cried out.   33

A deputy restrained me as the other one climbed onto the roof.   34
He stopped at a skylight, jagged edges on one of its sides. Shining a flashlight inside the building, the officer spotted Tino's mis-
shapen body on the floor, sprinkled over with shards of glass.

Expanding Vocabulary

Study the contexts in which the following words are used, or study
their definitions in your dictionary, and then use each word in a separate sentence. The number in parentheses is the number of the paragraph in which the word appears.

elongated (3)	smudged (26)
scaled (7)	hauntingly (27)
obstacle (14)	irate (27)
interspersed (15)	scurried (27)

Understanding Content

1. Briefly summarize the situation of the narrative by answering the
   reporter's questions: who, what, where, when.
2. What happens to Tino?

Drawing Inferences about Thesis and Purpose

1. Although both Tino and Luis are ten years old, their relationship
   does not seem quite equal. Which one seems to be the leader?
   How do you know?

2. Since Tino is already on the court, why does Luis say, in paragraph 13, "What are you waiting for?" What does he want to accomplish?
3. What is Rodriguez's purpose in writing? What is his thesis?

Analyzing Strategies and Style

1. Examine the author's opening three paragraphs. What do we learn about the narrator from the opening? What tone do the paragraphs establish?
2. Rodriguez includes several metaphors and images in his writing. Find three and explain each one's meaning and contribution.

Thinking Critically

1. Are you surprised by Tino's assertion that the police will beat the boys if they are caught? Do you think that he overstates and over-reacts? If you think so, how would you explain your views to Rodriguez? If you agree with Rodriguez, do you have evidence to support your views?
2. Rodriguez writes that the many "hunters" blur into one. Included are teachers "who jumped on us Mexicans." Does this statement surprise you? Why or why not?
3. What are some strategies young people can use to try to cope with gangs, with drug dealers, and with prejudiced teachers?

Death of an Officer

GAYE WAGNER

Gaye Wagner is a detective with the child abuse unit in the San Diego Police Department. She holds a master's degree and previously worked in children and youth services in New Hampshire. "Death of an Officer" was first published in *The American Enterprise* magazine in May 1995. Through narration Wagner examines issues of a police officer's commitment and perspective and shows us how we can learn and grow through reflection on telling moments in our lives, regardless of our age.

Questions to Guide Your Reading and Reflection

1. How did Officer Wagner feel after Officer Davis's death? What was the difference between her training experience and this experience?

2. Reflect on a time you cried in front of others. How did you
feel then? What are your reflections on the incident now?

When Officer Ron Davis was shot in the dark, foggy   1
predawn of September 17, 1991, I momentarily lost my perspective on why I've chosen to do what I'm doing. For a time, I
focused on just one dimension of my job as a police officer: the
possibility of a violent death, for me or people I care about.

Despite the graphic slides and blow-by-blow descriptions of   2
on-duty deaths that we sat through in the Academy, I still must
have believed deep down that I, and those alongside me, were
invincible. Then the faceless gloom of mortality took the place of
a fallen comrade. The streets became an evil, threatening place.

Before I felt the blow of a co-worker's death, I looked on   3
each shooting, stabbing, and act of violence as any rubber-
necker would—with a certain detachment. I was living the ul-
timate student experience: Social Wildlife 101. What better way
to understand problems of crime and justice than to immerse
yourself in the 'hood. I was there, but I was still an onlooker
peering inside some kind of fence. I watched, probed each
tragic or bizarre incident with curiosity, and pondered the
problems I faced.

With the death of a comrade, I understood that I was inside   4
the fence. I'm no longer an outsider looking in. The shadow of
death stalks all of us who walk in the valley of drugs, guns, alcohol, hopelessness, and hate. Police, addicts, hustlers, parents
trying to build futures for their children, good people struggling—we all risk falling into the firing line of desperation, ap-
athy, or corruption.

For a while, my response to the new threats I saw around me   5
was to treat all people like they were the enemy. Since an "us"
and "them" mentality can be a self-fulfilling prophecy, some of
my contacts with people were a little bumpy. Normally my approach is courteous, in one of several variations: either as sym-
pathizer, "just the facts, Bud" chronicler, or all-ears naive
airhead who can hardly believe that you, yes you, could do a
dastardly deed . . . ("how did this all happen my friend?").

But suddenly I just wasn't as enamored with this job as I had   6
been. Let's face it, a sense of contributing to society, the excitement of racing cars with lights and sirens, helping folks, and the

drama of never knowing what's next place a poor second to living long enough to count grey hairs and collect Social Security.

7   I had trouble getting an impersonal all-units bulletin about someone I knew out of my head. I read these bulletins every day, but the words now stung: "187 Suspect . . . Arrest in Public for 187 P.C.—Homicide of a Police Officer . . . Suspect Description: Castillo, Arno . . . On September 17, 1991, at 05:15 hours, Castillo was contacted by two officers in regard to a domestic violence call. As the officers approached, Castillo opened fire with a .45 cal. automatic weapon, fatally wounding one officer."

8   It was a routine incident that any one of us could have gone to, in an apartment complex that we've all been to. A victim mired in her own problems—a broken collar bone and a life crushing down around her—forgot to tell officers that her crazed, abusive boyfriend had fled with a gun. What followed happened fast. Thick fog and darkness shrouded the complex parking lot where Davis and his partner stopped to contact a driver backing out of the lot.

9   Ron took a bullet in the neck as he stepped out of his passenger side door. The bullet bled him faster than any resuscitating efforts could counteract. He died while his partner hopelessly tried to breathe life back into his bloody, weakening body. Medics said that even if they'd been there when it happened, there would have been nothing they could do to save his life.

10   The next week brought a crush of support for our division. The chief, the field operations commander, psychological services counselors, and peer support counselors all came to our lineups to say we're here man, and we know it doesn't feel good. The lineup room looked like a wake with its display of food, flowers, and cards that showered in from other divisions, other departments, and the citizens of our division.

11   Ron's squad was placed on leave, so officers came from other divisions to help us cover manpower shortages. And on the day of the funeral, officers volunteered from all over the city to cover our beats so that everyone in our division could go to the service.

12   The funeral procession filled the three miles from Jack Murphy Stadium to the church with bumper-to-bumper police units flashing red and blue overhead lights. Police cars came from San Diego, the Border Patrol, the U.S. Marshals, El Cajon, La

Mesa, Chula Vista, National City, Riverside, Los Angeles, seemingly everywhere. The sight we made sent chills up my spine.

For the breadth of that three-mile procession, for a few minutes at least, drivers couldn't keep racing in their usual preoccupied frenzy. Traffic had to stop. In those frozen freeway moments, a tiny corner of the world had to take time out to notice our mourning at the passing of Ronald W. Davis, age 24, husband, father of two, San Diego police officer. The citizens held captive by the procession responded with heart. There was no angry beeping, there were no cars nosing down breakdown lanes. Drivers turned off ignitions in anticipation of a long wait and watched patiently. Many got out of their cars and waved or yelled words of sympathy.

The pastor's words at the funeral have stayed with me, because he began stretching my perspective back to a more fruitful, hopeful size. "Life is not defined by the quantity of years that we are on this earth, but by the quality of the time that we spend here."

I never cried at the funeral. I cried three weeks later in front of a second grade class.

Staring at the bulletin board one day drinking my coffee, I noticed a sheaf of papers with big, just-learned-to-write letters on them. The papers were letters to the Officers of Southeastern from Ms. Matthews's second grade class at Boone Elementary:

Dear Friends of Officer Davis,

We hope this letter will make you feel better. We feel sad about what happened to Officer Davis. We know he was a nice man and a good cop. We thank you for protecting our neighborhood. We know you try to protect every one of us. We know Officer Davis was a good father. We're sorry.

Your friend, Jeffrey

Dear Friends of Officer Davis,

We feel sorry about Officer Davis. I know you feel sorry for what happened when the bad guy killed your friend, Officer Davis. Thank you for protecting us. I know that he's dead and

I know you feel sorry about it. I'm glad you got the bad guy. Do you think this would happen again? I'm sure not. Please protect yourself.

Your friend,

Henry

P.S. I live in Meadowbrook apartments.

Thank you.

Dear Friends of Officer Davis,

We feel sad about Officer Davis being killed. The man that killed Officer Davis got killed right behind our house. We live in front of Meadowbrook apartments. It is really sad that Officer Davis got killed. Last year when my brother was in sixth grade and he was playing basketball with his friends, two kids came and took the ball away. They broke his basketball hoop. Officers helped find the two kids. We are thankful you are trying to protect us.

Your friend,

Travis

Dear Friends,

I hope you will feel better. I know how you feel, sad. Was Officer Davis your friend? Well, he was my friend, too. When I saw the news I felt very sad for him. When I grow up, I might be a police officer. I'll never forget Officer Davis. I know how losing a friend is. When you lose a friend you feel very sad. I know how losing a friend is cause my best friend moved away to Virginia. They wrote to me once and I still miss her and I miss Officer Davis, too.

Your Friend,

Jennifer L.

Dear Officers,

I hope you feel a little better with my letter. We feel sorry that Officer Davis was killed. I heard that he got shot on his neck

when he was just getting out of his car. I also heard that Officer Davis was an officer for two years and that he has two children. That one is one years old and the other five years old. I
want to say thank you for protecting us and for helping us. We
all wish that Officer Davis was still alive.

Your friend always,

Arlene

Dear Officers,

We were so sad that your friend Officer Davis died. Last night
on 9-17-91 I couldn't sleep because I was thinking all about
your friend Officer Davis. When I heard about Officer Davis
getting shot I was so sad. I know how it feels when a friend is
gone. I wish that Officer Davis could hear this but he can't right
now. Officer Davis and the rest of the force do a great job.

Sincerely,

Jasper

    Those letters brought feelings up from my gut. The next day   17
I visited Room B-17 to deliver thank you notes to the authors.
Ms. Matthews was so excited with my visit that she asked me
to speak to the class. She explained that the letters were a class
exercise to help the students deal with fears they had expressed
to her after the shooting. Because many of her students lived in
the apartments where Ron was shot, the shooting was very
personal to them. Some couldn't sleep, others were afraid to
walk to school, and some were shocked at the realization that
the "good guys" get killed too.
    I hadn't expected to give a speech, and wasn't really ready   18
to give one on this particular topic. When I faced the class, I
saw 32 sets of Filipino, Latino, white, and African-American
eyes fixed on me. Their hands all sat respectfully in their laps.
In those young faces, I saw an innocence and trust that I didn't
want to shake. I thought of the sympathy in their letters; I
pictured them passing by the large, dark stain of Officer
Davis's blood that still scarred the parking lot pavement; and
I wondered what young minds must think when a force of

blacked-out SWAT officers sweeps through nearby homes in search of the "bad guy" who shot the "good guy."

19   I wondered how many of the children had been home looking out their windows when the suspect, Arnanda Castillo, was shot by a volley of officers' gunfire as he sprung out of his hiding place in the late afternoon of September 17. I couldn't imagine what these children must be thinking, because a second grader growing up in rural New Hampshire in 1962 didn't witness such events. I could only think that second graders of any generation in any place in the world shouldn't have to witness or ponder the senselessness of human violence.

20   When I finally opened my mouth to speak, my eyes watered and no words would come out. I could say nothing. Each time I tried to push my voice, my eyes watered more. I looked helplessly at Ms. Matthews and the vice principal, who had come to listen to me. Ms. Matthews came to my rescue by starting to talk to the class about strong feelings and the importance of letting feelings out so we don't trap sadness inside ourselves. "Even police officers know that crying can be a strong thing to do." Her reassurances to them reassured me and made me smile at the image of myself, "the big, brave cop" choked up by a second grade class.

21   We talked for a time about the shooting, about having someone to talk to about scary things, and about how important their thoughtful letters had been in a time of sadness. By the time I left, they were more enchanted with my handcuffs and nunchakus than they were concerned by death. Ahhh, the lure for us kids of all ages conjured up by cops and robbers, catching bad guys, rescuing good guys, and having a belt full of cop toys. Through Ron's death, I grew to have a more mature, realistic view of my job.

22   Through the eyes of the pastor at the funeral and Ms. Matthews's second grade class, I recovered perspective and belief in the value of what I do. It's important for me to live my life doing something I believe is important for this thing we call humanity. And I believe that what I do is important because of people like Henry, Jasper, Jennifer L., Jeffrey, Travis, Arlene, Ms. Matthews, and all of the kids in Room B-17.

Expanding Vocabulary

Examine the following words in their contexts in the essay and then write a brief definition or synonym for each one. (Do not use a dictionary; try to guess the word's meaning from its context.) The number in parentheses is the number of the paragraph in which the word appears.

invincible (2)	shrouded (8)
rubbernecker (3)	resuscitating (9)
bizarre (3)	nunchakus (21)
dastardly (5)	conjured (2l)
enamored (6)	

Understanding Content

1. Where does the author work, and what does she do?
2. What was her initial response to Officer Davis's death?
3. What did she do in response to reading the students' letters? Then what happened?

Drawing Inferences about Thesis and Purpose

1. What did the author receive from the young students? How did they help her change her thinking?
2. What is Wagner's thesis?

Analyzing Strategies and Style

1. Describe Wagner's chronology. How could the order be altered? What does Wagner gain with her chronology?
2. Near the end, Wagner writes that the students seem most interested in her "cop toys." What does she gain by including this detail?

Thinking Critically

1. Have you experienced violence in your family, neighborhood, or school? If so, how did the experience make you feel? If not, can you describe how you think the second graders from the neighborhood where Officer Davis was shot may have felt?
2. Has it occurred to you that police officers may doubt their commitment or fear for their safety? Should officers express their feelings as Wagner has? Why or why not?
3. Is it fair to say that there are some truths we have to "learn" several times before we really understand? Is there any age limit to

learning tough truths? How hard is it to learn, to gain perspective, to grow wiser? Be prepared to discuss your answers to these questions.

How Mr. Dewey Decimal Saved My Life

BARBARA KINGSOLVER

Barbara Kingsolver grew up in rural Kentucky, obtained a degree from DePauw University, worked abroad, settled in Tucson, Arizona, and obtained an MA degree in biology from the University of Arizona. As a novelist she draws on her rural roots, her time spent living abroad, and the southwestern world of her adult years. Her first big novel was *Pigs in Heaven* (1994), and she received much acclaim for *The Poisonwood Bible* (1999) as well. The following essay comes from her collection of essays, *High Tide in Tucson: Essays from Now or Never* (1994).

Questions to Guide Your Reading and Reflection

1. Who or what is Mr. Dewey Decimal?
2. Who has most influenced your life? What did that person do for you?

1   A librarian named Miss Truman Richey snatched me from the jaws of ruin, and it's too late now to thank her. I'm not the first person to notice that we rarely get around to thanking those who've helped us most. Salvation is such a heady thing the temptation is to dance gasping on the shore, shouting that we are alive, till our forgotten savior has long since gone under. Or else sit quietly, sideswiped and embarrassed, mumbling that we really did know pretty much how to swim. But now that I see the wreck that could have been, without Miss Richey, I'm of a fearsome mind to throw my arms around every living librarian who crosses my path, on behalf of the souls they never knew they saved.

2   I reached high school at the close of the sixties, in the Commonwealth of Kentucky, whose ranking on educational spending was I think around fifty-first, after Mississippi and whatever

was below Mississippi. Recently Kentucky has drastically changed the way money is spent on its schools, but back then, the wealth of the county decreed the wealth of the school, and few coins fell far from the money trees that grew in Lexington. Our county, out where the bluegrass begins to turn brown, was just scraping by. Many a dedicated teacher served out earnest missions in our halls, but it was hard to spin silk purses out of a sow's ear budget. We didn't get anything fancy like Latin or Calculus. Apart from English, the only two courses of study that ran for four consecutive years, each one building upon the last, were segregated: Home Ec for girls and Shop for boys. And so I stand today, a woman who knows how to upholster, color-coordinate a table setting, and plan a traditional wedding—valuable skills I'm still waiting to put to good use in my life.

As far as I could see from the lofty vantage point of age six-   3
teen, there was nothing required of me at Nicholas County High that was going to keep me off the streets; unfortunately we had no streets, either. We had lanes, roads, and rural free delivery routes, six in number, I think. We had two stoplights, which were set to burn green in all directions after 6 P.M., so as not, should the event of traffic arise, to slow anybody up.

What we *didn't* have included almost anything respectable   4
teenagers might do in the way of entertainment. In fact, there was one thing for teenagers to do to entertain themselves, and it was done in the backs of Fords and Chevrolets. It wasn't upholstering skills that were brought to bear on those backseats, either. Though the wedding-planning skills did follow.

I found myself beginning a third year of high school in a   5
state of unrest, certain I already knew what there was to know, academically speaking—all wised up and no place to go. Some of my peers used the strategy of rationing out the Science and Math classes between periods of suspension or childbirth, stretching their schooling over the allotted four years, and I envied their broader vision. I had gone right ahead and used the classes up, like a reckless hiker gobbling up all the rations on day one of a long march. Now I faced years of Study Hall, with brief interludes of Home Ec III and IV as the bright spots. I was developing a lean and hungry outlook.

We did have a school library, and a librarian who was surely   6
paid inadequately to do the work she did. Yet there she was, every afternoon, presiding over the study hall, and she noticed

me. For reasons I can't fathom, she discerned potential. I expect she saw my future, or at least the one I craved so hard it must have materialized in the air above me, connected to my head by little cartoon bubbles. If that's the future she saw, it was riding down the road on the back of a motorcycle, wearing a black leather jacket with "Violators" (that was the name of our county's motorcycle gang, and I'm not kidding) stitched in a solemn arc across the back.

7   There is no way on earth I really would have ended up a Violator Girlfriend—I could only dream of such a thrilling fate. But I was set hard upon wrecking my reputation in the limited ways available to skinny, unsought-after girls. They consisted mainly of cutting up in class, pretending to be surly, and making up shocking, entirely untrue stories about my home life. I wonder now that my parents continued to feed me. I clawed like a cat in a gunnysack against the doom I feared: staying home to reupholster my mother's couch one hundred thousand weekends in a row, until some tolerant myopic farm boy came along to rescue me from sewing-machine slavery.

8   Miss Richey had something else in mind. She took me by the arm in study hall one day and said, "Barbara, I'm going to teach you Dewey Decimal."

9   One more valuable skill in my life.

10   She launched me on the project of cataloging and shelving every one of the, probably, thousand books in the Nicholas County High School library. And since it beat Home Ec III by a mile, I spent my study-hall hours this way without audible complaint, so long as I could look plenty surly while I did it. Though it was hard to see the real point of organizing books nobody ever looked at. And since it was my God-given duty in those days to be frank as a plank, I said as much to Miss Richey.

11   She just smiled. She with her hidden agenda. And gradually, in the process of handling every book in the room, I made some discoveries. I found *Gone With the Wind*, which I suspected my mother felt was kind of trashy, and I found Edgar Allan Poe, who scared me witless. I found that the call number for books about snakes is 666. I found William Saroyan's *Human Comedy*, down there on the shelf between Human Anatomy and Human Physiology, where probably no one had touched it since 1943. But I read it, and it spoke to me. In spite of myself

I imagined the life of an immigrant son who believed human kindness was a tangible and glorious thing. I began to think about words like *tangible* and *glorious*. I read on. After I'd read all the good ones, I went back and read Human Anatomy and Human Physiology and found that I liked those pretty well too.

It came to pass in two short years that the walls of my high 12 school dropped down, and I caught the scent of a world. I started to dream up intoxicating lives for myself that I could not have conceived without the books. So I didn't end up on a motorcycle. I ended up roaring hell-for-leather down the backroads of transcendent, reeling sentences. A writer. Imagine that.

Expanding Vocabulary

Match each word in column A with its definition in column B. When in doubt, first find the word in the essay and look for context clues to aid your understanding of the word's meaning. Then, if necessary, use your dictionary to complete the matching exercise. The number in parentheses is the number of the paragraph in which the word appears.

Column A	Column B
heady (1)	strategically superior
sideswiped (1)	out of one's good sense
decreed (2)	recognized, detected
missions (2)	hit with a glancing blow
vantage (3)	out loud
fathom (6)	thrilling, intoxicating
discerned (6)	comprehend, understand
surly (7)	special assignments, vocations
myopic (7)	exalted, mystical
audible (10)	established, determined
witless (11)	dizzying
transcendent (12)	ill-humored, nasty
reeling (12)	nearsighted

Understanding Content

1. What period in her life does the author discuss in this essay?
2. How does Kingsolver describe education at her school?
3. What did teens do for "entertainment" in the author's community?
4. What did the author initially yearn to be or do?
5. What did the high school librarian have Kingsolver do?
6. What was the consequence of this experience for Kingsolver?

Drawing Inferences about Thesis and Purpose

1. What can we conclude about the world the author grew up in?
2. Kingsolver sums up her Home Ec classes as having taught her "how to upholster, color-coordinate a table setting, and plan a traditional wedding—valuable skills I'm still waiting to put to good use in my life." What can we infer about her life? What seems to be Kingsolver's attitude toward her Home Ec education?

Analyzing Strategies and Style

1. Kingsolver uses several clever, perhaps unusual, expressions. Explain the idea in each of the following.
   a. "hard to spin silk purses out of a sow's ear budget" (2)
   b. "used the classes up, like a reckless hiker gobbling up all the rations on day one of a long march" (5)
   c. "I clawed like a cat in a gunnysack" (7)
   d. "in two short years . . . the walls of my high school dropped down" (12)
   e. "I ended up roaring hell-for-leather down the backroads of transcendent, reeling sentences" (12)

Thinking Critically

1. Have you had someone older, a teacher or friend's parent for example, significantly change the direction of your life? If so, what did they do to help you change?
2. When Kingsolver writes that reading books allowed her to catch "the scent of a world," what does she suggest that books give us?
3. Have you found some particular book or books that have given you "the scent of a world"? If so, what books did this for you—and what world did they show you?
4. Many young people are not reading much these days. Is this a problem? Why or why not? If it is a problem, what can we do to correct the problem?

Captivated

MEREDITH F. SMALL

A professor of anthropology at Cornell University, Meredith F. Small is a primatologist whose current studies concentrate on the connections between biology and culture. She has written both scholarly and popular articles in addition to four popular books that include *Kids: How Biology and Culture Shape the Way We Raise Our Children* (2001). The following brief essay appeared November 2003 in *Natural History* magazine.

Questions to Guide Your Reading and Reflection

1. What feelings about her experience do you expect Small to communicate? How do you know?
2. What interest, hobby, or area of study do you feel intensely about? What is the source of your fascination?

I'm sitting on a bench in New York City's Central Park, wait- 1
ing for the zoo to open. I have spent years observing macaque monkeys in the field, but these days I only teach and write about what they do, and I miss them. So whenever I'm in Man-hattan, I hang out here with the snow monkeys (*Macaca fuscata*).

I've been visiting this troop for years. I have seen them in 2
sunshine and snow; stood in the rain and watched them lick drops of wetness off their fur; held short business meetings in front of their exhibit; forced friends to meet me here. Unbe-knownst to them, these furry gray monkeys from Japan have become my primate touchstone.

On this visit it's clear and sunny, and through the entrance 3
gates I see the macaques jumping around their island exhibit. A path of rocks breaks the surface of the retaining pond that surrounds their enclosure, and a young female hops from one to another, leapfrogging over her troopmates as she goes.

Finally the gates open, and as I approach the group my pro- 4
fessional observing skills click in. By the time I reach them, my training as an observer—and that touch of magic I always feel in the presence of monkeys—has locked out the world; all that matters is the movement of these animals.

Today I count nine adults, one juvenile, and no babies. I 5
know that fall is breeding season, and the females are signal-ing their fertility with red behinds. To my right a status inter-action is unfolding—a female turns her rear to another female, indicating her lower position. I lean across the rail and get into the Zen of figuring out what these monkeys already know about each other: who is related to whom, how do they rank, which pair will be the next to mate?

6   My primatological reverie is interrupted by a crowd of visitors. I hear one woman call a male "she," and I'm compelled to
correct her, "It's the shape of his face," I tell her, "and his size—
and those bright red testicles." But I should know better than
to be so patronizing, such a know-it-all. Several years ago, on
one frozen January day, I asked some of the zoo's wild-animal
keepers why the snow monkeys were indoors. After all, I told
them, these monkeys are accustomed to crawling through
snowdrifts in their native Japan. "If the pond froze over," they
patiently responded, "the monkeys would simply walk out of
the zoo," Humbled. I went to see the polar bear.

7   When I have the monkeys to myself again, I walk up the hill
behind the exhibit and lean over the granite wall overlooking
their enclosure, focusing on a pair of females. One is stretched out
on a rock, arms and legs splayed in relaxation. Her eyelids droop.
She is at peace. The other methodically moves a hand across her
partner's belly, separating each strand of hair, gently touching
each exposed patch of skin. Monkeys have done this to me, sitting on my shoulders with their handlike feet pressed against my
neck, picking through my hair. I know it feels like heaven.

8   Concentrating on the grooming females, I stretch my own
arms across the wall and feel the reflected warmth of the sun

seep up from the granite slab. I, too, let my eyelids droop in contentment. For a few precious minutes I pretend that I have done nothing for the past few months but watch this group, that we know each other intimately, observer and observed. Monkey noises, their barks and calls, fill my ears. The familiar, musty odor of monkey fur at close quarters fills my nostrils.

I am, once again, renewed.   9

Expanding Vocabulary

Examine the following words in their contexts in the essay and then write a brief definition or synonym for each one. (Do not use a dictionary; try to guess the word's meaning from its context.) The number in parentheses is the number of the paragraph in which the word appears.

primate (2)   reverie (6)
touchstone (2)   patronizing (6)
Zen (5)   splayed (7)

Understanding Content

1. Summarize the basics of Small's narrative by answering the questions: Who? What? Where? When?
2. What has been Small's relationship to snow monkeys in the past?
3. What monkey behaviors capture her attention on this visit to the zoo?

Drawing Inferences about Thesis and Purpose

1. Small writes: "I am, once again, renewed." In what way is she renewed?
2. What does the author want to suggest to readers about the sources of renewal in our lives? Do we all need to visit the snow monkeys at the zoo? If not, then what?

Analyzing Strategies and Style

1. Small includes, in paragraph 6, her correcting of some zoo visitors and then a discussion with some of the zoo keepers. Why does she included these two events in her essay? What does she wish to accomplish?
2. Examine the sentence style in paragraphs 6, 7, and 8. What kinds of sentences dominate? What is their effect?

Thinking Critically

1. Small writes about an experience that we might say is less dramatic or life-changing than others presented in this chapter. Are there lessons to be learned from "quieter" moments? Explain your answer.
2. What advice might Small give to bored young people who spend too much time in front of computers and on their cell phones?

MAKING CONNECTIONS

---

1. How important are names? Do names help to shape our characters? Do you know people whose names do not seem to fit them? Do you think that your name fits you? Be prepared for a class discussion on the topic of "names."
2. Luis Rodriguez and N. Scott Momaday write of dangerous experiences that led to greater awareness and a loss of innocence. Most of us, though, do not face such dramatic moments. We need to learn and grow from being made to feel different (Rau), from experiences on the job (Wagner), or when we travel (Small). Reflect on how we gain insight and mature from seemingly insignificant encounters with life. Why do some young people seem more grown up than others? What is required of us to grow from our experiences? What do the authors suggest on this subject? What can you add from your experience and reflection?
3. Luis Rodriguez, Santha Rama Rau, and N. Scott Momaday have written autobiographies. Select one from your library and read it. Think about what more you learn about the writer's life from reading the complete memoir. Prepare a two-page summary of the memoir.
4. Barbara Kingsolver had a kind of mentor in the school librarian, and she was helped enormously by this person. Would you like to be a mentor, to help a younger person? What mentoring programs are available on your campus or in your community? Schools and churches often provide mentoring opportunities. There is also the national Big Brother/Big Sister program. You can learn more about them online at *http://www.bbbsa.org*.

TOPICS FOR WRITING

1. Several writers in this chapter write of dangerous experiences. Have you ever experienced a situation of physical danger? If so, what were your thoughts and feelings at the time? What were your reactions to the experience after the danger had passed? Did the experience change you in any way? Select the important details of your experience, decide on a point of view, and write a narrative essay in which you let the details of the experience reveal much, if not all, of the effect of the experience on you.

2. Barbara Kingsolver reveals the influences in our society that affect us, especially when we are young and trying to find our way through adolescence: parents and peers. Do you have a story to tell about the influence of either parents or a social group or clique in your school or community? If so, select one narrative moment to retell to show the influence on—or pressure to influence—you. Your essay can reveal how you resisted the influence and the consequences or how you were influenced and the consequences.

3. Think of a situation, or period in your life, in which you felt unattractive or physically different from others in some way. (For example, you were big for your age, or short for your age, or had to wear braces.) How did the situation affect you at the time? Later? Reflect on what you might share from that time with readers and then plan your narrative essay to develop and support those reflections.

4. Think of your years in school. Was there a special teacher who made a difference in your attitude toward education or about yourself? If so, reflect on the incidents involving that teacher and then select either several important moments in that teacher's class or one particular event to serve as a narrative basis for your reflections. Decide whether you want to take your reader back to that time to present only your understanding then, or whether you want to blend your emerging awareness at the time with your greater understanding as an adult.

5. If you came to America as a young person or were born here of parents who were recent immigrants, think of the

stories you might tell of growing up in the midst of two cultures. Did you experience discrimination in any way? Did you experience feeling torn between two cultures? How did these situations make you feel then? Now? If you maintained elements of your family's culture, how has that benefited you? If you rejected your family's culture, what, from your perspective now, do you think you have lost? Reflect on these questions as a way to select your essay's subject and thesis. Resist the urge to write in general about your childhood. Rather, focus on one incident or short period.

6. Can you recall an incident in which one of your parents embarrassed you, or in which you embarrassed your parent? If you have experienced either one of these situations, think about your feelings both at the time and now. If you were embarrassed by a parent, do you think, on reflection, that you should have felt embarrassment? If you embarrassed a parent, were you aware of it at the time or only on looking back? What insights into the parent/child relationship or into the problems of growing up have you gained from reflecting on these incidents? Those insights can serve as the thesis of your narrative essay. Focus your retelling only on the important elements of the incident, those parts that will guide your reader to the insight you have gained.

7. Recall an event in your life from which you learned a lesson, perhaps a painful one. What was the lesson? How much did you understand at the time? Did you try to deny the lesson, or did you accept it? Construct your narrative so that your retelling carries your point. Offer some reflection but avoid stating the lesson as a simple moral, such as "I learned that one shouldn't steal."

8. Recall a particular event or period in your life that resulted in your losing some of your innocence, in your rather suddenly becoming much more grown up. What romantic or naive view of life did you lose? What more adult view was forced on you? You will probably want to place your reader back in that time of your growing up. Use chronological order and focus your attention on the key stages in the event that moved you from innocence to awareness.

A CHECKLIST FOR NARRATION ESSAYS

Invention

- ☐ Have I selected a topic and approach consistent with the instructor's guidelines for this assignment?
- ☐ Have I chosen, among the possible topics, one that fits with my experiences?
- ☐ Have I reflected on that experience and the assignment to create a tentative thesis that is clear, focused, and interesting to others?
- ☐ Have I chosen an effective perspective, a position in time from which to best present my experience?
- ☐ Have I recognized and selected the key incidents and rejected those that will distract from advancing my thesis?

Drafting

- ☐ Have I succeeded in completing a first draft at one sitting so that I can "see" the whole?
- ☐ Do I have enough—enough to meet assignment demands and enough to develop and support my thesis? If not, do I need new paragraphs or more details or reflection in existing paragraphs?
- ☐ Does the order work? If not, what needs to be moved—and where?
- ☐ Am I satisfied with the way I have expressed the insights to be gained? Do the details or incidents carry my point? Have I been too heavy-handed with a message?

Revision

- ☐ Have I made any needed additions, deletions, or changes in order based on answering the questions above about my draft?
- ☐ Have I revised my draft to produce coherent paragraphs, using transition words, especially time words, to guide readers?
- ☐ Have I eliminated wordiness and clichés?
- ☐ Have I avoided or removed any discriminatory language?
- ☐ Have I used my word processor's spell check and proofread a printed copy with great care?
- ☐ Do I have an appropriate and interesting title?

Using Description

Reflecting on People and Places

Good writing is concrete writing. Good writers *show* readers what they mean; they do not just tell them. Vague and abstract words may be confusing and often fail to engage readers. "The tawny-colored cocker spaniel with big, floppy ears" has our attention in ways that "The dog" will never achieve. We can see the "spaniel"; what "dog" are we to imagine? Thus, descriptive details are a part of all good writing, whatever its primary purpose or form.

When to Use Description

Sometimes writers use description to make the general concrete and to engage readers. But sometimes a writer's primary purpose is to describe—to show us—what a particular person, place, or thing looks like. Many instructors like to assign descriptive essays both because they are fun to write and because they provide good practice for using concrete language in other essays.

The descriptive essay can be viewed as a painting in words. (Not surprisingly, you will find some paintings reproduced in this chapter.) Like the artist who draws or paints, the artist working with words must be a perceptive observer. Some people actually see more than others. Can you close your eyes and "see" your writing classroom? The college library? Your history instructor? How carefully have you looked at the world around you? Some people go to a restaurant because they are hungry.

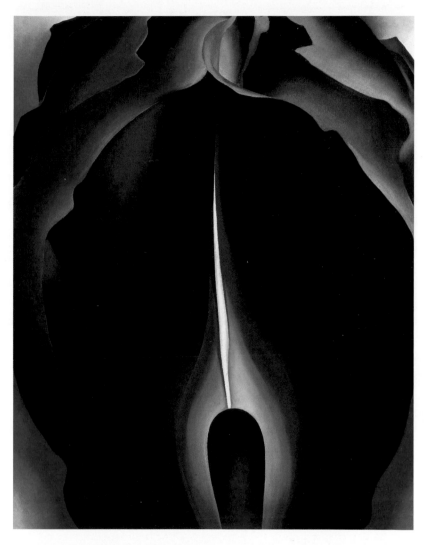

Georgia O'Keeffe, *Jack-in-the-Pulpit No. IV*, 1930, oil on canvas, 1.016 x .762 (40" x 30"); National Gallery of Art, Washington. Alfred Stieglitz Collection, Bequest of Georgia O'Keeffe. Photo by Richard Carafelli.

The American O'Keeffe (1887–1986), who spent much of her time in the Southwest, created many stunning canvases of flowers that combine poetic fluidity with such sharp focus that we seem to see deep within the plant, almost at its molecular level.

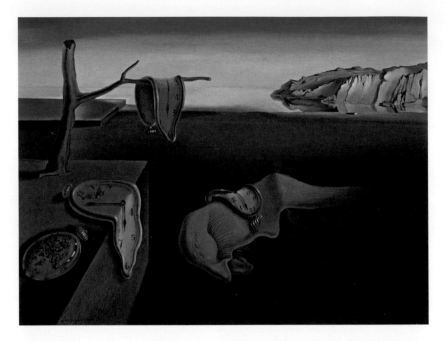

Salvador Dali, *The Persistence of Memory* [*Persistance de la mémoire*], 1931. Oil on canvas, 9-1/2″ x 13″ (24.1 x 33 cm). Digital image copyright the Museum of Modern Art/Licensed by SCALA/Art Resource, NY. Copyright © 2007 Salvador Dali, Gala-Salvador Dali Foundation/Artists Rights Society (ARS), New York.

Salvador Dali (1904–1989), a native of the Spanish province of Catalan, drew on dream imagery to create his surrealist canvases.

Pablo Picasso, *The Three Dancers*, 1925. Tate Gallery, London/Art Resource, NY. Copyright © 2007 Estate of Pablo Picasso/Artists Rights Society (ARS), New York.

Perhaps the best-known of twentieth-century painters, Picasso (1881–1973) was born in Spain but lived most of his life in France. His many canvases provide lessons in modern art's movements from Impressionism to Expressionism.

Vincent Van Gogh, *The Night Café*, 1888. Approx. 28 1/2" x 36 1/4". Yale University Art Gallery, New Haven, Connecticut (bequest of Stephen Carlton Clark, B.A., 1903).

Hollander Van Gogh (1853–1890) spent most of his painting years either in Paris or the south of France. His paintings blend impressionistic techniques with an expressionistic use of color.

Edgar Degas, *The Dance Class*, c. 1873–1876. Oil on canvas, 85 x 75 cm. Musée d'Orsay, Paris, France. Copyright Erich Lessing/Art Resource, NY.

One of the best known of the French Impressionists, Degas (1834–1917) is known for his interest in capturing movement, an interest that led to many studies of dancers and racehorses.

Francisco de Goya y Lucientes, *Third of May, 1808*, 1814. Approximately 8′ 8″ x 11′ 3″. Museo del Prado, Madrid, Spain. Copyright Scala/Art Resource, NY.

A Spaniard, Goya (1746–1828) lived and painted at the Spanish court of Charles II. His paintings reveal an unsentimental, tough-minded observation of human life.

The food critic goes to a restaurant not just to have dinner but to observe the color of the walls, the politeness of the waiters, the taste of the food. The food critic does not want to write, in her Sunday column, that the service was "okay." She needs to decide whether the waiters were formally polite, chatty, intrusive, uninformed. To generate details for good essays you will need to see more of the world around you and to store those visual impressions in your memory.

How to Use Descriptive Details

Descriptive Language

Really seeing what you want to describe is the necessary first step to writing a good descriptive essay. But, just as the artist must transfer impressions into forms and colors on canvas, so you must transfer your impressions into words. To help your reader see what you see, you need to choose words that are accurate, concrete, and vivid. If you are describing your backyard, for example, you want descriptive details so precise that a reader could easily draw a picture of your yard. If you were to write that you have "a large yard that goes to a creek," you would not be helping your reader to see much. How large is large? To an apartment dweller, the fifteen-by-twelve-foot deck of a townhouse might seem large. Better to describe your backyard as "gently sloping seventy feet from the screened-in back porch to a narrow creek that marks the property line." Now we can begin to see—really to see—your yard.

Take time to search for just the right word. The food critic will soon lose her column if she writes that the walls of a restaurant are "a kind of beige with pink." She needs to write, instead, that they are "salmon-colored." Do not settle for describing a lake as "bluish green." Is the water aquamarine? Or a deeper turquoise? Is its surface mirror-like or opaque? You might notice that some of these examples are actually metaphors: "salmon-colored" and "mirror-like." Fresh, vivid comparisons (not worn-out clichés) will help readers see your world and will leave a lasting impression on them. Lance Morrow, describing an East African wildlife preserve, writes that "a herd of elephants moves like a dense gray cloud . . . a mirage of floating boulders" and "a lion prowls in lion-colored grasses."

Finding Unity

When your primary purpose is to write a description, one way to get started is to list all the details that come to mind. However, to shape those details into a unified essay, you will eventually want to eliminate some and develop others. Remember that a list of details, no matter how vivid, does not make an essay. First, select the *telling details*, the specifics that really work to reveal your subject. Second, be sure that your essay has a thesis. Select the details that, taken together, create a unified impression, that make a point. In an essay on her father, British novelist Doris Lessing wants to show that war kills the spirit if not the body of those who have to fight. To support her thesis, she first draws the portrait of her father as a vigorous young man, full of life, and then presents the unpleasant details of the angry, sick, shattered man whom she knew after the war.

Organization

Remember to organize details according to some principle so that readers can follow the developing picture. You need to decide on a perspective from which the details will be "seen" by the reader. In describing a classroom, for example, you could create the impression of someone standing at the door by presenting details in the order in which the person's eyes move around the room. Spatial patterns are numerous. You can move from foreground to background, from the center out, from left to right. Descriptions of people are sometimes more challenging to organize, because in addition to physical details you need possessions, activities, and ways of speaking—the telling details of character. You could take the perspective of a new acquaintance, presenting what one would see first and then what details of personality emerge as a relationship develops. Whatever pattern you choose, develop it consistently and use connecting words (e.g., *from* the left, *below* the penetrating eyes, *next* to the rose bushes) to guide your reader. It's your canvas;

get to know your subject well, select your colors with care, and pay close attention to each brushstroke.

WRITING FOCUS:
IT'S ALL ABOUT WORDS

As we have noted, good writing is concrete and specific. In addition to taking time to search for vivid language, though, you need to be sure to select the *right* word. There are many simple, frequently used words that writers confuse. Learn to use the following words correctly. Consult a handbook for a longer list of words in each category.

Possessive Pronouns	*Contractions*
its *(Its message is clear.)*	it's *(it is)*
their *(Their books are on the table.)*	they're *(they are)*
whose *(Whose jacket is this?)*	who's *(who is)*
your *(Your time is up.)*	you're *(you are)*

Homonyms (Words that sound alike but are spelled differently and have different meanings.)

which *(one of a group)*	witch *(female sorcerer)*
roll *(move by turning over; bread)*	role *(part played)*
aisle *(passage between rows)*	isle *(island)*
bare *(naked)*	bear *(to carry; an animal)*
course *(path; part of a meal)*	coarse *(rough)*
cite *(refer to)*	sight *(vision)* site *(a place)*
capital *(major city; wealth)*	capitol *(government building)*
principal *(first; school head)*	principle *(basic truth/belief)*
stationery *(paper)*	stationary *(not moving)*
weather *(climatic condition)*	whether *(if)*

> **Pseudohomonyms (words that are similar in sound and often confused)**
>
> accept *(to receive)*   except *(other than)*
>
> affect *(to influence)*   effect *(result; to bring into existence)*
>
> then *(at that time; next)*   than *(in comparison with)*
>
> allusion *(indirect reference)*   illusion *(misleading image, idea)*
>
> conscience *(sense of right behavior)*   conscious *(aware; awake)*
>
> loose *(not tight)*   lose *(to misplace)*
>
> sense *(perception)*   since *(from then until now)*

Getting Started: Reflections on a Painting

After page 80, at the beginning of this chapter, you will find reprints of six paintings representing a range of time, styles, and subjects. Examine them, reflect on them, and then select the one you find most appealing or most startling. Write briefly (in your journal or class notebook), explaining what attracted you to the particular painting you selected. Then read at least one biographical entry about the painter (in an encyclopedia or art book—including online) and add a paragraph on the painter to your journal or notes. Your paragraph should include information that goes beyond the brief details included with the painting. Be prepared to share your information about the painter and your reactions to the work with classmates.

Mrs. Zajac

TRACY KIDDER

In his Pulitzer Prize–winning book *The Soul of a New Machine* (1981), Tracy Kidder makes complex technical material about computers clear and interesting. He perfected his talent for clarity by writing articles on a variety of complex topics for the *Atlantic,* where he has served as a contributing editor. His most recent book is *Old Friends* (1993). Kidder's portrait of Mrs. Zajac comes from his best-seller, *Among Schoolchildren* (1988), a compassionate study of a year in Mrs. Zajac's fifth-grade classroom. As you read, pay close attention to Kidder's telling details, the details that reveal character.

Questions to Guide Your Reading and Reflection

1. What is the italic print of the opening paragraph designed to represent? What is effective about beginning this way?
2. Close your eyes and visualize a favorite teacher. What telling details of appearance and character do you "see"?

Mrs. Zajac wasn't born yesterday. She knows you didn't do your 1
*best work on this paper, Clarence. Don't you remember Mrs. Zajac
saying that if you didn't do your best, she'd make you do it over? As
for you, Claude, God forbid that you should ever need brain surgery.
But Mrs. Zajac hopes that if you do, the doctor won't open up your
head and walk off saying he's almost done, as you just said when
Mrs. Zajac asked you for your penmanship, which, by the way, looks
like who did it and ran. Felipe, the reason you have hiccups is, your
mouth is always open and the wind rushes in. You're in fifth grade
now. So, Felipe, put a lock on it. Zip it up. Then go get a drink of
water. Mrs. Zajac means business, Robert. The sooner you realize she
never said everybody in the room has to do the work except for
Robert, the sooner you'll get along with her. And . . . Clarence. Mrs.
Zajac knows you didn't try. You don't just hand in junk to Mrs.
Zajac. She's been teaching an awful lot of years. She didn't fall off the
turnip cart yesterday. She told you she was an old-lady teacher.*

She was thirty-four. She wore a white skirt and yellow 2
sweater and a thin gold necklace, which she held in her fingers, as if holding her own reins, while waiting for children to answer. Her hair was black with a hint of Irish red. It was cut short to the tops of her ears, and swept back like a pair of folded wings. She had a delicately cleft chin, and she was short—the children's chairs would have fit her. Although her voice sounded conversational, it had projection. She had never acted. She had found this voice in classrooms.

Mrs. Zajac seemed to have a frightening amount of energy. 3
She strode across the room, her arms swinging high and her hands in small fists. Taking her stand in front of the green chalk-

board, discussing the rules with her new class, she repeated sentences, and her lips held the shapes of certain words, such as "home-work," after she had said them. Her hands kept very busy. They sliced the air and made karate chops to mark off boundaries. They extended straight out like a traffic cop's, halting illegal maneuvers yet to be perpetrated. When they rested momentarily on her hips, her hands looked as if they were in holsters. She told the children, "One thing Mrs. Zajac expects from each of you is that you do *your* best." She said, "Mrs. Zajac gives homework. I'm sure you've all heard. The old meanie gives homework." *Mrs. Zajac.* It was in part a role. She worked her way into it every September.

4   At home on late summer days like these, Chris Zajac wore shorts or blue jeans. Although there was no dress code for teachers here at Kelly School, she always went to work in skirts or dresses. She dressed as if she were applying for a job, and hoped in the back of her mind that someday, heading for job interviews, her students would remember her example. Outside school, she wept easily over small and large catastrophes and at sentimental movies, but she never cried in front of students, except once a few years ago when the news came over the intercom that the Space Shuttle had exploded and Christa McAuliffe had died—and then she saw in her students' faces that the sight of Mrs. Zajac crying had frightened them, and she made herself stop and then explained.

5   At home, Chris laughed at the antics of her infant daughter and egged the child on. She and her first-grade son would sneak up to the radio when her husband wasn't looking and change the station from classical to rock-and-roll music. "You're regressing, Chris," her husband would say. But especially on the first few days of school, she didn't let her students get away with much. She was not amused when, for instance, on the first day, two of the boys started dueling with their rulers. On nights before the school year started, Chris used to have bad dreams: her principal would come to observe her, and her students would choose that moment to climb up on their desks and give her the finger, or they would simply wander out the door. But a child in her classroom would never know that Mrs. Zajac had the slightest doubt that students would obey her.

The first day, after going over all the school rules, Chris 6
spoke to them about effort. "If you put your name on a paper,
you should be proud of it," she said. "You should think, This is
the best I can do and I'm proud of it and I want to hand this in."
Then she asked, "If it isn't your best, what's Zajac going to do?"

Many voices, most of them female, answered softly in uni- 7
son, "Make us do it over."

"Make you do it over," Chris repeated. It sounded like a chant. 8

"Does anyone know anything about Lisette?" she asked 9
when no one answered to that name.

Felipe—small, with glossy black hair—threw up his hand. 10

"Felipe?" 11

"She isn't here!" said Felipe. He wasn't being fresh. On those 12
first few days of school, whenever Mrs. Zajac put the sound of
a question in her voice, and sometimes before she got the question out, Felipe's hand shot up.

In contrast, there was the very chubby girl who sat nearly mo- 13
tionless at her desk, covering the lower half of her face with her
hands. As usual, most of their voices sounded timid the first day,
and came out of hiding gradually. There were twenty children.
About half were Puerto Rican. Almost two-thirds of the twenty
needed the forms to obtain free lunches. There was a lot of long
and curly hair. Some boys wore little rattails. The eyes the children lifted up to her as she went over the rules—a few eyes were
blue and many more were brown—looked so solemn and so
wide that Chris felt like dropping all pretense and laughing.
Their faces ranged from dark brown to gold, to pink, to pasty
white, the color that Chris associated with sunless tenements
and too much TV. The boys wore polo shirts and T-shirts and
new white sneakers with the ends of the laces untied and tucked
behind the tongues. Some girls wore lacy ribbons in their hair,
and some wore pants and others skirts, a rough but not infallible indication of religion—the daughters of Jehovah's Witnesses
and Pentecostals do not wear pants. There was a lot of prettiness
in the room, and all of the children looked cute to Chris.

Expanding Vocabulary

Examine the following words in their contexts in the essay. Then
write a brief definition or synonym for each one. (Do not use a dictionary; try to guess the word's meaning from its context.) The

number in parentheses is the number of the paragraph in which the word appears.

projection (2)   egged . . . on (5)
karate (3)   unison (7)
maneuvers (3)   pretense (13)
perpetrated (3)   infallible (13)
holsters (3)

Understanding Content

1. The excerpt you have read comes from the first four pages of Kidder's book. Why does Kidder begin his study in this way? What, exactly, does he accomplish in these opening pages?
2. What specific details do we get about Mrs. Zajac? List them. (Consider age, physical appearance, personality traits, values.)
3. Why does Mrs. Zajac go to school in a skirt or dress?
4. What details do we get about the children? List them.

Drawing Inferences about Thesis and Purpose

1. What is effective about Kidder's last sentence? What does it tell us about Mrs. Zajac's attitude toward teaching?
2. What can you conclude about the Kelly School neighborhood from details about the children?
3. What is the author's attitude toward his subject? Does he present Mrs. Zajac in a positive or negative way? As a good or bad teacher?

Analyzing Strategies and Style

1. Kidder offers some contrasts between Mrs. Zajac's classroom behavior and her behavior at home and with her children. How do these contrasts help us to understand Mrs. Zajac?
2. Can you find any sentences that contain general or abstract ideas?
3. What does your answer to question 2 tell you about Kidder's style of writing? Is this writing primarily general or specific? Abstract or concrete?

Thinking Critically

1. Would you have enjoyed being in Mrs. Zajac's fifth-grade class? Why or why not?
2. Mrs. Zajac emphasizes being proud of work you sign your name to. Is it ever too early to teach this idea? Is it ever too late?
3. Are you usually proud of the work you hand in? If not, why do you hand it in that way?

4. Mrs. Zajac believes in dressing properly for her job. Should students have a dress code or wear uniforms? How can clothes make a difference in the classroom or on the job?

Lost Lives of Women

AMY TAN

Amy Tan was born in California shortly after her parents immigrated to the United States from China. Tan started a career in consulting on programs for disabled children and then turned to writing short stories, some of which became part of her first and best-selling novel *The Joy Luck Club.* Her second novel, *The Kitchen God's Wife,* appeared in 1991. In the following article, which appeared in the April 1991 issue of *Life* magazine, Tan captures the stories of several women, relatives of hers, grouped in an old photo.

Questions to Guide Your Reading and Reflection

1. Tan tells us in paragraph 5 that the women in the photo "were not peasant women but big city people, very modern." Why does she include this comment? Why is this a telling detail?
2. If you were going to take a family photograph, who would you include and how would you arrange them?

When I first saw this photo as a child, I thought it was exotic   1
and remote, of a faraway time and place, with people who had no connection to my American life. Look at their bound feet! Look at that funny lady with the plucked forehead!

The solemn little girl is, in fact, my mother. And leaning   2
against the rock is my grandmother, Jingmei. "She called me Baobei," my mother told me. "It means Treasure."

The picture was taken in Hangzhou, and my mother believes   3
the year was 1922, possibly spring or fall, judging by the clothes. At first glance, it appears the women are on a pleasure outing.

But see the white bands on their skirts? The white shoes?   4
They are in mourning. My mother's grandmother, known to the others as Divong, "The Replacement Wife," has recently

died. The women have come to this place, a Buddhist retreat, to perform yet another ceremony for Divong. Monks hired for the occasion have chanted the proper words. And the women and little girl have walked in circles clutching smoky sticks of incense. They knelt and prayed, then burned a huge pile of spirit money so that Divong might ascend to a higher position in her new world.

5   This is also a picture of secrets and tragedies, the reasons that warnings have been passed along in our family like heirlooms. Each of these women suffered a terrible fate, my mother said. And they were not peasant women but big city people, very modern. They went to dance halls and wore stylish clothes. They were supposed to be the lucky ones.

6   Look at the pretty woman with her finger on her cheek. She is my mother's second cousin, Nunu Aiyi, "Precious Auntie." You cannot see this, but Nunu Aiyi's entire face was scarred from smallpox. Lucky for her, a year or so after this picture was taken, she received marriage proposals from two families. She turned down a lawyer and married another man. Later she divorced her husband, a daring thing for a woman to do. But then, finding no means to support herself or her young daughter, Nunu eventually accepted the lawyer's second proposal— to become his number two concubine. "Where else could she

go?" my mother asked. "Some people said she was lucky the lawyer still wanted her."

Now look at the small woman with a sour face *(third from left)*. There's a reason that Jyou Ma, "Uncle's Wife," looks this way. Her husband, my great-uncle, often complained that his family had chosen an ugly woman for his wife. To show his displeasure, he often insulted Jyou Ma's cooking. One time Great-Uncle tipped over a pot of boiling soup, which fell all over his niece's four-year-old neck and nearly killed her. My mother was the little niece, and she still has that soup scar on her neck. Great-Uncle's family eventually chose a pretty woman for his second wife. But the complaints about Jyou Ma's cooking did not stop. 7

Doomma, "Big Mother," is the regal-looking woman seated on a rock. (The woman with the plucked forehead, far left, is a servant, remembered only as someone who cleaned but did not cook.) Doomma was the daughter of my great-grandfather and Nu-pei, "The Original Wife." She was shunned by Divong, "The Replacement Wife," for being "too strong," and loved by Divong's daughter, my grandmother. Doomma's first daughter was born with a hunchback—a sign, some said, of Doomma's own crooked nature. Why else did she remarry, disobeying her family's orders to remain a widow forever? And why did Doomma later kill herself, using some mysterious means that caused her to die slowly over three days? "Doomma died the same way she lived," my mother said, "strong, suffering lots." 8

Jingmei, my own grandmother, lived only a few more years after this picture was taken. She was the widow of a poor scholar, a man who had the misfortune of dying from influenza when he was about to be appointed a vice-magistrate. In 1924 or so, a rich man, who liked to collect pretty women, raped my grandmother and thereby forced her into becoming one of his concubines. My grandmother, now an outcast, took her young daughter to live with her on an island outside of Shanghai. She left her son behind, to save his face. After she gave birth to another son she killed herself by swallowing raw opium buried in the New Year's rice cakes. The young daughter who wept at her deathbed was my mother. 9

At my grandmother's funeral, monks tied chains to my mother's ankles so she would not fly away with her mother's 10 ghost. "I tried to take them off," my mother said. "I was her treasure. I was her life."

11   My mother could never talk about any of this, even with her closest friends. "Don't tell anyone," she once said to me. "People don't understand. A concubine was like some kind of prostitute. My mother was a good woman, high-class. She had no choice."

12   I told her I understood.

13   "How can you understand?" she said, suddenly angry. "You did not live in China then. You do not know what it's like to have no position in life. I was her daughter. We had no face! We belonged to nobody! This is a shame I can never push off my back." By the end of the outburst, she was crying.

14   On a recent trip with my mother to Beijing, I learned that my uncle found a way to push the shame off his back. He was the son my grandmother left behind. In 1936 he joined the Communist party—in large part, he told me, to overthrow the society that forced his mother into concubinage. He published a story about his mother. I told him I had written about my grandmother in a book of fiction. We agreed that my grandmother is the source of strength running through our family. My mother cried to hear this.

15   My mother believes my grandmother is also my muse, that she helps me write. "Does she still visit you often?" she asked while I was writing my second book. And then she added shyly, "Does she say anything about me?"

16   "Yes," I told her. "She has lots to say. I am writing it down."

17   This is the picture I see when I write. These are the secrets I was supposed to keep. These are the women who never let me forget why stories need to be told.

Expanding Vocabulary

Define each of the following words and then use each one in a sentence. The number in parentheses is the number of the paragraph in which the word appears.

exotic (1)
heirlooms (5)
concubine (6)
shunned (8)
muse (15)

Understanding Content

1. When and where was the picture taken?
2. Who are the women in the photo? That is, what is their relationship to the author?
3. Why are the women together? What have they gathered to do?
4. What was the author's initial reaction to the photo?

Drawing Inferences about Thesis and Purpose

1. What reaction does Tan want readers to have after they read her descriptions of the women? What do the women share, other than family connections?
2. Explain the last line of the essay.
3. What is Tan's thesis?

Analyzing Strategies and Style

1. What details do you consider to be especially important? Why do you select them?
2. Tan gives each woman's Chinese name and then its meaning in English. What does she gain from this strategy?
3. Tan uses a metaphor in paragraph 5. Explain the metaphor.

Thinking Critically

1. Do you have stories to tell about your family? If you have a family album, find a picture in it that you think holds a secret or tells a story, and write that story in your journal.
2. Why is it important to write the stories of these women? What does Tan gain for herself? For others?
3. Why is it important for humans generally to tell stories? What does each culture, each age, gain from making stories?

Remembering Lobo

PAT MORA

Educated at Texas Western College and the University of Texas at El Paso, Pat Mora has published several children's books and volumes of poetry. Her essays have been collected in *Nepantla: Essays from the Land in the Middle* (1993), from which "Remembering Lobo" comes. Look for the telling details that Mora presents to develop and reveal the character of her aunt.

Questions to Guide Your Reading and Reflection

1. What is Mora's purpose in writing? What does she want to share with readers?
2. If you were going to write a descriptive essay about someone in your family, who would you chose? Why?

---

1   We called her *Lobo*. The word means "wolf" in Spanish, an odd name for a generous and loving aunt. Like all names it became synonymous with her, and to this day returns me to my childself. Although the name seemed perfectly natural to us and to our friends, it did cause frowns from strangers throughout the years. I particularly remember one hot afternoon when on a crowded streetcar between the border cities of El Paso and Juarez, I momentarily lost sight of her. "Lobo! Lobo!" I cried in panic. Annoyed faces peered at me, disappointed at such disrespect to a white-haired woman.

2   Actually the fault was hers. She lived with us for years, and when she arrived home from work in the evening, she'd knock on our front door and ask, "*¿Dónde están mis lobitos?*" "Where are my little wolves?"

3   Gradually she became our *lobo*, a spinster aunt who gathered the four of us around her, tying us to her for life by giving us all she had. Sometimes to tease her we would call her by her real name. "*¿Dónde está Ignacia?*" we would ask. Lobo would laugh and say, "She is a ghost."

4   To all of us in nuclear families today, the notion of an extended family under one roof seems archaic, complicated. We treasure our private space. I will always marvel at the generosity of my parents, who opened their door to both my grandmother and Lobo. No doubt I am drawn to the elderly because I grew up with two entirely different white-haired women who worried about me, tucked me in at night, made me tomato soup or hot *hierbabuena* (mint tea) when I was ill.

5   Lobo grew up in Mexico, the daughter of a circuit judge, my grandfather. She was a wonderful storyteller and over and over told us about the night her father, a widower, brought his

grown daughters on a flatbed truck across the Rio Grande at the time of the Mexican Revolution. All their possessions were left in Mexico. Lobo had not been wealthy, but she had probably never expected to have to find a job and learn English.

When she lived with us, she worked in the linens section of   6
a local department store. Her area was called "piece goods and bedding." Lobo never sewed, but she would talk about materials she sold, using words I never completely understood, such as *pique* and *broadcloth*. Sometimes I still whisper such words just to remind myself of her. I'll always savor the way she would order "sweet milk" at restaurants. The precision of a speaker new to the language.

Lobo saved her money to take us out to dinner and a movie,   7
to take us to Los Angeles in the summer, to buy us shiny black shoes for Christmas. Though she never married and never bore children, Lobo taught me much about one of our greatest challenges as human beings: loving well. I don't think she ever discussed the subject with me, but through the years she lived her love, and I was privileged to watch.

She died at ninety-four. She was no sweet, docile Mexican   8
woman dying with perfect resignation. Some of her last words before drifting into semiconsciousness were loud words of annoyance at the incompetence of nurses and doctors.

"*No sirven.*" "They're worthless," she'd say to me in Spanish.   9

"They don't know what they're doing. My throat is hurt-   10
ing and they're taking X rays. Tell them to take care of my throat first."

I was busy striving for my cherished middle-class polite-   11
ness. "Shh, shh," I'd say. "They're doing the best they can."

"Well, it's not good enough," she'd say, sitting up in anger.   12

Lobo was a woman of fierce feelings, of strong opinions.   13
She was a woman who literally whistled while she worked. The best way to cheer her when she'd visit my young children was to ask for her help. Ask her to make a bed, fold laundry, set the table or dry dishes, and the whistling would begin as she moved about her task. Like all of us, she loved being needed. Understandable, then, that she muttered in annoyance when her body began to fail her. She was a woman who found self-definition and joy in visibly showing her

family her love for us by bringing us hot *té de canela* (cinnamon tea) in the middle of the night to ease a cough, by bringing us comics and candy whenever she returned home. A life of giving.

14   One of my last memories of her is a visit I made to her on November 2, *El Día de los Muertos,* or All Souls' Day. She was sitting in her rocking chair, smiling wistfully. The source of the smile may seem a bit bizarre to a U.S. audience. She was fondly remembering past visits to the local cemetery on this religious feast day.

15   "What a silly old woman I have become," she said. "Here I sit in my rocking chair all day on All Souls' Day, sitting when I should be out there. At the cemetery. Taking good care of *mis muertos,* my dead ones.

16   "What a time I used to have. I'd wake while it was still dark outside. I'd hear the first morning birds, and my fingers would almost itch to begin. By six I'd be having a hot bath, dressing carefully in black, wanting *mis muertos* to be proud of me, proud to have me looking respectable and proud to have their graves taken care of. I'd have my black coffee and plenty of toast. You know the way I like it. Well browned and well buttered. I wanted to be ready to work hard.

17   "The bus ride to the other side of town was a long one, but I'd say a rosary and plan my day. I'd hope that my perfume wasn't too strong and yet would remind others that I was a lady.

18   "The air at the cemetery gates was full of chrysanthemums: that strong, sharp, fall smell. I'd buy tin cans full of the gold and wine flowers. How I liked seeing aunts and uncles who were also there to care for the graves of their loved ones. We'd hug. Happy together.

19   "Then it was time to begin. The smell of chrysanthemums was like a whiff of pure energy. I'd pull the heavy hose and wash the gravestones over and over, listening to the water pelting away the desert sand. I always brought newspaper. I'd kneel on the few patches of grass, and I'd scrub and scrub, shining the gray stones, leaning back on my knees to rest for a bit and then scrubbing again. Finally a relative from nearby would say, '*Ya, ya, Nacha,*' and laugh. Enough. I'd stop, blink

my eyes to return from my trance. Slightly dazed, I'd stand slowly, place a can of chrysanthemums before each grave.

"Sometimes I would just stand there in the desert sun and listen. I'd hear the quiet crying of people visiting new graves; I'd hear families exchanging gossip while they worked. 20

"One time I heard my aunt scolding her dead husband. She'd sweep his gravestone and say, '*¿Porqué?* Why did you do this, you thoughtless man? Why did you go and leave me like this? You know I don't like to be alone. Why did you stop living?' Such a sight to see my aunt with her proper black hat and her fine dress and her carefully polished shoes muttering away for all to hear. 21

"To stifle my laughter, I had to cover my mouth with my hands." 22

Expanding Vocabulary

Examine the following words in their contexts in the essay. Then write a brief definition or synonym for each one. (Do not use a dictionary; try to guess each word's meaning from its context.) The number in parentheses is the number of the paragraph in which the word appears.

synonymous (1)   semiconsciousness (8)
spinster (3)   bizarre (14)
nuclear (4)   pelting (19)
archaic (4)   trance (19)
precision (6)

Understanding Content

1. How did the author know her "Lobo"?
2. What are some of the telling details of Lobo's character? What activities or moments in her life reveal these character traits?

Drawing Inferences about Thesis and Purpose

1. When the author and her siblings called Lobo by her real name, Lobo answered that "she is a ghost." Why did she say that to the children?
2. What does Mora mean by "loving well"? What can we infer to be the characteristics of a person who loves well?

Analyzing Strategies and Style

1. Several times Mora uses Spanish words or phrases, which she then translates into English. What does she gain by including the Spanish?
2. Mora ends with Lobo's own account of visiting family graves. What does the author accomplish by ending with Lobo's own words?

Thinking Critically

1. Do you live in an extended family? If so, do you have an older family member whom you especially care for? What do we gain from extended families? What do we lose? Do the advantages outweigh the disadvantages?
2. What do you think are the marks of a meaningful life?
3. Without having read this essay, would you have included "loving well" as a mark of a meaningful life? Do you think it should be on everyone's list? Why or why not?

Let It Snow!

DIANE ACKERMAN

Diane Ackerman has been a staff writer at *The New Yorker* and a writer in residence at several colleges. She has published books of poetry and natural history, including a book on bats. Her latest book is *Cultivating Delights: A Natural History of My Garden* (2001), from which the following excerpt is taken, having appeared as an essay in *Parade* magazine, where she is a contributing editor.

Questions to Guide Your Reading and Reflection

1. What is Ackerman's purpose in writing? What does she want readers to see?
2. Visualize looking out a window in your home; what do you see? Describe the scene.

1   It's snowing like white pepper. At noon, several hours ago, it was 60 degrees. Now the bench drips a thin white glaze, the quaking aspens keen and sway. As a steady sift of snow falls

straight down and sticks, the wire fence begins to look crocheted. The wind poofs a snowdrift until it sprays flour. Powder snow, they call it—the skier's friend. To me, it just looks like small white grains, but I know it's really a blend of column- and plate-shaped crystals that prevent the snow from packing down.

The shape of the crystal determines whether the snow will stick 2 or pack down hard. Crystals clustered together form snowflakes, and there are many crystalline shapes. The best known are "dendritic," or branching—the classic star snowflake design that one finds on sweaters and many Christmas ornaments.

But snow crystals form many shapes that aren't always visi- 3 ble to the naked eye. Most people didn't know what snowflakes looked like until the 19th-century publication of *Cloud Crystals*, with sketches by "A Lady," who realized she could catch flakes on a black background and peer at them through a magnifying glass. Then, in 1931, Wilson Alwyn Bentley published an atlas of thousands of crystals he had photographed through a microscope, calling it simply *Snow Crystals*.

Depending on temperature, humidity and wind, snow crys- 4 tals can develop into stars, columns, plates, needles, asymmetricals, capped columns or strange combinations, such as "bullets," variants of columns topped by pyramids or "stellar dendrites," which are six-pointed stars.

Columns are hollow crystals, spatial dendrites are three-di- 5 mensional crystals, and needles are solid crystals. As they fall, they hit other crystals, break apart, build new forms, and soon a flurry thickens into heavy snow.

When I was little, my mother would turn off the lights in the 6 house, and she and I would sit on the rug in the living room, watching snowflakes dance like dervishes under the porch light. As flurry became blizzard, I knew there was a good chance I'd be staying home from school and building a snow house.

I like snow's odd quality of pouring over and around things 7 without breaking up, so that it creates pockets of air, overhanging eaves and accidental igloos where garden animals huddle to keep warm. I like how solidly snow packs, and how tiny flakes of it can bring a large city to a halt when snow is nothing but water and air, mostly air. I like how well snow insulates, despite its essential coldness.

No Two Are Alike...

Though unique, a snow crystal falls into a category of shapes: here, examples of the type "stellar plates."

Most people didn't know what snow crystals looked like until a book of sketches, *Cloud Crystals*, appeared in 1855, In 1931, Wison Alwyn Bentley published an atlas of crystals he had photographed through a microscope.

Photo: Camazine/Photo Researchers

8   I like the many names people have given snow. With each name, I learn to see snow in a slightly different way. The Inuits (a group of northern indigenous people also called Eskimos), famous for a vocabulary of snow, have words for drifting snow (*siqoq*), falling snow (*aniu*), wind-whipped snow (*upsik*), crusty melting freeze snow (*siqoqtoaq*), fine smooth snow (*saluma roaq*) and even the place where snow has blown away (*sich*), among many others.

9   Soon snow quilts the ground and talcs the trees, muffling sound and stifling scent. For many people, gardeners included, winter can be a challenge. I like the contrast of hot and cold: the warm-blooded animals trekking across the snow; the heat of a furnace or fire keeping one snug through a blizzard; tropical plants, such as amaryllis and orchids, blooming on the windowsill while snow falls invitingly beyond the panes of glass.

Expanding Vocabulary

Write a definition for each of the following words. Then select five of the words and use each one of those in a separate sentence of your own. The number in parentheses is the number of the paragraph in which the word appears.

quaking (1)	insulates (7)
crocheted (1)	indigenous (8)
asymmetricals (4)	stifling (9)
dervishes (6)	trekking (9)

Understanding Content

1. What scene does the author describe at the beginning?
2. What kind of snow is falling?
3. What are some of the kinds of shapes that snow crystals form? Which shape do we most commonly see at Christmas?
4. Who first explained the many shapes of snowflakes?
5. What other details of snow does Ackerman provide in addition to appearance?

Drawing Inferences about Thesis and Purpose

1. Ackerman begins and ends with descriptive details, but within the essay she includes scientific information about snowflakes. How would you state her subject?
2. What is the essay's thesis? Try to write a sentence or two that covers the several purposes that the author has.

Analyzing Strategies and Style

1. Ackerman begins with a metaphor. Find two other metaphors in the essay and then explain all three metaphors.
2. How does the author move from describing a scene of snow falling to presenting information about the various shapes of snowflakes? What makes her transition an effective one?
3. Where does Ackerman place us as we look at the falling snow—both at the beginning and end of her essay? How does that placement contribute to the feelings she wants readers to have?
4. Look again at her final three paragraphs. What does she repeat that helps to convey her attitude toward snow?

Thinking Critically

1. Why do you suppose that Inuits have so many names for snow?
2. When you see snow falling, what do you usually think about? Do you picture the various shapes of snow crystals? Do you find metaphors to describe to yourself the scene created by the falling snow? Something else?
3. What role does attitude play in how we respond to a situation or event?

Africa

LANCE MORROW

Journalist Lance Morrow is a senior writer at *Time* magazine who contributes to cover stories and the *Time* essay section. Morrow has also written several books, including *The Chief: A Memoir of Fathers and Sons* (1985), a study of the author's relationship with his famous journalist father Hugh Morrow. In 1981, Morrow received the National Magazine Award for his *Time* essays. In "Africa," published in the February 23, 1987, issue of *Time,* Morrow re-creates in words what he saw, felt, and reflected about while on safari in East Africa.

Questions to Guide Your Reading and Reflection
1. Morrow uses many images of light and dark—"blinding clarities" and "shadows." How do these images help him portray the landscape and its animal inhabitants?
2. What is your favorite wild animal? Why?

1   The animals stand motionless in gold-white grasses—zebras and impala, Thomson's gazelles and Cape buffalo and hartebeests and waterbuck and giraffes, and wildebeests by the thousands, all fixed in art naïf, in a smiting equatorial light. They stand in the shadowless clarity of creation.

2   Now across the immense African landscape, from the distant escarpment, a gray-purple rainstorm blows. It encroaches upon the sunlight, moving through the air like a dark idea. East Africa has a genius for such moments. Wildlife and landscape here have about them a force of melodrama and annunciation. They are the *Book of Genesis* enacted as an afternoon dream.

3   In Amboseli,[1] under the snow-covered dome of Mount Kilimanjaro, a herd of elephants moves like a dense gray cloud, slow motion, in lumbering solidity: a mirage of floating boulders. Around them dust devils rise spontaneously out of the desert, like tornadoes that swirl up on the thermals and go jittering and rushing among the animals like evil spirits busy in the primal garden.

[1]A game reserve in Kenya—Ed.

Later, in the sweet last light of the afternoon, a lion prowls 4
in lion-colored grasses and vanishes into the perfect camouflage—setting off for the hunt, alert, indolent and somehow ab-
stracted, as cats are. A rhinoceros disappears: the eye loses it
among gray boulders and thorn trees. . . .

To the human eye, the animals so often seem mirages: now 5
you see them, now you don't. Later, just after dusk, Abyssin-
ian nightjars discover the magic wash of the headlight beams.
The birds flit in and out of the barrels of light, like dolphins
frisking before a boat's prow. The Land Cruiser jostles, in four-
wheel drive, across black volcanic stones toward the camp, the
driver steering by the distant light-speck of the cooking fire.

And then the African night, which, more than elsewhere, 6
seems an abnegation of the conscious world. MMBA, "miles and
miles of bloody Africa," and it all falls into black magic void.

The world stills, for the longest time. Then, at the edge of 7
sleep, hyenas come to giggle and whoop. Peering from the tent
flap, one catches in the shadows their sidelong criminal slouch.
Their eyes shine like evil flashlight bulbs, a disembodied
horror-movie yellow, phosphorescent, glowing like the children of the damned. In the morning, one finds their droppings:
white dung, like a photographic negative. Hyenas not only eat
the meat of animals but grind up and digest the bones. The
hyenas' dung is white with the calcium of powdered bones.

Africa has its blinding clarities and its shadows. The clari- 8
ties proclaim something primal, the first days of life. The shadows lie at the other extreme of time: in the premonition of last
days, of extinction. Now you see the animals. Soon, perhaps,
you won't.

Africa is comprehensive: great birth, great death, the begin- 9
ning and the end. The themes are drawn, like the vivid, abstract hide of the zebra, in patterns of the absolute.

The first question to ask is whether the wildlife of Africa 10
can survive.

The second question is this: If the wild animals of Africa van- 11
ish from the face of the earth, what, exactly, will have been lost?

The Africa of the animals is a sort of dream kingdom. Carl 12
Jung traveled to East Africa in 1925 and wrote of a "most intense sentiment of returning to the land of my youth," of a
"recognition of the immemorially known." Africa, he said, has
"the stillness of the eternal beginning."

13   Earliest man lived in these landscapes, among such animals, among these splendid trees that have personalities as distinct as those of the animals: the aristocratic flat-topped acacia, the gnarled and magisterial baobab. Possibly scenes from that infancy are lodged in some layer of human memory, in the brilliant but preconscious morning. . . .

14   It is easy to fall in love not only with the shapes and colors of the animals but with their motions, their curving and infinitely varied gaits. The zebra moves with a strong, short-muscled stride. It is a sleek, erotic beast with vigorous bearing. The zebra's self-possession is a likable trait. It is human habit to sort the animals almost immediately into orders of preference. The animals are arranged in people's minds as a popularity contest. Some animals are endearing, and some repulsive. One wants to see the lion first, and then the elephant and after that the leopard, then rhino . . . and so on. One wants to see some animals because they are fierce, and some because they are lovable and soft. It is hard to explain the attractions and preferences. It is possible that human feelings about wild animals reflect the complexities of sexual attractions. Certain animals are admired for their majestic aggressions, and others for softer qualities. The lion is a sleek piece of violence, the waterbuck a sweet piece of grace.

15   Some of the animals move in deep slow motion, as if traversing another medium, previous to air, and thicker—an Atlantis of time. The elephant goes sleeping that way across the spaces. The medium through which it moves can be seen as time itself, a thicker, slower time than humans inhabit, a prehistoric metabolism. The giraffe goes with undulous slow motion, a long waving that starts with the head and proceeds dreamily, curving down the endless spine. The giraffe is motion as process through time. It is delicate, intelligent and eccentric, and as Karen Blixen said, so much a lady. Each of the animals has its distinct gait. The Grant's gazelle's tail never stops switching, like a nervous windshield wiper. The hartebeest moves off, when startled, in an undulous hallumph.

16   For days in Masai Mara,[2] the visitor watched the wildebeests. Ungainly and pewter colored, they are subject to sudden electric jolts of panic, to adrenal bursts of motion that can make them seem half crazed as a tribe. Now they were engaged not so much

[2]A game reserve in Kenya.—Ed.

in migration as in vagrancy, wandering across the plain on strange but idiotically determined vectors. Wildebeests smell monsters on the afternoon breeze, take sudden fear and bolt for Tanzania or Uganda or the Indian Ocean, anywhere to get away.

Sometimes, of course, the monsters are there. The veldt is lit- 17 tered with the corpses that the lion or cheetah has killed and dined on. But sometimes the herding wildebeests seem to be caught in a collective shallow madness. A fantasy of terror shoots through a herd, and all the beasts are gone: hysteria of hooves. The wildebeests thunder by the thousands across rivers and plains, moving like a barbarian invasion. They follow their instinct for the rains, for better grass. And they mow the grass before them. If they know where rain is, the wildebeests are relentless. Otherwise, they march with an undirected rigor, without destination, like cadets on punishment, beating a trail in the parade ground. The wildebeest's bisonlike head is too large for its body, its legs too thin and ungainly. It looks like a middle-aged hypochondriac, paltry in the loins and given to terrible anxiety attacks, the sort of creature whose hands (if it had hands) would always be clammy. God's genius for design may have faltered with the wildebeest.

In Masai Mara, vultures wheel dreamily in the air, like a slow 18 motion tornado of birds. Below the swirling funnel, a cheetah has brought down a baby wildebeest. The cheetah, loner and fleet aristocrat, the upper-class version of the hyena, has opened up the wildebeest and devoured the internal organs. The chee- tah's belly is swollen and its mouth is ringed with blood as it breathes heavily from the exertion of gorging. A dozen vultures flap down to take their turn. They wait 20 yards away, then wad- dle in a little toward the kill to test the cheetah. The cheetah, in a burst, rushes the vultures to drive them off, and then returns to the baby wildebeest. The vultures grump and readjust their feathers and wait their turn, the surly lumpen-carrion class.

The skeleton of an elephant lies out in the grasses near a 19 baobab tree and a scattering of black volcanic stones. The thick- trunked, gnarled baobab gesticulates with its branches, as if trying to summon help. There are no tusks lying among the bones, of course; ivory vanishes quickly in East Africa. The ele- phant is three weeks dead. Poachers. Not far away, a baby ele- phant walks alone. That is unusual. Elephants are careful mothers and do not leave their young unattended. The skeleton is the mother, and the baby is an orphan. . . .

20   The wild animals fetch back at least 2 million years. They represent, we imagine, the first order of creation, and they are vividly marked with God's eccentric genius of design: life poured into pure forms, life unmitigated by complexities of consciousness, language, ethics, treachery, revulsion, reason, religion, premeditation or free will. A wild animal does not contradict its own nature, does not thwart itself, as man endlessly does. A wild animal never plays for the other side. The wild animals are a holiday from deliberation. They are sheer life. To behold a bright being that lives without thought is, to the complex, cross-grained human mind, profoundly liberating. And even if they had no effect upon the human mind, still the wild animals are life—other life.

21   John Donne asked, "Was not the first man, by the desire of knowledge, corrupted even in the whitest integrity of nature?" The animals are a last glimpse of that shadowless life, previous to time and thought. They are a pure connection to the imagination of God.

Expanding Vocabulary

1. Match each word in column A with its definition in column B. When in doubt, first find the word in the essay and look for context clues to aid your understanding of the word's meaning. Then, if necessary, use your dictionary to complete the matching exercise. The number in parentheses is the number of the paragraph in which the word appears.

Column A	*Column B*
naïf (1)	original
escarpment (2)	sensual
annunciation (2)	irregular
thermals (3)	luminous
primal (3)	directions
abnegation (6)	open grassland
phosphorescent (7)	excessively worried about health
premonition (8)	
gnarled (13)	current of warm air
magisterial (13)	unqualified or unaffected
erotic (14)	natural simplicity
Atlantis (15)	authoritative

metabolism (15)	meager
undulous (15)	forewarning
eccentric (15)	expresses through gestures
adrenal (16)	twisted and knotty
vectors (16)	mythical island
veldt (17)	worthless
hypochondriac (17)	religious significance
paltry (17)	process of generating energy in
lumpen-carrion (18)	an organism
gesticulates (19)	sudden charge of energy
unmitigated (20)	rejection
	clifflike ridge of land or rock
	wavelike

2. Morrow mentions three people he expects his readers to know. After checking a dictionary or encyclopedia (in print or online), add a one-sentence biographical statement to your text for Carl Jung, Karen Blixen, and John Donne.

Understanding Content

1. In the first thirteen paragraphs, Morrow "paints" the East Africa game preserve landscape. What are the predominant colors of this landscape? What does the land look like?
2. Morrow devotes paragraph 7 to the hyenas. What image of this animal emerges? How does the detail of the hyenas romping in the darkness help to create Morrow's view of the hyenas?
3. In paragraphs 14 through 19 Morrow describes the animals' movements. Read these paragraphs again, picturing each animal's movements as Morrow presents them. Which animals would you want to see first? Why?
4. Morrow notes what others have also experienced when on safari in a group: members of the group have animal favorites. Morrow suggests that preferences may be connected to sexual attractions. Is this a new idea for you? Does it seem to make sense?
5. Morrow ends the section on movement with nonmovement: a dead elephant and lonely baby elephant. How does this detail contribute to the image of East Africa that he seeks to develop? If the animals become extinct, what will we have lost?

Drawing Inferences about Thesis and Purpose

1. Is there one sentence in the essay that could stand as Morrow's thesis? If you don't think so, then state the essay's thesis in your own words.

2. After several paragraphs about the wildebeests, Morrow concludes that "God's genius . . . may have faltered." Why? What details lead to this conclusion?
3. Why, in Morrow's view, are the animals "pure forms" and "sheer life"? How do they differ from humans? What do they represent in the development of life forms?

Analyzing Strategies and Style

1. Look at Morrow's opening paragraphs. What does the first paragraph accomplish? As the camera rolls on, what is added in paragraph 2? How do these two scenes announce the complex world of the game preserve that Morrow develops in the rest of the essay?
2. Examine Morrow's organization. Is it appropriate to say that Morrow first shows us photographs of his trip and then a videotape? Why?
3. How many paragraphs at the beginning of the essay give us photographs? How many separate photos are needed? What is the organizing principle of the photos?
4. Morrow presents some details as contrasts, almost contradictions. Find some examples. Is a landscape of contrasts simple or complex? Boring or awesome? What sense of this world does the author give us?
5. Morrow uses some striking metaphors to develop his description. Find three that you particularly like and explain why they are effective.

Thinking Critically

1. Has Morrow rekindled, or awakened, in you an interest in the wildlife of East Africa? If so, but you cannot afford to go on safari, what can you do to see these animals and learn more about them? List as many sources of information and experience as you can.
2. On the basis of Morrow's description—or your experiences— which of the big game is your favorite animal? Why? What attracts you to that animal? List the characteristics that you find appealing.
3. Closer to home, what domestic animal is or would be your favorite pet? Why? List the characteristics that you find appealing.
4. Should we be concerned about the possible extinction of the African elephant or rhino, the two most seriously threatened species of the big game in East Africa? What can you learn about the problem online?

Ground Zero

JONATHAN SCHELL

Jonathan Schell has taught at Princeton University, New York University, and Wesleyan University and has been a writer and editor of *The New Yorker*. He is the author of many articles and books; among his books are *The Fate of the Earth* (1982), a look at the potential horrors of nuclear war, and *The Unconquerable World* (2003). He is currently the Harold Willens Peace Fellow at the Nation Institute and author of a regular column in *The Nation*, "Letter from Ground Zero," begun after September 11, 2001, to explore and comment on issues that have arisen as a result of the Twin Towers attacks. The following is part of his first "Letter," published October 15, 2001.

Questions to Guide Your Reading and Reflection

1. What did we learn from the 9/11 attacks?
2. Many people have visited the site in lower Manhattan. Have you? If so, what was your reaction? If not, what do you think your reaction might be?

Of course there can be no such thing as a literal letter from ground zero—neither from the ground zeros of September 11 nor from the potential nuclear ground zero that is the origin of the expression. There are no letters from the beyond. (By now, "zero" has the double meaning of zero distance from the bombardier's assigned coordinates and the nothingness that's left when his work is done.) As it happens, though, I live six blocks from the ruins of the north tower of the World Trade Center, which is about as close as you can be to ground zero without having been silenced. My specific neighborhood was violated, mutilated. As I write these words, the acrid, dank, rancid stink—it is the smell of death—of the still-smoking site is in my nostrils. Not that these things confer any great distinction—they are merely the local embodiment of the circumstance, felt more or less keenly by everyone in the world in the aftermath of the attack, that in our age of weapons of mass destruction every square foot of our globe can become such a ground zero in a twinkling. We have long known this intellectually, but now we know it viscerally, as a nausea in the pit of the stomach that is unlikely to go away. What to do to change this condition, it seems to me, is the most important of the practical tasks that the crisis requires us to perform.

2   It takes time for the human reality of the losses to sink in. The eye is quick but the heart is slow. I had two experiences this week that helped me along. It occurred to me that I would be a very bad journalist and maybe a worse neighbor if, living just a few blocks from the catastrophe, I did not manage to get through the various checkpoints to visit the site. A press pass was useless; it got me no closer than my own home. A hole in the storm-fence circling the site worked better. I found myself in the midst of a huge peaceable army of helpers in a thousand uniforms—military and civilian. I was somehow unprepared by television for what I saw when I arrived at ground zero. Television had seemed to show mostly a low hillock of rubble from which the famous bucket brigade of rescuers was passing out pieces of debris. This proved to be a keyhole vision of the site. In fact, it was a gigantic, varied, panoramic landscape of destruction, an Alps of concrete, plastic and twisted metal, rising tier upon tier in the smoky distance. Around the perimeter and in the surrounding streets, a cornucopia of food, drinks (thousands of crates of spring water, Gatorade, etc.) and other provisions contributed by well-wishers from around the country was heaped up, as if some main of consumer goods on its way to the Trade Center had burst and disgorged its flood upon the sidewalks. The surrounding buildings, smashed but still standing, looked down eyelessly on their pulverized brethren. The pieces of the facade of the towers that are often shown in photographs—gigantic forks, or bent spatulas— loomed surprisingly high over the scene with dread majesty. Entry into the ruins by the rescue workers was being accomplished by a cage, or gondola, suspended by a crane, as if in some infernal ski resort. When I arrived at the southern rim, the rescuers were all standing silent watching one of these cages being lifted out of the ruins. Shortly, a small pile of something not shaped like a human being but covered by an American flag was brought out in an open buggy. It was the remains, a solemn nurse told me, of one of the firemen who had given his life for the people in the building. And then the slow work began again. Although the site was more terrible even than I

had imagined, seeing was somehow reassuring. Unvisited, the site, so near my home, had preyed on my imagination.

A few days later—one week after the catastrophe—I took my dog for a walk in the evening in Riverside Park, on the upper West Side. Soft orange clouds drifted over the Hudson River and the New Jersey shore. In the dim, cavernous green of the park, normal things were occurring—people were out for walks or jogging, children were playing in a playground. To the south, a slender moon hung in the sky. I found myself experiencing an instant of surprise: So it was still there! It had not dropped out of the sky. That was good. After all, our local southern mountain peaks—the twin towers—had fallen. The world seemed to steady around the surviving moon. "Peace" became more than a word. It was the world of difference between the bottom half of Manhattan and the top. It was the persistence of all the wonderful, ordinary things before my eyes.

Curiously, it was only after this moment of return to confidence in the continuity of life that the shape and size of the change that had been wrought in the world a week before began to come into view. The very immensity of that change— and, what was something different, the news coverage of that change—was itself a prime fact of the new situation. In an instant and without warning on a fine fall morning, the known world had been jerked aside like a mere slide in a projector, and a new world had been rammed into its place. I have before me the *New York Times* of September 11, which went to press, of course, the night before the attack. It is news from Atlantis.[1] "Key Leaders," were talking of "Possible Deals to Revive Economy," a headline said, but who was paying attention now? Were "School Dress Codes" still in a struggle with "A Sea of Bare Flesh"? Yes, but it was hard to give the matter much thought. Was "Morning TV" still a "Hot Market" in "a Nation of Early Risers"? It was, but not for the reasons given in the article. Only one headline—"Nuclear Booty: More Smugglers Use Asia Route"—seemed fit for the day's events.

Has the eye of the world ever shifted more abruptly or completely than it did on September 11? The destruction of Hiroshima of course comes to mind. It, too, was prepared in secrecy and fell like a thunderbolt upon the world. But it came

3

4

5

---

[1]A legendary island—Ed.

after years of a world war and ended the war, whereas the September 11 attack came in a time of peace and—so our President has said—started a war. The assassination of Archduke Ferdinand on June 28, 1914, starting the First World War, is another candidate. Yet the possibility of war among the great powers had long been discussed, and many previous crises—in the Far East, in the Mediterranean, in the Balkans—had threatened war. It was not the event but the aftermath (we are still living in it)—the war's ferocity and duration and the war-born horrors that sprang out of it to afflict the entire twentieth century—that changed the world. Also, whereas the guns of August touched off a chain of events—the invocation of a web of treaty agreements, the predetermined mobilization schedules of great armies—that statesmanship and diplomacy seemed powerless to prevent, today little seems predetermined, and the latitude of choice, ranging from international police work to multifront major war, seems exceptionally wide.

Expanding Vocabulary

Match each word in column A with its definition in column B. When in doubt, first find the word in the essay and look for context clues to aid your understanding of the word's meaning. Then, if necessary, use your dictionary to complete the matching exercise. The number in parentheses is the number of the paragraph in which the word appears.

Column A	Column B
acrid (1)	unbroken view
embodiment (1)	that which gives shape to
viscerally (1)	a small hill
hillock (2)	reduced to dust
panoramic (2)	spewed out
cornucopia (2)	appeal to
pulverized (2)	unpleasantly sharp
disgorged (2)	abundance
invocation (5)	emotionally, instinctively

Understanding Content

1. What is the author's relationship to the "ground zero" of the 9/11 site?
2. Why did he feel compelled to visit the site?

3. How did the site affect him before he visited? How did visiting make him feel?
4. What did Schell do a week after the attacks? How did this activity make him feel?

Drawing Inferences about Thesis and Purpose

1. Schell's opening and concluding paragraphs suggest that his primary purpose is something more than description. What is his purpose in writing?
2. Is there a sentence (or two) in paragraph 1 that serves as a thesis? If yes, underline it; if no, write a thesis statement for the essay.

Analyzing Strategies and Style

1. Reread Schell's description of ground zero. What details strike you as most vivid, most effective? Why?
2. Schell uses a number of metaphors. Select two and explain each one.
3. What do the historical details of paragraph 5 contribute to the essay?

Thinking Critically

1. In paragraph 4, the author lists headlines from a newspaper published the morning of 9/11. Why does he include these details What point does he want to make?
2. What is the connection between the details in paragraph 3 and those in paragraph 2? Why does Schell include the details in paragraph 3?
3. How did 9/11 affect you initially? Are there ways in which it continues to affect you? In what ways has the country been affected by that day?

STUDENT ESSAY—DESCRIPTION

TIME'S TROPHY
Alexa Skandar

There is something timeless and comforting about an old face. The face of my grandmother is built of a thousand weathered wrinkles. She doesn't smile too

Subject introduced through details of aging.

often anymore. On those rare occasions when we are lucky enough to catch her smile, her eyes seem to completely disappear behind the folds of time, yet somehow they still radiate that light that always attracted everyone to her.

My grandmother smells of rose oil and lettuce cream. She keeps her yellowed white hair permed and short and slicks it back with water every so often. Her skin is like the leather of her brown sandals, and her hands reveal the years of toil she has survived. Veins show like ancient flowing rivers through her aged skin. The index finger of her right hand is curved. "It's from years of crocheting," her daughter once explained to me in whispers. Her small, frail body, bent like her finger by the hands of time, seems to reflect pain and hardship in her past.

Celuta Quiroga de Skandar wears black every day, black to mourn her dead husband. Every day she prays for him. Every day her cloudy hazel eyes show her grief that has been there since he passed away close to thirty years ago. She used to go to church every day and to visit his grave every Sunday, but she has grown too old for that now. Instead she sits in a chair in the corner, rosary beads in

Subject is now identified—her grandmother.

Good use of metaphors to describe physical details.

Grandmother's name and widowed state revealed.

hand, eyes partially closed, pupils rolled back, whispering her "Hail Mary's" as she rocks herself back and forth. Senile though she is, sometimes she gets serious, and her eyes become clear, as if she has broken out of some kind of trance for a moment, and she admits that she prays every day for God to take her to be with her husband. Then her eyes cloud over and her words become meaningless again.

My grandmother is very old now. Little matters to her anymore. She has stopped living on the same plane of existence as the rest of us. She sits down *Example of her* to tell us the same stories over and *senility.* over. She goes to bed at eight in the evening only to wake up a few hours later, make her bed, and get dressed. She often makes her way to the kitchen and is fixing breakfast before she is found and told gently, "Abuelita, it's still nighttime. Time to sleep. Let's put you back to bed." A confused look comes over her face, but she obliges, often just to get back up and repeat the morning routine a few hours later.

She used to be a strong and active woman. "Dona Celu," as they called her in her small village, was a mother, a

nurse, a midwife, a farmer, a cook, and
a storyteller. People who remember how
she used to be tell stories of her great-
ness, making me proud to be her grand-
daughter. They recount how she organized
the building of the first swimming pool
in the valley in which she lived and how
she saved the lives of new mothers and
their infants from the complications of
small-town childbirth. They tell of how
she took in the neighbors' orphaned children when they had nowhere else to turn,
and raised them as her own. Now her fee-
ble attempts to sneak out of the house
and stumble to church inspire pity in all
of us. She has become a mere shadow of
the strong and determined woman she once
was. But, there is a certain strength in
the lines that time has etched in her
face, a kind of beauty that she has attained as a trophy for all she has been
through in her years of existence. For
one, a wonderful grandmother.

Details given to reveal the person she once was.

Thesis stated at end.

MAKING CONNECTIONS

1. Degas and Picasso both depict dancers in their paintings. (See reproductions following p. 80.) How do their paintings differ? How do the differences in presentation change the viewer's "picture" of dancers? Can one painting be said to be more realistic than the other? If so, what is meant by *realistic*?

2. Study the essays of Kidder, and Mora. What conclusions can you draw about effective strategies for presenting telling details of character?

3. Santha Rama Rau (pp. 46–52) was shaped by where she grew up and also by her ethnicity. Luis Rodriguez (pp. 56–59) and Amy Tan in this chapter (pp. 89–92) were influenced by growing up as minorities in American culture. Think about what these writers say—or imply—about the shaping of personality. Reflect: What are the strongest forces in the molding of character?

4. Select one of the painters represented in the chapter and learn more about him or her, using your library's reference books or going online. Learn about the painter's life and time, the kind of painting he or she is known for, and something about that style or type of painting. Be able to answer the question: What makes this painter famous in the history of art? You can do a keyword search using the artist's last name to locate books in your library's book catalog, to find current articles in your library's online databases, or to locate information online.

5. What place in the world would you like to visit for the first time? Go online and see what you can learn about your choice. Find out how you can get there and what you can see and do there. Be prepared to share your information with classmates.

TOPICS FOR WRITING

1. Describe a place you know well and that has a special significance for you. (Possibilities include your backyard, the path you walked to school, a favorite park, playground, vacation spot, city street.) Give the details that will let your reader see this place clearly. But also provide the telling details that will let your reader understand why this place has (or had) significance for you, why it is (or was) special.

2. Describe a place you have visited that produced a strong reaction in you, a place that you fell in love with (e.g., Fifth Avenue in New York City the week before Christmas), heartily disliked (e.g., Los Angeles in heavy smog), found incredibly

beautiful or awe-inspiring or special in some way (e.g., the Florida Everglades, Niagara Falls, the green hills of Vermont). Give enough details to let readers who have not been there see the place, but concentrate on presenting those details so that readers will want to visit—or never visit—depending on your thesis.

3. Have you been in an earthquake or hurricane or seen a tornado? If so, re-create the event in words so that readers can see it and feel the accompanying human emotions. Do not write a narrative account; rather select a moment or two and describe that time vividly.

4. Diane Ackerman describes the snow falling outside her home. Describe a specific scene during one of the seasons. Possibilities include your garden in autumn, a city park in summer, a city center at holiday time, your campus in the spring.

5. Describe a room on your campus to develop and support the thesis that the room fulfills—or fails to fulfill—its purpose or function. Possibilities include a classroom, science lab, learning lab, writing center, cafeteria, or library. If your library is a large and separate building, select one section of it, such as the periodicals room. Resist the urge to describe a large building, such as the entire student center. Instead, focus on one place and present details to support your thesis.

6. Lance Morrow offers readers some detailed and moving descriptions of animals he saw in the East Africa game preserves. If you enjoy wildlife, either in the wild or in a nearby zoo, take some time to watch one of your favorite animals. Or, if you have a pet, reflect on that animal. Then write a description of the animal you have selected, giving many details but also the telling details that will support a thesis about the animal. Reflect on what is central to the animal's way of life or personality to arrive at your thesis. Is the animal funny? Endearing? Inspiring? Mean? Intelligent or clever?

7. How well do you see someone close to you—a family member, friend, colleague, teacher? Select telling physical and biographical details to create an interesting and thoughtful portrait of the person you select. Pay close attention to the details that shape personality.

8. Select one of the paintings reproduced in this text or find a color reproduction of a favorite painting in your library's art book collection. Explain how the details in the painting work to create the painting's dominant effect. You will need to reflect on the painting's effect, or the artist's attitude toward the subject. Then ask yourself: How is that effect achieved by the details—the objects, composition, color, and brushwork—that make up the painting?

A CHECKLIST FOR DESCRIPTION ESSAYS

Invention

☐ Have I selected a topic and approach consistent with the instructor's guidelines for this assignment?

☐ Have I chosen, among the possible topics, one that fits my knowledge?

☐ Have I reflected on my knowledge of person or place or painting to create a tentative thesis that is clear, focused, and interesting to others?

☐ Have I recognized, from my reflection, the *telling details* that will best reveal my subject?

☐ Do I have an order for my descriptive details—spatial or by type of detail?

Drafting

☐ Have I succeeded in completing a first draft at one sitting so that I can "see" the whole?

☐ Do I have enough—enough to meet assignment demands and enough to develop and support my thesis? If not, do I need new paragraphs or more details or reflection in existing paragraphs?

☐ Does the order work? If not, what needs to be moved—and where?

☐ Am I satisfied with the way I have expressed the insights to be gained? Do the details carry my point? Have I been too heavy-handed with a message?

Revision

- ☐ Have I made any needed additions, deletions, or changes in order based on answering the questions about my draft?
- ☐ Have I revised my draft to produce coherent paragraphs, using transition words, including spatial terms if I am writing about a place or painting, to guide readers?
- ☐ Have I eliminated wordiness and clichés?
- ☐ Have I avoided or removed any discriminatory language?
- ☐ Have I used my word processor's spell check and proofread a printed copy with great care?
- ☐ Do I have an appropriate and interesting title?

Using Comparison and Contrast
Ways of Learning

When we compare we examine similarities; when we contrast we examine differences. These are strategies frequently used— whether in thinking for ourselves or communicating with others—to organize information or ideas about two (or more) similar subjects. When you think about why you like your biology course more than your chemistry course, you begin to note points of difference between them. You begin to use contrast. When shopping for a stereo system, you might read a consumer guide or gather information from friends so that you can contrast several models for cost, reliability, and sound.

When to Use Comparison and Contrast

Let's see what we have said about thinking comparatively. First, it is a strategy for organizing information and ideas. You may be able to think more clearly about problems in your chemistry course if you contrast those problems with your successes in biology. Second, you have a reason to examine similarities or differences between subjects. Your goal, in our example, is to understand why you are doing better in biology than in chemistry. Perhaps you came to college thinking that you would major in chemistry. Rethinking career goals may be aided by a careful listing of specific differences in your study of chemistry and biology. (One difference is the amount of math needed in the study of chemistry. Could that be the problem?) Third, we compare or contrast items that are similar. There seems to be little purpose in contrasting your chemistry course with doing your laundry. We compare or contrast two cities, two schools, two jobs, two dorms. We probably do not contrast living in Louisville with living in a frat house because there is no point to such a contrast. (You might have good reason, though, to contrast living at home with living away at school.) Finally, a useful comparison or contrast focuses on important similarities or differences. If you have plenty of space for your new stereo, then contrasting the sizes of different systems is unimportant. But unless you have unlimited funds, the cost of each unit is quite important, important to your purpose for choosing the best stereo for you.

Remember that an organizing principle such as comparison or contrast does not supply a purpose for writing. Rather it is a strategy that needs to grow logically out of your topic and purpose. Nancy Sakamoto contrasts American and Japanese conversations to show why sometimes Japanese and Americans have trouble communicating or being comfortable in conversation with one another. Her contrast structure is a strategy, not an end in itself.

How to Use Comparison and Contrast

Sometimes writers combine comparison and contrast, but more often their goal is to show either similarities or differences. Thus the student who asserts that there are good reasons for parents to move their children from McLean to Langley High School has a thesis that announces a contrast purpose. Although the schools certainly have some similarities—both are high schools in northern Virginia—readers will expect to learn about the significant differences between the two schools.

Organization

How should points of difference between two high schools (or any two items) be organized in an essay? You have two basic plans from which to choose. Suppose you want to show differences in the two buildings, in the courses offered, and in the extracurricular activities. If we assign "A" to McLean and "B" to

Langley and number the points of difference 1, 2, and 3, we can diagram the two patterns as follows:

Whole by Whole	*Part by Part*

A. McLean
   1. McLean Physical Plant
   2. McLean Courses
   3. McLean Activities
B. Langley
   1. Langley Physical Plant
   2. Langley Courses
   3. Langley Activities

A. Physical Plant
   1. McLean
   2. Langley
B. Courses
   1. McLean
   2. Langley
C. Activities
   1. McLean
   2. Langley

Observe that the whole-by-whole pattern organizes the essay first by school and then by points of difference, whereas the part-by-part pattern organizes the paper by the three (in this example) points of difference.

As you will see in the essays in this chapter, professional writers do not always strictly follow one plan or the other. Your instructor, however, may want you to practice using either the whole-by-whole or part-by-part structure. In fact, many instructors believe that, for most contrast topics, the part-by-part pattern is the best choice because it keeps writers focused on the business of explaining points of difference.

Transitions

When you read articles that have a comparison or contrast purpose, you may want to label the two subjects A and B and then, in the margin of your book, assign a number to each point of similarity or difference as you read. Then remember when you are writing a contrast essay that you want your reader to be able to recognize the parts of your contrast structure. This means that you will need to use appropriate transitions to mark the parts of your contrast structure. Consider these possibilities and other similar expressions to guide your reader:

| by contrast | on the other hand |
| another difference | a third similarity |

Metaphors and Analogies

When we think about the strategies of comparison and contrast, two related terms come to mind: metaphor (or simile) and analogy. We have said that we compare or contrast similar items: two schools, two courses, and so on. A *metaphor* (or a *simile*) differs in that it compares two items that are essentially unlike. When the poet writes the simile: "My love is like a red, red rose," he asks us to consider the ways that love (a feeling) can be like a rose (a flower). (To express the idea as a metaphor, the poet can write: "My love blooms.") In either case, we understand that a feeling isn't really like a flower. This is why a metaphor or a simile is called a *figure of speech*—we are speaking figuratively, not literally. The cleverness of a fresh metaphor delights us, sometimes surprises us, and affects us emotionally. You will find the essayist E. B. White using metaphors effectively to express feelings about his subjects.

In Linda Pastan's poem at the end of this chapter, she has a grading system to comment on family relationships. She uses, in other words, the same figurative idea throughout the poem. In an essay, the use of an extended metaphor is called an *analogy*. Think of an analogy as fanciful (like a metaphor) but developing a number of points of similarity or difference to support a thesis. Both metaphors and analogies, when original and thoughtful, enrich our writing. Some of this chapter's exercises will give you a chance to practice both strategies.

WRITING FOCUS:
COHERENCE IS CRUCIAL

We have noted that it is important to use transition words to guide readers through your contrast essay. But writers need to use *coherence strategies* in all of their writing, not just to show contrast. Think of each body paragraph (excluding the opening and concluding paragraphs) as a "mini"-essay; each one needs both *unity* and *coherence*. *Unity* means that all sentences in each paragraph are on that paragraph's topic. *Coherence* means using strategies that *show* readers how each body paragraph holds together. Make a point to use coherence strategies. They are illustrated and labeled in the following sample paragraph and then listed for you.

> During the Cretaceous Period (about 160 million to 65 million years ago) in North America, you would have found some familiar plants—for example, ferns, palm trees, and redwoods—and you would have been surprised by the mix of animals. At that time you would have found many birds, including giant flying pterosaurs. In the sea, you would have seen an interesting mix, for example, sharks and turtles along with giant marine lizards and fishlike ichthyosaurs. On land there were insects and small, furry mammals, but also the dinosaurs. Although some dinosaurs were already extinct, others still roamed North America, for instance, duck-bills, *Triceratops*, and the famous *Tryannosaurus rex*.

[Margin annotations: paragraph's topic sentence; repetition of subject key words; Transition words/phases; Clear structure of material—air, sea, land]

Coherence Strategies

1. Clear organization (e.g., air, sea, land)
2. Repetition of key words (e.g., "North America")
3. Use of transition worlds (e.g., "at that time")
4. Consistent person (e.g. "*you* would")

Getting Started: Reflecting on Expectations of College

Although you may not have been at college for long, still you have probably had some experiences that were not what you expected. Reflect on what you expected college to be like and how your experiences have, in part, differed from those expectations. In your journal or class notebook make two columns—one of expectations and one of what you have actually experienced. Have most of your expectations been met? Only some of them? Is there one important difference that is bothering you? You may want to write about that difference in another journal entry, or perhaps in an essay.

Conversational Ballgames

NANCY MASTERSON SAKAMOTO

American-born Sakamoto (b. 1931) lived with her Japanese husband in Osaka and taught English to Japanese students. She is currently a professor at Shitennoji Gakuen University in Hawaii. "Conversational Ballgames" is a chapter from her textbook on conversational English, *Polite Fictions*, published in 1982. Her contrasts of English and Japanese styles of conversation and her strategy for developing that contrast make us aware of the effect of cultural conditioning on the ways we learn to use language.

Questions to Guide Your Reading and Reflection

1. What differences between American culture and Japanese culture are suggested in Sakamoto's discussion of conversation?
2. How would you characterize conversation in a language other than English or Japanese? Or, how would you describe the conversation of young children and their parents?

1   After I was married and had lived in Japan for a while, my Japanese gradually improved to the point where I could take part in simple conversations with my husband and his friends and family. And I began to notice that often, when I joined in, the others would look startled, and the conversational topic would come to a halt. After this happened several times, it became clear to me that I was doing something wrong. But for a long time, I didn't know what it was.

2   Finally, after listening carefully to many Japanese conversations, I discovered what my problem was. Even though I was speaking Japanese, I was handling the conversation in a western way.

3   Japanese-style conversations develop quite differently from western-style conversations. And the difference isn't only in the languages. I realized that just as I kept trying to hold western-style conversations even when I was speaking

Japanese, so my English students kept trying to hold Japanese-style conversations even when they were speaking English. We were unconsciously playing entirely different conversational ballgames.

A western-style conversation between two people is like a   4
game of tennis. If I introduce a topic, a conversational ball, I expect you to hit it back. If you agree with me, I don't expect you simply to agree and do nothing more. I expect you to add something—a reason for agreeing, another example, or an elaboration to carry the idea further. But I don't expect you always to agree. I am just as happy if you question me, or challenge me, or completely disagree with me. Whether you agree or disagree, your response will return the ball to me.

And then it is my turn again. I don't serve a new ball from   5
my original starting line. I hit your ball back again from where it has bounced. I carry your idea further, or answer your questions or objections, or challenge or question you. And so the ball goes back and forth, with each of us doing our best to give it a new twist, an original spin, or a powerful smash.

And the more vigorous the action, the more interesting and   6
exciting the game. Of course, if one of us gets angry, it spoils the conversation, just as it spoils a tennis game. But getting excited is not at all the same as getting angry. After all, we are not trying to hit each other. We are trying to hit the ball. So long as we attack only each other's opinions, and do not attack each other personally, we don't expect anyone to get hurt. A good conversation is supposed to be interesting and exciting.

If there are more than two people in the conversation, then   7
it is like doubles in tennis, or like volleyball. There's no waiting in line. Whoever is nearest and quickest hits the ball, and if you step back, someone else will hit it. No one stops the game to give you a turn. You're responsible for taking your own turn.

But whether it's two players or a group, everyone does his   8
best to keep the ball going, and no one person has the ball for very long.

A Japanese-style conversation, however, is not at all like tennis or volleyball. It's like bowling. You wait for your turn. And   9
you always know your place in line. It depends on such things as whether you are older or younger, a close friend or a relative

stranger to the previous speaker, in a senior or junior position, and so on.

10   When your turn comes, you step up to the starting line with your bowling ball, and carefully bowl it. Everyone else stands back and watches politely, murmuring encouragement. Everyone waits until the ball has reached the end of the alley, and watches to see if it knocks down all the pins, or only some of them, or none of them. There is a pause, while everyone registers your score.

11   Then, after everyone is sure that you have completely finished your turn, the next person in line steps up to the same starting line, with a different ball. He doesn't return your ball, and he does not begin from where your ball stopped. There is no back and forth at all. All the balls run parallel. And there is always a suitable pause between turns. There is no rush, no excitement, no scramble for the ball.

12   No wonder everyone looked startled when I took part in Japanese conversations. I paid no attention to whose turn it was, and kept snatching the ball halfway down the alley and throwing it back at the bowler. Of course the conversation died. I was playing the wrong game.

13   This explains why it is almost impossible to get a western-style conversation or discussion going with English students in Japan. I used to think that the problem was their lack of English language ability. But I finally came to realize that the biggest problem is that they, too, are playing the wrong game.

14   Whenever I serve a volleyball, everyone just stands back and watches it fall, with occasional murmurs of encouragement. No one hits it back. Everyone waits until I call on someone to take a turn. And when that person speaks, he doesn't hit my ball back. He serves a new ball. Again, everyone just watches it fall.

15   So I call on someone else. This person does not refer to what the previous speaker has said. He also serves a new ball. Nobody seems to have paid any attention to what anyone else has said. Everyone begins again from the same starting line, and all the balls run parallel. There is never any back and forth. Everyone is trying to bowl with a volleyball.

16   And if I try a simpler conversation, with only two of us, then the other person tries to bowl with my tennis ball. No wonder foreign English teachers in Japan get discouraged.

Now that you know about the difference in the conversa- 17
tional ballgames, you may think that all your troubles are over.
But if you have been trained all your life to play one game, it
is no simple matter to switch to another, even if you know the
rules. Knowing the rules is not at all the same thing as playing
the game.

Even now, during a conversation in Japanese I will notice 18
a startled reaction, and belatedly realize that once again I
have rudely interrupted by instinctively trying to hit back
the other person's bowling ball. It is no easier for me to "just
listen" during a conversation than it is for my Japanese students to "just relax" when speaking with foreigners. Now I
can truly sympathize with how hard they must find it to try
to carry on a western-style conversation.

If I have not yet learned to do conversational bowling in 19
Japanese, at least I have figured out one thing that puzzled me
for a long time. After his first trip to America, my husband
complained that Americans asked him so many questions and
made him talk so much at the dinner table that he never had a
chance to eat. When I asked him why he couldn't talk and eat
at the same time, he said that Japanese do not customarily
think that dinner, especially on fairly formal occasions, is a
suitable time for extended conversation.

Since westerners think that conversation is an indispensable 20
part of dining, and indeed would consider it impolite not to
converse with one's dinner partner, I found this Japanese custom rather strange. Still, I could accept it as a cultural difference
even though I didn't really understand it. But when my husband added, in explanation, that Japanese consider it extremely
rude to talk with one's mouth full, I got confused. Talking with
one's mouth full is certainly not an American custom. We think
it very rude, too. Yet we still manage to talk a lot and eat at the
same time. How do we do it?

For a long time, I couldn't explain it, and it bothered me. But 21
after I discovered the conversational ballgames, I finally found
the answer. Of course! In a western-style conversation, you hit
the ball, and while someone else is hitting it back, you take a
bite, chew, and swallow. Then you hit the ball again, and then
eat some more. The more people there are in the conversation,
the more chances you have to eat. But even with only two of
you talking, you still have plenty of chances to eat.

22   Maybe that's why polite conversation at the dinner table has never been a traditional part of Japanese etiquette. Your turn to talk would last so long without interruption that you'd never get a chance to eat.

Expanding Vocabulary

Study definitions of each of the following words and then use each one in a separate sentence. The number in parentheses is the number of the paragraph in which the word appears.

elaboration (4)	belatedly (18)
murmuring (10)	customarily (19)
registers (10)	etiquette (22)

Understanding Content

1. When Sakamoto first participated in Japanese conversations, what happened? What was the cause of her problem?
2. What are the characteristics of an American-style conversation?
3. What are the characteristics of a Japanese-style conversation?
4. How do the Japanese feel about conversing during dinner? How do Americans feel about dinner conversation?

Drawing Inferences about Thesis and Purpose

1. How hard is it to converse in another language after one has "learned" the language?
2. What is Sakamoto's thesis? Where is it stated?

Analyzing Strategies and Style

1. What strategy does Sakamoto use as an opening? What makes it effective?
2. Explain each analogy. How is American-style conversation like a tennis game, and how is Japanese-style conversation like bowling? What other game comparison does the author use?
3. Who is Sakamoto's primary audience? (Be sure to read the headnote.) What makes her writing style appropriate for her audience and purpose?

Thinking Critically

1. Did the author's analogies help you to see the differences between American and Japanese conversational styles? If not, why not? If the analogies did help you, can you explain why?

2. Had you thought before about the way we carry on conversations? After reflection, do you agree with the author's description of American conversation patterns? Why or why not?

3. What might we conclude about the relationship between language and cultural traits and values? What else do we learn when, as children, we learn our primary language?

Education

E. B. WHITE

One of the finest of modern essayists, E. B. White (1899–1985) made his name as a writer for *The New Yorker*. He also published many of his best-loved essays, including "Education," from 1938 to 1943 in *Harper's* and then collected them in *One Man's Meat* (1943). White the essayist may be best known for his now-classic children's stories: *Stuart Little, Charlotte's Web*, and *The Trumpet of the Swan*. You can learn much about essay writing by observing White's variation of contrast organization to reinforce thesis and by his use of examples and metaphors.

Questions to Guide Your Reading and Reflection

1. In his second sentence, White lists activities over which the country school teacher is guardian. What is White's point with this seemingly odd list?

2. When you think of your elementary school, what images come to mind?

I have an increasing admiration for the teacher in the country school where we have a third-grade scholar in attendance. She not only undertakes to instruct her charges in all the subjects of the first three grades, but she manages to function quietly and effectively as a guardian of their health, their clothes, their habits, their mothers, and their snowball engagements. She has been doing this sort of Augean task for twenty years, and is both kind and wise. She cooks for the children on the stove that heats the room and she can cool their passions or warm their soup with equal competence. She conceives their costumes, cleans up their messes, and shares their confidences.

1

My boy already regards his teacher as his great friend, and I think tells her a great deal more than he tells us.

2   The shift from city school to country school was something we worried about quietly all last summer. I have always rather favored public school over private school, if only because in public school you meet a greater variety of children. This bias of mine, I suspect, is partly an attempt to justify my own past (I never knew anything but public schools) and partly an involuntary defense against getting kicked in the shins by a young ceramist on his way to the kiln. My wife was unacquainted with public schools, never having been exposed (in her early life) to anything more public than the washroom of Miss Winsor's. Regardless of our backgrounds, we both knew that the change in schools was something that concerned not us but the scholar himself. We hoped it would work out all right. In New York our son went to a medium-priced private institution with semi-progressive ideas of education, and modern plumbing. He learned fast, kept well, and we were satisfied. It was an electric, colorful, regimented existence with moments of pleasurable pause and giddy incident. The day the Christmas angel fainted and had to be carried out by one of the Wise Men was educational in the highest sense of the term. Our scholar gave imitations of it around the house for weeks afterward, and I doubt if it ever goes completely out of his mind.

3   His days were rich in formal experience. Wearing overalls and an old sweater (the accepted uniform of the private seminary), he sallied forth at morn accompanied by a nurse or a parent and walked (or was pulled) two blocks to a corner where the school bus made a flag stop. This flashy vehicle was as punctual as death: seeing us waiting at the cold curb, it would sweep to a halt, open its mouth, suck the boy in, and spring away with an angry growl. It was a good deal like a train picking up a bag of mail. At school the scholar was worked on for six or seven hours by half a dozen teachers and a nurse, and was revived on orange juice in mid-morning. In a cinder court he played games supervised by an athletic instructor, and in a cafeteria he ate lunch worked out by a dietician. He soon learned to read with gratifying facility and discernment and to make Indian weapons of a semi deadly nature. Whenever one of his classmates fell low of a fever the news was put on the wires and

there were breathless phone calls to physicians, discussing periods of incubation and allied magic.

In the country all one can say is that the situation is different, and somehow more casual. Dressed in corduroys, sweatshirt, and short rubber boots, and carrying a tin dinner-pail, our scholar departs at crack of dawn for the village school, two and a half miles down the road, next to the cemetery. When the road is open and the car will start, he makes the journey by motor, courtesy of his old man. When the snow is deep or the motor is dead or both, he makes it on the hoof. In the afternoons he walks or hitches all or part of the way home in fair weather, gets transported in foul. The schoolhouse is a two-room frame building, bungalow type, shingles stained a burnt brown with weather-resistant stain. It has a chemical toilet in the basement and two teachers above stairs. One takes the first three grades, the other the fourth, fifth, and sixth. They have little or no time for individual instruction, and no time at all for the esoteric. They teach what they know themselves, just as fast and as hard as they can manage. The pupils sit still at their desks in class, and do their milling around outdoors during recess.

There is no supervised play. They play cops and robbers (only they call it "Jail") and throw things at one another—snowballs in winter, rose hips in fall. It seems to satisfy them. They also construct darts, pinwheels, and "pick-up sticks" (jackstraws), and the school itself does a brisk trade in penny candy, which is for sale right in the classroom and which contains "surprises." The most highly prized surprise is a fake cigarette, made of cardboard, fiendishly lifelike.

The memory of how apprehensive we were at the beginning is still strong. The boy was nervous about the change too. The tension, on that first fair morning in September when we drove him to school, almost blew the windows out of the sedan. And when later we picked him up on the road, wandering along with his little blue lunch-pail, and got his laconic report "All right" in answer to our inquiry about how the day had gone, our relief was vast. Now, after almost a year of it, the only difference we can discover in the two school experiences is that in the country he sleeps better at night—and *that* probably is more the air than the education. When grilled on the subject of school-in-country *vs.* school-in-city, he replied that the chief difference is that the day seems to go so much quicker in the country. "Just like lightning," he reported.

Expanding Vocabulary

Study the definitions of each of the following words in your dictionary and then write the definition that fits the word's use in White's essay. Select five words and write a sentence for each word, using it in the same way that White does. The number in parentheses is the number of the paragraph in which the word appears.

Augean (1)	kiln (2)
conceives (1)	giddy (2)
involuntary (2)	seminary (3)
ceramist (2)	sallied (3)
dietician (3)	allied (3)
facility (3)	esoteric (4)
discernment (3)	laconic (6)
incubation (3)	

Understanding Content

1. Using "A" for the country school and "B" for the city school, outline White's organization paragraph by paragraph. Which contrast structure does White most closely follow?
2. How does White vary the contrast structure he has selected? What does he gain by this variation?
3. List the specific points of difference between the two school experiences (including travel, recess, etc.).

Drawing Inferences about Thesis and Purpose

1. Because White's son has attended only one city school and one country school, White cannot claim to be contrasting all (or most) city and country schools. What, then, is he contrasting about education?
2. What is White's thesis?

Analyzing Strategies and Style

1. The boy remembers the fainting Christmas angel from his city-school days. Why does White give us this detail? What is its significance?

2. White reveals his implied thesis in part through contrasting details. Find several sentences that express differences between the schools. How are the sentences similar? How do they differ? How do the differences in wording emphasize the differences between the schools?
3. White's metaphors may be his best strategy for expressing attitude. Find two metaphors in paragraph 3, state the two items being compared, and explain how these metaphors express White's attitude toward the city school.
4. White chooses words carefully, not only for meaning but for sound—and the emphasis gained by repeating sounds. List all the words in paragraph 1 that begin with the same first letter. (This technique is called *alliteration*.) What does White accomplish by having these words connected through sound?

Thinking Critically

1. Which school described by White do you think you would have preferred? Why?
2. White is contrasting elementary schools. Do you think his attitude would be different if he were contrasting an old, rural high school (without a gym, cafeteria, science labs, specialized teachers) and a modern, well-equipped suburban high school with specially trained teachers? Should his attitude be different?
3. In your view, how important are a school's facilities? How important are the teachers?

What Adolescents Miss When We Let Them Grow Up in Cyberspace

BRENT STAPLES

Holding a Ph.D. in psychology from the University of Chicago, Brent Staples is currently an editorial writer, specializing in politics and culture, for *The New York Times*. He has written a memoir, *Parallel Time: Growing Up in Black and White* (1994), and his essays and columns are widely published in textbooks. The following column appeared in *The New York Times* on May 29, 2004.

Questions to Guide Your Reading and Reflection
1. What do teens miss when they spend large amounts of time in cyberspace?
2. Do you think that e-mail has made you more—or less—connected to others? What do you mean by "connected"?

1   My 10th-grade heartthrob was the daughter of a fearsome steelworker who struck terror into the hearts of 15-year-old boys. He made it his business to answer the telephone—and so always knew who was calling—and grumbled in the background when the conversation went on too long. Unable to make time by phone, the boy either gave up or appeared at the front door. This meant submitting to the intense scrutiny that the girl's father soon became known for.

2   He greeted me with a crushing handshake, then leaned in close in a transparent attempt to find out whether I was one of those bad boys who smoked. He retired to the den during the visit, but cruised by the living room now and then to let me know he was watching. He let up after some weeks, but only after getting across what he expected of a boy who spent time with his daughter and how upset he'd be if I disappointed him.

3   This was my first sustained encounter with an adult outside my family who needed to be convinced of my worth as a person. This, of course, is a crucial part of growing up. Faced with the same challenge today, however, I would probably pass on meeting the girl's father—and outflank him on the Internet.

4   Thanks to e-mail, online chat rooms and instant messages—which permit private, real-time conversations—adolescents have at last succeeded in shielding their social lives from adult scrutiny. But this comes at a cost: teenagers nowadays are both more connected to the world at large than ever, and more cut off from the social encounters that have historically prepared young people for the move into adulthood.

5   The Internet was billed as a revolutionary way to enrich our social lives and expand our civic connections. This seems to have worked well for elderly people and others who were isolated before they got access to the World Wide Web. But a growing body of research is showing that heavy use of the Net can actually isolate younger socially connected people who un-

wittingly allow time online to replace face-to-face interactions with their families and friends.

Online shopping, checking e-mail and Web surfing—mainly   6
solitary activities—have turned out to be more isolating than watching television, which friends and family often do in groups. Researchers have found that the time spent in direct contact with family members drops by as much as half for every hour we use the Net at home.

This should come as no surprise to the two-career couples   7
who have seen their domestic lives taken over by e-mail and wireless tethers that keep people working around the clock. But a startling body of research from the Human-Computer Interaction Institute at Carnegie Mellon has shown that heavy Internet use can have a stunting effect outside the home as well.

Studies show that gregarious, well-connected people actually   8
lost friends, and experienced symptoms of loneliness and depression, after joining discussion groups and other activities. People who communicated with disembodied strangers online found the experience empty and emotionally frustrating but were nonetheless seduced by the novelty of the new medium. As Prof. Robert Kraut, a Carnegie Mellon researcher, told me recently, such people allowed low-quality relationships developed in virtual reality to replace higher-quality relationships in the real world.

No group has embraced this socially impoverishing trade-   9
off more enthusiastically than adolescents, many of whom spend most of their free hours cruising the Net in sunless rooms. This hermetic existence has left many of these teenagers with nonexistent social skills—a point widely noted in stories about the computer geeks who rose to prominence in the early days of Silicon Valley.

Adolescents are drawn to cyberspace for different reasons   10
than adults. As the writer Michael Lewis observed in his book *Next: The Future Just Happened,* children see the Net as a transformational device that lets them discard quotidian identities for more glamorous ones. Mr. Lewis illustrated the point with Marcus Arnold, who, as a 15-year-old, adopted a pseudonym a few years ago and posed as a 25-year-old legal expert for an Internet information service. Marcus did not feel the least bit guilty, and wasn't deterred, when real-world lawyers discovered his secret and accused him of being a fraud. When asked whether he had actually read the law, Marcus responded that

he found books "boring," leaving us to conclude that he had learned all he needed to know from his family's big-screen TV.

11   Marcus is a child of the Net, where everyone has a pseudonym, telling a story makes it true, and adolescents create older, cooler, more socially powerful selves any time they wish. The ability to slip easily into a new, false self is tailor-made for emotionally fragile adolescents, who can consider a bout of acne or a few excess pounds an unbearable tragedy.

12   But teenagers who spend much of their lives hunched over computer screens miss the socializing, the real-world experience that would allow them to leave adolescence behind and grow into adulthood. These vital experiences, like much else, are simply not available in a virtual form.

Expanding Vocabulary

Match each word in column A with its definition in column B. When in doubt, first find the word in the essay and look for context clues to aid your understanding of the word's meaning. Then, if necessary, use your dictionary to complete the matching exercise. The number in parentheses is the number of the paragraph in which the word appears.

Column A	Column B
transparent (2)	assumed name
outflank (3)	not intending
unwittingly (5)	ties that limit one's range of mobility
tethers (7)	outgoing
stunting (7)	commonplace, ordinary
gregarious (8)	obvious
hermetic (9)	prevented from acting
quotidian (10)	limiting the growth of
pseudonym (10)	maneuver around
deterred (10)	sealed off from outside influence

Understanding Content

1. What advantages did people see in the Internet? Who has benefited from these advantages? Who has been hurt by them?
2. What about cyberspace seems especially appealing to teens?
3. What is the contrast Staples makes? Make A "teens without the Internet" and B "teens with the Internet." List specific points of difference between the two.

Drawing Inferences about Thesis and Purpose

1. What is Staples's thesis? Is there a sentence in the essay that serves as the author's thesis? If not, write a thesis statement for the essay.
2. Evaluate the author's sources. If you are unfamiliar with Carnegie Mellon, see what you can learn about the university online.

Analyzing Strategies and Style

1. Staples opens with three paragraphs of personal anecdote. What is the point of his experience? What about his presentation makes this a clever opening?
2. What do we learn from the example of Marcus Arnold in paragraph 10? How are we to read the paragraph's last sentence? What is its tone?

Thinking Critically

1. Staples describes Marcus as "a child of the Net, where everyone has a pseudonym, telling a story makes it true, and adolescents create older, cooler, more socially powerful selves any time they wish." Comment on each of his three points. Is this an insightful comment on our "electronic" times? Why or why not?
2. Have you ever felt the isolation of the electronic environment? If so, have you changed your behavior in any way? If not, how would you respond to Staples?

Boys and Girls:
Anatomy and Destiny

JUDITH VIORST

Judith Viorst is a poet, journalist, and author of books for both children and adults. She has published several volumes of poetry and more than a dozen books. Viorst may be best known as a contributing editor to *Redbook* magazine; she has received several awards for her *Redbook* columns. Her book *Necessary Losses* (1986) is an important book for adults about coping with the changes we experience at different times in our lives. The following is an excerpt from *Necessary Losses*.

Questions to Guide Your Reading and Reflection

1. What are the incorrect beliefs about males and females, according to Maccoby and Jacklin?
2. Make a list of what you think are differences between males and females (other than anatomy) and compare your list to Viorst's.

---

1   It is argued that sex-linked limits have been culturally produced. It is argued that sex-linked limits are innate. What gender-identity studies seem to strongly suggest, however, is that—from the moment of birth—both boys and girls are so clearly treated as boys or as girls that even very early displays of "masculine" or "feminine" behavior cannot be detached from environmental influences.

2   For parents make a distinction between boys and girls.

3   They have different ways of holding boys and girls.

4   They have different expectations for boys and girls.

5   And as their children imitate and identify with their attitudes and activities, they encourage or discourage them, depending on whether or not they are boys or girls.

6   Are there, in actual fact, *real* sex-linked limits? Is there an inborn male or female psychology? And is there any possible way of exploring such tricky questions unbiased by culture, upbringing or sexual politics? . . .

7   Sigmund Freud . . . went on record as saying that women are more masochistic, narcissistic, jealous and envious than men, and also less moral. He saw these qualities as the inevitable consequences of the anatomical differences between the sexes—the result of the fact (fact?) that the original sexuality of the little girl is masculine in character, that her clitoris is merely an undeveloped penis and that she correctly perceives herself as nothing more than a defective boy. It is the girl's perception of herself as a mutilated male that irrevocably damages her self-esteem, leading to resentments and attempts at reparation which produce all the subsequent defects in her character.

8   Well, as his friends say, who can be right about everything?

9   For in the years since this was written, science has established that while genetic sex is determined at fertilization by our chromosomes (XX for girls; XY for boys), all mammals, in-

cluding humans, *regardless of their genetic sex,* start out female in nature and in structure. This female state persists until the production, some time later in fetal life, of male hormones. It is only with the appearance of these hormones, at the right time and in the right amount, that anatomical maleness and postnatal masculinity become possible.

While this may not tell us much about the psychology of femaleness and maleness, it does put a permanent crimp in Freud's phallocentricity. For, far from little girls starting out as incomplete little boys, in the beginning all human beings are female. 10

Despite his phallocentricity, however, Freud was smart enough to note at the time that his comments on the nature of women were "certainly incomplete and fragmentary." 11

He also said: "If you want to know more about femininity, enquire from your own experiences of life, or turn to the poets, or wait until science can give you deeper and more coherent information." 12

Two Stanford psychologists have tried to do just that in a highly regarded book called *The Psychology of Sex Differences.* Surveying and evaluating a broad range of psychological studies, authors Eleanor Maccoby and Carol Jacklin conclude that there are several widely held but dead-wrong beliefs regarding the ways in which males and females differ: 13

That girls are more "social" and more "suggestible" than boys. That girls have lower self-esteem. That girls are better at rote learning and simple repetitive tasks and boys more "analytic." That girls are more affected by heredity and boys by environment. That girls are auditory and boys are visual. And that girls lack achievement motivation. 14

Not true, say authors Maccoby and Jacklin. These are myths. 15

Some myths, however—or are they myths?—have not yet been dispelled. Some sexual mysteries remain unsolved: 16

Are girls more timid? Are they more fearful? More anxious? 17

Are boys more active, competitive and dominant? 18

And is it a female quality—in contrast to a male quality—to be nurturing and compliant and maternal? 19

The evidence, the authors say, is either too ambiguous or too thin. These tantalizing questions are still open. 20

There are, however, four differences which they believe to be fairly well established: That girls have greater verbal ability. 21

That boys have greater math ability. That boys excel in visual-spatial ability. And that verbally and physically, boys are more aggressive.

22   Are these innate differences, or are they learned? Maccoby and Jacklin reject this distinction. They prefer to talk in terms of biological predispositions to learn a particular skill or kind of behavior. And talking in these terms, they designate only two sexual differences as clearly built upon biological factors.

23   One is boys' better visual-spatial ability, for which there is evidence of a recessive sex-linked gene.

24   The other is the relationship that exists between male hormones and the readiness of males to behave aggressively.

25   However, even that has been disputed. Endocrinologist Estelle Ramey, professor of physiology and biophysics at Georgetown Medical School, told me:

26   "I think hormones are great little things and that no home should be without them. But I also think that virtually all the differences in male and female behavior are culturally, not hormonally, determined. It's certainly true that *in utero* sex hormones play a vital role in distinguishing male from female babies. But soon after birth the human brain takes over and overrides *all* systems, including the endocrine system. It is said, for instance, that men are innately more aggressive than women. But conditioning, not sex hormones, makes them that way. Anyone seeing women at a bargain-basement sale— where aggression is viewed as appropriate, even endearing— sees aggression that would make Attila the Hun turn pale."

27   Although Maccoby and Jacklin's survey also concludes that little girls are no more dependent than boys, the female-dependency issue will not go away. A few years ago Colette Dowling's best-selling book *The Cinderella Complex* struck a responsive chord in women everywhere with its theme of a female fear of independence.

> Here it was—the Cinderella Complex. It used to hit girls of six-teen or seventeen, preventing them, often, from going to college, hastening them into early marriages. Now it tends to hit women after college—after they've been out in the world a while. When the first thrill of freedom subsides and anxiety rises to take its place, they begin to be tugged by that old yearning for safety: the wish to be saved.

Dowling argues that women, in contrast to men, have a 28
deep desire to be taken care of and that they are unwilling to
accept the adult reality that they alone are responsible for their
lives. This tendency toward dependency, Dowling maintains,
is bred into them by the training of early childhood, which
teaches boys that they're on their own in this difficult, challenging world and which teaches girls that they need and
must seek protection.

Girls are trained *into* dependency, says Dowling.   29
Boys are trained *out* of it.   30
Even in the mid-1980s, at an Eastern liberal-elite private 31
school where the mothers of students are doctors and lawyers
and government officials and the students themselves are full
of feminist rhetoric, there are echoes of the Cinderella Complex. One of the teachers, who gives a course in human behavior to the high school seniors, told me that he has asked them,
for the last several years, where they expect to see themselves
at age thirty. The answers, he said, are consistently the same.
Both boys and girls expect that the girls will be bearing and
rearing children, while also engaged in some interesting *part-
time* work. And although the boys express a desire to have a
great deal of freedom at that age, the girls routinely place the
boys in successful *full-time* jobs, supporting their families.

Now it surely is true that a great many women live with a 32
someday-my-prince-will-take-care-of-me fantasy. It is true that
the way girls are raised may help explain why. But we also
need to consider that the source of female dependence may run
deeper than the customs of early child care. And we also need
to remember that dependence isn't always a dirty word.

For female dependence appears to be less a wish to be pro- 33
tected than a wish to be part of a web of human relationships, a
wish not only to get—but to give—loving care. To need other
people to help and console you, to share the good times and bad,
to say "I understand," to be on your side—*and also to need the re-
verse, to need to be needed*—may lie at the heart of women's very
identity. Dependence on such connections might be described as
"mature dependence." It also means, however, that identity—for
women—has more to do with intimacy than with separateness.

In a series of elegant studies, psychologist Carol Gilligan 34
found that while male self-definitions emphasized individual

achievement over attachment, women repeatedly defined themselves within a context of responsible caring relationships. Indeed, she notes that "male and female voices typically speak of
the importance of different truths, the former of the role of separation as it defines and empowers the self, the latter of the ongoing process of attachment that creates and sustains the human
community." It is only because we live in a world where matu-
rity is equated with autonomy, argues Gilligan, that women's
concern with relationships appears to be a weakness instead of
a strength.

35   Perhaps it is both.

36   Claire, an aspiring physician, finds essential meaning in attachment. "By yourself, there is little sense to things," she says.
"It is like the sound of one hand clapping. . . . You have to love
someone else, because while you may not like them, you are in-
separable from them. In a way, it is like loving your right hand.
They are part of you; that other person is part of that giant collection of people that you are connected to."

37   But then there is Helen who, talking about the end of a relationship, reveals the risks inherent in intimacy. "What I had to
learn . . . ," she says, "wasn't only that I had a Self that could
survive it when Tony and I broke up; but that I had a Self *at all!*
I wasn't honestly sure that, when we two were separate, there
would be anything there that *was me.*"

38   Freud once observed that "we are never so defenseless
against suffering as when we love, never so helplessly unhappy as when we have lost our loved object or its love."
Women will find these words particularly true. For women, far
more often than men, succumb to that suffering known as depression when important love relationships are through. The
logic thus seems to be that women's dependence on intimacy
makes them, if not the weaker sex, the more vulnerable one.

Expanding Vocabulary

Match each word in column A with its definition in column B.
When in doubt, first find the word in the essay and look for context clues to aid your understanding of the word's meaning. Then,
if necessary, use your dictionary to complete the matching exercise.
The number in parentheses is the number of the paragraph in
which the word appears.

Column A

masochistic (7)
narcissistic (7)
mutilated (7)
irrevocably (7)
reparation (7)
crimp (10)
phallocentricity (10)
coherent (12)
auditory (14)
compliant (19)
predispositions (22)
autonomy (34)
inherent (37)
succumb (38)
vulnerable (38)

Column B

impossible to retract or change
held together, logically connected
to have a hampering effect on
idea of the central role of the penis—or lack
   of one—in shaping one's psychology
tending to yield to others
independence, self-direction
getting pleasure from being dominated
   or abused
submit or yield to something
   overwhelming
easily affected
deprived of a limb or essential part
existing as an essential characteristic
process of making amends
advance inclinations to something
having excessive love of oneself
related to sense of hearing

Understanding Content

1. What do gender-identity studies suggest about how we become masculine or feminine?
2. How did Freud explain the "defects" in women's characters?
3. How do all mammals begin their development?
4. For what myths about males and females is there still inadequate evidence?
5. What is the "Cinderella Complex"?
6. How can dependency be seen as a strength? What seems to matter more to women than to men?

Drawing Inferences about Thesis and Purpose

1. What is Viorst's subject? What is her purpose in writing?
2. What is her position on differences between males and females and on the source(s) of those differences?

Analyzing Strategies and Style

1. Examine Viorst's opening. How does it both establish her subject and get reader interest?
2. The author uses many brief paragraphs. When does she use them? What does she gain by using them?

Thinking Critically

1. How many of the myths about male and female differences have you believed? Has Viorst convinced you that most are unsupported by evidence? Why or why not?
2. Observe how the author introduces the specialists on whom she draws. Are you prepared to accept them as reliable sources? Can they be reliable and still leave readers with questions and concerns? If so, why?
3. Do you see female "dependence" or desire for close relationships as a weakness or strength? Explain your views.
4. Why do we have so much trouble sorting out similarities and differences among males and females? What are some of the issues that get in the way?

Who Says a Woman Can't Be Einstein?

AMANDA RIPLEY

Amanda Ripley is a reporter for *Time* magazine. The following article, slightly condensed, was the cover story on March 7, 2005, probably in response to the issue raised by Harvard President Larry Summers over possible reasons for so few women pursuing careers in math, science, and engineering.

Questions to Guide Your Reading and Reflection

1. What does the title suggest to you about the article's subject matter? What does the title suggest about the writer's attitude toward the subject?
2. What may be some of the reasons why women do not choose careers in the sciences in the same numbers as men?

1   Now that scientists are finally starting to map the brain with some accuracy, the challenge is figuring out what to do with that knowledge. The possibilities for applying it to the classroom, workplace and doctor's office are tantalizing. "If something is genetic, it means it must be biological. If we can figure out the biology, then we should be able to tweak the biology," says Richard Haier, a psychology professor who studies intelligence at the University of California at Irvine. . . .

Lesson 1: Function Over Form

Scientists have been looking for sex differences in the brain   2
since they have been looking at the brain. Many bold decrees
have been issued. In the 19th century, the corpus callosum, a
bundle of nerve fibers that connects the two hemispheres of the
brain, was considered key to intellectual development. Accordingly, it was said to have a greater surface area in men.
Then, in the 1980s, we were told that no, it is larger in women—
and that explains why the emotional right side of women's
brains is more in touch with the analytical left side. Aha. That
theory has since been discredited, and scientists remain at odds
over who has the biggest and what it might mean. Stay tuned
for more breaking news.

But most studies agree that men's brains are about 10% big-   3
ger than women's brains overall. Even when the comparison is
adjusted for the fact that men are, on average, 8% taller than
women, men's brains are still slightly bigger. But size does not
predict intellectual performance, as was once thought. Men and
women perform similarly on IQ tests. And most scientists still
cannot tell male and female brains apart just by looking at them.

Recently, scientists have begun to move away from the ob-   4
session with size. Thanks to new brain-imaging technology, researchers can get a good look at the living brain as it functions
and grows. Earlier studies relied on autopsies or X-rays—and
no one wanted to expose children or women, who might be
pregnant, to regular doses of radiation.

The deeper you probe, the more interesting the differences.   5
Women appear to have more connections between the two
brain hemispheres. In certain regions, their brain is more
densely packed with neurons. And women tend to use more
parts of their brain to accomplish certain tasks. That might explain why they often recover better from a stroke, since the
healthy parts of their mind compensate for the injured regions.
Men do their thinking in more focused regions of the brain,
whether they are solving a math problem, reading a book or
feeling a wave of anger or sadness.

Indeed, men and women seem to handle emotions quite dif-   6
ferently. While both sexes use a part of the brain called the
amygdala, which is located deep within the organ, women
seem to have stronger connections between the amygdala and
regions of the brain that handle language and other higher-level

functions. That may explain why women are, on average, more likely to talk about their emotions and men tend to compartmentalize their worries and carry on. Or, of course, it may not.

7   "Men and women have different brain architectures, and we don't know what they mean," says Haier. By administering IQ tests to a group of college students and then analyzing scans of their brain structure, Haier's team recently discovered that the parts of the brain that are related to intelligence are different in men and women. "That is in some ways a major observation, because one of the assumptions of psychology has been that all human brains pretty much work the same way," he says. Now that we know they don't, we can try to understand why some brains react differently to, say, Alzheimer's, many medications and even teaching techniques, Haier says.

8   Even more interesting than the brain's adult anatomy might be the journey it takes to get there. For 13 years, psychiatrist Jay Giedd has been compiling one of the world's largest libraries of brain growth. Every Tuesday evening, from 5 o'clock until midnight, a string of children files into the National Institutes of Health outside Washington to have their brains scanned. Giedd and his team ease the kids through the MRI procedure, and then he gives them a brain tour of their pictures—gently pointing out the spinal cord and the corpus callosum, before offering them a copy to take to show-and-tell.

9   Most of the kids are all business. Rowena Avery, 6, of Sparks, Nev., arrived last week with a stuffed animal named Sidewalk and stoically disappeared into the machine while her mom, dad and little sister watched. In preparation, she had practiced at home by lying very still in the bathtub. Her picture came out crystal clear. "The youngest ones are the best at lying still. It's kind of surprising," Giedd says. "It must be because they are used to hiding in kitchen cabinets and things like that."

10   Among the girls in Giedd's study, brain size peaks around age 11/12. For the boys, the peak comes three years later. "For kids, that's a long time," Giedd says. His research shows that most parts of the brain mature faster in girls. But in a 1999 study of 508 boys and girls, Virginia Tech researcher Harriet Hanlon found that some areas mature faster in boys. Specifically, some of the regions involved in mechanical reasoning, visual targeting and spatial reasoning appeared to mature four to eight years earlier in boys.

The parts that handle verbal fluency, handwriting and recognizing familiar faces matured several years earlier in girls. . . .

Lesson 2: The Segregation of the Senses

So how do we explain why, in study after study, boys and 11 men are still on average better at rotating 3-D objects in their minds? As for girls and women, how do we explain why they tend to have better verbal skills and social sensitivities?

The most surprising differences may be outside the brain. "If 12 you have a man and a woman looking at the same landscape, they see totally different things," asserts Leonard Sax, a physician and psychologist whose book *Why Gender Matters* came out last month. "Women can see colors and textures that men cannot see. They hear things men cannot hear, and they smell things men cannot smell." Since the eyes, ears and nose are portals to the brain, they directly affect brain development from birth on.

In rats, for example, we know that the male retina has more 13 cells designed to detect motion. In females, the retina has more cells built to gather information on color and texture. If the same is true in humans, as Sax suspects, that may explain why, in an experiment in England four years ago, newborn boys were much more likely than girls to stare at a mobile turning above their cribs. It may also help explain why boys prefer to play with moving toys like trucks while girls favor richly textured dolls and tend to draw with a wider range of colors, Sax says.

Likewise, women's ears are more sensitive to some noises. 14 Baby girls hear certain ranges of sound better. And the divergence gets even bigger in adults. As for smell, a study published in the journal *Nature Neuroscience* in 2002 showed that women of childbearing age were many times more sensitive than men to several smells upon repeated exposure. (Another study has found that heterosexual women have the most sensitive smell and homosexual men have the least.)

Rest assured, Sax says: none of that means women are, over- 15 all, better than men at perception. It just means the species is internally diverse, making it more likely to survive. "The female will remember the color and texture of a particular plant and be able to warn people if it's poisonous. A man looking at the same thing will be more alert to what is moving in the periphery," he says. "Which is better? You need both."

Lesson 3: Never Underestimate the Brain

16   Until recently, there have been two groups of people: those who argue sex differences are innate and should be embraced and those who insist that they are learned and should be eliminated by changing the environment. Sax is one of the few in the middle—convinced that boys and girls are innately different and that we must change the environment so differences don't become limitations.

17   At a restaurant near his practice in Montgomery County, Md., Sax spreads out dozens of papers and meticulously makes his case. He is a fanatic, but a smart, patient one. In the early 1990s, he says, he grew alarmed by the "parade" of parents coming into his office wondering whether their sons had attention-deficit/hyperactivity disorder. Sax evaluated them and found that, indeed, the boys were not paying attention in school. But the more he studied brain differences, the more he became convinced that the problem was with the schools. Sometimes the solution was simple: some of the boys didn't hear as well as the girls and so needed to be moved into the front row. Other times, the solution was more complex.

18   Eventually, Sax concluded that very young boys and girls would be better off in separate classrooms altogether. "[Previously], as far as I was concerned, single-sex education was an old-fashioned leftover. I thought of boys wearing suits and talking with British accents," he says. But coed schools do more harm than good, he decided, when they teach boys and girls as if their brains mature at the same time. "If you ask a child to do something not developmentally appropriate for him, he will, No. 1, fail. No. 2, he will develop an aversion to the subject," he says. "By age 12, you will have girls who don't like science and boys who don't like reading." And they won't ever go back, he says. "The reason women are underrepresented in computer science and engineering is not because they can't do it. It's because of the way they're taught."

19   So far, studies about girls' and boys' achievements in same-sex grammar schools are inconclusive. But if it turns out that targeting sex differences through education is helpful, there are certainly many ways to carry it out. Says Giedd:

"The ability for change is phenomenal. That's what the brain does best." A small but charming 2004 study published in *Nature* found that people who learned how to juggle increased the gray matter in their brains in certain locations. When they stopped juggling, the new gray matter vanished. A similar structural change appears to occur in people who learn a second language. . . .

In a recent experiment with humans at Temple University, [20] women showed substantial progress in spatial reasoning after spending a couple of hours a week for 10 weeks playing *Tetris*, of all things. The males improved with weeks of practice too, says Nora Newcombe, a Temple psychologist who specializes in spatial cognition, and so the gender gap remained. But the improvement for both sexes was "massively greater" than the gender difference. "This means that if the males didn't train, the females would outstrip them," she says.

Of course, we already manipulate the brain through drugs— [21] many of which, doctors now realize, have dramatically different effects on different brains. Drugs for improving intelligence are in the works, says Haier, in the quest to find medication for Alzheimer's. "We're going to get a lot better at manipulating genetic biology. We may even be better at manipulating genetic biology than manipulating the environment."

Until then, one solution to overcoming biological tendencies [22] is to consciously override them, to say to yourself, "O.K., I may have a hard time with this task, but I'm going to will myself to conquer it." Some experiments show that baby girls, when faced with failure, tend to give up and cry relatively quickly, while baby boys get angry and persist, says Witelson at Ontario's Michael G. DeGroote School of Medicine at McMaster University. "What we don't know is whether that pattern persists into adulthood," she says. But in her experience in academia, she says she knows of at least a couple of brilliant women who never realized their potential in science because they stopped trying when they didn't get grants or encountered some other obstacle. "It's much better," she says, "for people to understand what the differences are, act on their advantages and be prepared for their disadvantages."

Lesson 4: Expectations Matter

23 We have a tendency to make too much of test-score differences between the sexes (which are actually very small compared with the differences between, say, poor and affluent students). And regardless of what happens in school, personality and discipline can better predict success when it comes to highly competitive jobs.

24 One thing we know about the brain is that it is vulnerable to the power of suggestion. There is plenty of evidence that when young women are motivated and encouraged, they excel at science. For most of the 1800s, for example, physics, astronomy, chemistry and botany were considered gender-appropriate subjects for middle-and upper-class American girls. By the 1890s, girls outnumbered boys in public high school science courses across the country, according to *The Science Education of American Girls,* a 2003 book by Kim Tolley. Records from top schools in Boston show that girls outperformed boys in physics in the mid-19th century. Latin and Greek, meanwhile, were considered the province of gentlemen—until the 20th century, when lucrative opportunities began to open up in the sciences.

25 Today, in Iceland and Sweden, girls consistently outperform boys in math and physics. In Sweden the gap is widest in the remote regions in the north. That may be because women want to move to the big cities farther south, where they would need to compete in high-tech economies, while men are focused on local hunting, fishing and forestry opportunities, says Niels Egelund, a professor of educational psychology at the Danish University of Education. The phenomenon even has a name, the Jokkmokk effect, a reference to an isolated town in Swedish Lapland.

26 Back in the States, the achievement gap in the sciences is closing, albeit slowly. Female professors have been catching up with male professors in their publishing output. Today half of chemistry and almost 60% of biology bachelor of science degrees go to females. Patience is required.

Expanding Vocabulary

Examine the following words in their contexts in the essay and then write a brief definition or synonym for each one. (Do not use a dictionary; try to guess the word's meaning from its context.)

meticulously (17)   vulnerable (24)
fanatic (17)   lucrative (24)
cognition (20)   albeit (26)

Understanding Content

1. How do the brains of men and women differ in size overall? Is this difference considered significant?
2. What are the key differences in brain functioning? What inferences are drawn from these differences? How confident are researchers about these inferences?
3. What are the differences in brain development?
4. What differences has Sax found among men's and women's senses?
5. What do studies suggest about the effect of teaching?
6. What roles do motivation and social expectations play?

Drawing Inferences about Thesis and Purpose

1. This cover article on gender differences and the brain was motivated by some politically unwise statements made by president of Harvard Lawrence Summers. How does this article address the question of why more men than women excel in the sciences?
2. What seems to be Ripley's primary purpose in writing, her primary focus?
3. Write a thesis statement for the article.

Analyzing Strategies and Style

1. In paragraph 2, Ripley provides a brief history of brain size studies and their conclusions. After studies revealed that women's hemisphere connections were larger, a new inference was drawn. Why does Ripley write "Aha" after providing this information? What does she imply?
2. How has Ripley organized her material? Look at the four headings in the article. What unites each section? What is significant about the order of information and discussion through the four lessons?

Thinking Critically

1. Did you find new ideas and information here? If so, what new idea or fact seems most important to you? Why?
2. What information is most important for parents to know? For teachers to know? For everyone—society—to know? Why?

Surveying the Damage on Campus USA

COLBERT I. KING

Deputy Editor of the Editorial page of the *Washington Post* and a syndicated columnist, Colbert King is also a regular on the political talk show *Inside Washington*. The following column appeared in the *Post* on November 30, 2002.

Questions to Guide Your Reading and Reflection

1. Contemporary American college students are compared to two other groups: what are they?
2. If you were a college president, how would you handle your students' destruction of property, both on campus and in the neighborhood?

1   It's sad to see what prompts student unrest on American university campuses these days. On recent weekends, we've seen glasses and bottles flying in Pullman, Wash., and students arrested in Berkeley, Calif.—and in Raleigh, N.C., too. A woman and a cop were hurt in Clemson, S.C., and cars were set afire, furniture was burned and dozens were arrested in Columbus, Ohio. Then there are the student riots last year in College Park.

2   And what is causing America's future leaders to abandon civility, embrace violence and convert their campuses into war zones? What injustice has moved them so?

3   Suppression of student rights? Incursions on speech, assembly, academic freedom? Nah. On American campuses, students are fistfighting and smashing and burning over what else? Sports. Yep. They're socking it to the town over football and basketball. (In Gainesville, Fla., the University of Florida stations a German shepherd at each corner of the football field.) In stadiums across America, the frenzy to win is driving responsibility out the window. The fear of losing is trumping respect. And indulgence in personal excess is the ruling ethic.

4   Contrast that kind of campus behavior with the university scene in Iran. Thousands of Iranian students have been bravely taking on their country's oppressive Islamic regime, openly

criticizing the supreme leader Ayatollah Ali Khamenei and other hard-line Muslim clerics for standing in the way of social and political reforms. Unlike the drunken hooliganism on the grounds of American academe, students in Iran have been seriously and soberly engaged in a power struggle against Islamic hard-liners. And it's no weekend affair.

It's not cost-free either. Unlike their American counterparts, Iranian students aren't waging their battle with credit cards in their pockets and with protective and indulging school administrations covering their backsides. In Iran, student demonstrators and their courageous professors are up against the country's police, Islamic courts and militiamen—armed foes who will break their heads at the order of the conservative Islamic regime.

America's students riot over the defeat of a legendary rival. Iranian students are in the streets over the sentencing to death of a history lecturer, Hashem Aghajari, who had the nerve to criticize the regime in a speech. The American collegiate sports fans erupt in rowdyism in pursuit of fun. The Iranian students put it on the line in the name of democracy.

They are a different breed. The supreme religious leader denounced their protests as the work of the devil. He ordered the movement suppressed and student leaders arrested. They responded to the crackdown by announcing a symbolic referendum on the Islamic regime to be held next week among students attending more than a dozen universities in Tehran. Now they are in even deeper trouble with the conservative hard-liners, who are mobilizing thousands of their supporters and paramilitary units to stare down and frighten off the pro-reformers.

Ah, but who can think of stuff like that in Iran when here at home there are beers to be drunk, goal posts to be torn down, fires to be started, and sofas and chairs to be burned. Today is a far cry from that time in America when students built shantytowns on their campuses and marched on their administration buildings to demand that their schools cut ties with companies that invested in apartheid South Africa. Then students were all about raising consciousness about South Africa's oppression. Today it's all about losing consciousness in a fog of alcohol on Saturday night.

9   And when the football team isn't so hot, there are other fun ways to pass the time at school. How about a party? A dress-up party? A party where fraternity guys and sorority gals can paint their faces black like they used to do in minstrel shows back in the good ol' days. Where you can dress in tennis outfits and come in blackface as Venus and Serena Williams, the two African American tennis champions. Or, if you have a patriotic bent, you can dress as Uncle Sam, of course with black makeup. That's the way they did it last month at a fraternity-sponsored Halloween party at the University of Virginia.

10   What do they know? What do they care about college students who sat at lunch counters, conducted read-ins in public libraries, kneel-ins in churches, stand-ins at movie theaters, wade-ins in public swimming pools, because, as they said in the '60s, "Education without freedom is useless"? Are they even fazed by a movement started by African American students that was joined by hundreds of white students from across the country, which saw 1,700 student demonstrators standing trial in 1960 alone?

11   That was then. Nowadays, for some in America's next generation of leaders, when it comes to sheer emotional fulfillment, nothing quite matches the act of tearing up the campus or coloring the skin and lips to exaggerate black features.

12   Welcome to American college daze, 2002.

Expanding Vocabulary

Write a definition for each of the following words. Then use each word in a separate sentence of your own. The number in parentheses is the number of the paragraph in which the word appears.

incursions (3)	hooliganism (4)
frenzy (3)	rowdyism (6)
indulgence (3)	apartheid (8)

Understanding Content

1. What are contemporary college students in the United States making headlines for doing? How does King evaluate their actions?
2. What are Iranian students doing? How does King evaluate their cause?

3. What did American students do in the 1960s? How are their actions evaluated by King?

Drawing Inferences about Thesis and Purpose

1. What is King's purpose? What does he want to accomplish through his contrasts?
2. Write a thesis statement for the essay that reveals the contrast structure.

Analyzing Strategies and Style

1. What does King want to underscore when he describes the American students as "America's future leaders"?
2. How are we to understand paragraph 11? What writing strategy for emphasis does King use in this paragraph?
3. What play on words does King employ in his final sentence? What is its effect?

Thinking Critically

1. Which of the two kinds of actions of American students do you think is the less excusable: rioting after games or dressing to look like black personalities at parties? Why? Explain your reasoning.
2. King, in rhetorical questions in paragraph 10, suggests that today's American students neither know nor care about the demonstrations for change of students from the past. Is he right? Do you know about student actions of the 1960s? Do you think those actions were significant? What about your fellow students?

Marks

LINDA PASTAN

A graduate of Radcliffe College and Brandeis University, Linda Pastan (b. 1932) is the author of eight books of poetry. Many of her poems, such as the one that follows from *The Five Stages of Grief Poems* (1978), examine the complexity and problems of family life.

Questions to Guide Your Reading and Reflection

1. Who is speaking—or more accurately thinking—the words
   of the poem? What relationships does the speaker refer to in
   the poem?
2. How would you grade your relationships with your parents?

My husband gives me an A
for last night's supper,
an incomplete for my ironing,
a B plus in bed.
My son says I am average,   5
an average mother, but if
I put my mind to it
I could improve.
My daughter believes
in Pass/Fail and tells me   10
I pass. Wait 'til they learn
I'm dropping out.

Understanding Content and Strategies

1. What marks does the speaker receive? For what activities? Who
   does the speaker's son sound like when he says that she "could
   improve" if she put her "mind to it"?
2. The poem is organized and developed, then, by using what extended metaphor? The speaker is being compared to what?
3. What is the speaker's attitude toward her situation? What lines
   reveal her attitude?

Drawing Inferences about Theme

1. Whose perspective on family responsibilities and chores are we
   given in the poem?
2. What observations about family life is Pastan making?

Thinking Critically

1. Do you think the views of family life expressed here are fairly
   widespread? What evidence do you have for your opinions?

2. Have you ever felt as though you were being graded by family members or rated on a scale from 1 to 10? If so, how did that make you feel?

3. Try your hand at a short, free-verse poem similar to Pastan's. In your poem create a speaker who is a teenager being "graded" by other family members.

STUDENT ESSAY—CONTRAST

THE FADED STAIN
Denisse M. Bonilla

"The plantain stain on a 'jíbaros' back can never be erased," says an old Puerto Rican proverb. "Jíbaros," or Puerto Rican peasants, is what my compatriots fondly call each other. The proverb is most commonly used to illustrate their feeling that, regardless of where a Puerto Rican lives, a Puerto Rican always remains a Puerto Rican. But reflecting on my own experiences, I have read a different meaning into the old proverb. My compatriots could be saying that once a Puerto Rican has lived on the island, she or he can never forget it. However, in saying this, one must ponder what happens to the stain itself. Does it look like a plantain for the rest of the jíbaros' life, or does it change over time? Perhaps it starts resembling a

Student uses a proverb as an attention-getting opening.

banana, looking similar but not exactly the same.

Coming back to Puerto Rico as an adult, I found a place quite different from the one I thought I had left behind. The memories I had were those of a child who had never lived outside the island. Because I lived in Puerto Rico as an insular child, I had the memories of such a child. Youth had shaped my perception when I lived there; then time further confused my memory, neutralizing the colors of the countryside, creating indistinguishable Puerto Rican cities, sharpening the soft accent of the people. When I came back as an adult, what I saw was not what I expected to see.

Thesis stated: What I saw on a return visit to Puerto Rico was different from my youthful memories. The thesis clearly emphasizes contrast.

I remembered the trip from San Juan to Ponce, a trip crossing the island from north to south, as an incredibly long and painful ordeal. Impatient to get to my grandmother's house in Ponce, I would look out the car window, some times noticing the small towns or the way the sea peeked out from in-between the mountains. The mountains that I saw during the beginning of the trip were green, seeming to remain in the landscape for hours. I would anxiously await

First difference: the trip to Ponce was not as long or unpleasant as it seemed in her memories.

the golden mountains to the south, which to me were an indication of the end of our trip.

When I returned as an adult, I remembered and expected the same grueling and unexciting trip, but was happily disappointed. The trip south was not as long as I remembered; it was over in two hours. Perhaps it did not seem as long as it did in my youth because I had become accustomed to driving longer distances in the large North American continent. But I accredited my newfound tolerance to the enchanting beauty of the Caribbean countryside! The vegetation in the north was a lush shade of green, growing profusely and becoming a tangle of startling color. The houses on the outskirts of the small towns we passed seemed to blossom out of the foliage, their old-fashioned charm reminiscent of a bygone time when the Puerto Rican economy was more dependent on agriculture. In what seemed like a short distance, the mountains changed to golden hues and a softer green. The Caribbean Sea appeared to be a watercolor painting framed by the dry southern mountains. The beauty of the trip

Student analyzes causes for the differences between youthful memories and adult realities.

bewildered me, causing me to recollect in disbelief the impatience I had felt as a young girl. Had I been colorblind when I was young?

The Puerto Rican cities I remembered from my youth were <u>also different</u> when viewed through my adult eyes. I remembered Old San Juan as a beautiful old city, <u>comparing</u> it in my memory to places such as Old Town Alexandria. I <u>also</u> saw generic streets in my recollections, remembering how as a young girl I used to imagine that the bigger roads looked exactly like the ones in the United States. <u>But in contrast to my recollections,</u> neither Old San Juan nor the streets of the other cities were similar to those in the U.S. Taking a stroll down the narrow, cobblestoned streets of Old San Juan, I often discovered hidden parks and nicely shaded plazas in which old gentlemen sat to chat, play dominoes, or feed doves. Wooden fruit stands brimming with delectable tropical fruits stood on many corners. The pastel-colored ambiance of Old San Juan, bespeaking Spanish ancestry and Caribbean sensibility, <u>could not be compared</u> to the somber ambiance of the old American cities in the north. As for my recollections of Puerto Rican streets

Second difference: cities and streets were different than remembered.

Observe transition words and phrases.

that looked exactly like the ones in the United States, to my eyes accustomed to the large, smooth highways of North America, the streets of Puerto Rico looked humble and in need of repair.

The people of Puerto Rico proved to be equally changed to my adult eyes and ears. In the memories of a young insular child, Puerto Rican manners were just like American manners and Puerto Rican Spanish was bland, without any distinguishable accent. In contrast, I found my people to be more physically demonstrative than Americans. Their faces and bodies would remain mobile through an entire conversation, allowing someone standing a few feet away to guess what they were talking about. They spoke Spanish with a funny melodic sound, characterized by relaxed pronunciation. The Puerto Rican people were more flamboyant than I had noticed as a child.

Although the plantain stain on my back faded after I left my country, the experience of rediscovering its many hues left me with an even bigger impression. To notice the essence of a country, one must spend time outside it. My recollections were bland when compared to what I later saw. What I saw when I came back

Third difference: the people—and their way of speaking Spanish—are different than remembered.

Conclusion refers again to the proverb and extends the thesis to suggest that one's country is best understood when one spends time away from it.

to Puerto Rico left a moist, green, ripe
plantain stain on my back, a stain that
will never fade.

MAKING CONNECTIONS

1. Viorst and Ripley examine gender differences. Ripley provides updates of studies and Viorst gives some explanations of behavioral differences. Study both articles and see if you find any connections between the two discussions. Make a list of all connections you find.
2. Sakamoto discusses differences in American and Japanese conversational styles. What are some of the ways that cultural and class differences may affect students in the classroom? What are some ways that instructors and students can ease some of the problems created by cultural and class differences?
3. Ripley raises the issues of motivation and expectations in education. How important are effort and desire to succeed? How important is intellectual curiosity? How much difference can facilities and dedicated teachers make if students are unmotivated to learn? If parents and society do not place a high value on education?
4. Ripley writes in response to remarks by Harvard president Summers; King writes about American students in the 1960s and Iranian students in 2002. Select one of these references to the past and get the facts on the event or time. Turn to U.S. history texts for the 1960s, to your library's electronic databases for articles on any one of the events, or search the Internet for information. Prepare a one- or two-page fact sheet for your classmates. Cite your source(s) according to MLA guidelines for documentation.
5. We know that Asian (and European) students regularly outscore American students in math and science. We also know that, as a group, students from more affluent school districts outscore students from less affluent districts. What are four strategies for improving American education that you would seek to implement if you were appointed "Education Czar"? What might be some political problems you would have trying to implement your four-point plan?

TOPICS FOR WRITING

1. In an essay, contrast two stories, two movies, or two TV shows you know well. Select two works that have something in common but differ in important and/or interesting ways so that you have a clear purpose in writing.
2. If you have attended two schools that differed significantly or if you have lived in two quite different places, draw on one of these experiences for a contrast essay. Organize your essay by specific points of difference that together support a thesis statement that announces your contrast purpose. (Example: California and Virginia are not just miles apart; they are worlds apart.)
3. Do you know a neighborhood, city, or area of the country that has changed significantly for better or worse? If so, develop an essay that contrasts specific differences between the place you once knew and the place as it is now. Your purpose is to demonstrate that the changes have made the place either better or worse. (Example: The _____ neighborhood of _____ is no longer the attractive, family-oriented community in which I grew up.)
4. You have had many teachers during your years of schooling. Think of ones you liked and ones you didn't like. Think about why you enjoyed some but not others. Then select two to contrast for the purpose of revealing traits that make a good teacher. Write about specific traits (e.g., knowledge of field, energy, clarity, fairness, humor), not just generalizations (e.g., she was nice).
5. How do you view today's college students—or some portion of them? What traits, characteristics, attitudes toward learning, and reasons for being in school do you see? Can you think of an animal, fantasy creature, individual, or group from history who in your view has the traits that are more appropriate for college students? If so, then you can develop an analogy. Remember to have specific differences between students and the animal, creature, or historical figure you are using.
6. As a variation of topic 5, develop an analogy that compares rather than contrasts today's students with some animal, fantasy creature, or historical figure. Use specific

points of similarity and establish a point to the comparison, a thesis about students that is supported through the fanciful comparison.

7. Most of us have had at least one experience that did not turn out as we thought it would. Sometimes, nervous about a new situation, we expect the worst only to discover that we are happy or successful participating in the actual experience. Probably more often we look forward to an upcoming event only to be disappointed. Or, we have childhood memories that are inconsistent with our re-experiencing a place or person from the past. Reflect about any experience you have had that fits the pattern of contrast between perception (expectation) and reality. (Possible experiences include a first date, a special event such as Thanksgiving or a wedding, a first experience with a new sport, a recent reunion with a childhood friend, or a return to your childhood home.)

The point of your contrast is to offer some insight into why we so often have expectations that do not match reality. Why do we remember our grandparents' old house as larger and more exciting than it appears to us today? The student essay in this chapter is an example of one student's response to this topic.

A CHECKLIST FOR COMPARISON AND CONTRAST ESSAYS

Invention

☐ Have I selected a topic and comparison or contrast approach consistent with the instructor's guidelines for this assignment?

☐ Have I chosen among the possible topics one that fits my knowledge and experience?

☐ Have I reflected on the topic to create a tentative thesis that establishes my main idea in a clear comparison or contrast structure?

☐ Have I found, from my reflection, specific points of similarity or difference?

☐ Have I given thought to a specific order in which to present the points of similarity or difference?

Drafting

☐ Have I succeeded in completing a first draft at one sitting so that I can "see" the whole?

☐ Do I have enough—enough to meet assignment demands and enough to develop and support my thesis? If not, do I need new paragraphs or more details or reflection within paragraphs?

☐ Does the order work? If not, what needs to be moved—and where?

☐ Am I satisfied with the way I have expressed the insights to be gained? Have I been too heavy-handed with a message?

☐ Do I have adequate, effective details to illustrate each point of similarity or difference?

Revision

☐ Have I made any needed additions, deletions, or changes in order based on answering the questions about my draft?

☐ Have I revised my draft to produce coherent paragraphs, using transition and connecting words that reveal my comparison or contrast structure?

☐ Have I eliminated wordiness and clichés?

☐ Have I avoided or removed any discriminatory language?

☐ Have I used my word processor's spell check and proofread a printed copy with great care?

☐ Do I have an appropriate and interesting title?

Explaining and Illustrating
Examining Media Images

"How do you know that?" "Where is your evidence?" "Can you be specific?" These questions are raised by the avid dinner companion who wants you to illustrate and support your ideas. As a writer, you need to keep in mind that the engaged reader is going to ask the same kinds of questions. For you to be an effective writer, you must answer these questions; you must provide examples.

Illustrating ideas and opinions with examples seems so obvious a way to develop and support views that you may wonder why the strategy warrants its own chapter. Even though providing examples may be the most frequently used writing technique, as with many "obvious truths," we can all benefit from being reminded of its importance.

When to Use Examples

The smart writer searches for examples as part of the process of generating ideas. Indeed, when brainstorming or in other ways inventing ideas for an essay, you may find that specifics come to mind more easily than general points. Whether you are a generalizer who needs to find illustrations for ideas or a generator of specifics who needs to reflect on what the examples illustrate, the end result will be a blend of general points and concrete examples. When should you select the use of examples as your primary strategy of development? When you are presenting information or discussing ideas that can best be understood and absorbed by readers with the aid of specifics. And that's just about any time you write.

How to Use Examples

To use examples effectively, think about what kinds of examples are needed to develop your thesis, about how many you need, and about how to introduce and discuss them effectively. First, the *kinds* of examples. You will need to find illustrations that clearly and logically support your generalizations. When Gloria Steinem asserts that advertisers give orders to women's magazines, we expect her to explain and illustrate those orders. And this is exactly what Steinem does. If she had not used five major companies' demands as examples, we may have doubted her claim of advertisers' control over women's magazines.

We also expect *enough* examples. If Stephanie Mencimer mentioned only one "action chick" in the movies, we would probably doubt her thesis. Occasionally, a writer will select one *extended* example rather than a number of separate examples. Jack McGarvey uses one extended example, his and his students' experience of being on TV, to show the celebrity-making power of television. To develop his example, McGarvey uses techniques of narration and description, reminding us that few pieces of writing are developed using only one strategy. Typically, though, the writer who develops a thesis primarily through illustration presents a goodly number of appropriate examples. How many make a "goodly" number will vary with each essay, but be assured that few writers include too many examples.

How many examples an essay needs depends in part on how they are introduced and discussed and on how many facets of a topic need to be covered. Gloria Steinem does not just list five advertisers but gives details of their demands. After all, if all the examples were so obvious that just a brief listing would work, we would already have reached the writer's conclusions and would not need to read the article. As common to our lives as advertising, television, movies, and song lyrics are, we still have much to learn from this chapter's writers because they are the ones who have looked closely at and listened intently to the swirl of words and images bombarding us through the media. Sometimes examples are startling enough to speak for themselves. Usually the writer's task is not only to present good illustrations but to explain how they support the essay's main ideas.

When presenting and explaining illustrations, give some thought to ordering them and to moving smoothly from one to another to create coherence. Look first for some logical basis for organizing your examples. If there is no clear reason to put one example before another, then you are probably wise to put your most important example last. Examples that add to your point can be connected by such transitions as

for instance	in addition
also	next
another example	moreover
further	finally

Ocassionally, brief examples can be listed as a series in one sentence. Examples that offer contrast need contrast connectors:

by contrast	on the other hand
however	instead

Remember that a list does not make an essay. Explain *how* your examples support your thesis.

WRITING FOCUS:
VARY YOUR SENTENCES

Effective writing stays focused on a controlling idea (thesis), is concrete and vivid, and shows a command of grammar, mechanics, and correct word choice. Yet readers recognize that although two essays may follow these guidelines, one essay will "read" better than another. What accounts for the difference? One answer is content; some writers are more insightful than others. Another answer is style, the selection and arrangement of words into sentences. Do not settle for the first way that you write down an idea or detail; revise and polish sentences for both variety and emphasis. Think about ways to restructure a series of short sentences into fewer sentences—even one sentence—creating variety but also greater power.

In a comparison of the life of the squirrel with her students, Liane Ellison Norman could have opened her essay this way:

> The squirrel is curious. He darts around. He looks partially at me and stays alert for enemies. So, I see only one bright black eye.

Notice that each sentence begins with subject and verb, and all have about the same weight or feel. But, here is what Norman actually wrote:

> The squirrel is curious. He darts and edges, profile first, one bright black eye on me, the other alert for his enemies on the other side.

The first sentence is arresting in its brevity. Then the next few ideas have been gathered into one longer, more dramatic sentence.

Consider the following details: *It was a battered face. But it was a noble face. It commanded immediate respect.* There are several ways these ideas can be shaped into one sentence, one more interesting and effective than the three brief sentences. Here are two possibilities:

> It was a battered but noble face, commanding immediate respect.

> A battered but noble face, it commanded immediate respect.

Which of these two sentences is, in your view, the most effective? Why?

Here are some guidelines for improving your sentences:

1. Combine short sentences on the same subject into longer sentences.
2. Use more than one way to combine; instead of just joining two short sentences with "and," use a dependent clause, verbal phrases, or modifying words (adjectives and adverbs).
3. Do not always begin a sentence with its subject; instead use an introductory clause or phrase (e.g., *A battered but noble face*).

> 4. Vary sentence lengths. Use short sentences for emphasis along with longer sentences.
> 5. Be sure to keep the most important idea in the main clause, putting less important ideas into modifying clauses, phrases, and words.

Getting Started: Thinking About Advertising

Here are eight questions to help you think about advertising, one of the topics of this chapter and represented by the four ads that follow. Reflect on these examples of current advertising by answering the questions for each ad.

Questions

1. What are the ad's purposes? To sell a product? An idea? An image of the company? Some combination?
2. What audience is the ad designed to reach?
3. What kind of relationship does it establish with its audience?
4. What social values does it express?
5. To what degree are those values held by the target audience? To what degree are they the values of a different social class or group?
6. Does the ad use metaphors? Puns? Rhyme? Does the company establish and repeat a logo or slogan for the product? How well known are the logo, the slogan, or both?
7. Does the ad use symbols? To what extent do the symbols help express the ad's social values? How is their association with the product appropriate?
8. Is the ad's appeal primarily direct and explicit or indirect and associative?

WOULD IT
SURPRISE YOU TO KNOW
THAT GROWING SOYBEANS CAN
HELP THE ENVIRONMENT?

Biotech soybeans have been widely
planted by American farmers and they
help preserve our natural resources.
Plant biotechnology makes it easier to
control weeds and plow soybean fields
less—which means less soil erosion.

But before those soybean seeds could
be planted, it took years of research and
testing to ensure that biotech crops
were safe for people and the environment. Extensive testing by scientists
shows foods derived from plant
biotechnology are as safe to eat as
traditional foods.

In fact, three government agencies
share the authority to evaluate the safety
of new biotech products from incep-
tion to approval—the U.S.
Department of Agriculture
(USDA), the Environmental Protection
Agency (EPA), and the Food and Drug
Administration (FDA). If you want to
learn more, we invite you to call or
visit our Web site.

WWW.WHYBIOTECH.COM
1-800-980-8660

Biotech
Soybean

COUNCIL FOR
BIOTECHNOLOGY
INFORMATION

good ideas are growing

To Be or Not to Be as Defined by TV

JACK McGARVEY

Jack McGarvey completed his master's degree at the University of Connecticut and taught in the Westport, Connecticut school system for many years. He has also published many articles, short stories, and poems in the *New York Times, McCall's, Parents,* and other newspapers and magazines. The following article, a report on his experience with the power of television, appeared in 1982 in the journal *Today's Education.*

Questions to Guide Your Reading and Reflection

1. What is the source of part of the author's title? What does he gain by his reference to that source?
2. Do you view people who appear on TV talk shows as celebrities? Why or why not?

A couple of years ago, a television crew came to film my ninth grade English class at Bedford Junior High School in Westport, Connecticut. I'm still trying to understand what happened.   1

I was doing some work with my students, teaching them to analyze the language used in television commercials. After dissecting the advertising claims, most of the class became upset over what they felt were misleading—and in a few cases, untruthful—uses of language. We decided to write to the companies that presented their products inaccurately or offensively. Most of them responded with chirpy letters and cents-off coupons. Some did not respond at all.   2

I then decided to contact *Buyline,* a consumer advocate program aired on New York City's WNBC-TV at the time. The show and its host, Betty Furness, were well-known for their investigation of consumer complaints. I sent off a packet of the unanswered letters with a brief explanation of the class's work.   3

About a week later, the show's producer telephoned me. She said that she'd seen the letters and was interested in the   4 class's project. Could she and her director come to Westport to have a look?

5   I said sure and told her about a role-playing activity I was planning to do with my students. I said I was going to organize my class of 24 students into four committees—each one consisting of two representatives from the Federal Trade Commission (FTC), the agency that monitors truth in advertising; two advertising executives anxious to have their material used; and two TV executives caught somewhere in the middle—wanting to please the advertisers while not offending the FTC. Then, I would ask each committee to assume that there had been a complaint about the language used in a TV commercial, and that the committees had to resolve the complaint. "That sounds great! I'll bring a crew," she said.

6   I obtained clearance from my school district's office, and the next morning, as I was walking into the school, I met one of my students and casually let out the word: "WNBC's coming to film our class this afternoon."

7   I was totally unprepared for what happened. Word spread around school within five minutes. Students who barely knew me rushed up to squeal, "Is it true? Is it really, really true? A TV crew is coming to Bedford to film?" A girl who was not in my class pinned me into a corner near the magazine rack in the library to ask me whether she could sit in my class for the day. Another girl went to her counselor and requested an immediate change in English classes, claiming a long-standing personality conflict with her current teacher.

8   Later, things calmed down a bit, but as I took my regular turn as cafeteria supervisor, I saw students staring wide-eyed at me, then turning to whisper excitedly to their friends. I'd become a celebrity simply because I was the one responsible for bringing a TV crew to school.

9   Right after lunch, the show's producer and director came to my class to look it over and watch the role-playing activity; they planned to tape near the end of the school day. The two women were gracious and self-effacing, taking pains not to create any disturbance; but the students, of course, knew why they were there. There were no vacant stares, no hair brushes, no gum chewers, and no note scribblers. It was total concentration, and I enjoyed one of my best classes in more than 15 years of teaching.

After the class, I met with the producer and director to plan 10
the taping. They talked about some of the students they'd seen
and mentioned Susan. "She's terribly photogenic and very,
very good with words." They mentioned Steve. "He really
chaired his committee well. Real leadership there. Handsome
boy, too." They mentioned Jim, Pete, Randy, and Jenny and
their insights into advertising claims. Gradually I became
aware that we were engaged in a talent hunt; we were looking
for a strong and attractive group to be featured in the taping.

We continued the discussion, deciding on the players. We 11
also discussed the sequencing of the taping session. First, I'd
do an introduction, explaining the role-playing activity as if the
class had never heard of it. Then, I'd follow with the conclusion—summarizing remarks ending with a cheery "See you tomorrow!"—and dismiss the class. The bit players would leave
the school and go home. We'd then rearrange the set and film
the photogenic and perceptive featured players while they discussed advertising claims as a committee. Obviously, this is not
the way I'd conduct an actual class, but it made sense. After all,
I wanted my students to look good, and I wanted to look good.

"It'll be very hard work," the producer cautioned. "I trust
your students understand that."   12

"It's already been hard work," I remarked as I thought of
possible jealousies and bruised feelings over our choices of fea- 13
tured players.

About a half hour before school's end, the crew set up cameras and lights in the hall near the classroom we'd be working 14
in, a room in an isolated part of the building. But as the crew
began filming background shots of the normal passing of students through the hall, near chaos broke out.

Hordes of students suddenly appeared. A basketball star
gangled through the milling mob to do an imitation of 15
Nureyev,[1] topping off a pirouette by feigning a couple of jump
shots. A pretty girl walked back and forth in front of the cameras at least a dozen times before she was snared by a home
economics teacher. Three boys did a noisy pantomime of opening jammed lockers, none of which were theirs. A faculty member, seen rarely in this part of the building, managed to work
his way through the crowd, smiling broadly. And as members

[1]Famous ballet star—Ed.

of my class struggled through the press of bodies, they were hailed, clutched at, patted on the back, and hugged.

16   "Knock 'em dead!" I heard a student call.

17   It took the vice-principal and five teachers 10 minutes to clear the hall.

18   We assembled the cast, arranged the furniture, erased several mild obscenities from the chalkboard, and pulled down the window shades—disappointing a clutch of spectators outside. The producers then introduced the crew and explained their work.

19   I was wired with a mike and the crew set up a boom microphone, while the girls checked each other's make-up and the boys sat squirming.

20   Finally, the taping began. It was show business, a performance, a total alteration of the reality I know as a teacher. As soon as I began the introduction, 26 pairs of eyes focused on me as if I were Billy Joel about to sing. I was instantly startled and self-conscious. When I asked a question, some of the usually quieter students leaped to respond. This so unsettled me that I forgot what I was saying and had to begin again.

21   The novelty of being on camera, however, soon passed. We had to do retakes because the soundman missed student responses from the rear of the room. The director asked me to rephrase a question and asked a student to rephrase a response. There were delays while technicians adjusted equipment.

22   We all became very much aware of being performers, and some of the students who had been most excited about making their TV debut began to grumble about the hard work. That pleased me, for a new reality began to creep in: Television is not altogether glamorous.

23   We taped for almost five hours, on more than 3,200 feet of videotape. That is almost an hour-and-a-half's worth, more than double a normal class period. And out of that mass of celluloid the producer said she'd use seven minutes on the program!

24   Two days later, five students and I went to the NBC studios at Rockefeller Center to do a taping of a final segment. The producer wanted to do a studio recreation of the role-playing game. This time, however, the game would include real executives—one from advertising, one from the NBC network, and one from the FTC. We'd be part of a panel discussion moder-

ated by Betty Furness. My students would challenge the TV
and the advertising executives, asking them to justify some of
the bothersome language used in current commercials.

This was the most arduous part of the experience. The tap- 25
ing was live, meaning that the cameras would run for no longer
than eight minutes. As we ate turkey and ham during a break
with Ms. Furness and the guest executives, I realized that we
were with people who were totally comfortable with television. I began to worry. How could mere 14-year-olds compete
in a debate with those to whom being on television is as ordinary as riding a school bus?

But my concern soon disappeared. As Ms. Furness began 26
reading her TelePrompTer, Susan leaned over and whispered,
"This is fun!" And it was Susan who struck first. " 'You can see
how luxurious my hair feels' is a perfect example of the silly
language your ad writers use," she said with all the poise of a
Barbara Walters. "It's impossible to *see* how something feels,"
she went on.

That pleased me, for as an English teacher, I've always em- 27
phasized the value of striving for precision in the use of language.
The work we'd done with TV commercials, where suggestibility
is the rule, had taken hold, I thought, as the ad executive fumbled
for a response. The tension vanished, and we did well.

The show aired two weeks later, and I had it taped so the class 28
could view it together. It was a slick production, complete with
music—"Hey, Big Spender"—to develop a theme for Ms. Furness' introduction. "Teens are big business these days," she said.
"Does television advertising influence how they spend their
money?" Then followed a shot of students in the hall—edited to
show none of the wildness that actually occurred. Next, three of
my students appeared in brief clips of interviews. They were
asked, "Have you ever been disappointed by television advertising?" The responses were, "Yes, of course," and I was pleased
with their detailed answers. Finally, the classroom appeared,
and there I was, lounging against my desk, smiling calmly. I
looked good—a young, unrumpled Orson Bean, with a cool
blue-and-brown paisley tie. My voice was mellifluous. Gee, I
thought as I saw the tape, I could have been a TV personality.

Now, I am probably no more vain than most people. But 29
television does strange things to the ego. I became so absorbed

in studying the image of myself that the whole point of the show passed me by. I didn't even notice that I'd made a goof analyzing a commercial until I'd seen the show three times. The students who participated were the same; watching themselves on videotape, they missed what they had said. I had an enormous struggle to get both them and me to recall the hard work and to see the obvious editing. It was as if reality had been reversed: The actual process of putting together the tape was not real, but the product was.

30   I showed the tape again last year to my ninth grade class. I carefully explained to this delightful gang of fault-finders how the taping had been done. I told them about the changed sequence, the selection of the featured players, the takes and retakes. They themselves had just been through the same role-playing activity, and I asked them to listen carefully to what was said. They nodded happily and set their flinty minds to look at things critically. But as the tape ended, they wanted to tease me about how ugly and wrinkled I looked. They wanted to say, "That's Randy! He goes to Compo Beach all the time." "Jenny's eye shadow—horrible!" "When will you get us on TV?"

31   The visual image had worked its magic once again: They had missed the point of the show altogether. And, as I dismissed them, I felt something vibrating in their glances and voices—the celebrity image at work again. I was no longer their mundane English teacher: I was a TV personality.

32   I decided to show the tape again the next day. I reviewed the hard work, the editing, the slick packaging. I passed out questions so we could focus on what had been said on the program. I turned on the recorder and turned off the picture to let them hear only the sound. They protested loudly, of course. But I was determined to force them to respond to how effectively the previous year's class had taken apart the language used in the claims of commercials. This was, after all, the point of the program. And it worked, finally.

33   As class ended, one of the students drifted up to me. "What are we going to do next?" she asked.

34   "We're going to make some comparisons between TV news shows and what's written in newspapers," I replied.

35   "Do they put together news shows the way they filmed your class?"

"It's similar and usually much quicker," I answered.   36

She smiled and shook her head. "It's getting hard to believe   37
anything anymore."

In that comment lies what every TV viewer should have—a   38
healthy measure of beautiful, glorious skepticism. But as I said,
I'm still trying to understand that taping session. And I'm
aware of how hard it is to practice skepticism. Every time I see
the *Buyline* tape, I'm struck by how good a teacher TV made
me. Am I really that warm, intelligent, creative, and good looking? Of course not. But TV made me that way. I like it, and
sometimes I find myself still hoping that I am what television
defined me to be.

I sometimes think children have superior knowledge of   39
TV. They know, from many years of watching it, that the
product in all its edited glory is the only reality. Shortly after
the program aired on that February Saturday two years ago,
our telephone rang. The voice belonged to my daughter's 11-
year-old friend. She said, "I just saw you on TV. May I have
your autograph?"

I was baffled. After all, this was the boisterous girl who   40
played with my daughter just about every day and who
mostly regarded me as a piece of furniture that occasionally
mumbled something about lowering your voices. "Are you serious?" I croaked.

"May I have your autograph?" she repeated, ignoring my   41
question. "I can come over right now." Her voice was without guile.

She came. And I signed while she scrutinized my face, her   42
eyes still aglow with Chromacolor.

To Stephanie, television had transformed a kindly grump   43
into something real. And there is no doubt in my mind what-
soever that in the deepest part of her soul is the fervent dream
that her being, too, will someday be defined and literally af-
firmed by an appearance on television.

Lately, my ninth grade class has been growing restless. Shall I   44
move up the TV unit and bring out the tape again? Shall I remind
them what a great teacher they have? Shall I remind myself what
a fine teacher I am? Shall I renew their—and my—hope?

To be or not to be as defined by TV? Does that question sug-   45
gest what makes television so totally unlike any other medium?

Expanding Vocabulary

Match each word in column A with its definition in column B. When in doubt, first find the word in the essay and look for context clues to aid your understanding of the word's meaning. Then, if necessary, use your dictionary to complete the matching exercise. The number in parentheses is the number of the paragraph in which the word appears.

Column A	*Column B*
dissecting (2)	smoothly flowing
advocate (3)	attractive when photographed
photogenic (10)	examined carefully
sequencing (11)	walked with long-legged awkwardness
gangled (15)	careless mistake
pirouette (15)	separating, analyzing
snared (15)	ordinary
pantomime (15)	full spin of the body on the toes or
arduous (25)	ball of the foot (in ballet)
mellifluous (28)	speak in favor of
goof (29)	act of communicating with bodily or
flinty (30)	facial expressions and gestures
mundane (31)	trapped, caught
skepticism (38)	cunning, deceit
boisterous (40)	very difficult
guile (41)	emotional, zealous
scrutinized (42)	arranging in a series
fervent (43)	hard, tough
	loud, unrestrained
	doubting, questioning attitude

Understanding Content

1. What had McGarvey's English class been studying before the TV crew came? What response did the class receive from their letters to companies?
2. What was the response of students to the news of the coming crew? How did McGarvey's students behave with the crew watching their classes?
3. How did the TV producer want to sequence the class discussion? On what basis did they select students to tape? How long did the taping take? How representative of a typical class would the taped version be?

4. How did McGarvey respond when he watched the finished tape?   45
   How did his class respond? And future classes?

Drawing Inferences about Thesis and Purpose

1. What attitude, according to McGarvey, should we hold toward
   what we see on TV? Why did he, and his students, have trouble
   maintaining that attitude?
2. What is McGarvey's thesis, the main points he wants to make
   about television?

Analyzing Strategies and Style

1. McGarvey develops his observations about TV through one example, one event that he recounts at length. What makes one long
   example an effective way to illustrate his thesis?
2. McGarvey includes a clever description of students (and teachers)
   showing off for the TV cameras in the school hallway. Examine
   this passage again (paragraphs 14 and 15). What makes this an effective description? What strategies does the author use here?

Thinking Critically

1. Are you skeptical about everything you see on television? That is,
   do you understand that much of what is presumably "live" has
   been taped and carefully edited? If you aren't skeptical, should
   you be?
2. Do you want to be on TV? If so, why? If not, why not?
3. Is there something wrong with a society in which a seven-minute TV
   segment can suddenly turn an ordinary person into a celebrity? Why
   are celebrities so appealing? Do we put too much emphasis on them?

Sex, Lies, and Advertising

GLORIA STEINEM

Editor, writer, and lecturer, Gloria Steinem has been cited in
World Almanac as one of the twenty-five most influential
women in America. She is the cofounder of *Ms.* magazine and
was its editor from 1972 to 1987. She is the cofounder of the National Women's Political Caucus and is the author of a number
of books, including *Outrageous Acts and Everyday Rebellions*

(1983), *Revolution from Within: A Book of Self-Esteem* (1992), and *Moving Beyond Words* (1993). In "Sex, Lies, and Advertising," first published in *Ms.* in 1990, Steinem "tells all" about the strategies advertisers use to control much of the content and appearance of women's magazines.

Questions to Guide Your Reading and Reflection

1. What does Steinem want readers to do about the control advertisers have?
2. What do you expect to learn about advertisers' demands from women's magazines?

1   When *Ms.* began, we didn't consider *not* taking ads. But we wanted to ask advertisers to come in *without* the usual quid pro quo of "complementary copy"—editorial features praising their product area.

2   We knew this would be hard. Food advertisers have always demanded that women's magazines publish recipes and articles on entertaining (preferably ones that name their products) in return for their ads; clothing advertisers expect to be surrounded by fashion spreads (especially ones that credit their designers); and shampoo, fragrance, and beauty products insist on positive editorial coverage of beauty subjects, plus photo credits besides. That's why women's magazines look the way they do.

3   Advertisers who demand such "complementary copy" clearly are operating under a double standard. The same food companies place ads in *People* with no recipes. Cosmetics companies support *The New Yorker* with no regular beauty columns.

4   In recent years, advertisers' control over the editorial content of women's magazines has become so institutionalized that it is sometimes written into "insertion orders" or dictated to ad salespeople as official policy. The following are typical orders given to women's magazines:

5   • Dow's Cleaning Products stipulated that ads for its Vivid and Spray 'n Wash products should be adjacent to "children or fashion editorial"; ads for Bathroom Cleaner should be next to "home furnishings/family" features; and so on. "If a magazine fails for ½ the brands or more," the Dow order warns, "it will be omitted from further consideration."

- C. Johnson & Son, makers of Johnson Wax, lawn and laundry prod- 6
  ucts, insect sprays, hair sprays, and so on, insisted that its ads
  "should not be opposite extremely controversial features or material anti-
  thetical to the nature/copy of the advertised product." (Italics theirs.)
- Maidenform, manufacturer of bras and other women's apparel, left 7
  a blank for the particular product and stated: "The creative concept
  of the _____ campaign, and the very nature of the product itself
  appeal to the positive emotions of the reader/consumer. Therefore,
  it is imperative that all editorial adjacencies reflect that same positive tone. The editorial must not be negative in content or lend itself contrary to the _____ product imagery/message (e.g.,
  editorial relating to illness, disillusionment, large size fashion, etc.)."
  (Italics mine.)
- The De Beers diamond company, a big seller of engagement rings, 8
  prohibited magazines from placing its ads with "adjacencies to
  hard news or anti/love-romance themed editorial."
- Procter & Gamble, one of this country's most powerful and di- 9
  versified advertisers, stands out in the memory of Anne Summers and Sandra Yates [who ran the company that published *Ms.*
  in the late 1980s]: its products were not to be placed in *any* issue
  that included *any* material on gun control, abortion, the occult,
  cults, or the disparagement of religion. Caution was also demanded in any issue that included articles on sex or drugs, even
  for educational purposes.

Those are the most obvious chains around women's maga- 10
zines. There are also rules so understood they needn't be written down: for instance, an overall "look" compatible with
beauty and fashion ads. Even "real" nonmodel women photographed for a women's magazine are usually made up,
dressed in credited clothes, and retouched out of all reality.
When editors do include articles on less-than-cheerful subjects
(for instance, domestic violence), they tend to keep them short
and unillustrated. The point is to be "upbeat." Just as women
in the street are asked, "Why don't you smile, honey?"
women's magazines acquire an institutional smile.

Within the text itself, praise for advertisers' products has be- 11
come so ritualized that fields like "beauty writing" have been
invented. One of its frequent practitioners explained seriously
that "It's a difficult art. How many new adjectives can you
find? How much greater can you make a lipstick sound? The
FDA restricts what companies can say on labels, but we create

illusion. And ad agencies are on the phone all the time push-
ing you to get their product in."

12   Often, editorial becomes one giant ad. An issue of *Lear's* featured an elegant woman executive on the cover. On the con-
tents page, we learn she is wearing Guerlain makeup and
Samsara, a new fragrance by Guerlain. Inside are full-page ads
for Samsara and Guerlain antiwrinkle cream. In the article about
the cover subject, we discover she is Guerlain's director of public relations and is responsible for launching, you guessed it, the
new Samsara. When the *Columbia Journalism Review* cited this
example in one of the few articles to include women's magazines in a critique of ad influence, editor Frances Lear was
quoted as defending her magazine because "this kind of thing
is done all the time."

13   Advertisers are also adamant about where in a magazine
their ads appear. When Revlon was not placed as the first
beauty ad in one Hearst magazine, for instance, Revlon
pulled its ads from *all* Hearst magazines. Ruth Whitney, editor in chief of *Glamour,* attributes some of these demands to
"ad agencies wanting to prove to a client that they've
squeezed the last drop of blood out of a magazine." She also
is, she says, "sick and tired of hearing that women's magazines are controlled by cigarette ads." Relatively speaking,
she's right. To be as censoring as are many advertisers for
women's products, tobacco companies would have to demand articles in praise of smoking and expect glamorous
photos of beautiful women smoking their brands.

14   I don't mean to imply that the editors I quote here share my
objections to ads: most assume that women's magazines have
to be the way they are. But it's also true that only former editors can be completely honest. "Most of the pressure came in
the form of direct product mentions," explains Sey Chassler,
who was editor in chief of *Redbook* from the sixties to the eighties. "We got threats from the big guys, the Revlons, blackmail
threats. They wouldn't run ads unless we credited them.

15   "But it's not fair to single out the beauty advertisers because these pressures come from everybody. Advertising
wants to know two things: What are you going to charge me?
What *else* are you going to do for me? It's a holdup. For in-

stance, management felt that fiction took up too much space. They couldn't put any advertising in that. For the last ten years, the number of fiction entries into the National Magazine Awards has declined.

"I also think advertisers do this to women's magazines especially," he concluded, "because of the general disrespect they have for women." [16] [17]

What could women's magazines be like if they were as editorially free as books? as realistic as newspapers? as creative as films? as diverse as women's lives? We don't know.

We'll only find out if we take women's magazines seriously. [18] If readers were to act in a concerted way to change traditional practices of *all* women's magazines and the marketing of *all* women's products, we could do it. After all, they are operating on our consumer dollars; money that we now control. You and I could:

- refuse to buy products whose ads have clearly dictated their surroundings, and write to tell the manufacturers why; [19]
- write to editors and publishers (with copies to advertisers) that we're willing to pay *more* for magazines with editorial independence, but will *not* continue to pay for those that are just editorial extensions of ads; [20]
- write to advertisers (with copies to editors and publishers) that we want fiction, political reporting, consumer reporting—whether it is, or is not, supported by their ads; [21]
- put as much energy into breaking advertising's control over content as into changing the images in ads, or protesting ads for harmful products like cigarettes; [22]
- support only those women's magazines and products that take us seriously as readers and consumers. [23]

Those of us in the magazine world can also use the carrot- [24] and-stick technique. The stick: if magazines were a regulated medium like television, the demands of advertisers would be against FCC rules. Payola and extortion would be penalized. As it is, there are potential illegalities. A magazine's postal rates are determined by the ratio of ad-to-edit pages, and the former costs more than the latter. Counting up all the pages that are *really* ads could make an interesting legal action.

The carrot means appealing to enlightened self-interest. [25] Many studies show that the greatest factor in determining an ad's effectiveness is the credibility of its surroundings. The "higher the rating of editorial believability," concluded a 1987 survey by the *Journal of Advertising Research*, "the higher the rating of the advertising." Thus, an impenetrable wall between edit and ads would also be in the best interest of advertisers.

26   Even as I write this, I get a call from a writer from *Elle,* who is doing a whole article on where women part their hair. Why, she wants to know, do I part mine in the middle?

27   It's all so familiar. A writer trying to make something of a nothing assignment; an editor laboring to think of new ways to attract ads; readers assuming that other women must want this ridiculous stuff; more women suffering for lack of information, insight, creativity, and laughter that could be on these same pages.

28   I ask you: Can't we do better than this?

Expanding Vocabulary

Examine the following words in their contexts in the essay and then write a brief definition or synonym of each one. Avoid using a dictionary; try to guess each word's meaning from its context. The number in parentheses is the number of the paragraph in which the word appears.

stipulated (5)	adjacencies (7)
antithetical (6)	diversified (9)
ritualized (11)	extensions (20)
launching (12)	Payola (24)
critique (12)	extortion (24)
adamant (13)	impenetrable (25)
concerted (18)	

Understanding Content

1. Do advertisers make demands with other kinds of magazines similar to those with women's magazines?
2. What are some of the more subtle "understood" "rules" of advertisers in women's magazines?
3. What have advertisers done to get their way?
4. What can those in the magazine business do about the control advertizers have?

Drawing Inferences about Thesis and Purpose

1. Explain the idea of using a carrot-and-stick approach.

2. What is Steinem's purpose in writing? Does she have more than one? What does she want to accomplish?
3. What is Steinem's thesis?

Analyzing Strategies and Style

1. Steinem uses bullets in two places. What does she gain by using this organizational strategy?
2. The author concludes by mentioning a call from an *Elle* writer. What is effective about this example as a way to conclude?

Thinking Critically

1. How many of the controlling strategies of advertisers are new to you? Which one is the most surprising or shocking to you? Why?
2. Steinem suggests that advertisers place their extreme demands on women's magazines because they lack respect for women. Does this seem a good explanation of their double standard? If you disagree, how would you account for the advertisers' demands on women's magazines?
3. Steinem lists several actions we can take to change advertisers' mistreatment of women's magazines. Which suggestion do you think is the best one? Why? Are there other suggestions you would make? Explain.

Violent Femmes

STEPHANIE MENCIMER

A former writer for *Legal Times* and *Washington City Paper*, Stephanie Mencimer has a degree in journalism from the University of Oregon. She has left *The Washington Monthly*, where she was an editor, to return to school to seek her MA and a future teaching career. Her essay on an interesting change in action movies appeared in *The Washington Monthly* in September 2001.

Questions to Guide Your Reading and Reflection

1. What is Mencimer's topic? Be specific.
2. What are some of the reasons for the popularity of films such as *Crouching Tiger, Hidden Dragon*?

1   This spring, while *Lara Croft: Tomb Raider* was breaking box-office records and feminists were arguing over the merits of the female action hero, no one noticed the dogs playing in theaters elsewhere. *Exit Wounds,* the latest Steven Seagal flick, opened with a paltry $19 million—his best in years, but a poor showing for an action film. While he's mercifully cut off the pony-tail, Seagal is showing all of his 50 years, wearing a pastiche of orange pancake makeup and sporting heft not attributable to muscle mass.

2   In *Exit Wounds,* the martial-arts aficionado and star of macho classics *Hard to Kill* and *Out for Justice* employed Hong Kong kung-fu-movie wire tricks made famous in *The Matrix* and now standard fare in action-chick flicks. But where the wires only added to the grace and agility of lithesome Zhang Zi Yi in *Crouching Tiger, Hidden Dragon,* they seemed to strain just to get Seagal off the ground.

3   Meanwhile, *Driven,* the latest by Sylvester Stallone, the quintessential beefcake action hero, was dying from neglect. The car-racing movie went almost straight to video, and so far has grossed only $32 million, a far cry from the $47 million *Tomb Raider* made in its very first weekend. *Driven's* returns were actually an improvement over Stallone's last disaster, *Get Carter,* which in 2000 earned all of $15 million, barely what his 1981 classic, *Nighthawks,* grossed back when ticket-prices were a lot cheaper.

4   And then there's poor Arnold Schwarzenegger. Last fall, his cloning film, *The Sixth Day,* disappeared with similar returns—this from a guy behind one of the all-time box-office blowouts, *Terminator 2: Judgment Day.* Schwarzenegger had better luck last year playing the voice of a bug in the animated film, *Antz,* which pulled in $90 million.

5   This year, the muscle-bound stars of action-film blockbusters of the '80s and '90s have found themselves ungraciously drop-kicked out of the genre by, of all things, a bunch of girls. Girl-power flicks like *Charlie's Angels, Crouching Tiger,* and *Tomb Raider* are topping the $100 million mark once dominated by men like Schwarzenegger. *Charlie's Angels* has brought in $125 million; *Crouching Tiger* is up to $179 million; and *Tomb Raider,* only open since mid-June, stands at $126 million. Even last year's cheerleading movie, *Bring It On,* trumped the traditional male stars, grossing $68 million.

Action chicks are taking over prime time television as   6
well. *Buffy the Vampire Slayer, Xena: Warrior Princess,* and *La
Femme Nikita*—all WB or UPN fodder—are about to be joined
on a major network by *Alias,* a show about Sydney Bristow,
a kung-fu-chopping female agent for a top-secret division of
the CIA.

The enormous popularity of women as film enforcers has   7
stirred much debate over what these films say about women,
feminism, Hollywood, and violence, and whether it's
progress or exploitation. But no one has answered a more interesting question: What does this say about men? After all,
none of the big female hits could have achieved its staggering
popularity without nabbing a significant male audience,
those same guys who were once the primary consumers of
Die Hard, First Blood, and *Commando.* If men once lived vicar-
iously through the escapades of John Rambo and Col. Matrix—in movies where women were mainly crime victims or
in need of rescue—what does it mean when they love watching Lara Croft kick some bad-boy ass? It's a pretty sharp turn
from misogyny to masochism.

The cynics say men will watch hot babes do just about any-   8
thing, whether it's Jell-O wrestling or kickboxing men, and that
the dominatrix has always been part of the male fantasy. Certainly, that must be part of it. But while simple sex appeal
might explain why men like Lara Croft, it doesn't explain why
they no longer love Schwarzenegger, to whom they'd been so
loyal, suffering through everything from *Predator* to *Junior.* Nor
does the hot-babe theory explain why no obvious successors
have stepped in to replace Jean Claude Van Damme and the
other aging beef boys.

More to the point, though, the pat male-fantasy explanation   9
doesn't answer the question: Why now? Women have been
playing action heroes for more than a decade, but they have
never achieved *Tomb Raider's* level of success until just last year.
In fact, earlier films where women played the lead roles as
strong (and sexy) action heroines dropped like bombs.

Neither Demi Moore's 1997 *G.I. Jane* nor *The Long Kiss Good-*   10
night in 1996, starring Geena Davis as a highly trained government assassin, spawned any TV spin-offs or plans for sequels.
And neither came anywhere near the $100 million box-office
benchmark of *Charlie's Angels* or *Crouching Tiger. The Long Kiss*

grossed only $33 million; *G.I. Jane*, despite Moore's star-power and new breasts, garnered only $48 million.

11   Part of the appeal of the new action genre, of course, is that the old beefcake films were getting tired and repetitive, and their stars Reagan-era relics. It's not just that their stars are getting old—most are in their 50s now—but for men on the silver screen these days, being buff just isn't what it used to be.

12   If you don't believe that studs on steroids have lost their Hollywood appeal, all you have to do is watch *Copland*, the 1997 indie film in which Stallone tried to revive his flagging career by going against character and starring as a fat guy. He wasn't bad either, playing Freddy Hefflin, the sensitive, half-deaf New Jersey sheriff who adores Sibelius violin concertos. Still, there was only so much the Italian Stallion could do; Schwarzenegger had already exhausted the cutesy roles for inarticulate lugs (remember *Kindergarten Cop?*).

13   The meathead movie really flourished at a time when men were desperately clinging to their traditional male roles in the world even as those roles were quickly disappearing. The action heroes like John Rambo or *Commando's* Col. Matrix represented an ideal, and also nostalgia for a time when men built bridges, defended helpless broads, and were worshiped for their physical conquests—sexual and otherwise. They thrived during the '80s, when military might made a comeback and Bruce Springsteen dedicated albums to steelworkers.

14   Technology and the sexual revolution, though, have combined to make the muscleman—and his movie—obsolete. Wires have allowed Lucy Liu and Cameron Diaz to high-kick, jump, and fly better than Seagal ever could, and the girls didn't have to become body-builders in the process. The lithe titanium bodies of Angelina Jolie and *Crouching Tiger's* Zhang Zi Yi make men like Schwarzenegger look like lumps of heavy, slow-moving steel. Their kind of over-tanned, sweat-sheened, macho muscularity has all but disappeared from the screen. Who sweats in action films these days? . . .

Barbarella Bites Back

15   *T2* also foreshadowed the emergence of the action babe, with tank-top-clad Linda Hamilton opening the film doing very manly chin-ups. It took a while before Hollywood got the formula right—*G.I. Jane* and *The Long Kiss Goodnight* were fledgling

efforts to bring a woman to the center of the action, but those films were fatally flawed in terms of the mass-marketing success formula for an action film.

The key to any good action film is an inverse relationship be- 16 tween the amount of special effects and the amount of dialogue. Talk too much and the heroine loses her mystique and starts to remind men of their ex-wives. *Tomb Raider* certainly scores on that front. Angelina Jolie couldn't have more than five lines—all snappy ones, of course, which is also a prerequisite for a good action flick.

The other critical requirement for a successful action movie 17 is for the audience to be able to suspend disbelief enough to enjoy the fantasy. Even with a minimum of dialogue, it's unlikely that male movie audiences 20 years ago would have been willing to accept the preposterous idea of Angelina Jolie engaged in hand-to-hand combat with a man—and winning. With the women's movement beginning to make men uncomfortable men probably weren't eager to see women back up their political threat (or even divorce threats) with good roundhouse kicks to the head.

Today, women everywhere seem to be kicking ass, and men 18 don't seem to mind, within reason. You only have to look to the tennis court to see the change. Women's tennis has never been more powerful—or popular. Venus and Serena Williams are smashing 100-mile-an-hour serves that John McEnroe would have had a hard time returning in his heyday. Lindsey Davenport could eat Lara Croft for lunch.

Oddly enough, while women's sports have paved the way for 19 Lara Croft to gross $100 million at the box office, they have also made Rambo and his expression of male physical power the more laughable movie scenario. Rambo's reliance on brute force, jungle warfare, and big pipes seems so passé, especially when dorks like Bill Gates run the world. Muscles on men have become somewhat irrelevant unless the men happen to be mopping the floors at Microsoft. (Perhaps one of the slyest commentaries on the state of the modern American male came a few years back in the film *American Beauty,* when Kevin Spacey decides to try getting in shape and has to ask the neighborhood gay guys for workout advice.)

The average straight American male today is the doughy 20 white guy who sits in a suburban office park most of the day before driving his SUV home to the wife and kids and online stock reports. Shooting hoops and bench-pressing in the garage just don't figure into the equation. And why should they, when women are more interested in the size of men's portfolios than the size of their pecs anyway?

Conan the Librarian

21   It's easy to see how Stallone and company have lost their male audience. What's harder to understand is why men aren't more threatened by the arrival of powerful heroines. Of course, a closer viewing of these films suggests that, for all their killer moves and rippling muscles, the action babes still aren't really creating a new world order. . . .

22   And when the action babe does meet her male match, the fighting becomes more like foreplay than a duel to the death, as with Zhang Zi Yi and Chang Chen, wrestling across the sand dunes over a stolen comb in *Crouching Tiger*. More than just a good martial-arts scene, the fight is fraught with the excitement of sexual conquest that has all but disappeared with the sexual revolution.

23   No doubt our action heroines have come a long way since Wonder Woman, but the feminist critics are right: Women are still only allowed to be violent within certain parameters largely prescribed by what men are willing to tolerate. To be sure, what men will tolerate has certainly changed a good deal. But in the old action films, at the end, the male hero always walks away from a burning building looking dirty, bleeding, sweaty yet vindicated (Remember Bruce Willis' bloody feet after walking through broken glass barefoot in *Die Hard?*).

24   None of today's action chicks come near that level of messiness. The violence is sterilized—it is, after all, PG-13, aimed mostly at 12-year-olds. They rarely mess up their hair, nor do they really fight—or perhaps gun down—significant bad guys like, say, Rutger Hauer or Wesley Snipes, which would seriously upset the balance of power. Often they end up sparring with other women. Their motives are always pure and they never use unnecessary violence the way Arnold and the boys get to. The body count in *Commando* topped 100; *Charlie's Angels* couldn't have had a single real corpse.

Women playing real action figures who menace *real* men still   25
don't sell, as Geena Davis discovered in *Long Kiss Goodnight*. In
the opening scene, Davis does something unbelievably unla-
dylike: She kills Bambi, snapping a deer's neck with her bare
hands. That scene alone probably sank her movie. Men may
have accepted women as action figures, but only when those
action figures are a cross between Gidget and Bruce Lee. To
achieve box-office success, the new action babes have to celebrate women's power without being so threatening that men
would be afraid to sleep with the leading lady.

Expanding Vocabulary

Match each word in column A with its definition in column B. When
in doubt, first find the word in the essay and look for context clues
to aid your understanding of the word's meaning. Then, if necessary, use your dictionary to complete the matching exercise. The
number in parentheses is the number of the paragraph in which the
word appears.

Column A	*Column B*
flick (1)	form, type
pastiche (1)	to use unethically, selfishly
aficionado (2)	dominating female
lithesome (2)	mix, blend
quintessential (3)	gave rise to
genre (5)	hatred of women
fodder (6)	pleasure from being mistreated
exploitation (7)	or dominated
nabbing (7)	movie
vicariously (7)	requirement
misogyny (7)	purest form or version
masochism (7)	reversed in order
dominatrix (8)	longing for the past
spawned (10)	one who cares deeply for something
lugs (12)	no longer in fashion; dated
nostalgia (13)	catching
inverse (16)	nerds
prerequisite (16)	feeling as if one were living
passé (19)	another's experiences
dorks (19)	moves easily and gracefully
	clumsy fools
	food, usually for livestock

Understanding Content

1. Who are the three male actors whose latest films are not financially competitive with "girl-power flicks"?
2. What female action movies are given as examples of this genre's success?
3. Where else do we now find "action chicks"?
4. What question does Mencimer think is the most interesting one to ask about the female action movies?
5. How do the cynics answer her key question? What is the author's response to their answer?
6. What reasons does Mencimer offer for the current popularity with men of female action movies? Why have the male actors lost their following? Why are men accepting the female action stars?

Drawing Inferences about Thesis and Purpose

1. What is Mencimer's thesis? Consider her topic, the questions she raises, and then how she answers those questions.
2. The author asserts that the action babes aren't creating a new world order. What world order did the action guys create—or help sustain and justify? How has that world changed in our time?

Analyzing Strategies and Style

1. Mencimer not only refers to many films and their leading men and women; she also includes how much money these films have made. What purpose do the money references serve? How do these facts support Mencimer's thesis?
2. The author uses a number of informal or slang terms—"lugs," "dorks," "flicks," "ass"—to mention only four. What do they contribute to the style and tone of the essay?

Thinking Critically

1. Do any of the movie earnings figures surprise you? Shock you? Why or why not?
2. What connection does Mencimer see between women's tennis and the new action movies? Is this a new idea for you? Does it make sense? Why or why not?
3. The author concludes by observing that the action chicks are actually limited in their physical dominance over men, and that's why men will watch these films. First, do you think her explana-

tion makes sense? Second, do you think that the movies reflect our society—that is, that women can do more than 30 years ago but are still restricted in their power and in the ways they can show that power? Reflect on this issue.

More Powerful Than . . . Ever: On-Screen and Off, Superheroes Are a Force to Reckon With

VINCENT P. BZDEK

Vincent Bzdek has been the *Washington Post*'s news editor for six years. He occasionally writes articles on popular culture for the paper and has had articles published in the Asian and European editions of the *Wall Street Journal* and *Wired* magazine. His degree is in English literature from Colorado College. First published February 6, 2005, his essay here is a somewhat shortened version of a richly detailed study of popular films featuring superheroes.

Questions to Guide Your Reading and Reflection
1. What is the basis for Bzdek's title—what does it refer to?
2. Do you enjoy superhero films, such as *Spiderman*? If so, why?

Holy spandex, Batman.   1

Seventy years after a pair of Cleveland teenagers created the   2 first superhero out of a primordial soup of pulp magazines, rough neighborhoods and absent dads, primary-colored crime-fighters are more popular than ever. Just ask Hollywood.

No fewer than 18 big-budget movies scheduled for release   3 this year were inspired by comic books or superheroes, including, this spring and summer, *Batman Begins, Fantastic Four, Constantine, Sin City, Ultraviolet* and *Sky High*.

The boom was already well underway last year. Eight su-   4 perhero movies made it to multiplexes in 2004, led by two of the year's five biggest box-office draws, *Spider-Man 2* and *The*

Incredibles. Together, *Spider-Man* (2002) and *Spider-Man 2* have made more than $1.6 billion in the United States, making them the sixth and eighth most popular movies ever here.

5   And the hero worship doesn't seem likely to stop any time soon. *Superman Returns,* under the direction of Bryan Singer (*X-Men, X2*), is scheduled for release in 2006, the first new Superman movie in 20 years. DC Comics hopes to release films of *Wonder Woman, The Flash* and *Shazam* in the next couple of years. Its rival, Marvel Comics, has ambitious plans to bring more of its wards to the big screen, too, including *Captain America, The Phantom, Ghost Rider,* and sequels—or additional sequels—to *Hulk, X-Men* and *Spider-Man.*

6   If you look at the success of *Spider-Man* and the success of *The Incredibles,* Hollywood is saying: "Hey, there's gold in them thar hills," said Joe Quesada, editor in chief of Marvel Comics. "The superhero genre is today's western."

7   Gerard Jones, who sits on the advisory board of the MIT Comparative Media Studies program, recently published *Men of Tomorrow,* a book that chronicles the history of superheroes, the birth of comic books and their impact on American culture.

8   "No other icon comes back so strong again and again after so many decades, and just keeps going," Jones says. "Adults aren't embarrassed anymore about their interest in a genre that used to be regarded as kid stuff," he said, adding that superheroes are "one of the major shaping influences of pop culture."

9   So why have tights-clad geek fantasies vaulted to the pinnacle of Mediapolis at this moment in history? And how to explain their superhuman resonance and longevity in a culture with the attention span of a newt?

10   For one thing, the caped crusaders have a great pedigree. "The familiarity and built-in nostalgia of superheroes makes them a relatively safe bet in an increasingly risk-averse studio system," said David Cook, author of *A History of Narrative Film* and director of film studies at Emory University.

11   "These stories are presold," Cook says. "There's a public out there that is already familiar with the narrative and characters. More and more, Hollywood tends to recycle and borrow icons from popular culture. They ran out of ideas 50 years ago."

12   Though a few superhero movies have bombed recently (*Catwoman* and *Elektra* come to mind), the two *Spider-Man* and *X-*

Men films seem to have cured producers of their qualms about the genre after the Batman sequels went bust in the early '90s.

Another reason for the proliferation of super-films now is 13 simply that technology is catching up to subject matter. With the evolution of computer animation, directors are finally able to realistically simulate the fantastic feats that comic artists dreamed up on pulp. . . .

At the same time, the super stunts have grown extraordi- 14 narily realistic and engaging in the past few years. Seeing Spider-Man swing convincingly through the real-life canyons of Manhattan certainly wows children, but it also satisfies a deep-seated desire of many adults to see how the movie version of their favorite superhero stacks up with the image that has been locked inside their heads since their comics-reading childhood.

That ability to cross generational lines is a large part of why 15 superhero movies do so well when done right. Thanks to the repeat showings made possible by videos and DVD, children's movies have become one of the primary vehicles by which children and parents bond. Watching superhero movies together, the kids get to dream about being more powerful than Mom and Dad, and the parents get to laugh at the inside jokes while resampling the joys of their own childhoods.

Four of the five most lucrative movies of 2004 were nomi- 16 nally children's movies: *Spider-Man 2, The Incredibles, Shrek 2* and *Harry Potter and the Prisoner of Azkaban.* Together they made more than $1.3 billion at the box office worldwide. . . .

Many of the shapers of pop culture today were weaned on 17 Marvel Comics, which enjoyed its heyday 40 years ago when Spider-Man, the X-Men, the Fantastic Four and the Incredible Hulk all came into being.

"You have no idea how many closet comics lovers there 18 are," says Avi Arad, president of Marvel Studios.

"The thing about comics and graphic novels, they're ready- 19 made storyboards for movies," says Cook. "They lend themselves incredibly well to filmic adaptation.". . .

Few in Hollywood turn up their noses at superhero films 20 these days. Christian Bale, not yet a major star, is this season's Bruce Wayne in *Batman Begins*—but that movie will also feature Academy Award winner Michael Caine and Oscar nominees Morgan Freeman and Liam Neeson, as well as director

Christopher Nolan (*Memento*). Kevin Spacey has signed on to be Lex Luthor in *Superman Returns,* and British actor Ioan Gruffudd, the lead in A&E's *Horatio Hornblower* films, is Mr. Fantastic in *Fantastic Four* this summer.

21   Well-regarded filmmakers, Quentin Tarantino, Robert Rodriguez and Bryan Singer among them, have used comic books as source material in recent work. Kevin Smith, director of *Clerks* and *Jay and Silent Bob Strike Back,* is writing and producing the upcoming *Green Hornet.* Michael Chabon, the novelist who won a Pulitzer Prize in 2001 for *The Amazing Adventures of Kavalier and Clay,* his fictionalized history of the birth of the superhero, co-wrote the screenplay for last year's *Spider-Man 2.* . . .

22   Jones thinks superhero fans have helped trigger a huge shift in how popular culture is created. "This geek-nerd culture that they were part of really has taken over as the shaping, dominant force in pop culture," he says.

23   These fans have erected an entire industry of consumer mass-market fantasy. Comic-book characters are being converted not just into movies but into entertainment franchises, replete with profitable tie-ins such as video games, computer games, toys, action figures and costumes. Related comic books and graphic novels also get a bump when a superhero movie succeeds. . . .

24   Superhero Web sites such as SuperheroHype.com, Efavata.com and SuperheroTimes.com keep the fan base stoked, tracking all the latest developments in the world of comic books and superheroes. A popular new Internet game, *City of Heroes,* even allows players to create their own superheroes and do battle against each other in cyberspace.

25   Reality TV is next on the bandwagon. This month MTV will start producing *Who Wants to be a Superhero?,* a show in which contestants will dress, act and compete as superheroes against other wannabe superheroes and an assortment of stock villains. The grand prize winner's invented character will be published in a comic book. . . .

26   But there may be something deeper afoot. During the past century, Americans often turned to superheroes as an escape in times of national jitteriness. The comic book *Superman* made its debut in 1938, as war clouds were gathering over Europe. Within five years of Action Comics No. 1, 90 percent of kids were reading superhero comic books, which enjoyed a kind of golden age during World War II.

"The desire for some big, bright escape that had something   27
to do with fighting off big, bad scary things was a big part of
that," Jones says.

Superheroes nearly disappeared from pop culture after the   28
war, but reemerged in a new, more morally complicated way
during the Vietnam War. The Marvel superheroes who made
their debuts in the '60s often found they did more harm than
good with their powers.

Spider-Man, the Hulk and Daredevil "were real people first,   29
acting in real places, like New York and Brooklyn," and dealing with real-world problems, Quesada says. "Their alter egos
became the real story."

And now, as we wring our hands over Iraq and terrorism,   30
America's superheroes have arrived en masse on movie
screens. . . .

Rainer points out that Hollywood has always been evasive   31
about portraying what's going on in the real world—in real
time—when it's grim news. Hardly any movies during Vietnam were directly about Vietnam. Instead, movies deal with
the violence and anxiety of such periods in code. "This is how
Hollywood talks about Iraq: with superheroes," he says.

Superheroes are experiencing something more than just a   32
new round of popularity, however. They've evolved into much
more complex and ambiguous beings in recent movies. They're
being taken seriously by critics, directors and scholars as a
unique American storytelling form.

"The cruel irony is that these superheroes are more compli-   33
cated than many real actors in live action movies today,"
Rainer says. "They have more shades of feeling, and there is
tremendous psychic conflict that they come out of."

X-Men was really a story about prejudice, substituting mu-   34
tants as the persecuted and cast-out minority. Ang Lee, the director of *Sense and Sensibility* and *The Ice Storm,* made *Hulk*
(2003), a story about the wounds that egomaniacal parents can
inflict on their children. And on one level, *The Incredibles* was a
meditation on midlife crises.

In his book *Superman on the Couch,* Danny Fingeroth identi-   35
fies several different mythological archetypes in superhero
movies, such as the angry young man (Wolverine of *X-Men*),
the avenging orphan (Batman), the dual personality (Superman) and the empowered Amazon (Wonder Woman).

36　Other countries, too, have superheroes—Turkey, in particular, has a love affair with low-budget superhero movies, and Japan prints millions more comic books a year than does the United States. But most foreign-born heroes are derivative of America's. It's here that they started and here that they maintain their strongest pull.

37　Arad makes an analogy to jazz, which was once regarded by cultural arbiters as junk music but gained acceptance and cachet over time until it achieved a reputation as one of America's most original art forms."Superheroes are the jazz of art history," Arad says.

38　Still, their metamorphosis into icons wouldn't have happened if they hadn't touched some primal nerves from the get-go.

39　Fingeroth, Jones, Cook, and others speculate that we're drawn to superheroes because they tap strongly felt emotions clustered around helplessness, identity issues, and an ancient ache to connect to something more powerful, higher and nobler. . . .

40　Superheroes also express our "hope (and fear) that there may be more to this world than what we see," Fingeroth writes in *Superman on the Couch*. Religion taps the same yearning, in a different, more serious and ritualistic way.

41　Jerry Siegel created Superman when he was in his late teens, a time when a person's limitations are keenly felt in contrast to his powers. Siegel may have felt the helplessness that results from that power gap more than others. In *Men of Tomorrow*, Jones reveals that just a few years before Siegel and his artist/partner Joe Shuster committed their first Superman stories and sketches to paper, Siegel's father had been shot and killed in his Cleveland haberdashery. It was a crime that was never solved, and an incident Siegel never talked about publicly the rest of his life.

42　Instead he created a bulletproof father figure who brought the bad guys to justice over and over again. What Siegel gave us was a playful format for the expression of a very painful and universal human frustration.

43　Siegel's creation of the first superhero didn't provide him the kind of catharsis and pleasure he brought to so many others, until very late in his life. Shortly after Superman first appeared, Siegel and Shuster sold the rights to their invention for

$130. For 40 years they received none of the royalties that accrued to America's most popular fictional character.

It was the movies that finally brought Siegel a measure of 44
vindication. In 1975, when he heard that Warner Bros. was paying $3 million for the rights to film *Superman* and he wasn't getting a penny, Siegel began a full-out public campaign for better compensation, reviving efforts to settle a lawsuit that had languished for a decade.

The press soon picked up the story, which touched a nerve 45
in a public fed up with corporate scandals and Watergate. The pressure built until Warner Bros. and DC Comics decided it was best to clear the decks of the Siegel lawsuit before the movie opened.

On Dec. 19, 1975, Siegel and Shuster received a settlement of 46
more than $20,000 a year for life. More important, they were promised credit as the creators of Superman on all printed matter, TV and movies in perpetuity. When *Superman Returns* comes out next year, at some point the screen will announce: "The character of Superman was created by Jerry Siegel and Joe Shuster."

Expanding Vocabulary

Match each word in column A with its definition in column B. When in doubt, first find the word in the essay and look for context clues to aid your understanding of the word's meaning. Then, if necessary, use your dictionary to complete the matching exercise. The number in parentheses is the number of the paragraph in which the word appears.

Column A	*Column B*
icon (8)	continuance, powerful influence
genre (8)	anxieties, doubts
pinnacle (9)	businesses
resonance (9)	altogether
pedigree (10)	those judging, deciding
nostalgia (10)	illustrative history
qualms (12)	mark of distinction
proliferation (13)	image or representation
franchises (23)	excessively focused on the self
en masse (30)	purging of painful memories
evasive (31)	type or category, often applied
egomaniacal (34)	to literary types

arbiters (37)   intentionally vague
cachet (37)   bittersweet longing for the past
catharsis (43)   highest point
                                extensive increase

Understanding Content

1. What is Bzdek's subject?
2. What is the source of most film superheroes?
3. How successful have the superhero movies been?
4. What reasons does the author give for these films' current popularity? Be able to state each reason in your own words.
5. Explain the concept of the "primal nerves" that superheroes touch in us.

Drawing Inferences about Thesis and Purpose

1. What is Bzdek's primary purpose in writing? What additional purpose does he have? (See paragraph 9.)
2. Write a thesis statement for the essay that includes both purposes.

Analyzing Strategies and Style

1. A good use of examples, we've said, means having "enough" and making them relevant to the support of the thesis. Does the author succeed in providing enough appropriate examples to develop and support his ideas? What is one good lesson you can learn from Bzdek?
2. Bzdek also presents the views of various people in the film or comic business. How does this strategy add to his essay?
3. Find three examples of clever or amusing word choice in the essay and explain why you have made your choice.

Thinking Critically

1. Many cultures of the past have stories about heroes. Why do you think humans feel a need to create such tales? Has Bzdek given you some increased insight into the causes? Explain.
2. There are many interesting studies of "the hero," the traits, experiences, and goals necessary to get the label. See what you can find in your library's book or periodicals collection or on the Internet to help you define the hero. How well does your definition fit the superheroes of comics and film mentioned by Bzdek?
3. Suppose someone said to you that these films are silly children's fluff. How would you respond to that comment?

Bad Raps: Music Rebels Revel in Their Thug Life

SUZANNE FIELDS

Suzanne Fields (b. 1936) is a syndicated op-ed columnist with a twice-weekly column in the *Washington Times*. She holds a Ph.D. in literature from Catholic University and is trained in social psychology. A collection of her columns was published by the *Washington Times* in 1996. Her article on rap music appeared on May 21, 2001, in *Insight on the News*.

Questions to Guide Your Reading and Reflection

1. How does Sinatra differ from current rappers?
2. What if anything, draws you to rap music?

Nothing in the culture wars makes a stronger argument for   1
the defense of conservative values than rap music. Rap expresses the worst kind of images emanating from a postmodern society that has consigned a generation of young men and women to the darkest dramas of the desperately lost.

The megastars of this genre are not about to sing of "you and   2
me and baby makes three." Their lyrics come from a world of broken families, absent fathers, illegitimate children and matriarchal dominance, often subsidized by welfare.

For the men who denigrate women as "bitches" and "ho's,"   3
this is not merely misogyny (though it is that), but alienation from common humanity and community. The lyrics employ vulgar street idioms because both the language and experience of poetry or romance are absent from the lives of the rappers and their audience as well.

Frank Sinatra grew up on the mean streets of New Jersey   4
and he knew the Mafia well, but when he sang "You're the top, You're the Tower of Pisa. . . . You're the Mona Lisa" he aspired to sophistication and wanted others to see him as debonair. (Is there a rapper alive who knows the difference between the Tower of Pisa and a towering pizza?) When Frankie was bad, literally, he didn't want his fans to hear

about it. He wasn't as innocent as his lyrics, but he cultivated that impression.

5   Rappers Sean "Puffy" Combs and Eminem, by contrast, must live like they sing. They're rich, but their attraction resides in perverse behavior on and off stage. When as adults they tap into adolescent rebellion, they dumb down both their emotions and their economic success.

6   Shelby Steele, a black scholar, has their number when he writes that to keep their audience they can't just sing about alienation—they had better experience it as well, either with the audience or for the audience.

7   "The rappers and promoters themselves are pressured toward a thug life, simply to stay credible," Steele writes in the *Wall Street Journal*. "A rap promoter without an arrest record can start to look a lot like Dick Clark."

8   A rapper such as Eminem, who revels in affecting a white-trash identity, has defenders, too. They find irony, satire and poetic metaphor in his lyrics, but it's difficult to see how most of his fans take those lyrics as anything but straight. Lurking in them is a cruel depravity that seeks ways to go over the line by singing of macho brutality—of raping women, holding gay men with a knife at their throats and helping a group of friends to take a little sister's virginity.

9   These lyrics are powerful, but the power resides in psychological defensiveness that provides a perverse rationalization for brutality: If you don't love you can't be rejected, so you might as well hate and rape.

10   Every generation since Elvis has driven through adolescence on popular music—looking for the new sound and sensibility that rejects what their parents liked. Elvis was the cutting edge of the sexual revolution, innovative then, but tame and hardly even titillating today. It's hard to believe that for his first appearance on the *Ed Sullivan Show*, the maestro wouldn't allow the cameras to focus below the singer's waist.

11   Elvis brilliantly combined the black, blues and sex rhythms of the honky-tonks of the backroads South of his time, liberating teen-age rebels in dance and song. But nearly every music hero and heroine after him has had to push the envelope or raise the ante to be a big winner. For some teenagers the explicit meanness may provide an imaginary escape, the permission to

act in a dark, forbidden drama of their imaginations. For these young men and women, the incentives to "act out" may be no more aggressive than dyeing hair purple or wearing ugly clothes. For others, "acting out" as in "men behaving badly," may be the preferred response in human relationships.

Rappers, rollers and rockers who tap into the big time with bite   12
and bitterness draw millions to their records and concerts for different reasons. The teen-age and young-adult Zeitgeist is made up of rebels with and without causes. It didn't hurt Eminem that his mother sued him for $10 million for using lyrics such as "my mom smokes more dope than I do." (It might have been Eminem's press agent's idea.) That's on the same track in which he ponders which Spice Girl he would prefer to "impregnate."

There are lots of other popular singers who get less notice by   13
being less bizarre. They make up a popular lifestyle that eventually will morph into a healthy nostalgia. The pity is that the nasty stuff of violent rap may never reach the nostalgic mode but congeal into a brutal life perspective.

In one of Eminem's hits he sings of a deranged fan. Eminem   14
suggests the fan get counseling, but the fan doesn't. Instead he kills himself and his pregnant girlfriend. Fantasy or reality?

Expanding Vocabulary

Match each word in column A with its definition in column B. When in doubt, first find the word in the essay and look for context clues to aid your understanding of the word's meaning. Then, if necessary, use your dictionary to complete the matching exercise. The number in parentheses is the number of the paragraph in which the word appears.

Column A	Column B
emanating (1)	form, type
consigned (1)	attack the reputation of,
megastars (2)	put down
genre (2)	pleasurably exciting, arousing
denigrate (3)	conductor, head of the show
misogyny (3)	the stake to be paid to play
debonair (4)	given over to, set apart
perverse (5)	coming from
titillating (10)	spirit of the times

maestro (10)	insane
honky-tonks (11)	really big stars
ante (11)	change form
Zeitgeist (12)	hatred of women
morph (13)	perverted, wrong-headed
deranged (14)	cheap, noisy bars or dance halls
	suave, cultured and urbane

Understanding Content

1. What are the subjects of rapper lyrics?
2. What does Frank Sinatra have in common with modern rappers?
3. What is the relationship between Combs and Eminem's music and their lifestyles? How are their lifestyles a series of contradictions?
4. What image does Eminem like to present? How does the author describe his image?
5. What were the sources of Elvis's music? How was he innovative for his time?
6. What, according to Fields, eventually happens to each era's adolescent music? Does she expect the same process to take place with teens growing up on rap music?

Drawing Inferences about Thesis and Purpose

1. What is Field's thesis? Where does she state it?
2. Fields asserts that rap lyrics provide a "perverse rationalization for brutality." Explain her idea.

Analyzing Strategies and Style

1. The author quotes Shelby Steele, who says that rap promoters need an arrest record so as not to be like Dick Clark. Who is Dick Clark? What makes this reference effective?
2. Fields uses two examples to contrast with today's rappers—Sinatra and Elvis. What makes these popular singers particularly useful examples to show how rappers differ from popular singers of the past?

Thinking Critically

1. Do you agree with the author that "the language and experience of poetry or romance are absent from the lives of rappers and their audiences"? Is this one of the realities of our postmodern society? Explain your views.
2. Do you agree that teens influenced by rap music will be affected into adulthood by a music that alienates them from "common

humanity"? If so, how do you suggest that we keep teens from this influence?

3. Do you listen to rap music? If so, how would you defend your choice? If not, why not?

Call Hating

DAVE BARRY

A humor columnist for the *Miami Herald* since 1983, Dave Barry is now syndicated in more than 150 newspapers although he is currently taking a break from his weekly column. A Pulitzer Prize–winner in 1988 for commentary, Barry has several books, including *Dave Barry Slept Here* (1989), a collection of his columns. The following column appeared in 2001.

Questions to Guide Your Reading and Reflection

1. What is Barry's primary purpose in writing? Can he be said to have more than one purpose?
2. Should cell phones be banned from use in public places? In cars?

It was a beautiful day at the beach—blue sky, gentle breeze, 1 calm sea. I knew these things because a man sitting five feet from me was shouting them into his cellular telephone, like a play-by-play announcer.

"IT'S A BEAUTIFUL DAY," he shouted. "THE SKY IS BLUE, AND 2 THERE'S A BREEZE, AND THE WATER IS CALM, AND . . ."

Behind me, a woman, her cell phone pressed to her ear, was 3 pacing back and forth.

"She DIDN'T," she was saying. "No. She DIDN'T. She DID? Re- 4 ally? Are you SERIOUS? She did NOT. She DID? No she DIDN'T. She DID? NO she . . ."

And so on. This woman had two children, who were frolick- 5 ing in the surf. I found myself watching them, because the woman surely was not. A giant squid could have surfaced and snatched the children, and this woman would not have noticed. Or, if she had noticed, she'd have said, "Listen, I have to go, be- cause a giant squid just . . . No! She didn't! She DID? No! She . . ."

6   And next to me, the play-by-play man would have said: "... AND A GIANT SQUID JUST ATE TWO CHILDREN, AND I'M GET-TING A LITTLE SUNBURNED, AND ..."

7   It used to be that the major annoyance at the beach was the jerk who brought a boom box and cranked it up so loud that the bass notes caused sea gulls to explode. But at least you knew where these jerks were; you never know which beachgo-ers have cell phones. You'll settle next to what appears to be a sleeping sunbather, or even (you hope) a corpse, and you'll sprawl happily on your towel, and you'll get all the way to the second sentence of your 467-page book before you doze off to the hypnotic surge of the surf, and ...

8   BREEP! BREEP! The corpse sits up, gropes urgently for its cell phone, and shouts, "Hello! Oh hi! I'm at the beach! Yes! The beach! Yes! It's nice! Very peaceful! Very relaxing! What? She did? No she didn't! She DID? No she ..."

9   Loud cell-phoners never seem to get urgent calls. Just once, I'd like to hear one of them say: "Hello? Yes, this is Dr. John-son. Oh, hello, Dr. Smith. You've opened the abdominal cav-ity? Good! Now the appendix should be right under the ... What? No, that's the liver. Don't take *that* out, ha ha! Oh, you did? Whoops! Okay, now listen very, very carefully ..."

10   The good news is, some politicians want to ban cell-phone use. The bad news is, they want to ban it in cars, which is the one place where innocent bystanders don't have to listen to it. Granted, drivers using cell phones may cause accidents ("I gotta go, because I just ran over a man, and he's bleeding from the ... What? She DID? NO she didn't. She DID? No she ..."). But I frankly don't believe that drivers yakking on cell phones are nearly as dangerous as drivers with babies in the back seat. I'm one of those drivers, and we're definitely a menace, espe-cially when our baby has dropped her Elmo doll and is scream-ing to get it back, and we're steering with one hand while groping under the back seat with the other. ("Groping for Elmo" would be a good name for a rock band.)

11   So we should, as a long-overdue safety measure, ban babies. But that is not my point. My point is that there is good news on the cell-phone front, which is that several companies—including Image Sensing Systems and Net-

Line—are selling devices that jam cell-phone signals. Yes! These devices broadcast a signal that causes every cell phone in the immediate vicinity to play the 1974 hit song "Kung Fu Fighting."

No, that would be too wonderful. But, really, these devices, 12 which start at around $900, cause all nearby cellular phones to register NO SERVICE.

Unfortunately, there's a catch. Because of some outfit call- 13 ing itself the "Federal Communications Commission," the cell-phone jamming devices are illegal in the United States. I say this stinks. I say we should all contact our congresspersons and tell them that if they want to make it up to us consumers for foisting those lousy low-flow toilets on us, they should put down their interns for a minute and pass a law legalizing these devices, at least for beach use.

I realize some of you disagree with me. I realize you have 14 solid reasons—perhaps life-and-death reasons—why you *must* have your cellular phone working at all times, everywhere. If you're one of those people, please believe me when I say this: I can't hear you.

Expanding Vocabulary

Examine the following words in their contexts in the essay. Then write a brief definition or synonym for each one. (Do not use a dictionary; try to guess the word's meaning from its context.) The number in parentheses is the number of the paragraph in which the word appears.

frolicking (5)
cranked (7)
hypnotic (7)
yakking (10)
menace (10)
foisting (13)

Understanding Content

1. Where, in particular, would Barry like to see an end to cell-phone use?
2. Does Barry really want to make jamming devices legal? Explain.

Drawing Inferences about Thesis and Purpose

1. What exactly is Barry's thesis?
2. Does the author believe that most cell-phone use is necessary, that people really have to have their phones on all the time? How do you know the answer to this question?

Analyzing Strategies and Structures

1. At what point in your reading are you aware that Barry is using humor?
2. What passages do you find especially funny? Why?
3. How does Barry cleverly blend and overlap his examples of cell-phone conversations? What makes this use of repetition funny?
4. One strategy for humor is Barry's introducing something that doesn't fit the discussion, that seems completely disconnected. Find examples of this strategy.

Thinking Critically

1. Are you bothered by intrusive cell-phoners who talk loudly about, apparently, nothing important? If no, how would you respond to Barry? If yes, what suggestions do you have for dealing with the situation?
2. Why do you think some people have to talk loudly and repeatedly into their cells while at the beach or in a restaurant? What may explain this behavior?
3. What guidelines for the courteous use of cell phones would you recommend? Draw up a list to share with classmates.

STUDENT ESSAY—USING EXAMPLES

RAP'S REFUSAL OF INJUSTICE
Michael King

The caustic manner in which rap music questions its surroundings provides most critics with a dilemma: does one focus on the negative or the positive qualities of the genre? Rap's frequent revelry in

Introduction recognizes negative attitudes toward rap.

misogyny, homophobia, and violence blunts its virtues, and its preoccupation with the rejection of contemporary paradigms rather than a synthesis of new and old ideas has hindered progress in dialogues about race. Still, for all of its bravado, hip-hop's move away from the overly didactic writing of the civil rights era and into a period of angry rejection is the inevitable reaction to continued inequality. The rage found in rap music is a reaction to continued injustice and a means of empowerment. It is, therefore, politically significant.

Opening paragraph moves to a thesis statement.

Unfortunately, the dynamic nature of rap music makes defining its political importance a challenge. While today's better rap groups continue to reflect the rage associated with inequality, one risks generalizing by placing every group into one category. However, three groups stand out for their use of rage as a political tool. Although their expression of rage differed, Public Enemy, N.W.A., and Scarface have become archetypal rather than stereotypical, representing the best rap has to offer.

Transitional paragraph introduces the three examples.

Formed somewhere between the Black Nationalist movement of the seventies and New York's economic collapse in the

eighties, Public Enemy's sonic and political rage moved hip-hop from a benign
oddity to a force that uprooted the cultural norms of the time. Labeled by many
critics as hateful, Public Enemy's refusal to accept the superficial truce between the haves and have-nots represented
not only a move away from white America
but moderate black America as well. In
Public Enemy's world, middle class values, the de facto norms of American culture, were tantamount to racism. Their
support of former Black Panther and political exile Assata Shakur on "Rebel
Without a Pause" and their vilification
of both Elvis and John Wayne in the
group's best known song, "Fight the
Power," successfully redefined the cultural heroes of the time, giving both
black and white youth a new, more culturally diverse value system. Similarly,
their song, "Black Steel in the Hour of
Chaos," dealing with the imprisonment and
eventual escape of a black war objector,
jettisoned the values rooted in America's
white hierarchy, while the group's support of Minister Farrakhan in "Bring the
Noise" implicitly rejected the goal of
integration of the more moderate civil
rights leaders.

First example:
Public Enemy

Three songs by
Public Enemy
analyzed.

While Public Enemy searched for ideological empowerment, N.W.A.'s first album, <u>Straight Out of Compton</u>, took a more visceral but nonetheless important stand against injustice. At first glance, the group's brand of reaction seemed to be little more than violent hedonism, a juvenile reaction to a complex problem, but the group's behavior represented an important shift in approach. N.W.A. removed the shackles of propriety and rooted its raps in both the language and reality of ghettos across the country. Even the title of their album suggested a geographical context, and in doing so, N.W.A. identified with the residents of Compton. Seemingly unredeemable songs like "Gangsta Gangsta" found solace in its populist approach to empowerment. No longer were communities like Compton places for their residents to be embarrassed about; instead "Gangsta Gangsta" insisted that Compton, long ignored by politicians and citizens alike, must redefine their goals and produce their own--albeit equally corrupt--brand of success. In confronting police brutality in their most controversial song, "_ _ _ _ Tha Police," the group further defied cultural norms by outlining the tension

Second example: NWA

First album and two songs analyzed

between minorities and police. Justice, the song cried, was not found behind a badge, and with each chorus sung, "_ _ _ _ Tha Police" warned of the impending 1992 L.A. riots.

Perhaps the most worrisome rapper of the nineties, Houston's Scarface became the most easily made case for censorship. His vivid tales of murder and violence were not without redemption. His exploration of psychological desperation revealed a source for the rage first articulated by N.W.A., and through shocking detail exposed the humanity of violence. "Diary of a Madman," his first solo effort, presented listeners with a character so void of opportunity that he descends into madness. Confessional in nature, the song served as both an apologetic exploration of insanity and a critique of the opportunities presented to the poor. Similarly, "I Seen a Man Die" expanded the theme developed in "Diary of a Madman," producing a more sophisticated analysis of desperation. Unlike previous gangsta rap songs that removed the ugliness of violence, "I Seen a Man Die" forced listeners to confront the victim, making it impossible to romanticize the act, and refusing the larger paradigm of

Third example introduced.

Two songs analyzed.

remorseless murderers. Ultimately, Scarface's success lay in his ability to show
not only the consequences of violence but
also the consequences of inequality.

With seventeen years since the release
of both Public Enemy's <u>It Takes a Nation
of Millions to Hold Us Back</u> and N.W.A.'s
<u>Straight Out of Compton</u>, and thirteen
years since the release of Scarface's
first solo effort, rap music's relevance
continues to rest in its ability to reflect the cultural disconnects found in
race, economics, age, and ideology.
Whether one finds rap's presentation de-
praved or acceptable, the insights provided in the music are essential to
understanding the community that em-
braces the music.

Conclusion reminds readers of the three examples of rap artists and restates the essay's thesis.

MAKING CONNECTIONS

1. Mencimer and Fields both write about violence in the
   media, whether in song lyrics or the movies. Because children and teenagers are big listeners and watchers, they
   are growing up exposed to a considerable amount of violence. Of course, fairy tales also contain much violence,
   but some experts believe that their violence is healthy for
   children. Are there different kinds or levels of violence?
   Should distinctions be made, and some kinds of violence
   banned or available to adults only? Consider the examples these writers use and those you know, and then try
   to define the kinds of violence that may be tolerated and
   the kinds that should be controlled in some way. To aid

your reflection, find some statistics on violence in the media. Explore essays in electronic databases in your library or do an online search.

2. If violence in lyrics and on television should be controlled, who should do the controlling? Is the task one for parents, for education through the schools and TV, for voluntary control by the media, for federal guidelines and restrictions? Decide on the approaches you would take if you were "media czar."

3. McGarvey and Steinem are stating or implying the power of the media. The media create images that sanction the dress, language, and behavior presented in those images. And children are not the only ones influenced by those images, as McGarvey's experience demonstrates. How should children be instructed to understand the media, especially television, movies, and advertising, so that they can distinguish between image and reality? Consider the suggestions stated or implied in this chapter and reflect on other possibilities as well.

4. Gloria Steinem examines some ways that advertising misleads. How can we know what is accurate and reliable? Think about strategies readers can use to guide their reading of both magazines and Websites.

5. Studies show that TV programs are filled with stereotypes. What about advertising? Conduct an online search to see what you can learn about stereotyping in print or TV ads, or in television shows. Search with keywords such as "advertising and stereotyping." One useful site to visit is: *http://www.media-awareness.ca.*

TOPICS FOR WRITING

---

1. What makes your favorite type of television program so good, or what makes your least favorite type of program so bad? Do you most enjoy (or least enjoy) watching news, sports, sitcoms, soaps, a movie channel? Select your most (or least) favorite type and then support a thesis with specific examples from particular shows.

2. The columnist George Will has described the names of some foods as "printed noise." (Think of the names of ice cream flavors, for example.) Are there other words or pictures that should be labeled verbal or visual litter—words or pictures that are silly, inaccurate, overstated, childish? Think about product commercials; political advertising; repeated coverage of particular issues in the media; repeated "lectures" from teachers, parents, friends that you now simply tune out.

3. Examine current political campaigns to see whether any use negative advertising that distorts the issues and misleads voters. For evidence, listen to radio and TV ads for specific examples with which to develop your essay. Your thesis will be that the _____ campaign uses misleading negative tactics, or the _____ campaign uses only fair and accurate campaign tactics.

4. Suzanne Fields is concerned about violence in song lyrics and in the lives of rap musicians. Are you? Examine examples of lyrics and/or TV images (e.g., MTV videos), decide on your point of view, and then support it.

5. Do you watch "live" TV shows—game shows, talk shows, competitions, survivor shows? If so, reflect on what these shows have in common and what attracts viewers to them. Develop and support a thesis about "live" TV.

6. In this chapter you have read some articles about the power of advertising and image making. When a product's name is clever, that name becomes an ongoing advertisement for the product. Many product names are highly connotative or suggestive, such as Lestoil cleaner. Think about the names used for one type of product, such as cleaning materials, perfumes, diet foods, or cigarettes. (You may want to explore your favorite grocery store or shopping mall for ideas.) In an essay, explain the effects of the various product names, grouping the names by their different effects (their purpose or the desired impact on buyers), and illustrate those effects with specific examples. You probably need at least ten specific items (e.g., White Shoulders) in the product category (e.g., perfumes).

7. Writing fables or parables to make a point about human character traits or about morality can be fun. Try writing

one to make some point about advertising or about what motivates humans to buy particular products. Think, for example, about the many different car models—what types of people are drawn to each model—or the array of sports equipment or kinds of drinks. When planning your story, follow these guidelines: (a) keep your story short, no more than two or three pages; (b) make it a story—not an essay—with characters, dialogue, and a sequence of events; (c) remember that characters do not have to be human; (d) fill your story with specific details; (e) avoid any direct statement of your story's point; (f) consider using humor as a way to imply your point.

A CHECKLIST FOR ESSAYS USING EXAMPLES

Invention
- [ ] Have I selected a topic consistent with the instructor's guidelines for this assignment?
- [ ] Have I chosen among the possible topics one that fits my knowledge and experience?
- [ ] Have I reflected on the topic to write a tentative thesis that invites the use of examples for support?
- [ ] Have I generated a good list of possible examples to use?
- [ ] Have I given thought to a meaningful order in which to introduce each example?

Drafting
- [ ] Have I succeeded in completing a first draft at one sitting so that I can "see" the whole?
- [ ] Do I have enough—enough to meet assignment demands and enough to develop and support my thesis? If not, do I need new paragraphs or more examples or reflection within paragraphs?
- [ ] Have I explained how the examples support my thesis?
- [ ] Does the order work? If not, what needs to be moved—and where?
- [ ] Am I satisfied with the way I have expressed the insights to be gained? Have I been too heavy-handed with a message?

Revision

☐ Have I made any needed additions, deletions, or changes in order based on answering the questions about my draft?

☐ Have I revised my draft to produce coherent paragraphs, using transition and connecting words that reveal my use of several examples?

☐ Have I eliminated wordiness and clichés?

☐ Have I avoided or removed any discriminatory language?

☐ Have I used my word processor's spell check and proofread a printed copy with great care?

☐ Do I have an appropriate and interesting title?

6

Using Process Analysis
How We Work and Play

How does it work? How do we do it? How did it happen? These questions are answered when you provide a process analysis. You live with process analysis every day. The directions to the library that you give to a visitor, the mechanic's explanation of how your car engine is supposed to be working, your history text's account of the planning and execution of the D-Day invasion of Normandy, the biology instructor's explanation of the steps to follow in dissecting a frog: All of these directions, accounts, and instructions are examples of process analysis.

When to Use Process Analysis

The label "process analysis" tells us about this kind of writing. It is, first, *process* because we are talking about an activity or procedure that takes us from one situation to another, that results in some change, some goal reached. You follow the instructions on the recipe card to produce the desired carrot cake, or on the box to put together the new bookcase. You listen to the instructor's guidelines carefully so that you will end with a properly dissected frog. Process is also a type of *analysis* because the good writer of process breaks down the activity into a clear series of steps or stages. Getting the steps in a process right—absolutely right!—is essential. You have come to value the person who gives clear directions, the instructor whose guidelines help you through the stages that shaped an important period in history. You value those who write process analyses well because you have probably experienced more than one occasion of frustration over directions that were unclear, incomplete, or just plain wrong. When you have a topic that can most logically be developed as steps or stages in a process, then you will want to be one of those writers who presents the steps or stages clearly and completely for your readers.

How to Use Process Analysis

To write a clear, effective process analysis you need to keep several points in mind. First, when you are assigned a process analysis—or, more accurately, topics that can best be developed by using process analysis—you are not writing a *list* of instructions. You are writing an essay. This means that you must begin the way you begin any essay—with decisions about audience and purpose. You would not give the same directions for using a camera to a fifth-grade class that you would give to an advanced photography class at an adult education center. Similarly, when planning a process essay, you must assess your readers' knowledge of the subject as a basis for deciding how much background information and explanation are appropriate. These are really two separate decisions. One answers the question: Where do I start? The other answers the question: How detailed is my discussion of each step or stage in the process? Many "how-to" books are not really written for beginners, as you may have discovered. Instead, the author assumes more background than the beginner has.

When the process is complex, the writing challenge lies in giving sufficient explanation of each step so that readers are not too confused with step one to comprehend step two. Unless you are given an assignment that calls for a particular audience, think of directing your essays to a general adult audience made up of people like your classmates. Few of them are likely to be as knowledgeable as you are about a topic you select for your process analysis. When planning the essay, take time to include the background and explanations needed by readers who are not likely to have your knowledge and expertise.

The good essay is not only directed to a clearly defined audience; it is also unified around a clear thesis. In those instructions with the bookcase pieces, the implied thesis is: If you follow these directions you will put the bookcase together correctly. In a process essay, the thesis extends beyond the completing of the process. You must ask yourself why a reader should be interested in learning about the process topic you have selected. Ernest Hemingway wants to keep inexperienced campers from having so miserable a time that they will swear never to camp again. John Aigner explains a process for preparing for a job interview so that readers will be able to do well in their interviews and get the job.

Finally, the good essay is the interesting essay. The *HTML for Dummies* manual doesn't have to be interesting; it just has to be clear so that the computer user can complete the desired documents. But the essay, whatever its purpose or organizational strategy, needs to engage its reader, to make an audience for itself through clear explanations and interesting details. Be sure to guide your reader through the time sequence that is your basic organizational strategy. Search for transitions that are more lively than "the first step," "the second step," and so on. Here are some transition words that often appear in process essays:

after	following	second	before
later	next	then	finally
last	now	when	

In addition, when you present each step or stage, provide vivid details and concrete examples. Hemingway does not tell us in general terms to fry in the frying pan and boil in the kettle. He prepares trout and pancakes and macaroni, and an apple pie. The reader, mouth watering, is ready to start packing. Make your analysis right, make it clear, but, above all, make it interesting.

WRITING FOCUS:
PUNCTUATING PROPERLY

When you punctuate sentences properly, you show readers how the parts connect and what groups of words go together. Incorrect punctuation can confuse readers—and sometimes create unintended humor. There are many rules, but only a handful cover most situations. Here they are.

1. **Use commas to separate items in a series.**
   Winston Churchill spoke of blood, sweat, toil, and tears.
   It was Mario's idea, Ruth's organization, and Brian's technical skill that produced the winning project.
2. **Use commas to separate adjectives modifying the same noun.**
   The frisky, black, floppy-eared spaniel trotted next to her youthful, happy owner.
3. **Use a comma to set off lengthy introductory phrases and clauses.**
   Struggling to get his sentences punctuated properly, the student carefully reviewed the rules.
   Although the deli's sandwiches are just okay, their pizza is really good.
   Avoid using commas to set off short introductory elements.
   No: Yesterday, a little, old lady bought a new, red Miata.
4. **Use commas to set off parenthetical material, or interrupters.**
   Chuck, who will lose his job, is lazy.
   Do not set off restrictive material:
   Workers who are lazy will lose their jobs.
5. **Use a comma with a coordinating conjunction (and, or, but, for, nor, yet, so) to separate two independent clauses. (Independent clauses can stand alone as complete sentences.)**
   Some say Woods is the greatest golfer ever, but others argue that the honor still goes to Nicklaus.
6. **Use a semicolon (NOT a comma) to separate two independent clauses not joined with a coordinating conjunction.**
   Some say Woods is the greatest golfer ever; others argue that the honor still goes to Nicklaus.
7. **DO NOT use a comma between compound words or phrases.**
   The boat sailed out of the cove⊘and into the bay.
   The football team trotted onto the field⊘and prepared for the opening kickoff.

8. **Use a comma to prevent misreading.**
   Inside, the church was dimly lit.
   While the dog ate, the cat hid under the sofa.

Getting Started: Reflections on Your Favorite Game

If you were going to teach some element of your favorite game or sport to a beginner, how would you break down the element into steps to be taught in sequence? For example, if you were to teach the tennis serve, you might go through the following steps: the stance, the toss, the backswing, contact with the ball, and the follow-through. List steps in the process of teaching some movement, play, or strategy in your favorite game. Try this process analysis in your journal or prepare it for class discussion.

Putting Your Job Interview into Rehearsal

JOHN P. AIGNER

A graduate of City College of New York, John Aigner (b. 1937) is the founder and president of Network Résumés, a New York City career services firm. Aigner has taught courses for career counselors in addition to running his company, which helps job seekers with the process of finding desired positions. His article on preparing for a job interview was originally published in the *New York Times* on August 16, 1983.

Questions to Guide Your Reading and Reflection
1. What are the three broad steps in preparation for a job interview?
2. Have you rehearsed before interviews or class presentations

1   No actor would be so foolish as to walk onto a stage in front of a first-night audience without weeks of rehearsal. Yet every day thousands of job seekers at all stages of their careers walk

into interviews without even a minimum of preparation. Hours of effort and expense invested in an effective résumé that successfully obtained the interview are thrown away through lack of preparation.

There are three key areas in which preparation can pay big   2
dividends:

- Creating and rehearsing a personal script.
- Developing a "power vocabulary."
- Researching information about the job, company and industry.

Creation of a script and a power vocabulary are essentially   3
one-time projects that will likely remain useful with only minor variations throughout a job search. General industry-oriented information also has an extended utility during a search. The gathering of information about the company or opportunity will need to be repeated for each occasion.

Persons who might be uncertain about the basic shoulds and   4
shouldn'ts preliminary to successful interviewing—proper dress, on-time arrival, appropriate greeting—might try reading *Sweaty Palms*, by Anthony Medley, or *How to Win in a Job Interview*, by Jason Robertson.

Preparing the Script

Devising a strategy for handling difficult questions will en-   5
able you to answer them calmly and with confidence. A particularly successful approach is to make a list of the most feared questions (some excellent examples may be found in *How to Turn an Interview Into a Job*, by Jeffrey G. Allen, or *Outinterviewing the Interviewer*, by Steven Merman and John McLaughlin), and prepare a written answer to each. Then record your answers on a cassette, listen to yourself and practice, practice, practice.

Be aware that most interviewers cover the same ground, and   6
the same basic questions will appear in most interviews. This makes it relatively simple to prepare your answers. Following are some difficult questions that job-seekers may encounter, with suggestions for answering them:

- "Why did you leave your last job?" or "Why do you want to leave your present job?" Remember to be positive, not defensive. Acceptable answers are: greater opportunity, changing conditions, seeking greater responsibility. The best answers are both honest and brief.

- "Why should we hire you?" You may say that from your research you have learned that the interviewer's company is a leader in your field and you believe that your skills and its needs are well matched.
- "What are your strengths and weaknesses?" For many interviewees this question is the most intimidating. This is where preparation and a positive approach are most rewarding. One of the best ways to deal with a weakness is to refer to it as "an area in which I am working to strengthen my skills." Some career advisers suggest responding with, "Well, I don't really have any major weaknesses, but . . ." This is not a satisfactory answer, and would annoy me if I were the interviewer.

7   One general rule is never to answer a serious or really difficult question off the top of your head. Ask for an opportunity to think the question over, and promise to get back to the interviewer the next day. This approach has the added benefit of giving you a follow-up, second opportunity to sell yourself.

8   Have a friend or relative ask you the questions as many times as necessary for you to feel comfortable with the answers. Three to six hours spent practicing in this way will result in greatly improved confidence during interviews. If you think of additional questions later or if an interviewer throws you a curve, you can update your recorded answers.

9   The interviewer controls the flow of an interview, but the interviewee controls the content. If you know what you want to say, you will be more likely to say it, and you will have provided yourself with a powerful tool to maintain control of even a difficult interview.

The Power Vocabulary

10   A survey conducted among personnel executives by the Bureau of National Affairs concluded that the interview was the single most important factor in landing a job and that most applicants were rejected because they didn't promote themselves well during the interview. They frequently preface their description of an experience with, "Well, I only . . ." or "That wasn't a major part of my job." By such a deprecating phrase, they devalue their experience.

11   This lack of confidence about self-promotion is particularly true of women, an American Management Association study

has concluded. Men, it seems, have had more practice at competition and are less reticent when it comes to advertising
their accomplishments.

You should consider the interviewer to be in the same cate-   12
gory as the tax auditor. He or she is not your friend, and you
are under no obligation to volunteer any information that
won't help you. In short, telling the truth and telling everything are not the same thing. If you performed well at a project,
such as setting up a computer installation or devising a new
method of taking inventory, it is not necessary to volunteer, for
example, that the project lasted only a short while. If asked directly, of course answer honestly.

The words you select to describe yourself during the inter-   13
view will have a powerful effect on the outcome. These words
can be planned in advance. In the same way that you planned
a script for the interview, you can also plan a vocabulary of
"power" words that will create an accumulation of positive impressions about you and your accomplishments.

Consider this example: "I reduced costs" versus "I trimmed   14
costs." The word "reduce" conjures up a fat person who is trying to lose weight. The word "trim" brings to mind someone
who is fit and healthy.

Or: "While at company X, I . . ." versus "I am proud of the   15
fact that while at company X, I . . ." The latter approach is much
stronger and more positive.

16   Use only positive words, ones that create strong mental im-   16
ages, adjectives such as accurate, dynamic, proficient, reliable,
thorough, and verbs such as expedite, generate, improve, mo-
tivate, persuade, solve. These descriptors will add spice if you
pepper your interview with them.

17   You can learn to develop a winning interview style by se-   17
lecting ten winning words each week and writing them on
index cards. Practice using them in sentences about yourself,
using one word per sentence. Select words with which you feel
comfortable and work them into phrases within your script.
You'll quickly discover that these words affect your self-image
and the image that others have of you.

18   Avoid complaints of any kind. Do not criticize your previ-   18
ous company, supervisor or position. A complaint is always
negative, and that is not the impression you wish to create.

Gathering Information

19   Valuable information about an industry, and about particular companies within it, can be acquired through a library source such as Standard & Poor's, or annual reports, or through the trade press. This is an excellent way to learn the jargon of an industry. These special-interest professional and business publications have mushroomed like cable channels, and are frequently overlooked by job seekers because most are not available on newsstands and are not sold to the general public. There are thousands of these publications—privately circulated newsletters, weekly newspapers, slick monthlies, annual directories and everything in between. They contain a wealth of insider information—for example, industrywide trends and concerns, corporate plans, new-product announcements, trade jargon.

20   A sample copy or even a free subscription is generally available for the asking. To track down the trade press in your industry, check the *Standard Periodical Directory, Gebbe Press All-in-One Directory, The Encyclopedia of Business Information Sources, Ayers Guide to Periodicals* or *Standard Rate and Data.* For articles on particular business subjects, check the *Business Periodicals Index.*

21   Being current on industry concerns in general and company problems in particular can go a long way toward making an interview successful.

Expanding Vocabulary

Examine the following words in their contexts in the essay and then write a brief definition or synonym of each one. (Do not use a dictionary; try to guess each word's meaning from its context.) The number in parentheses is the number of the paragraph in which the word appears.

preliminary (4)   accumulation (13)
intimidating (6)   descriptors (16)
deprecating (10)   jargon (19)
devalue (10)   mushroomed (19)
reticent (11)

Understanding Content

1. List the specific steps within the first step: preparing the script. Why is it possible to prepare basically one script?

2. List the specific steps for developing a power vocabulary.
3. Why does it help to think of the interviewer as similar to a tax auditor?
4. What is the procedure for gathering information? What are the advantages beyond preparation for a specific interview?

Drawing Inferences about Thesis and Purpose

10

1. What is Aigner's thesis—what is the point of his process analysis?
2. When advising people on how to sell themselves, one invites the charge of encouraging misrepresentation, of "packaging" the interviewee. How does Aigner seek to avoid this charge? How does he try to balance polishing one's interview skills with a fair presentation of one's qualifications?

11

Analyzing Strategies and Style

1. What analogy does Aigner use throughout his article? Where does he introduce the comparison? Where does he refer to it again? Is this an effective analogy? Why or why not? 12
2. Aigner's introduction runs to several paragraphs, but his conclusion is only one paragraph containing one sentence. Does it seem too abrupt to you? Can you make the case that it is an effective ending?
3. Examine Aigner's metaphors in paragraphs 1, 8, and 16. How are they effective? What do they contribute to the article?

Thinking Critically

1. Will you now prepare for an interview in any of the ways Aigner 13
suggests? If so, do you think the process helped you in the interview? If not, would you follow Aigner's steps the next time? Why or why not?
2. Is there one step in Aigner's process that would be especially important in your career field? If so, how would it make you a better interviewee in your career field?
3. Aigner emphasizes the similarity of most job interviews. Had you 14
thought about this point before? Does the idea seem sensible? How can understanding this characteristic of interviews help to make the interview process a little easier?
4. Aigner gives the most space to developing a power vocabulary. Is 15
there some good advice here that extends beyond the interview process? How important are positive attitudes about ourselves?

Improving Your Body Language Skills

SUZETTE H. ELGIN

A professor emeritus in linguistics from San Diego State University, Suzette Elgin (b. 1936) is the author of several books on language use, including *Try to Feel It My Way* (1996) and *How to Disagree without Being Disagreeable* (1997). She has also written several science fiction novels. "Improving Your Body Language Skills" is a section from Elgin's book *Genderspeak* (1997). Here Elgin offers guidelines for finding the most respected way of speaking American English and for understanding the messages in body language.

Questions to Guide Your Reading and Reflection

1. What are the characteristics of the ideal adult voice for American speakers of English?
2. When you speak, what do others "hear" in your voice?

1   Body language problems between men and women who are speakers of American Mainstream English [AME] today begin at the most basic of nonverbal levels: with the *pitch* of the voice. The admired voice for the AME culture is the adult male voice; the deeper and richer it is, and the less nasal it is, the more it is admired. Women tend to pitch their voices higher than men do, and this is a strike against them in almost every language interaction. Not because there is anything inherently wrong with high-pitched voices, but because AME speakers associate them with children. A high-pitched voice that's also nasal is heard as the voice of a *whiny* child. People know, of course, that they're hearing an adult woman (or, for the occasional man with a high-pitched voice, an adult male). But at a level below conscious awareness they tend to perceive the voice as the voice of a child. This perception, however much it is in conflict with reality, affects their response to and their behavior toward the speaker.

2   The contrast in voice pitch isn't really a *physiological* matter; the difference between adult male and female vocal tracts is too minor to account for it in the majority of people. In many other cultures, male voices are higher than those of AME-speaking men, although the physical characteristics of the males are the

same. When American adults speak to infants, they pitch their voices lower as they talk to boys, and the infants respond in the same way. Females learn, literally in the bassinet and playpen, that they are expected to make higher-pitched sounds than males are.

In addition to the difference in baseline pitch, AME-speaking women's voices have more of the quality called *dynamism:* They use more varied pitch levels, they move from one pitch to another more frequently, and they are more likely than men's voices are to move from one pitch to another that's quite a bit higher or lower. In other situations the term "dynamic" is a compliment, while "monotonous," its opposite, is a negative label. But not in language; not in the AME culture. The less monotonous a woman's voice is, the more likely it is that her speech will be described by others as "emotional" or "melodramatic." Monotony in the male voice, however, is ordinarily perceived as evidence of strength and stability. (For a detailed discussion of these differences, see McConnell-Ginet 1983.) 3

Certainly male/female body language differences go beyond the voice. There are positions and gestures and facial expressions that are more typical of one gender than of the other. But the effect one gender achieves by learning to use such items of body language from the other gender is rarely positive. A woman who hooks her thumbs into her belt, spreads her feet wide, and juts out her chin usually looks foolish, as does a man who carefully crosses his legs at the ankles. There are a few stereotypically feminine items that reinforce the "childish" perception which a woman can be careful *not* to use, such as giggling behind her hand or batting her eyelashes. But the most useful thing any woman—or man—can do to get rid of the perceptually filtered "I'm listening to a child" effect is to make the voice lower, and less nasal, and more resonant, so that it will be perceived as an *adult* voice. 4

This is something that anyone not handicapped by a physical disability that interferes with voice quality can do. One way to do it is to put yourself in the hands of a competent voice *coach.* If you have the time and money to do that, and you live where such experts are available, that's an excellent idea. On the other hand, it's also something you can do by yourself, using an ancient technique that in the *Gentle Art* system is called *simultaneous modeling. . . .* 5

6   Let me make one thing clear, however, before we go on. I'm not suggesting that anyone, of either gender, "should" try to change the quality of their voice. As is true for many linguistic questions, this is not a moral issue but an issue of cultural fashion. Low voices are not "better" than high voices. In the same way that some people insist on their right to wear jeans in an office where everyone else dresses more formally, people have every right to take the position that the voice they have is the voice they prefer to have. I approve of that, one hundred percent. However, because that decision can have grave consequences, people need to be aware that the consequences exist and that the choice is theirs to make.

7   It's unacceptable for someone to be unaware that the primary reason for his or her communication problems is a high-pitched voice, and to assume that the problems are caused by the lack of a "powerful vocabulary," or a thin enough body, or a sufficiently expensive blazer, or some such thing. It's also unacceptable for those who do realize what the problem is to believe they're helpless to do anything about it. Except in cases requiring medical attention, *anyone,* working alone, can change his or her voice to make it closer to what our culture perceives as the ideal and adult voice. When a medical condition complicates the issue, the potential for improvement may be less, but even limited change toward the ideal can bring about significant positive effects.

8   The facts about body language and its critical importance to communication can be frightening. We don't study body language in school, and few of us are given formal training in the subject. We read everywhere that "a more powerful vocabulary" is our ticket to communication success, and that seems easy—just buy a book or a software program and learn some new words. Improving our body language skills seems mysterious and difficult by contrast. But there's no need to be intimidated; it's simpler than you think.

9   Your internal grammar, the same one that you use to put the right endings on your words and arrange your words in the proper order in your sentences, contains all the rules for body language in your culture. You just haven't had convenient *access* to that information that would let you use it consciously and strategically. The sections that follow will help you establish that access.

Developing Your Observational Skills

The first step in developing observational skills for nonver-   10
bal communication is simply learning to PAY ATTENTION to
the speaker's body and voice. Men in the AME culture tend
not to do this, and to be unaware that it matters; when they do
pay attention they usually follow a rule that tells them to pay
attention only to the speaker's face. Women do somewhat better, not because they have any built-in biological advantage,
but because it is universally true that those having less power
pay more attention to the body language of those having more
power. (In the most primitive situations, this means being alert
to the movements of the powerful person so that you will be
able to get out of the way before the powerful person grabs or
hits you.)

This gender difference is well known. In 1975 a footnote in   11
the *Virginia Law Review* suggested that perhaps women should
be excluded from jury duty, because their skill at observing and
interpreting nonverbal communication might make them ex-
cessively vulnerable to body language effects, interfering with
the defendant's right to an independent and unbiased jury.
("Notes: Judges' Nonverbal Behavior in Jury Trials: A Threat to
Judicial Impartiality," *Virginia Law Review,* 1975, 61:1266–1298.
For a review of research and an account of experiments prov-
ing that the body language of trial judges has a significant impact on jury decisions, see Blanck et al. 1985.)

Sometimes this language skill is an advantage for women;   12
sometimes it's not. Like any other skill, it depends on how it is
used. Nobody likes the idea that another person is able to read
his or her mind. The woman who expresses in words what a
man's body language tells her—with claims such as "I can tell
by the look on your face that you don't want to go to St. Louis"
or "Don't try to tell me you want to go to St. Louis; the way you
keep wiggling your index fingers gives you away every
time"—is almost sure to provoke hostility. Such remarks are
equally counterproductive coming from men who have well-
developed body language reading skills.

The only way to learn to pay attention to body language is   13
to *practice.* You have to work at it consciously until you become
so skilled that you do it automatically, just as you would work
at your tennis or your golf or a favorite handicraft. If you're not

accustomed to body language observation, you'll find it extremely difficult at first. You'll keep *forgetting* to do it.

14   You've probably had the experience of "coming to" as you take the last highway exit on your drive home and realizing that you have no memory of your previous ten minutes on the road. In the same way, you'll start out carefully observing someone's body language and then suddenly realize that it's been five minutes since you were consciously aware of anything but the words, and perhaps the facial expression, of the speaker. If you continue to work at it, however, you'll get past this stage. As a first practice partner, I strongly recommend your television set. Unlike living persons, the TV set doesn't get tired, doesn't wonder why you're staring at it, is always available at your convenience, and—best of all— never gets its feelings hurt.

Establishing Baseline Values—and Spotting Deviations from Them—in Body Language

15   Body language baselines are profiles of people's speech when they're relaxed, as in casual conversations with close friends. Baselines include such information as the typical pitch of the voice, rate of speed for speech, frequency of eyeblink, body posture, number of hand gestures, etc., for the individual you're interacting with, during *relaxed communication*. This information is important because a *deviation* from the baseline— a move away from these typical values—is a signal to be alert. It indicates some sort of emotional involvement, positive or negative; it indicates that something is happening; sometimes it indicates an attempt to deceive or mislead you.

16   You will have read books or listened to tapes telling you that when you see a person cross his arms or scratch her nose it *means* a particular thing. You'll read that crossed arms signal defensiveness and disagreement with what you're saying; you'll hear that scratching the nose signals anxiety. Sometimes that's true, of course; but much of the time it means the person you're observing is cold or has a nose that itches. When such items *are* reliable, they hold for a restricted population in specific circumstances—usually for the middle class or upper class dominant white male in a business situation. Learning to es-

tablish baseline values for the other person and spotting deviations from that baseline is a great deal more reliable, and will be useful to you in every communication situation, including interactions with people from outside your own culture.

For example, one of the most reliable clues to anxiety, a lack   17
of sincere commitment to what's being said, and a possible intention to deceive is a change to a higher voice pitch. But you won't know there's been a change unless you have first learned what pitch the speaker uses in normal everyday conversation. The same thing is true for other deviations from baseline values. Here are two simple and practical ways to get the necessary information:

- Make a phone call to the individual in advance of your meeting and discuss something entirely neutral, like how to get to the meeting site.
- When you're with the other person, don't begin by talking about anything important. Instead, spend five minutes—or as long as it takes—making small talk on neutral subjects.

Now we can move on to improving your body language   18
performance skills, as opposed to observation alone.

Simultaneous Modeling

When students learn t'ai chi, they learn not by watching the   19
teacher and then trying out the posture or movement by themselves but by watching and then moving *with* the teacher. This technique has been successful for thousands of years. If you've studied a foreign language, you're familiar with the traditional procedure: Listen to a sequence of the foreign language, and then, during the pause provided, repeat what you've just heard. At the University of California San Diego, instead of repeating the foreign language sequence *after* the recorded model, students listen to it several times to become familiar with the content and then speak simultaneously *with* the model. This technique (developed at UCSD by linguist Leonard Newmark) consistently produces results far superior to the traditional method. And there are many cultures in which people learn to do things (weaving, for example) by first watching someone who already knows how and then sitting down beside that person and working along with her or him.

20   These are all examples of *simultaneous modeling*. They take *advantage* of the way human brains work instead of fighting against it. When you change your behavior to make it like someone else's you have to make many small adjustments all over your body, all at once. You can't do that very well *consciously*. But your brain can do it competently and successfully, if you just stay out of its way. You can use this information and your brain's built-in skills to improve the quality of your voice, by adapting Newmark's foreign language teaching method.

21   Changing voice quality requires an array of small but crucial adjustments. You have to change the tension of the muscles of your tongue and throat and chest, you have to move the parts of your vocal tract in ways that you're not used to, and so on. When you listen to a foreign language sequence and try to repeat it afterward, you not only have to make all those adjustments but you have to *remember* the sequence. The final result is that you change your speech to match the sequence you *remember* instead of the one you actually heard. When you speak *with* the model voice instead of repeating on your own, this doesn't happen. Your brain takes over and does all the adjustments, matching your voice to the model.

Working with the Tape Recorder

22   You need a tape recorder (an inexpensive one will do), a few blank tapes, and a tape about thirty minutes long by someone of your own gender whose voice sounds the way you'd like to sound. For men, I recommend television anchorman Peter Jennings, or one of the male announcers on National Public Radio's regular news programs ("Morning Edition" or "All Things Considered," for example). For women I recommend a tape of Diane Sawyer or one of the female NPR newscasters. If you prefer someone else, either a public figure or someone in your own circle, that's fine. Just be sure the voice you choose as your model is one that you and others perceive as strong, resonant, pleasant, compelling, and—above all—the voice of a *mature adult*. Then follow the steps below, at your own convenience, at your own speed, and in privacy.

23   1. Make a twenty- to thirty-minute *baseline* tape of your own speech, write down the date on which it was made, and keep it for com-

parison with tapes you make later on. Don't read aloud, and don't say something memorized—just *talk.* Talk about your childhood, or why you have trouble communicating with people of the opposite sex, or anything else you can talk about easily and naturally.

2. Listen to the tape you've chosen as a model, all the way through, 24 to get a general idea of its content. Don't write it down, and don't try to memorize it—doing either of those things just gets in the way and keeps you from succeeding.

3. Choose a sentence of average length to work with, from any point 25 on the tape. Listen to it a couple of times, to become familiar with it. Then repeat it, SPEAKING ALONG WITH THE TAPE, SIMULTANEOUSLY. Rewind the tape and do it again, as many times as you feel are necessary—ten times is not in any way unusual. Your goal is to be able to speak smoothly and easily with the model. Don't *struggle.* Trust your brain and let it carry out its functions without interference.

4. When you're bored with the sentence you chose, pick another 26 sentence and repeat Step #3. You should also move on whenever you realize that you know a sentence so well that you've stopped needing the model voice; you aren't interested in learning to *recite* the tape. Continue in this way until you've finished the tape or achieved your goal, whichever happens first. (And go on to another model tape if you find that you need one.)

5. After about ten hours of practice (and after every additional five 27 or six hours), make a new baseline tape of your own speech. Listen to it, and compare it with the earlier ones. When you're satisfied with the change you hear, STOP. The point of this technique is to improve your *own* voice. You don't want people to think you're doing Peter Jennings or Diane Sawyer imitations when you talk; if you go on too long, that's exactly what will happen.

How long this will take will depend on the amount of time 28 you have for practice, how tired you are, whether you are a person who learns well by listening, and other individual factors. Try to make each practice session at least fifteen minutes long; thirty minutes is even better. Try to practice every other day, roughly. If all you can manage is ten minutes once a week, put in those ten minutes—just be prepared for it to take you much longer to achieve results on that basis. Remember: It doesn't make any *difference* how long it takes. You're not paying by the hour when you use this technique, and there won't be a final exam. Relax and let it take as long as it takes. Some of my clients have noticed substantial improvement in six weeks; others have needed six months or more for the same results.

29   The fact that you can't just take a Voice Quality Pill and change instantly is actually a good thing. The people you interact with regularly (and especially the person or persons you live with) need to be able to get used to the change in your voice gradually. You don't want your partner to leave in the morning, accustomed to the voice you've always had, and come home that night to someone who sounds like an entirely different person. A pleasant adult voice is a powerful tool for improving your relationships, but it shouldn't come as a *shock* to those around you.

30   **Note:** You can also use this procedure to learn to speak other varieties of English—other dialects or other registers—at will. If you feel that your native accent sometimes holds you back in the American Mainstream English environment, simultaneous modeling is a good way to learn a variety of English that's more helpful. Moving back and forth among varieties—called *codeswitching*—is a valuable skill.

Working with the Television Set

31   A voice coach (or an "image" coach) may be beyond the financial limits for many of us. It's fortunate that we have our television sets available to use as free coaches. In exactly the same way that you can improve your voice quality by speaking along with a tape recorded model, you can improve the rest of your body language by *moving* simultaneously with a model on videotape. Ideally, you will also have a VCR, so that you can work with a single tape over a period of time. If you have a video camera (or can rent one), to let you make a baseline video of your body language, that's also a plus. But if those items aren't available to you, choose as a model someone of your own gender that you can see on television several times a week, and practice moving simultaneously with that person at those times. As with voice quality, stop *before* you find yourself doing impersonations of your model.

32   I don't recommend that women try to learn "male body language" by working with a videotape of a male speaker, or that men work with a videotape of a woman to learn "female body language." (The fact that the latter alternative is wildly unlikely outside the entertainment field is consistent with the power relationships in our society.) Cross-gender modeling is a bad idea, full of hidden hazards and boobytraps, and it almost al-

ways backfires. If you're gifted with the sort of superb acting ability that would let you do this *well*, like Dustin Hoffman playing the heroine in the movie *Tootsie*, you're not someone who needs improved body language anyway. You will be far more successful with the body language of a strong and competent adult of your own gender.

If you believe you have a long way to go in acquiring satis- 33 factory body language skills, if you feel self-conscious trying to acquire them, if your opportunities to practice them are few and far between, by all means rely on the TV set. You can move on to practice with live partners when you feel more at ease.

Expanding Vocabulary

Study the definitions of any of the following words that are unfamiliar to you. Then use each of the words in a separate sentence. The number in parentheses is the number of the paragraph in which the word appears.

perceptually (4)   vulnerable (11)
resonant (4)   boobytraps (32)
intimidated (8)

Understanding Content

1. What are the characteristics of a "whiny child's" voice?
2. How hard is it to improve body language skills?
3. What is the first step to improving body language skills? What is a good way to practice?
4. What are body language baseline profiles? Why are they useful to establish?
5. How do you establish baseline profiles?
6. What is meant by "simultaneous modeling"? Why does it work well?
7. What can you change using simultaneous modeling?
8. Summarize the process of using a tape recorder to change your voice quality.
9. Summarize the process of working with a TV to improve your body language. What should be your standard to work with?

Drawing Inferences about Thesis and Purpose

1. What is Elgin's position on changing one's voice quality? Should the typical male voice be set as a standard for everyone?
2. What is Elgin's purpose in writing?
3. What is her thesis?

Analyzing Strategies and Style

1. What tone of voice do you "hear" in this essay? Do you respond to the author as a sympathetic teacher? Support your response.
2. Elgin uses italics and even all caps for some words. Why? What do they contribute?

Thinking Critically

1. Have you thought about the idea that the typical male voice is considered standard and that many women are perceived as talking like children? Does the idea make sense to you? Why or why not?
2. Why is it important to develop sensitivity to body-language messages?
3. Do you agree that women tend to be better at this sensitivity than men? Does Elgin's explanation for this tendency make sense? Why or why not?
4. Are you going to tape yourself and examine your voice quality and body language? Why or why not?

How to Turn No Into Yes!

CAROLINE HWANG

Caroline Hwang is an editor and writer whose essays have appeared in many publications including *Glamour, Redbook,* and *Newsweek.* She is a graduate of the University of Pennsylvania and holds a MFA degree from New York University. Her first novel, *In Full Bloom,* was published in 2003. In the following article, appearing originally in *Good Housekeeping,* Hwang provides good advice for both work and play situations.

Questions to Guide Your Reading and Reflection

1. What are the three situations for which Hwang offers advice?
2. What strategies do you usually use to try to get what you want? Do they work?

1   Can we be frank? Getting what you want isn't as easy as it used to be. Begging, badgering, and sulking may work, but only if you're under the age of ten. Don't necessarily count on

logical arguments either. Unless there are a lot of Supreme Court justices in your life, the people you need to persuade—your husband, a boss, a friend—won't base their decision on anything as simple as a preponderance of evidence. People factor in their own vested interest, as well as how they feel about the person making the request and what the consequences of saying yes will be. Persuasion is the key—and since every relationship has different power dynamics, you must tailor your tactics if you want to prevail, says Kathleen McGinn, Ph.D., a professor at Harvard Business School who teaches negotiation. So try these customized strategies—and get used to getting your way.

1. Persuade your husband

WHAT YOU WANT: His sign-off on a major expense.   2

After however many years of marriage, your wish has   3
stopped being his command. Yes, he loves you and wants you to be happy—but marriage is a gnarly knot of emotions and material interests and when it comes to money, the same man who promised to love, honor, and cherish may not immediately fall into line. So if you want his financial buy-in for, say, a new car or a major renovation—something you know the family can afford but that you want more than he does—negotiate as if this were a business deal.

Appeal to his self-interest. "Your position is vulnerable if the   4
best case you can make is 'I want it,'" says McGinn. In an argument over finances, concerns about solvency and security will trump either partner's desires. You'd feel the same if he wanted a Porsche.

A smarter approach, says McGinn, is to emphasize how   5
your husband and family will benefit: "You've got to show that what you're asking for isn't just for you." Bonnie Jacobson, Ph.D., a professor at New York University and a psychologist in private practice, agrees. One couple whom she counseled were fighting over remodeling their kitchen. "The husband didn't care about decorating, so he thought the whole thing was a waste of money," recalls Jacobson. But he was a devoted father, and after listening to his wife, "he realized that the kids would have a better-lit, more inviting space to do their homework." This approach could also work on the new-car front: If

you and the kids spend a lot of time on the road, driving to school and events, a newer model could make a big difference in your family's comfort and, often, safety.

6 Put the ball in his court. If your husband isn't sold on your pitch, fall back on the old forensics-team strategy of flipping the discussion. "Ask him to explain why your suggestion is a bad idea," says Kerry Patterson, Ph.D., coauthor of *Crucial Conversations*. Generally, it's harder to prove a negative, why the improvement should not be made, than a positive.

7 Share the credit. Once he agrees to the idea, immediately begin talking about the project or purchase as if you'd both thought of it. Including your husband should create a feeling of harmony between the two of you—which is what you want, says Jacobson; otherwise, you "could've just bulldozed forward without him."

8 DEAL BREAKER: "Don't you want me to be happy?"

9 DEAL MAKER: "This isn't for me. It's for the family."

2. Convince your boss

10 *WHAT YOU WANT: A flexible work arrangement.*

11 Bosses often expect us to act as if we don't have families," says Patterson. So when our personal needs intrude on business—for example, the baby-sitter breaks her leg, or you want to work from home one day a week—many of us are confused about how to approach our boss.

12 The most important thing you can do is behave in a businesslike way. That's because, even if you and your manager are chums, you're in what McGinn calls an exchange relationship. You're there for the paycheck—and your boss, however nice she may be, is there to make sure you get the work done. You shouldn't talk to her as if she's a friend or appeal to her as a fellow mother or wife.

13 Make your request in person. It's easy to e-mail a no; it's harder to say it right to someone's face.

14 Act strong, not weak. "Your attitude should be positive, engaged, and problem solving," says McGinn—not mopey, sad, and "woe is me."

15 Make it clear that the new arrangement won't affect your output. Need to take days off during a particularly busy time? Tell your boss exactly how you'll complete your work on

schedule. Want to come in late every Wednesday? Explain that one of your colleagues has agreed to cover for you until 10:00—and once you arrive, you'll work straight through without taking lunch.

Whatever you do, don't frame your request as a special 16 favor. "Managers are accustomed to thinking about policy—not about individuals," explains Rachel Croson, Ph.D., a negotiations professor at the Wharton School of the University of Pennsylvania. Undoubtedly, your boss will worry that if she gives you what you want, she'll have to give it to everyone. So if the company has ever agreed to a similar arrangement, remind your boss that there's a precedent for what you're asking.

Don't get emotional. Pouring out your heart about how your 17 kids rarely see you is counterproductive, says William Ury, author of *Getting Past No: Negotiating Your Way from Confrontation to Cooperation*. Instead, explain how Fridays at home will make you a more effective worker, then come up with a way to measure that—for instance, commit to a faster timetable for a project and suggest evaluating the new schedule after two months.

Don't promise too much. To convince your boss that you're 18 serious, you may find yourself offering to take on more than your regular workload. But that isn't necessary or even advisable. "Your argument should be that your boss will lose nothing by granting your request," says Croson. "And you should stick to that."

Have a fallback plan. If your idea to work from home on Fri- 19 days is nixed—and, realistically, it is a tough sell—suggest every other Friday, says Ury: "An effective negotiator has an alternative in her back pocket."

DEAL BREAKER: "I'm up the creek and I need your help." 20
DEAL MAKER: "With this new arrangement, I'll get more 21 done in a shorter period of time."

3. Win over your friend

WHAT YOU WANT: A big favor. 22
Unlike your boss, a friend is in your life purely because 23 she likes you. (We're talking close pals here—not someone in the carpool.) While this makes for a happy relationship, it's tough in a negotiation, because it means that even if your request is reasonable and within her power (watching your

kids a few days a week so you can take a class), you have no real leverage. If she says no, your only remaining weapon is to threaten to stop speaking to her—which wouldn't be very friendly on your part. You can tell her that if she helps you, you'll owe her, big-time. But friends don't usually call in chits—at least not explicitly, which is why you also can't remind her of the many times you've leaped to her aid. So how do you win this one?

24   Throw yourself on her mercy. "Friends care about each other, so if she sees how dire the situation is, she'll most likely feel inclined to do what she can," says McGinn.

25   Make your plea in a way that emphasizes how close you are. McGinn offers a recent experience of her own as an example: "When a friend asked to borrow money, she said to me, 'I hate doing this, but the only other people I can turn to are my parents.' Now, she and I have known each other since we were 16, and so I immediately said yes, because she was the person by my side when I was rebelling against my parents."

26   Raise the stakes. If your friend just won't say yes, it's probably because the cost to her seems higher than the benefit would be to you, says Croson. Your task, then, is to swing that balance by making it clear how very important this request is. Let her know that you need the class in order to get a better job, because you and your husband just aren't making enough to meet expenses. If you've asked to borrow money, tell her something you might have withheld up until now (that your husband lost money on a bad investment, or your mother needs financial help). If the benefit to you is clearly greater than the cost to her, a real friend won't be able to resist.

27   DEAL BREAKER: "How can you not help me, after all the times I've helped you?"

28   DEAL MAKER: "You're my only hope."

Expanding Vocabulary

Examine the following words in their contexts in the essay and then write a brief definition or synonym of each one. Avoid using a dictionary; try to guess each word's meaning from its context. The number in parentheses is the number of the paragraph in which the word appears.

preponderance (1) chits (23)
solvency (4) explicitly (23)
precedent (16) dire (24)
leverage (23)

Understanding Content

1. What steps should a wife take to persuade a husband? What should she *not* say?
2. What steps should you take to persuade a boss? What should you avoid saying?
3. What steps should you follow to get a favor from a friend? What should you *not* say?
4. Why is the negotiation with a friend often difficult?

Drawing Inferences about Thesis and Purpose

1. Hwang provides a "deal breaker" for each situation. What do the three have in common; that is, what, in general, are we being warned not to do?
2. What do the steps in each of the three situations have in common; that is, what are the key strategies to follow, regardless of the situation?
3. Write a thesis for the essay.

Analyzing Strategies and Style

1. Analyze the author's opening paragraph. What does it accomplish? What makes it successful?
2. Who is Hwang's primary audience? How can you tell from the way she presents her examples?
3. What is clever about each "deal breaker" and "deal maker"?

Thinking Critically

1. Have you thought of asking for something from a spouse or friend as similar to asking for something in the workplace? Does this idea make sense to you? Explain.
2. Reflect on the psychology involved in each negotiation. Does Hwang seem to you to be offering good advice—strategies that are likely to work? Why or why not?
3. Hwang asserts that logic, a good argument, may not help us achieve our goals. Is her power-play approach a realistic view of people, or too harsh? Support your response.

How to Get Unstuck Now!

GAIL SALTZ

Dr. Saltz is a psychoanalyst with a private practice; she is also on the faculty of the New York Presbyterian Hospital, is a health contributor to several TV shows, and writes a weekly column on *MSNBC.com*. Her first book, *Becoming Real: Defeating the Stories We Tell Ourselves That Hold Us Back,* was published in 2004. A book for children and parents is scheduled for 2005 publication. The following article was published in *Parade* magazine on March 20, 2005.

Questions to Guide Your Reading and Reflection

1. What kinds of people make up the two groups of procrastinators?
2. Do you ever procrastinate? If so, would you like to get "unstuck"?

1   David looks miserable as he tells me that, once again, he has to pay a late penalty for failing to turn in his taxes on time. He feels angry and guilty that this delay will now cost him the money he was saving for the family vacation. His family and friends have been calling him lazy for years. It seems to him that the harder he tries to "get it right," the worse his procrastinating gets. "It's ruining my relationships and holding me back at work," he says. "Why am I doing this?"

2   Maria, on the other hand, had always gotten things done on time—until she was up for a promotion. Suddenly, this very conscientious woman was late with her assignments. She knew that she was screwing up her chances for advancement yet was baffled as to why she kept doing it.

Who Procrastinates?

3   David is one of the 20 percent of Americans considered "chronic procrastinators." Maria, like the majority of us, is an occasional procrastinator whose repeated delays take place in a particular realm.

4   Almost everyone procrastinates some of the time. The results can range from annoyance to misery—for both the person doing it and those affected by it. Research has shown that procrastinators tend to feel extremely stressed, resulting in more

insomnia, colds and stomachaches than nonprocrastinators suffer. In one survey of 300 college students who confessed to being procrastinators, nearly half said they would rather donate blood than write an assigned paper; almost a third said they would rather visit the dentist; and more than one in five said they would rather pick up trash on campus.

Both men and women suffer from anxiety as a result of procrastination. Interestingly, women suffer from guilt as well—nearly twice as often as men. 5

Why We Procrastinate

Too often procrastinators receive the advice from professionals or others to just "quit it." Would that it were really that simple! The idea that procrastinators are simply lazy is a myth, and their behavior rarely is changed by just deciding to stop. Laziness might respond to giving yourself a good kick in the pants. Procrastination doesn't. 6

Unlike laziness, procrastination is caused by fears—the result of emotional stories that each of us carries around inside us. Understanding the reasons why you procrastinate ultimately can change your behavior and your life. To do that, think about what it means to you to get things done and about the stuff you're putting off. See which of the following stories resonates with you: 7

"I'm so afraid of failing that I would rather not try than to try but fail." Fear of failure probably is the most common story. If that's you, you may be a perfectionist who feels that doing a "just OK" task is mortifying. These types also believe that they need to please others in order to be accepted. In the extreme, they may believe that they are only lovable and worthwhile if their performance is outstanding. 8

"I'm afraid to be successful because people will envy me or see me as a threat, and then I'll lose them." Fear of success can lead to procrastination as well. You may imagine that if you succeed, you'll then be expected to be wildly successful all the time, or that you'll become a workaholic, or even that on some level you'll feel you are not deserving of success. All are common reasons for procrastination. 9

"I need to be defiant, or they will rule me and win." This too is a common story. If it's yours, you may believe that all of life is a battle for control. Perhaps you grew up in a home with an authoritarian parent who was extremely controlling. Some- 10 times people with this story respond to the whole world as if it were that parent and seek to passive-aggressively control that world by procrastinating.

11   "This task holds no interest for me unless it is so last-minute as to be perilous and thrilling." People who say this to themselves generally are chronic procrastinators who, unlike the others, do not appear anxious. They are the thrill-seeking, risk-taking drama lovers. If you are such a procrastinator, you may feel that the daily grind is boring, and boredom is terrifying. Waiting until the last moment lets thrill-seeking procrastinators shake things up by creating their own crisis.

Understanding Your Own Story

12   Figuring out what your fears are is an important first step. So is taking notice of which situations tend to trigger your procrastinating. Is it work, your love life, friends, your body or money? The specific arena of life in which you procrastinate is a clue as to where you feel most conflicted and afraid. That's likely to be the arena that is most important to you at this time.

13   David, the chronically late tax-filer, came to understand that he was afraid of failing. He imagined messing up his taxes, failing at his job and even disappointing his loved ones. So he avoided doing many things in order to spare himself the chance of failure. Eventually, he came to see that he had damaged them all by procrastinating. This understanding helped him to change his behaviors.

14   Maria tapped into her knowledge that her success threatened her competitive husband. Once she understood that, she was able to catch herself delaying her work and to forge ahead. She also was able to discuss the issue with her husband, who ultimately became more supportive.

Break the Pattern

15   These steps can help you (or someone you know) break the pattern of procrastination:

1. **Articulate what you get out of procrastinating**. (Examples: "I avoid risking failure"; "I can't stand to not have fun.") This is what keeps you locked in.
2. **Consider the problems your procrastination creates vs. what you think you get out of it**. (Example: "I like being a victim, but that means I never get ahead in life.")

3. **Start small**. Do the least-noxious task to get yourself rolling. Remind yourself along the way—or enlist someone else to remind you—that the actual cost of not doing it is greater than the imagined fear of getting it done.

4. **Help a procrastinator.** Living or working with a procrastinator can be exasperating. It's easier to be objective about someone else's state of mind than your own. Plus, you aren't being bogged down by anxiety or fear. But rather than blame the procrastinator in your life—which merely perpetuates the cycle of anxiety and delay—describe the story you see him or her acting out. Offer to help break the cycle.

Tackle It Now

- **Prioritize tasks**. If everything seems like a priority, you'll feel overwhelmed and get none of it done. And if nothing seems important, nothing will get done. Create a "to do" list, ranking tasks in order of priority. Marking a specific number of hours to work and to play on your calendar also helps.
- **Question your beliefs**. Do you tell yourself that you work better under pressure? Prove it. Do one task at the last minute and one ahead. Test other myths, such as "I don't have the ability" and "It has to be done perfectly."
- **Control your impulsiveness**. Most procrastinators jump from one task to the next and never finish anything. Make yourself complete one task before moving on to another.
- **Old habits die hard**. Don't expect it to change overnight. If you change one thing a week, you are making progress, and that progress will show you that more change is possible.

Expanding Vocabulary

Match each word in Column A with its definition in Column B. When in doubt, first find the word in the essay and look for context clues to aid your understanding of the word's meaning. Then, if necessary, use your dictionary to complete the matching exercise. The number in parentheses is the number of the paragraph in which the word appears.

Column A	Column B
procrastinating (1)	area, part of one's life
conscientious (2)	echoes, makes sense
realm (3)	annoying, frustrating
resonates (7)	steadily push ahead
mortifying (8)	unpleasant, poisonous

perilous (11)	putting off doing something
forge (14)	humiliating
articulate (16)	principled, thorough
noxious (18)	express in words
exasperating (19)	dangerous

Understanding Content

1. What are some consequences of procrastinating?
2. How does procrastination differ from laziness?
3. Explain each of the four "stories" that account for the behavior of most procrastinators.
4. What is the first—and most critical—step toward change? Explain the next four steps in your own words.

Drawing Inferences about Thesis and Purpose

1. Saltz opens with some interesting information about procrastination. What, though, is her primary purpose in writing? What does she want to accomplish?
2. Write a thesis for the essay that indicates that process analysis will be used as a structure for the essay.

Analyzing Strategies and Style

1. What formatting strategies aid the presentation of information? How do they help?
2. The author begins by introducing David and Maria. What does she accomplish with her opening strategy?

Thinking Critically

1. Are you a procrastinator? If so, have you found your "story"? Do you think recognizing the reasons for procrastinating will help a procrastinator change? Why or why not?
2. Saltz writes that many college students said they would rather donate blood or go to the dentist than write a paper. Does this describe your attitude toward writing? Or the attitude of students you know? How can you take Saltz's process steps and apply them specifically to paper assignments? Explain.
3. How important is it to understand the causes of our behavior? Explain.

Restoring Recess

CAROL KRUCOFF

A journalist, Carol Krucoff is a freelance writer on health and exercise topics, a syndicated health columnist, and the author of
Healing Moves (2000). Krucoff runs and holds a black belt in
karate. In "Restoring Recess," which appeared in the *Washington
Post*'s Health Section on January 12, 1999, Krucoff encourages
readers to treat daily exercise not as work but as play.

Questions to Guide Your Reading and Reflection
 1. How do adults who exercise regularly feel about it?
 2. How do you feel about regular exercise?

So here we are, just a few weeks into the new year, and if   1
you're like most Americans you're already struggling to keep
your resolution to shape up. Despite good intentions, the sad
fact is that half of all adults who start a new exercise program
drop out within six months.

Adopting a new habit isn't easy. As Sir Isaac Newton   2
pointed out, a body at rest will tend to remain at rest. Even the
promise of better health and improved appearance won't get
most people to exercise regularly.

But there is one motivator that can pry even the most con-   3
firmed "potato" off the couch. Freud called it the pleasure principle: People do things that feel good and avoid things that feel
bad. Most American adults get little or no exercise and more
than half are overweight because many of them consider exercise to be hard, painful work—a distasteful chore they must
force themselves to endure.

Yet as children we didn't feel this way about moving our   4
bodies. Most kids see physical pursuits, like skipping and running, as exciting play to be enjoyed.

So this year, meet your fitness goals by turning exercise   5
into child's play. Scratch the resolution to work out. Instead,
vow to play actively for 30 minutes most days. Think of it as

recess, and try to recapture the feeling you had as a child of being released onto the playground to swing, play ball or do whatever your little heart—and body—desired. Don't worry about flattening your abs or losing weight. Just enjoy the sensations of moving your body, breathing deeply and experiencing the moment.

6   This is your personalized playtime, so pick any form of movement that you like—a solitary walk, shooting hoops with a friend, a dance class, gardening, ping-pong, cycling. The options are vast, and nearly anything that gets you moving is fine, since even light-to-moderate exercise can yield significant health benefits.

7   The point is to stop thinking of your workout as one more demanding task you must cram into your busy day and start viewing it as a welcome recess that frees you from the confines of your chair. Most regular exercisers will tell you that this is the reason they remain active. Yes, they exercise to lose weight, build strong bones and all those other healthy reasons. But scratch deeper and most will admit that a central reason they're out there day after day is that it's fun—their exercise satisfies body and soul, and is a cherished highlight of their lives.

8   If you think this attitude adjustment is merely a mind game, you're right. Getting in shape is, after all, a matter of mind over body. But it's also a healthy way of approaching fitness, to enjoy the journey as much as reaching the destination. Goals can be helpful motivators to shape up. But once you drop a clothing size, then what?

9   So instead of being caught up in reaching a certain scale weight, view taking care of your physical self—which can play a key role in boosting your emotional self—as an opportunity for active play. This may be difficult in our culture, which considers play a frivolous time-waster. Yet "the ability to play is one of the principal criteria of mental health," wrote anthropologist Ashley Montague in his book, *Growing Young*.

10   Just as kids need the release of recess to get the "wiggles" out of the bodies, adults also need relief from the stiffness caused by sitting and the chance to oxygenate sluggish brains.

11   Next time a problem has you stumped, take it out on a walk in the fresh air—and bring along a pencil and paper. Solutions will appear on the move that eluded you at your desk.

To make your play breaks happen, schedule them into your   12
life. Lack of time is the main reason people say they don't exercise, and it's true that most of us lead very busy lives. But it's
also true that we find time for things that are important to us.
It's a matter of making choices.

You may need to get up a half hour earlier—and go to bed a   13
half hour earlier—to make your play break happen. You might
have to turn off the TV, cut short a phone call or eat lunch at
your desk to squeeze in recess. But if it's fun, it won't be a terrible sacrifice—it'll be a willing trade-off. Besides, as a wise
person once said, "If you don't make time to exercise, you'll
have to take time to be sick."

To keep your break fun, remember to: 14

1. Start slowly and progress gradually. If you've been inactive,   15
   begin with as little as five minutes of your chosen activity. Add
   on five more minutes each week with the goal of playing actively
   for 30 minutes on most days.
2. Avoid negative talk about yourself. Instead of obsessing about   16
   your thunder thighs, have an attitude of gratitude about your
   body and all that it does for you.
3. Choose a positive exercise environment. Just as fresh air and   17
   music may enhance your recess, mirrors may detract from your
   experience if you're self-critical. If so, play outdoors or in a mir-
   ror-free room.
4. Consider a few sessions with a personal trainer if you need help   18
   getting started. For a referral, call the American Council on Exercise's consumer hot line at 1-800-529-8227.
5. Vary your activity. If you like doing the same thing, day after day,   19
   great. But it's fine to move in different ways on different days, depending on your mood, the weather and other factors you find
   relevant.
6. Focus on behaviors, not on outcomes. If you consistently exercise   20
   and eat right, results will come.
7. Avoid rushing back to routine. Take a few minutes to breathe   21
   deeply and bring the refreshing spirit of playfulness back to your
   grown-up world.

Expanding Vocabulary

Study the definitions of any of the following words that are unfamiliar to you. Then use each of the words in a separate sentence. The

number in parentheses is the number of the paragraph in which the word appears.

pry (3)   oxygenate (10)
confines (7)   sluggish (10)
frivolous (9)   eluded (11)

Understanding Content

1. How many adults drop out of an exercise program within six months?
2. How many Americans are overweight?
3. How did most of us feel about movement and play when we were children?
4. How much exercise and what kinds of exercise does the author recommend?
5. What steps should we take to get back to "recess"?

Drawing Inferences about Thesis and Purpose

1. What are the advantages of exercise suggested throughout Krucoff's essay?
2. What is Krucoff's thesis?

Analyzing Strategies and Style

1. How does the author use New Year's resolutions as both an opening strategy and a way develop her essay?
2. Krucoff writes with brief paragraphs and ends with a list. What is the effect of these strategies? How does her style connect to audience and purpose?

Thinking Critically

1. Do you make New Year's resolutions to exercise more? If so, do you keep them? If not, why not?
2. Do you exercise regularly? If not, why not? How would you defend your inactivity to Krucoff?
3. Do you agree that we choose to do what is important to us? Do you think that most of us could find thirty minutes most days for exercise if we really wanted to? Explain your response.
4. Has Krucoff convinced you to treat exercise as play and to start playing more? Why or why not?

Camping Out

ERNEST HEMINGWAY

One of the most popular of twentieth-century fiction writers, Ernest Hemingway (1899–1961) is best known for his short stories and novels, especially *A Farewell to Arms, The Sun Also Rises,* and *The Old Man and the Sea.* Hemingway, winner of the Nobel Prize for Literature, began his writing career as a journalist and returned to journalism from time to time, most notably as a correspondent during the Spanish Civil War and World War II. His guidelines for a successful camping trip, first published in the *Toronto Star Weekly* in 1920, continue to provide good advice for today's campers.

Questions to Guide Your Reading and Reflection

1. What is Hemingway's purpose in writing about camping? What does he want to accomplish?
2. From your camping experience, what is one piece of advice you would give to other campers?

Thousands of people will go into the bush this summer to cut the high cost of living. A man who gets his two weeks' salary while he is on vacation should be able to put those two weeks in fishing and camping and be able to save one week's salary clear. He ought to be able to sleep comfortably every night, to eat well every day and to return to the city rested and in good condition.

But if he goes into the woods with a frying pan, an ignorance of black flies and mosquitoes, and a great and abiding lack of knowledge about cookery, the chances are that his return will be very different. He will come back with enough mosquito bites to make the back of his neck look like a relief map of the Caucasus. His digestion will be wrecked after a valiant battle to assimilate half-cooked or charred grub. And he won't have had a decent night's sleep while he has been gone.

He will solemnly raise his right hand and inform you that he has joined the grand army of never-agains. The call of the wild may be all right, but it's a dog's life. He's heard the call of the tame with both ears. Waiter, bring him an order of milk toast.

4   In the first place he overlooked the insects. Black flies, no-see-ums, deer flies, gnats and mosquitoes were instituted by the devil to force people to live in cities where he could get at them better. If it weren't for them everybody would live in the bush and he would be out of work. It was a rather successful invention.

5   But there are lots of dopes that will counteract the pests. The simplest perhaps is oil of citronella. Two bits' worth of this purchased at any pharmacist's will be enough to last for two weeks in the worst fly- and mosquito-ridden country.

6   Rub a little on the back of your neck, your forehead and your wrists before you start fishing, and the blacks and skeeters will shun you. The odor of citronella is not offensive to people. It smells like gun oil. But the bugs do hate it.

7   Oil of pennyroyal and eucalyptol are also much hated by mosquitoes, and with citronella they form the basis for many proprietary preparations. But it is cheaper and better to buy the straight citronella. Put a little on the mosquito netting that covers the front of your pup tent or canoe tent at night, and you won't be bothered.

8   To be really rested and get any benefit out of a vacation a man must get a good night's sleep every night. The first requisite for this is to have plenty of cover. It is twice as cold as you expect it will be in the bush four nights out of five, and a good plan is to take just double the bedding that you think you will need. An old quilt that you can wrap up in is as warm as two blankets.

9   Nearly all outdoor writers rhapsodize over the browse bed. It is all right for the man who knows how to make one and has plenty of time. But in a succession of one-night camps on a canoe trip all you need is level ground for your tent floor and you will sleep all right if you have plenty of covers under you. Take twice as much cover as you think that you will need, and then put two-thirds of it under you. You will sleep warm and get your rest.

10   When it is clear weather you don't need to pitch your tent if you are only stopping for the night. Drive four stakes at the head of your made-up bed and drape your mosquito bar over that, then you can sleep like a log and laugh at the mosquitoes.

Outside of insects and bum sleeping, the rock that wrecks 11
most camping trips is cooking. The average tyro's idea of cooking is to fry everything and fry it good and plenty. Now, a frying pan is a most necessary thing to any trip, but you also need
the old stew kettle and the folding reflector baker.

A pan of fried trout can't be bettered and they don't cost any 12
more than ever. But there is a good and bad way of frying them.

The beginner puts his trout and his bacon in and, over a 13
brightly burning fire, the bacon curls up and dries into a dry
tasteless cinder, and the trout is burned outside while it is still
raw inside. He eats them and it is all right if he is only out for
the day and going home to a good meal at night. But if he is
going to face more trout and bacon the next morning and other
equally well-cooked dishes for the remainder of two weeks, he
is on the pathway to nervous dyspepsia.

The proper way is to cook over coals. Have several cans of 14
Crisco or Cotosuet or one of the vegetable shortenings along that
are as good as lard and excellent for all kinds of shortening. Put
the bacon in and when it is about half cooked lay the trout in the
hot grease, dipping them in cornmeal first. Then put the bacon
on top of the trout and it will baste them as it slowly cooks.

The coffee can be boiling at the same time and in a smaller 15
skillet pancakes being made that are satisfying the other
campers while they are waiting for the trout.

With the prepared pancake flours you take a cupful of pancake 16
flour and add a cup of water. Mix the water and flour and as soon
as the lumps are out it is ready for cooking. Have the skillet hot
and keep it well greased. Drop the batter in and as soon as it is
done on one side loosen it in the skillet and flip it over. Apple butter, syrup or cinnamon and sugar go well with the cakes.

While the crowd have taken the edge from their appetites with 17
flapjacks, the trout have been cooked and they and the bacon are
ready to serve. The trout are crisp outside and firm and pink inside and the bacon is well done—but not too done. If there is anything better than that combination the writer has yet to taste it in
a lifetime devoted largely and studiously to eating.

The stew kettle will cook you dried apricots when they have 18
resumed their predried plumpness after a night of soaking, it will
serve to concoct a mulligan in, and it will cook macaroni. When
you are not using it, it should be boiling water for the dishes.

19   In the baker, mere man comes into his own, for he can make a pie that to his bush appetite will have it all over the product that mother used to make, like a tent. Men have always believed that there was something mysterious and difficult about making a pie. Here is a great secret. There is nothing to it. We've been kidded for years. Any man of average office intelligence can make at least as good a pie as his wife.

20   All there is to a pie is a cup and a half of flour, one-half teaspoonful of salt, one-half cup of lard and cold water. That will make piecrust that will bring tears of joy into your camping partner's eyes.

21   Mix the salt with the flour, work the lard into the flour, make it up into a good workmanlike dough with cold water. Spread some flour on the back of a box or something flat, and pat the dough around a while. Then roll it out with whatever kind of round bottle you prefer. Put a little more lard on the surface of the sheet of dough and then slosh a little flour on and roll it up and then roll it out again with the bottle.

22   Cut out a piece of the rolled-out dough big enough to line a pie tin. I like the kind with holes in the bottom. Then put in your dried apples that have soaked all night and been sweetened, or your apricots, or your blueberries, and then take another sheet of the dough and drape it gracefully over the top, soldering it down at the edges with your fingers. Cut a couple of slits in the top dough sheet and prick it a few times with a fork in an artistic manner.

23   Put it in the baker with a good slow fire for forty-five minutes and then take it out, and if your pals are Frenchmen they will kiss you. The penalty for knowing how to cook is that the others will make you do all the cooking.

24   It is all right to talk about roughing it in the woods. But the real woodsman is the man who can be really comfortable in the bush.

Expanding Vocabulary

Examine the following words in their contexts in the essay and then write a definition for each one. (Do not use a dictionary; try to guess the word's meaning from its context.) The number in parentheses is the number of the paragraph in which the word appears.

relief map (2)

Caucasus (2)

valiant (2)

assimilate (2)

grub (2)

dopes (5)

skeeters (6)

proprietary (7)

requisite (8)

rhapsodize (9)

browse bed (9)

tyro (11)

dyspepsia (13)

concoct (18)

mulligan (18)

Understanding Content

1. Explain the processes for coping with each of the first two problems Hemingway addresses.
2. Hemingway devotes most of his article to the third problem. Why?
3. How does he organize his guidelines for cooking?
4. When explaining pie-making, what misconception does Hemingway clear up?

Drawing Inferences about Thesis and Purpose

1. Hemingway's title announces the broad subject of camping but not his specific subject. State his subject by completing the phrase: "how to _____."
2. State a thesis for the essay.

Analyzing Strategies and Style

1. Hemingway has written a lively and entertaining essay, not a list of impersonal instructions. How did he make his process essay interesting? Discuss specific passages that you think are effective.
2. When Hemingway writes, in paragraph 4, "It was a rather successful invention," what writing technique is he using? What tone do we hear in the line?
3. Who is Hemingway's anticipated audience? Who does he think are potential campers among the newspaper's readers? What passages reveal his assumption?
4. Camping out has changed since the 1920s. Writers on this topic today would not assume a male audience, and they would be careful not to write in a sexist manner. How would this essay have to be edited to eliminate sexist writing? What specific changes would you make?
5. The essay's conclusion is brief—only two sentences. Why is it effective in spite of its brevity? How does it connect to the essay's thesis?

Thinking Critically

1. What reasons for camping does Hemingway suggest? Are these still the reasons most people camp out today?
2. Are the problems Hemingway addresses—bugs, uncomfortable sleeping, bad food—still the basic problems to be solved to enjoy a camping trip? What modern equipment can help campers with these problems?
3. Many people today go "camping" in well-equipped RVs. Is this really camping? What would Hemingway say? What do you say? Why?

MAKING CONNECTIONS

---

1. John Aigner and Caroline Hwang emphasize the importance of being prepared. Preparation is a major key to success. Does this make sense to you? If you agree, think how you would convince unprepared students of the value of preparation. If you disagree, think how you would challenge these writers.
2. John Aigner encourages interviewees to develop a power vocabulary and learn to speak only positively about themselves. Suzette Elgin gives directions for changing one's speech to be more effective. Are these writers providing useful self-help guidelines for success? Or, are they encouraging us to misrepresent ourselves to get ahead? Or, are they implying that society fails to accept diverse styles? Be prepared to debate these issues.
3. How are we expected to behave in the workplace today? Look for guides in your library's book collection or search online for advice on office behavior
4. Take an informal survey of those with whom you work or those you know at school to analyze their conversational styles. Are most direct or indirect in their speech? Are there other observations about conversational styles that are useful to note?
5. Select a company (e.g., Nike) or a sports organization (e.g., the United States Tennis Association) you are interested in and visit their Website. Analyze the Website, looking at color and graphics and the information. Does it provide useful information? Is it organized clearly? Is it engaging visually? Be prepared to discuss your Website analysis with classmates.

6. E-mailing is an important function in today's workplace. Do an online search of e-mail etiquette (netiquette) to see what you can learn about the appropriate way to use, write, and send e-mails. Consider: Should you follow these guidelines when e-mailing your professors?

TOPICS FOR WRITING

1. In an essay examine some process of change that has taken place in your life. Consider physical, emotional, intellectual, or occupational changes. Although you will use chronological order, make certain that you focus on specific *stages* or *steps* that led to the change so that you write a process analysis, not a narrative. Possible topics include: how you grew (or shrank) to the size you are now, how you developed your skill in some sport or hobby, how you changed your taste in music, how you decided on a career. Analyze the change into at least three separate stages. Explain and illustrate each stage. Reflect on *your* reason for writing about the change in your life. Then state your thesis in your first paragraph and restate it, enlarging on it, in your concluding paragraph.

2. Select a change in human society that has occurred in stages over time and that has had a significant effect on the way we live. Your thesis is the significance of the development—significance for good or ill. Develop that thesis by analyzing the process of change, the stages in development. Be sure to analyze the change into several distinct stages of development. Possible topics include technological changes (e.g., the generations of computers), changes in the classroom or school buildings, changes in recreation, and changes in dress.

3. Do you have advice to give someone preparing for a job interview, advice that is different from or in addition to the advice given by John Aigner in "Putting Your Job Interview into Rehearsal"? If so, organize your advice into a series of specific steps and write your guide to the successful interview. Your thesis, stated or implied, is that following these steps will improve one's chances of obtaining the desired position.

4. Have you taken the same type of vacation (camping, renting a beach house, sightseeing by car, traveling abroad)

several times? If so, you may have learned the hard way what to do and what not to do to have a successful vacation. In an essay, pass your knowledge along to readers. Organize your essay into a process—a series of steps or directions—but also approach your analysis by explaining both the wrong way and the right way to complete each step. Ernest Hemingway's "Camping Out" is your model for this topic.

5. Many people have misconceptions about processes or tasks they are unfamiliar with, particularly if those activities are a part of a different culture. Do you understand how to do something that others might have misconceptions about? If so, prepare a process analysis that will explain the activity and thereby clear up the reader's misconceptions. In your opening paragraph you might refer to the typical misconceptions that people have and then move on to explain how the task or activity is actually done. If your activity is part of a particular culture (how to cook with a wok, how to prepare pita bread, how to serve a Japanese dinner, how to wrap a sari), enrich your process analysis with appropriate details about that culture.

6. Some social situations can be difficult to handle successfully. If you have had success in one of them (such as asking someone for a date, meeting a close friend's or a fiancé's family, attending a large family reunion, attending the office Christmas party), then explain how to handle the situation with ease and charm. Select either a chronological ordering of steps or a list of specific instructions, including dos and don'ts. Humorous examples can be used with this topic to produce lively writing.

7. Prepare a detailed, knowledgeable explanation of a particular activity or task from your work or play for interested nonspecialists. You are the expert carefully explaining the process of, for example, bunting down the third-base line, booting up the computer, tuning an engine, building a deck, sewing a dress, or whatever you know well. Be sure to give encouragement as you give directions.

A CHECKLIST FOR PROCESS ESSAYS

Invention

- ☐ Have I selected a topic consistent with the instructor's guidelines for this assignment?
- ☐ Have I chosen among the possible topics one that fits my knowledge and experience?
- ☐ Have I reflected on the topic to write a tentative thesis that invites the use of process analysis for support?
- ☐ Have I organized my thinking into clear steps or stages?
- ☐ Have I considered my audience as a guide to where and when to start the process or how much information to include about each step?
- ☐ Do I have the correct order for the process?

Drafting

- ☐ Have I succeeded in completing a first draft at one sitting so that I can "see" the whole?
- ☐ Do I have enough—enough to meet assignment demands and enough to develop and support my thesis? If not, do I need new paragraphs or more examples or reflection within paragraphs?
- ☐ Do the steps in the process connect to and support my thesis?
- ☐ Does the order work? If not, what needs to be moved—and where? Have I left out any steps?
- ☐ Am I satisfied with the way I have expressed the insights to be gained? Have I been too heavy-handed with a message?

Revision

- ☐ Have I made any needed additions, deletions, or changes in order based on answering the questions about my draft?
- ☐ Have I revised my draft to produce coherent paragraphs, using transition and connecting words that reveal the steps or stages in the process?
- ☐ Have I eliminated wordiness and clichés?
- ☐ Have I avoided and removed any discriminatory language?
- ☐ Have I used my word processor's spell check and proofread a printed copy with great care?
- ☐ Do I have an appropriate and interesting title?

7

Using Division and Classification

Examining Human Connections— and Misconnections

You have probably discovered by now that your college library organizes its book collection not by the Dewey decimal system but by the Library of Congress *classification* system. And you are probably taking courses offered by several different departments. Those departments, English for example, may be further *classified* by colleges—the college of arts of sciences. If you needed to find an apartment near campus or a part-time job, you may have looked in the newspaper's *classified* section. We *divide* or separate individual items and then group or *classify* them into logical categories because order is more convenient than disorder and because the process helps us make sense of a complex world. Just think how frustrated you would be if you had to search through a random listing of want ads rather than being able to look under several headings for specific jobs, or if you had to search up and down shelves of books because they were not grouped by any system.

When to Use Division and Classification

Division and classification are not similar but distinct strategies, as are comparison and contrast. Rather, division and classification work together; they are part of the same thinking process that brings order to a mass of items, data, ideas, forms of behavior, groups of people, or whatever else someone chooses to organize. Division is another term for analysis, the breaking down of something into its parts. Division, or analysis, provides the plan or pattern of grouping. To devise a classification system for books, books have to be divided by type: books on history, or art, or botany. Then large categories need to be subdivided: U.S. history, British history, Russian history. Then each individual book can be given a number that is its very own but also shows into what categories it has been classified, twentieth-century U.S. history, for example. The categories have been developed after thoughtful analysis; each book can be placed in one of the established categories.

A thinking process that has served us so well, solving organizational problems from the biologist's classification of the animal kingdom to the phone company's classification of businesses in the Yellow Pages must surely be a useful strategy for writers. And indeed it is. If you have written essays using examples and have sought to group examples to support different parts of your topic, you have already started working with the process of division and classification. The difference between the essays in Chapter 5 ("Explaining and Illustrating") and those in this chapter lies in the rigor of the classification system. To use classification effectively, you need a logical, consistent principle of division, and your classification needs to be complete. So, when thinking about possible topics for an essay and when thinking about purpose in writing, ask yourself: Am I interested in giving some specific examples to develop an idea, or am I interested in analyzing a topic, dividing it logically into its parts?

How to Use Division and Classification

Thinking and Organizing

Suppose that you are asked to write about some element of campus life. Reflecting on the fun you have had getting acquainted with classmates over meals in nearby restaurants, you decide to write about the various restaurants available to college students. How many and how varied are the restaurants within walking distance of the campus? To be thorough, you may not want to trust your memory; better to walk around, making a complete list of the area restaurants. Next, analyze your list to see the possible categories into which the restaurants can be grouped. You may see more than one way to classify them, perhaps by type of food (French, Chinese, Italian) and by cost (cheap, moderate, expensive). You need to avoid overlapping categories and to classify examples according to the division you select. The following chart illustrates the general principle:

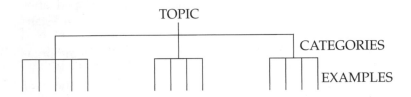

Thesis

The divisions and classifications you create must also support a thesis. What do you want to explain to your readers? This is the key question to answer in deciding on a classification pattern. If you decide to stress the variety of food available to students, for example, then you will want to classify your examples of restaurants by food type, not by cost.

In your essay on restaurants, division and classification provide an effective strategy for developing your thesis. Sometimes, though, a writer's thesis *is* the classification pattern. Put another way, what the writer has learned is that the subject can best be grasped by understanding the author's classification of that subject. Ralph Whitehead, writing about American class structure, asserts that the old categories are no longer accurate and that his new categories give us more insight into American society.

Much of what is important in your division and classification essay lies in your analysis, in the logical and perhaps new way you ask readers to examine your topic. This means that you may need to explain your categories to readers, to explain how and why you have divided your subject in your particular way and to show, if necessary, why the categories do not overlap. In "The Science and Secrets of Personal Space," Curt Suplee defines the required distances for each category or zone—intimate, personal, social, and public—but then explains how various cultures modify their space requirements. Remember, too, that you need to illustrate each of your divisions. In the essay on restaurants, the student needs to name and describe sample restaurants in each of the categories.

WRITING FOCUS:
WORDS TO LIVE WITHOUT!

Student writers have been known to assure instructors that they would revise more energetically if they only knew what to look for to change or toss out. Here are several categories of words, with some examples of each, that you can watch for in your drafts and get in the habit of cutting or changing. Indeed, you can improve your writing overnight if you will commit to live without these types of words.

Unnecessary Qualifiers

How often have you written:

In my opinion, it seems to me that gun laws . . .
I believe that possibly we should have a . . .
What I got out of the poem is just that the poet . . .

Whether the goal is padding or genuine concern about "being wrong," the writing suffers. Delete these kinds of words and phrases in all of your writing.

Vague, General Language

Some words that are hard to live without in casual speech do not belong in writing. These include such words as: *thing, good, bad, nice, aspects, factor.* In your writing you have the opportunity to substitute more powerful, concrete words for these overworked and now powerless words.

Loaded Words

Avoid language that puts down someone based on gender, age, race, ethnicity, or disability. Educated writers today make every effort to write in ways that do not offend, at least when that is not the point of the writing. Here are some examples and the edits you can make: *firemen* (firefighters), *man* (human), *poetess* (poet for both genders). Also avoid all racial or ethnic slur words and be careful about political name calling as well (e.g., *radical, right wing, communist, reactionary*).

Getting Started: Classifying Recent Reading or Viewing

Make a list of all the works (books, magazines, newspapers, texts, etc.) you have read in the past three months. Study your list, thinking of several classifying principles you could use to organize your reading. Consider: Which pattern seems the most logical and complete? Could several patterns work, depending on your purpose in classifying? Alternately, complete the same exercise for all the movies or all the television shows you have seen in the past three months.

The Plot Against People

RUSSELL BAKER

A graduate of Johns Hopkins University, Russell Baker began his journalism career with the *Baltimore Sun* and then moved to the *New York Times* to cover government and politics. In 1962 he began writing his "Observer" column for the *New York Times*, a column that ran for 36 years. Baker has won the Pulitzer Prize for his commentary as well as for his popular memoir *Growing Up* (1982). "The Plot Against People" was an "Observer" column in 1968.

Questions to Guide Your Reading and Reflection

1. What is Baker's primary purpose in writing?
2. What are some advantages of using humor in writing?

Inanimate objects are classified scientifically into three 1
major categories—those that break down, those that get lost,
and those that don't work.

The goal of all inanimate objects is to resist man and ultimately 2
to defeat him, and the three major classifications are based on the
method each object uses to achieve its purpose. As a general rule,
any object capable of breaking down at the moment when it is
most needed will do so. The automobile is typical of the category.

With the cunning peculiar to its breed, the automobile never 3
breaks down while entering a filling station which has a large
staff of idle mechanics. It waits until it reaches a downtown in-
tersection in the middle of the rush hour, or until it is fully
loaded with family and luggage on the Ohio Turnpike. Thus it
creates maximum inconvenience, frustration, and irritability,
thereby reducing its owner's lifespan.

Washing machines, garbage disposals, lawn mowers, fur- 4
naces, TV sets, tape recorders, slide projectors—all are in
league with the automobile to take their turn at breaking down
whenever life threatens to flow smoothly for their enemies.

Many inanimate objects, of course, find it extremely difficult 5
to break down. Pliers, for example, and gloves and keys are almost totally incapable of breaking down. Therefore, they have
had to evolve a different technique for resisting man.

They get lost. Science has still not solved the mystery of how 6
they do it, and no man has ever caught one of them in the act. The
most plausible theory is that they have developed a secret method
of locomotion which they are able to conceal from human eyes.

It is not uncommon for a pair of pliers to climb all the way 7
from the cellar to the attic in its single-minded determination to
raise its owner's blood pressure. Keys have been known to bur-
row three feet under mattresses. Women's purses, despite their
great weight, frequently travel through six or seven rooms to
find hiding space under a couch.

Scientists have been struck by the fact that things that break 8
down virtually never get lost, while things that get lost hardly
ever break down. A furnace, for example, will invariably break
down at the depth of the first winter cold wave, but it will
never get lost. A woman's purse hardly ever breaks down; it almost invariably chooses to get lost.

9   Some persons believe this constitutes evidence that inanimate objects are not entirely hostile to man. After all, they point out, a furnace could infuriate a man even more thoroughly by getting lost than by breaking down, just as a glove could upset him far more by breaking down than by getting lost.

10   Not everyone agrees, however, that this indicates a conciliatory attitude. Many say it merely proves that furnaces, gloves and pliers are incredibly stupid.

11   The third class of objects—those that don't work—is the most curious of all. These include such objects as barometers, car clocks, cigarette lighters, flashlights and toy-train locomotives. It is inaccurate, of course, to say that they *never* work. They work once, usually for the first few hours after being brought home, and then quit. Thereafter, they never work again.

12   In fact, it is widely assumed that they are built for the purpose of not working. Some people have reached advanced ages without ever seeing some of these objects—barometers, for example—in working order.

13   Science is utterly baffled by the entire category. There are many theories about it. The most interesting holds that the things that don't work have attained the highest state possible for an inanimate object, the state to which things that break down and things that get lost can still only aspire.

14   They have truly defeated man by conditioning him never to expect anything of them. When his cigarette lighter won't light or his flashlight fails to illuminate, it does not raise his blood pressure. Objects that don't work have given man the only peace he receives from inanimate society.

Expanding Vocabulary

Be able to define each of the following words. Then, select five words and use each one in a separate sentence. The number in parentheses is the number of the paragraph in which the world appears.

inanimate (1)	hostile (9)
plausible (6)	infuriate (9)
burrow (7)	conciliatory (10)
constitutes (9)	incredibly (10)

Understanding Content

1. What is the goal of inanimate objects, despite their classification, according to Baker?

2. What are the kinds of objects that fit into the first category?
3. Why are the objects that "get lost" not in the "break down" category? What are some of Baker's examples for this second category?
4. How does the "never work" category need to be qualified?
5. What is the most interesting theory to explain the third category?

Drawing Inferences about Thesis and Purpose

1. To decide on his thesis, you need to consider Baker's purpose or purposes in writing. Is it appropriate to say that he has two purposes? If so, what are they?
2. Baker's classification system is clear. What is his thesis?
3. When Baker says that "science is utterly baffled by the entire [third] category," does he mean this seriously? Explain.

Analyzing Strategies and Style

1. Baker describes the automobile as "cunning" and pliers as having climbed "all the way from the cellar to the attic." What strategy is he using when he writes this way of these objects?
2. At what point do you recognize that one of Baker's purposes is to amuse his readers? If he does not always mean what he writes, what strategy is he using?

Thinking Critically

1. Are you often frustrated by the "behavior" of inanimate objects? Which category of objects gives you the most grief? Do you have any explanation for this?
2. What makes Baker's approach, strategies, and tone engaging and effective?
3. In what situations can humor and irony be used to good effect?

The Roles of Manners

JUDITH MARTIN

Judith Martin is "Miss Manners." After graduating from Wellesley College, Martin began her career as a reporter for the *Washington Post*. She is best known now for her syndicated column, "Miss Manners." She has published ten books, including *Miss Manners' Guide to Rearing Perfect Children* (1984), *Common Courtesy* (1985), and *Miss Manners: A Citizens Guide to Civility*. In the following, a slightly shortened version of an article that appeared in the Spring 1996 issue of *The Responsive Community*, Martin analyzes the several roles of manners.

Questions to Guide Your Reading and Reflection

1. When you do not follow expected codes in society, how are you perceived? What do you appear to be doing?
2. What is your reaction to those who do not follow expected codes of behavior?

1   Ritual serves one of three major functions of manners. Oddly enough, the greatest scoffers at the traditions of American etiquette, who scorn the rituals of their own society as stupid and stultifying, voice respect for the custom and folklore of Native Americans, less industrialized peoples, and other societies they find more "authentic" than their own.

2   Americans who disdain etiquette in everyday life often go into an etiquette tailspin in connection with marriage. Although the premise on which the 20th-century American wedding forms were based—that a young girl is given by the father whose protection she leaves to a husband who will perform the same function—has changed, the forms retain their emotional value. If it happens that the bride has been supporting the bridegroom for years in their own household, she may well ask their own toddler age son to "give her away" just to preserve the ritual.

3   Ritual provides a reassuring sense of social belonging far more satisfying than behavior improvised under emotionally complicated circumstances. Rituals of mourning other than funerals have been nearly abandoned, but at a great emotional cost. Not only are the bereaved unprotected from normal social demands by customs of seclusion and symbols of vulnerability, but they are encouraged to act as if nothing had happened—only to be deemed heartless if they actually succeed.

4   A second function of manners is the symbolic one. It is the symbolic function that confuses and upsets people who claim that etiquette is "simply a matter of common sense" when actually the symbols cannot be deduced from first principles, but must be learned in each society, and, within that society, for different times, places, ages, and social classes.

Because symbols are arbitrary, it can happen that opposite   5
forms of behavior may symbolize the same idea, as when a
man takes off his hat to show respect in a church, but puts on
his hat to show respect in a synagogue. But once these rules are
learned, they provide people with a tremendous fund of nonverbal knowledge about one another, helping them to deal appropriately with a wide range of social situations and
relationships. Forms of greeting, dressing, eating, and restraining bodily functions can all be read as symbols of degrees of
friendliness or hostility, respect or contempt, solidarity with
the community or alienation from it. It is safe to assume that a
person who advances on you with an outstretched hand is
symbolizing an intent to treat you better than one who spits on
the ground at the sight of you.

The law, the military, diplomacy, the church, and athletics   6
have particularly strict codes of etiquette, compliance with
which is taken to symbolize adherence to the particular values
that these professions require: fairness, obedience, respect,
piety, or valor. And following the conventions of the society is
taken as a measure of respect for it—which is why people who
are facing juries are advised by their own lawyers to dress and
behave with the utmost convention.

It does not matter how arbitrary any of the violated rules   7
may be—ignoring them is interpreted as defiance of, or indif-
ference to, or antagonism toward, the interests of the person or
community whose standard is being ignored. The person who
wears blue jeans to a formal wedding, or a three-piece suit at a
beach party, may protest all he likes that his choice had only to
do with a clothing preference, but it is hard to imagine anyone
so naive as to believe that the people whose standards he is vi-
olating will not interpret the choice as disdain. In New York, a
15-year-old was shot on the street in a gang fight started over
his refusal to return another teenager's high five sign of greeting. "Dissin'," the current term for showing disrespect, is cited
as a leading provocation for modern murder.

The third function of etiquette is the regulative function,   8
which is less troublesome to the literal-minded, because those
rules can be understood functionally. Between them, etiquette and law divide the task of regulating social conduct in
the interest of community harmony, with the law addressing

grave conflicts, such as those threatening life or property, and administering serious punishments, while etiquette seeks to forestall such conflicts, relying on voluntary compliance with its restraints.

9   This is why etiquette restricts freedom of self-expression more than the law does (and why etiquette rejects encounter group theories of achieving harmony through total communication). It is within my legal right to tell you that you are ugly, or that your baby is, but this is likely to lead to ugly—which is to say dangerous—behavior, which it will require the law to address, no longer as a mere insult, but as a more serious charge of slander, libel, or mental cruelty.

10   But the danger of attempting to expand the dominion of the law to take over the function of etiquette—to deal with such violations as students calling one another nasty names, or protesters doing provocative things with flags—is that it may compromise our constitutional rights. For all its strictness, a generally understood community standard of etiquette is more flexible than the law and, because it depends on voluntary compliance, less threatening.

11   Jurisprudence itself cannot function without etiquette. In enforcing standards of dress, rules about when to sit and when to stand, restricting offensive language and requiring people to speak only in proper turn, courtroom etiquette overrides many of the very rights it may protect. So does the etiquette of legislatures, such as that specified in *Robert's Rules of Order.* This is necessary because the more orderly is the form of a social structure, the more conflict it can support. Etiquette requires participants in adversarial proceedings to present their opposing views in a restrained manner, to provide a disciplined and respectful ambience in which to settle conflicts peacefully.

Responding to Changing Times

12   That we cannot live peacefully in communities without etiquette, using only the law to prevent or resolve conflicts in everyday life, has become increasingly obvious to the public. And so there has been, in the last few years, a "return to etiquette," a movement for which I am not totally blameless. It has been hampered by the idea that etiquette need not involve self-restriction.

Those who must decry rudeness in others are full of schemes to punish those transgressors by treating them even more rudely in return. But the well-meaning are also sometimes stymied, because they understand "etiquette" to consist of the social rules that were in effect approximately a generation ago, when women rarely held significant jobs, and answering machines and Call Waiting had not yet been invented. As the same social conditions do not apply, they assume that there can be no etiquette system, or that each individual may make up his or her own rules.

One often hears that etiquette is "only a matter of being considerate of others," and that is certainly a good basis for good behavior. Obviously, however, it does not guide one in the realms of symbolic or ritual etiquette. And if each individual improvises, the variety of resulting actions would be open to misinterpretations and conflicts, which a mutually intelligible code of behavior seeks to prevent. 13

Yet many of the surface etiquette issues of today were addressed under the codes of earlier times, which need only be adapted for the present. . . . [A] system of precedence must exist, although it need not be "ladies first." One must regulate the access of others to one's attention—if not with a butler announcing the conventional fiction that "Madam is not at home," then by a machine that says, "If you leave a message after the beep. . . ." But dropping one unfinished conversation to begin another has always been rude, and that applies to Call Waiting. Usually, changes happen gradually, as, for example, most people have come to accept the unmarried couple socially, or to issue their wedding invitations in time for guests to take advantage of bargain travel prices. 14

There is, of course, ideologically motivated civil disobedience of etiquette, just as there is of law. But people who mean to change the behavior of the community for its own supposed benefit by such acts must be prepared to accept the punitive consequences of their defiance. They would be well advised to disobey only the rule that offends them, carefully adhering to other conventions, if they do not wish to have their protests perceived as a general contempt for other people. Thanks to her symbolic meaning, the well-dressed, soft-spoken grandmother is a more effective agitator than the unkempt, obscenity-spouting youth. 15

16   Ignorance of etiquette rules is not an easily accepted excuse, except on behalf of small children or strangers to the community. An incapacity to comply is acceptable, but only if convincingly explained. To refuse to shake someone's hand will be interpreted as an insult, unless an explanation, such as that one has crippling arthritis, is provided.

17   Such excuses as "Oh, I never write letters" or "I just wasn't in the mood" or "I'm not comfortable with that" are classified as insolence and disallowed. Etiquette cannot be universally abandoned in the name of individual freedom, honesty, creativity, or comfort, without social consequences.

18   In 1978, when I began chronicling and guiding the legitimate changes in etiquette, and applying the rules in specific cases, where there may be extenuating circumstances or conflicting rules—as a judge does in considering a case—it was difficult to get people to agree that etiquette was needed. Now it is only difficult to get people to comply with its rules.

Expanding Vocabulary

Match each word in column A with its definition in column B. When in doubt, first find the word in the essay and look for context clues to aid your understanding of the word's meaning. Then, if necessary, use your dictionary to complete the matching exercise. The number in parentheses is the number of the paragraph in which the word appears.

Column A	Column B
scoffers (1)	inflicting punishment
stultifying (1)	thwarted
tailspin (2)	left desolate, especially by death
bereaved (3)	unity of sympathies or interest within a group
arbitrary (5)	
solidarity (5)	state of estrangement, feeling of separation from others
alienation (5)	
adherence (6)	sudden deep decline or slump
naive (7)	simple, lacking worldliness
provocative (10)	act of inciting anger or stirring action
adversarial (11)	special atmosphere of a particular place
ambiance (11)	those expressing scorn
decry (12)	openly condemn

stymied (12)	antagonistic, behaving as an opponent
punitive (15)	determined by chance or whim
extenuating (18)	devotion to or commitment to
	providing partial excuses
	limiting or stifling

Understanding Content

1. What is often illogical about marriage rituals today? Why do we continue with these rituals anyway?
2. Why is it incorrect to insist that manners are simply common sense?
3. When you follow the codes of etiquette, diplomacy, or athletics, what does your behavior symbolize?
4. What is the relationship between the law and etiquette? What may happen if we try to get the law to take over the role of etiquette?
5. If you want to change particular etiquette, what should you do to be most successful?
6. Why is ignorance not usually accepted as an excuse for being unmannerly?

Drawing Inferences about Thesis and Purpose

1. What is Martin's purpose in writing? Does she have more than one? Try to write a thesis that makes her purpose clear.
2. Does Martin think that people today are more—or less—likely to follow codes of etiquette? How do you know?
3. What is the author's attitude toward Call Waiting? How do you know?

Analyzing Strategies and Style

1. Think about the ordering of the three roles of manners. What does the author gain by her choice of order?
2. Why does the author put *authentic* in quotation marks in paragraph 1? What do they signify to the reader?

Thinking Critically

1. Have you thought before about the ritual and symbolic roles of manners? If not, does Martin's explanation make sense to you?
2. Why are rituals helpful? Think of ways that the rituals of etiquette can aid us—and think of specific examples to illustrate your points.

3. Do you agree that etiquette can be a better choice than laws in controlling some kinds of behavior and that we should not turn to the law as a way to make people behave? Look specifically at Martin's examples and see whether you agree or disagree with her. Explain your position.
4. Many have argued that there has been a loss of manners in our time. What do you suggest that we do about the loss?

Hot Boxes for Ex-Smokers

FRANKLIN E. ZIMRING

Franklin Zimring completed his law degree at the University of Chicago in 1967 and taught there until 1985. He now teaches at the University of California at Berkeley's School of Law and directs the Center for Studies in Criminal Justice. Zimring has published extensively, both articles and books, usually on such legal issues as capital punishment, youth crime, the criminal justice system, and violence in society. An important recent book is *American Youth Violence* (1998). The following article, appearing in *Newsweek* on April 20, 1987, departs from legal issues to draw on the writer's experience as an ex-smoker.

Questions to Guide Your Reading and Reflection
1. Into which of his "boxes" does the author fit?
2. How would you describe the author's tone?

1   Americans can be divided into three groups—smokers, non-smokers, and that expanding pack of us who have quit. Those who have never smoked don't know what they're missing, but former smokers, ex-smokers, reformed smokers can never forget. We are veterans of a personal war, linked by that watershed experience of ceasing to smoke and by the temptation to have just one more cigarette. For almost all of us ex-smokers, smoking continues to play an important part in our lives. And now that it is being restricted in restaurants around the country and will be banned in almost all indoor public places in New York

state starting next month, it is vital that everyone understand the different emotional states cessation of smoking can cause. I have observed four of them; and in the interest of science I have classified them as those of the zealot, the evangelist, the elect, and the serene. Each day, each category gains new recruits.

Not all antitobacco zealots are former smokers, but a sub-   2
stantial number of fire-and-brimstone opponents do come from the ranks of the reformed. Zealots believe that those who continue to smoke are degenerates who deserve scorn, not pity, and the penalties that will deter offensive behavior in public as well. Relations between these people and those who continue to smoke are strained.

One explanation for the zealot's fervor in seeking to outlaw   3
tobacco consumption is his own tenuous hold on abstaining from smoking. But I think part of the emotional force arises from sheer envy as he watches and identifies with each lung-filling puff. By making smoking in public a crime, the zealot seeks reassurance that he will not revert to bad habits; give him strong social penalties and he won't become a recidivist.

No systematic survey has been done yet, but anecdotal ev-   4
idence suggests that a disproportionate number of doctors who have quit smoking can be found among the fanatics. Just as the most enthusiastic revolutionary tends to make the most enthusiastic counterrevolutionary, many of today's vitriolic zealots include those who had been deeply committed to tobacco habits.

By contrast, the antismoking evangelist does not condemn   5
smokers. Unlike the zealot, he regards smoking as an easily curable condition, as a social disease, and not a sin. The evangelist spends an enormous amount of time seeking and preaching to the unconverted. He argues that kicking the habit is not *that* difficult. After all, *he* did it; moreover, as he describes it, the benefits of quitting are beyond measure and the disadvantages are nil.

The hallmark of the evangelist is his insistence that he never   6
misses tobacco. Though he is less hostile to smokers than the zealot, he is resented more. Friends and loved ones who have been the targets of his preachments frequently greet the resumption of smoking by the evangelist as an occasion for unmitigated glee.

7   Among former smokers, the distinctions between the evangelist and the elect are much the same as the differences between proselytizing and nonproselytizing religious sects. While the evangelists preach the ease and desirability of abstinence, the elect do not attempt to convert their friends. They think that virtue is its own reward and subscribe to the Puritan theory of predestination.[1] Since they have proved themselves capable of abstaining from tobacco, they are therefore different from friends and relatives who continue to smoke. They feel superior, secure that their salvation was foreordained. These ex-smokers rarely give personal testimony on their conversion. They rarely speak about their tobacco habits, while evangelists talk about little else. Of course, active smokers find such bluenosed[2] behavior far less offensive than that of the evangelist or the zealot, yet they resent the elect simply because they are smug. Their air of self-satisfaction rarely escapes the notice of those lighting up. For active smokers, life with a member of the ex-smoking elect is less stormy than with a zealot or evangelist, but it is subtly oppressive nonetheless.

8   I have labeled my final category of former smokers the serene. This classification is meant to encourage those who find the other psychic styles of ex-smokers disagreeable. Serenity is quieter than zealotry and evangelism, and those who qualify are not as self-righteous as the elect. The serene ex-smoker accepts himself and also accepts those around him who continue to smoke. This kind of serenity does not come easily, nor does it seem to be an immediate option for those who have stopped. Rather it is a goal, an end stage in a process of development during which some former smokers progress through one or more of the less-than-positive psychological points en route. For former smokers, serenity is thus a positive possibility that exists at the end of the rainbow. But all former smokers cannot reach that promised land.

9   What is it that permits some former smokers to become serene? I think the key is self-acceptance and gratitude. The fully mature former smoker knows he has the soul of an addict and is grateful for the knowledge. He may sit up front in an air-

---

[1]Puritans believed that those of the elect, those saved, have been chosen by God.—Ed.
[2]Puritanical.—Ed.

plane, but he knows he belongs in the smoking section in back. He doesn't regret that he quit smoking, nor any of his previous adventures with tobacco. As a former smoker, he is grateful for the experience and memory of craving a cigarette.

Serenity comes from accepting the lessons of one's life. And 10 ex-smokers who have reached this point in their worldview have much to be grateful for. They have learned about the potential and limits of change. In becoming the right kind of former smoker, they developed a healthy sense of self. This former smoker, for one, believes that it is better to crave (one hopes only occasionally) and not to smoke than never to have craved at all. And by accepting that fact, the reformed smoker does not need to excoriate, envy, or dissociate himself from those who continue to smoke.

Expanding Vocabulary

Match each word in column A with its definition in column B. When in doubt, first find the word in the essay and look for context clues to aid your understanding of the word's meaning. Then, if necessary, use your dictionary to complete the matching exercise. The number in parentheses is the number of the paragraph in which the word appears.

Column A	*Column B*
watershed (1)	flimsy, uncertain
cessation (1)	deliberate self-restraint
zealot (1)	based on casual accounts rather than
degenerates (2)	strong evidence
tenuous (3)	one fanatically devoted to a cause
recidivist (3)	seeking to convert others from one belief
anecdotal (4)	to another
vitriolic (4)	self-satisfied
proselytizing (7)	turning point
sects (7)	scathing, caustic, sarcastic
abstinence (7)	mental, behavioral
foreordained (7)	declines in quality
smug (7)	denounce strongly
psychic (8)	ceasing, halt
excoriate (10)	narrowly defined religious groups
	predestined
	one who lapses into previous behavior

Understanding Content

1. How does the zealot feel about smokers? What motivates the zealot? What group of ex-smokers can often be found among the zealots?
2. What is the evangelist's attitude toward quitting? How do smokers feel about the evangelist?
3. How do the elect differ from evangelists? What attitude of the elect bothers smokers?
4. How do the serene differ from the other ex-smokers? How should ex-smokers view this category? What is the psychological state of the serene ex-smoker?

Drawing Inferences about Thesis and Purpose

1. What is the author's purpose in writng?
2. What is Zimring's thesis in his classification of ex-smokers?

Analyzing Strategies and Style

1. Zimring draws one word (*recidivist*) from his field, the law, but many of his words come from what other field or subject area? What does he gain from using so many words from this field?
2. Zimring announces early in his essay that he is an ex-smoker. Why is it important for him to tell this to readers?

Thinking Critically

1. Are you an ex-smoker? If so, do you see yourself in one of Zimring's categories? Are there other categories that he should add?
2. Are you a smoker? If so, do you recognize Zimring's classification of ex-smokers? Which type bothers you the most? (Why are you still smoking?)
3. Is it always best to serenely accept what others do—their habits, their speech, their lifestyles? Or is there a role for zealots or evangelists? Support your position.

The Science and Secrets
of Personal Space

CURT SUPLEE

Curt Suplee is a science writer and editor for the *Washington Post*. He has written *Everyday Science Explained* (1996) and *Physics in the 20th Century* (1999). His analysis of personal and public spaces appeared in the *Post's* Horizon Section on June 9, 1999.

Questions to Guide Your Reading and Reflection

1. How can the police use knowledge of personal space to aid their work?
2. What is your comfort level for personal space?

It's a free country, right? Well, not exactly. Every day, all day   1
long, the specific position of your body and the state of your mind are under the control of a powerful and authoritative force of which you are almost entirely unaware.

It's the system of personal space. Every culture has its own,   2
and some are so drastically different that they can cause friction—or at least extreme unease—when groups such as Arabs and northern Europeans get together.

Individual idiosyncracies and social context can modify the   3
rules slightly, as we shall see. But within a culture, the code usually is firmly imprinted by age 12 and remains surprisingly constant from town to town and region to region.

For the average American, according to anthropologist Ed-   4
ward T. Hall, there are four distinctive spacial zones, each with a well-understood spectrum of appropriate behavior.

The nearest Hall calls the "intimate" zone, which extends   5
outward from the skin about 18 inches. This is the range within which lovers touch and parents communicate with infants. At that distance, it is difficult to focus on another person's face, which appears larger than your entire field of vision. That is one reason why people often kiss with their eyes closed.

6   Within this zone, the sense of smell is important; and body heat is felt immediately. For example, sexual arousal customarily floods the abdomen with blood. Many people say they can sense the condition of a partner, even during cocktail conversation or formal ballroom dancing, by feeling the radiated heat.

7   The next, or "personal," zone, extends from 18 inches to about 4 feet. Within this range, you discuss private or serious matters and confer with literally "close" friends. Touch is easy throughout the nearest part of this space, up to about 30 inches. Alternatively, you can keep someone "at arm's length."

8   (Although you may be unaware of the rules of personal space, your language is not. Many of our familiar phrases reflect our cultural code and what happens when somebody is too close for comfort.)

9   Within the personal zone, you can focus sharply on another person's face and read very subtle details of expression. But you'll probably move your eyes a lot to focus on various parts of the other person's face. Watch somebody else talking at this distance, and you'll see his or her gaze flick rapidly from one spot to another.

10   You'll also notice that personal groups larger than two or three are very rare, because it becomes difficult to maintain appropriate spacing with more people.

11   Casual acquaintances or people who just want to tell you something relatively unimportant had better stay well outside the 30-inch inner personal zone. If they don't, they'll make you very uncomfortable, and you may find yourself inadvertently backing up until you're trapped against a wall.

12   One reason that economy-class air travel frequently is so ghastly is that the strangers who are your seatmates are way inside the close personal zone. Worse yet, side-by-side seating is widely felt to be the most intimate arrangement. Men will not voluntarily choose it unless the alternative is sitting too far apart to talk.

13   In one study, American, English, Dutch, Swedish and Pakistani subjects all ranked the side-by-side position as psychologically closest, followed by corner seating, face-to-face, and various diagonal arrangements.

14   The "social-consultive" zone, in which most day-to-day work and ordinary conversation occurs, starts at 4 feet and

goes to about 10 feet. In American culture, eight feet is the point at which you pretty much have to acknowledge another person's presence. Beyond that, you can ignore someone without giving obvious offense.

Usually, there are no smell or heat sensations at 4 to 10 feet, and much nonverbal information is conveyed by large-scale body language. The whole body is visible as a unit at about seven feet, although you can only focus on part because the clearest vision occurs in a cone of about 15 degrees from the eyeball.

Finally, there is an all-purpose "public" zone that begins at about 10 feet and extends to 25 feet. Thirty feet is the customary nearest distance for addresses by public officials or celebrities.

Studies have shown that people are more likely to interact with somebody who looks weird if that person stays well outside the personal zone. In one experiment, a researcher dressed as a punk rocker pretended to be looking for help from people sitting at tables in a shopping mall food court.

"Although only one in 15 people consented to help the punker when she sat right next to them, 40 percent agreed to help when she sat at a medium distance," the researchers found. But "80 percent of the people agreed to help her when she took the seat farthest away."

Over the Line

When someone does something that violates the tacit rules of the zone system, we are perplexed, annoyed or both. For example, if a person wanted a date with you and asked you out from 10 feet away—two feet beyond the farthest range of business conversation—you'd certainly think twice about agreeing, even if you were initially inclined to go.

On the other hand, a Latin American or French person, from a culture with a much closer personal interaction distance, could seem to be too "forward" or "coming on too strong" if he or she made the request from two feet away.

Sometimes, the resulting discomfort is intentional. Psychologist Robert Sommer notes in his book *Personal Space* that police interrogators are taught to intrude well inside the personal zone when questioning suspects.

22   Similarly, we often decide that someone is wearing "too much" perfume or cologne if the scent extends past the distance of personal space. So if you can smell a woman's perfume 8 feet away, you may find it irritating—not just because of the odor itself but because she is making what should be an intimate olfactory statement in public space. . . .

Size Does Matter

23   Variations abound. In much of India, there are only two zones: intimate and public. Some Mediterranean cultures have personal zones that begin much closer than those typical of Americans or northern Europeans. That's why Americans sometimes feel crowded or stressed in France or Italy.

24   And, of course, some cultures simply build things differently. Japanese rooms seem too small by Western standards, and the furniture tends to be placed in the center rather than along the walls. What we don't know is that the traditional Japanese room configuration can be changed by moving the lightweight walls.

25   Thus, what we perceive as a permanent space is merely a temporary arrangement from another perspective. Conversely, our fondness for big spaces with furniture at the edges can make Western rooms look barren to the Japanese eye.

26   In 1967, Hong Kong's housing authority was constructing apartments with 35 square feet per occupant. That's 5-by-7, about the size of a modern work "cubicle." When a westerner asked why the design was so stingy, a construction supervisor replied, "With 60 square feet per person, the tenants would sublet."

Birth and Turf

27   But each culture's rules arise from the same fundamental biological impetus, which extends throughout the animal kingdom—the tendency to mark and defend one's own territory or to avoid intruding on someone else's.

28   Think about that next time you sit down in a cafeteria or library. If you find an empty table that can seat six or eight, you're probably going to sit at one of the corner chairs—an "avoidance" position, according to psychologists—and you'll most likely face the door because some ancestral instinct says you might have to flee.

Dogs mark their territory by urinating at the boundaries. 29
Happily, human civilization has not evolved this trait. But
we're constantly doing the equivalent.

Everyone has been vaguely irritated by the person in a 30
movie theater who spreads coats and bags across six seats and
then goes off for popcorn. Nonetheless, we'll bypass any space
that faintly appears to be "marked" by an absentee squatter.
One study showed that, even in a busy and crowded library, a
simple stack of magazines in front of a chair kept that seat open
for more than an hour.

Analogously, you may find that when you enter someone's 31
home, you carefully avoid sitting in what seems to be the father's "personal" chair. Or you may notice how some passengers in the Metro system claim two spaces—an "aggressive"
position—by putting a briefcase next to them or taking the out-
ermost of the two side-by-side seats. . . .

Eyes Right

Space can be invaded by vision as well as another's pres- 32
ence, and visual territories also differ from culture to culture.
Unlike, say, the French, whose "frank" stares can be intimidating to outsiders, Americans rarely look directly at each other
for very long, even during intense conversation.

In the animal kingdom, an averted gaze often indicates a 33
passive stance. But in America, it is merely polite. We consider
it an invasion of personal space to "stare" at someone, even
briefly, and sensitivity varies by distance.

Thus, when the door closes on a crowded elevator, you'll 34
usually notice two behaviors. First, the occupants automatically adjust their positions to create the same amount of space
between each. Then most people either look down at their feet
or up at the floor indicator rather than at one another.

In fact, one experiment showed that people will sit closer to 35
a picture of a person with the eyes closed than to an otherwise
identical image with the eyes open.

The English, on the other hand, regard it as rude not to look 36
directly at the other person during conversation. To do otherwise makes it appear that you're not paying attention.

But in order to hold the head still and the gaze steady while 37
listening to someone, one has to be far enough away so the eyes

aren't constantly shifting around the other person's face. Thus the English tend to stand near the outer limits of American personal space, making them seem aloof, reserved or literally "stand-offish."

Expanding Vocabulary

Examine the following words in their contexts in the essay and then write a brief definition or synonym of each one. Do not use a dictionary; try to guess each word's meaning from the context. The number in parentheses is the number of the paragraph in which the word appears.

idiosyncracies (3)	interrogators (21)
spectrum (4)	olfactory (22)
inadvertently (11)	impetus (27)
tacit (19)	analogously (31)

Understanding Content

1. What are the characteristics of the intimate zone?
2. What are the dimensions and uses of the personal zone?
3. What terms have evolved from the dynamics of the personal zone?
4. How do most people view sitting next to strangers?
5. What are the dimensions and characteristics of the third zone? At what distance do we usually have to acknowledge another person?
6. What are the dimensions of the public zone?
7. What are some of the ways we "mark" our personal space?
8. How do American and British and French patterns differ regarding looking directly at someone?

Drawing Inferences about Thesis and Purpose

1. Why are we irritated by people who spread their belongings over several chairs?
2. What is Suplee's purpose in writing? State his thesis.

Analyzing Strategies and Style

1. What are the sources of the author's information? How does he provide this information for readers?
2. Describe the strategies Suplee uses to introduce each of his four space zones.
3. What *type* of information does the author provide for each of the zones?

Thinking Critically

1. Are you familiar with this information about personal space? If not, does Suplee's analysis make sense to you? Think about your own experiences on elevators and in movie theaters.
2. What information about zones is most helpful for our personal relationships? Explain your response.
3. What information is most helpful for our dealings with people we don't know? Explain your response.

The Ways We Lie

STEPHANIE ERICSSON

A screenwriter and advertising copywriter, Stephanie Ericsson is the author of *Companion Through the Darkness: Inner Dialogues on Grief* (1992) and *Companion into the Dawn: Inner Dialogues on Loving* (1994). After losing her husband while pregnant with their child, Ericsson kept a journal which has served as the basis for her writing and for her frequent speaking engagements on the subject of loss. The following analysis of the various types of lies we tell was published originally in the Nov./Dec. 1992 issue of the *Utne Reader*.

Questions to Guide Your Reading and Reflection

1. What is the definition of the term *lie*?
2. Do you define all false impressions as lies?

The bank called today and I told them my deposit was in the mail, even though I hadn't written a check yet. It'd been a rough day. The baby I'm pregnant with decided to do aerobics on my lungs for two hours, our three-year-old daughter painted the living-room couch with lipstick, the IRS put me on hold for an hour, and I was late to a business meeting because I was tired.

I told my client that the traffic had been bad. When my partner came home, his haggard face told me his day hadn't gone any better than mine, so when he asked, "How was your day?" I said, "Oh, fine," knowing that one more straw might break his back. A friend called and wanted to take me to lunch. I said

I was busy. Four lies in the course of a day, none of which I felt the least bit guilty about.

3   We lie. We all do. We exaggerate, we minimize, we avoid confrontation, we spare people's feelings, we conveniently forget, we keep secrets, we justify lying to the big-guy institutions. Like most people, I indulge in small falsehoods and still think of myself as an honest person. Sure I lie, but it doesn't hurt anything. Or does it?

4   I once tried going a whole week without telling a lie, and it was paralyzing. I discovered that telling the truth all the time is nearly impossible. It means living with some serious consequences: The bank charges me $60 in overdraft fees, my partner keels over when I tell him about my travails, my client fires me for telling her I didn't feel like being on time, and my friend takes it personally when I say I'm not hungry. There must be some merit to lying.

5   But if I justify lying, what makes me any different from slick politicians or the corporate robbers who raided the S&L industry? Saying it's okay to lie one way and not another is hedging. I cannot seem to escape the voice deep inside me that tells me: When someone lies, someone loses.

6   What far-reaching consequences will I, or others, pay as a result of my lie? Will someone's trust be destroyed? Will someone else pay penance because I ducked out? We must consider the *meaning of our actions*. Deception, lies, capital crimes, and misdemeanors all carry meanings. *Webster's* definition of *lie* is specific:

1. a false statement or action especially made with the intent to deceive;
2. anything that gives or is meant to give a false impression.

7   A definition like this implies that there are many, many ways to tell a lie. Here are just a few.

The White Lie

A man who won't lie to a woman has very little consideration for her feelings.

—Bergen Evans

8   The white lie assumes that the truth will cause more damage than a simple, harmless untruth. Telling a friend he looks

great when he looks like hell can be based on a decision that the friend needs a compliment more than a frank opinion. But, in effect, it is the liar deciding what is best for the lied to. Ultimately, it is a vote of no confidence. It is an act of subtle arrogance for anyone to decide what is best for someone else.

Yet not all circumstances are quite so cut and dried. Take, for 9 instance, the sergeant in Vietnam who knew one of his men was killed in action but listed him as missing so that the man's family would receive indefinite compensation instead of the lump-sum pittance the military gives widows and children. His intent was honorable. Yet for twenty years this family kept their hopes alive, unable to move on to a new life.

Facades

Et tu, Brute?

—Caesar

We all put up facades to one degree or another. When I put 10 on a suit to go to see a client, I feel as though I am putting on another face, obeying the expectation that serious business-people wear suits rather than sweatpants. But I'm a writer. Normally, I get up, get the kid off to school, and sit at my computer in my pajamas until four in the afternoon. When I answer the phone, the caller thinks I'm wearing a suit (though the UPS man knows better).

But facades can be destructive because they are used to se- 11 duce others into an illusion. For instance, I recently realized that a former friend was a liar. He presented himself with all the right looks and the right words and offered lots of new consciousness theories, fabulous books to read, and fascinating insights. Then I did some business with him, and the time came for him to pay me. He turned out to be all talk and no walk. I heard a plethora of reasonable excuses, including in-depth descriptions of the big break around the corner. In six months of work, I saw less than a hundred bucks. When I confronted him, he raised both eyebrows and tried to convince me that I'd heard him wrong, that he'd made no commitment to me. A simple investigation into his past revealed a crowded graveyard of disenchanted former friends.

Ignoring the Plain Facts

Well, you must understand that Father Porter is only human . . .
—A Massachusetts Priest

12   In the sixties, the Catholic Church in Massachusetts began hearing complaints that Father James Porter was sexually molesting children. Rather than relieving him of his duties, the ecclesiastical authorities simply moved him from one parish to another between 1960 and 1967, actually providing him with a fresh supply of unsuspecting families and innocent children to abuse. After treatment in 1967 for pedophilia, he went back to work, this time in Minnesota. The new diocese was aware of Father Porter's obsession with children, but they needed priests and recklessly believed treatment had cured him. More children were abused until he was relieved of his duties a year later. By his own admission, Porter may have abused as many as a hundred children.

13   Ignoring the facts may not in and of itself be a form of lying, but consider the context of this situation. If a lie is *a false action done with the intention to deceive*, then the Catholic Church's conscious covering for Porter created irreparable consequences. The church became a co-perpetrator with Porter.

Deflecting

When you have no basis for an argument, abuse the plaintiff
—Cicero

14   I've discovered that I can keep anyone from seeing the true me by being selectively blatant. I set a precedent of being upfront about intimate issues, but I never bring up the things I truly want to hide; I just let people assume I'm revealing everything. It's an effective way of hiding.

15   Any good liar knows that the way to perpetuate an untruth is to deflect attention from it. When Clarence Thomas exploded with accusations that the Senate hearings were a "high-tech lynching," he simply switched the focus from a highly charged subject to a radioactive subject. Rather than defending himself, he took the offensive and accused the country of racism. It was a brilliant maneuver. Racism is now politically incorrect in of-

ficial circles—unlike sexual harassment, which still rewards those who can get away with it.

Some of the most skillful deflectors are passive-aggressive   16 people who, when accused of inappropriate behavior, refuse to respond to the accusations. This you-don't-exist stance infuriates the accuser, who, understandably, screams something obscene out of frustration. The trap is sprung and the act of deflection successful, because now the passive-aggressive person can indignantly say, "Who can talk to someone as unreasonable as you?" The real issue is forgotten and the sins of the original victim become the focus. Feeling guilty of name-calling, the victim is fully tamed and crawls into a hole, ashamed. I have watched this fighting technique work thousands of times in disputes between men and women, and what I've learned is that the real culprit is not necessarily the one who swears the loudest.

Omission

The cruelest lies are often told in silence.
—R. L. Stevenson

Omission involves telling most of the truth minus one or   17 two key facts whose absence changes the story completely. You break a pair of glasses that are guaranteed under normal use and get a new pair, without mentioning that the first pair broke during a rowdy game of basketball. Who hasn't tried something like that? But what about omission of information that could make a difference in how a person lives his or her life?

For instance, one day I found out that rabbinical legends tell   18 of another woman in the Garden of Eden before Eve. I was stunned. The omission of the Sumerian goddess Lilith from Genesis—as well as her demonization by ancient misogynists as an embodiment of female evil—felt like spiritual robbery. I felt like I'd just found out my mother was really my stepmother. To take seriously the tradition that Adam was created out of the same mud as his equal counterpart, Lilith, redefines all of Judeo-Christian history.

Some renegade Catholic feminists introduced me to a view   19 of Lilith that had been suppressed during the many centuries when this strong goddess was seen only as a spirit of evil. Lilith was a proud goddess who defied Adam's need to control her, attempted negotiations, and when this failed, said adios and left the Garden of Eden.

20   This omission of Lilith from the Bible was a patriarchal strategy to keep women weak. Omitting the strong-woman archetype of Lilith from Western religions and starting the story with Eve the Rib has helped keep Christian and Jewish women believing they were the lesser sex for thousands of years.

Stereotypes and Clichés

Where opinion does not exist, the status quo becomes stereotyped and all originality is discouraged.

—Bertrand Russell

21   Stereotype and cliché serve a purpose as a form of shorthand. Our need for vast amounts of information in nanoseconds has made the stereotype vital to modern communication. Unfortunately, it often shuts down original thinking, giving those hungry for truth a candy bar of misinformation instead of a balanced meal. The stereotype explains a situation with just enough truth to seem unquestionable.

22   All the *isms*— racism, sexism, ageism, et al.—are founded on and fueled by the stereotype and the cliché, which are lies of exaggeration, omission, and ignorance. They are always dangerous. They take a single tree and make it a landscape. They destroy curiosity. They close minds and separate people. The single mother on welfare is assumed to be cheating. Any black male could tell you how much of his identity is obliterated daily by stereotypes. Fat people, ugly people, beautiful people, old people, large-breasted women, short men, the mentally ill, and the homeless all could tell you how much more they are like us than we want to think. I once admitted to a group of people that I had a mouth like a truck driver. Much to my surprise, a man stood up and said, "I'm a truck driver, and I never cuss." Needless to say, I was humbled.

Groupthink

Who is more foolish, the child afraid of the dark, or the man afraid of the light.

—Maurice Freehill

Irving Janis, in *Victims of GroupThink*, defines this sort of lie   23
as a psychological phenomenon within decision-making
groups in which loyalty to the group has become more important than any other value, with the result that dissent and the
appraisal of alternatives are suppressed. If you've ever worked
on a committee or in a corporation, you've encountered groupthink. It requires a combination of other forms of lying—ignoring facts, selective memory, omission, and denial, to name a few.

The textbook example of groupthink came on December 7,   24
1941. From as early as the fall of 1941, the warnings came in,
one after another, that Japan was preparing for a massive military operation. The Navy command in Hawaii assumed Pearl
Harbor was invulnerable—the Japanese weren't stupid
enough to attack the United States' most important base. On
the other hand, racist stereotypes said the Japanese weren't
smart enough to invent a torpedo effective in less than 60 feet
of water (the fleet was docked in 30 feet); after all, U.S. technology hadn't been able to do it.

On Friday, December 5, normal weekend leave was granted   25
to all the commanders at Pearl Harbor, even though the Japanese consulate in Hawaii was busy burning papers. Within the
tight, good-ole-boy cohesiveness of the U.S. command in
Hawaii, the myth of invulnerability stayed well entrenched. No
one in the group considered the alternatives. The rest is history.

Out-and-Out Lies

The only form of lying that is beyond reproach is lying for its own sake.
—Oscar Wilde

Of all the ways to lie, I like this one the best, probably be-   26
cause I get tired of trying to figure out the real meanings behind
things. At least I can trust the bald-faced lie. I once asked my
five-year-old nephew, "Who broke the fence?" (I had seen him
do it.) He answered, "The murderers." Who could argue?

At least when this sort of lie is told it can be easily confronted.   27
As the person who is lied to, I know where I stand. The bald-
faced lie doesn't toy with my perceptions—it argues with them. It
doesn't try to refashion reality, it tries to refute it. *Read my* lips . . .
No sleight of hand. No guessing. If this were the only form of

lying, there would be no such thing as floating anxiety or the adult-children of alcoholics movement.

Dismissal

Pay no attention to that man behind the curtain! I am the Great Oz!
—The Wizard of Oz

28   Dismissal is perhaps the slipperiest of all lies. Dismissing feelings, perceptions, or even the raw facts of a situation ranks as a kind of lie that can do as much damage to a person as any other kind of lie.

29   The roots of many mental disorders can be traced back to the dismissal of reality. Imagine that a person is told from the time she is a tot that her perceptions are inaccurate. *"Mommy. I'm scared."* "No you're not, darling." *"I don't like that man next door, he makes me feel icky."* "Johnny, that's a terrible thing to say, of course you like him. You go over there right now and be nice to him. "

30   I've often mused over the idea that madness is actually a sane reaction to an insane world. Psychologist R.D. Laing supports this hypothesis in *Sanity, Madness & The Family*, an account of his investigations into the families of schizophrenics. The common thread that ran through all of the families he studied was a deliberate, staunch dismissal of the patient's perceptions from a very early age. Each of the patients started out with an accurate grasp of reality, which, through meticulous and methodical dismissal, was demolished until the only reality the patient could trust was catatonia.

31   Dismissal runs the gamut. Mild dismissal can be quite handy for forgiving the foibles of others in our day-to-day lives. Toddlers who have just learned to manipulate their parents' attention sometimes are dismissed out of necessity. Absolute attention from the parents would require so much energy that no one would get to eat dinner. But we must be careful and attentive about how far we take our "necessary" dismissals. Dismissal is a dangerous tool, because it's nothing less than a lie.

Delusion

We lie loudest when we lie to ourselves.
—Eric Hoffer

I could write the book on this one. Delusion, a cousin of dis-   32
missal, is the tendency to see excuses as facts. It's a powerful
lying tool because it filters out information that contradicts
what we want to believe. Alcoholics who believe that the problems in their lives are legitimate reasons for drinking rather
than results of the drinking offer the classic example of de-
luded thinking. Delusion uses the mind's ability to see things
in myriad ways to support what it wants to be the truth.

But delusion is also a survival mechanism we all use. If we   32
were to fully contemplate the consequences of our stockpiles of
nuclear weapons or global warming, we could hardly function
on a day-to-day level. We don't want to incorporate that much
reality into our lives because to do so would be paralyzing.

Delusion acts as an adhesive to keep the status quo intact.   34
It shamelessly employs dismissal, omission, and amnesia,
among other sorts of lies. Its most cunning defense is that it
cannot see itself.

> *The liar's punishment . . . is that he cannot believe anyone else.*
> —George Bernard Shaw

These are only a few of the ways we lie. Or are lied to. As I   35
said earlier, it's not easy to entirely eliminate lies from our lives.
No matter how pious we may try to be, we will still embellish,
hedge, and omit to lubricate the daily machinery of living. But
there is a world of difference between telling functional lies and
living a lie. Martin Buber once said, "The lie is the spirit committing treason against itself." Our acceptance of lies becomes a
cultural cancer that eventually shrouds and reorders reality until
moral garbage becomes as invisible to us as water is to a fish.

How much do we tolerate before we become sick and tired   36
of being sick and tired? When will we stand up and declare our
right to trust? When do we stop accepting that the real truth is
in the fine print? Whose lips do we read this year when we vote
for president? When will we stop being so reticent about making judgments? When do we stop turning over our personal
power and responsibility to liars?

Maybe if I don't tell the bank the check's in the mail I'll be   37
less tolerant of the lies told to me every day. A country song I
once heard said it all for me: "You've got to stand for something or you'll fall for anything."

Expanding Vocabulary

Match each word in column A with its definition in column B. When in doubt, first find the word in the essay and look for context clues to aid your understanding of the word's meaning. Then, if necessary, use your dictionary to complete the matching exercise. The number in parentheses is the number of the paragraph in which the word appears.

Column A	Column B
travails (4)	careful and precise
hedging (5)	love of children that is abusive
penance (6)	cause to turn aside, to blunt the force of
facades (10)	impossible to repair
plethora (11)	those who hate women
pedophilia (12)	prolong the existence of
irreparable (13)	many
blatant (14)	struggles
perpetuate (15)	strong, solid
deflect (15)	abnormal condition often marked
misogynists (18)	by withdrawal
obliterated (22)	something that conceals
staunch (29)	deceptive appearances
meticulous (29)	completely wiped out
catatonia (29)	atonement for one's sins
foibles (30)	super-abundance
myriad (31)	offensively obvious
shrouds (34)	minor weaknesses of character
	making an ambiguous statement

Understanding Content

1. What is the fundamental problem with the white lie?
2. What is destructive about facades?
3. How can ignoring obvious facts be a form of lying?
4. How does the lie by deflecting work? What makes it effective?
5. How do we lie by omission?
6. What lying strategies underlie the stereotype? Groupthink?
7. What happened on December 7, 1941?
8. Why is dismissal dangerous?
9. What is useful about delusion? What is dangerous about it?
10. Who may suffer the most from our lying? Why?

Drawing Inferences about Thesis and Purpose

1. Ericsson begins paragraph 6 with three questions. How are we supposed to answer these questions?
2. What is Ericsson's purpose in writing?
3. Write a thesis that reveals the author's use of a classification strategy.

Analyzing Strategies and Style

1. The author begins by recounting four lies she told in one day. What does she gain by this opening?
2. In paragraph 21 Ericsson uses a metaphor to make her point. Explain the metaphor.
3. The author introduces each category of lying with a quotation. How do these quotations contribute to the essay?

Thinking Critically

1. Ericsson suggests that lying is self-destructive. Does this idea make sense to you? Why or why not?
2. Which types of lies seem to have the greatest potential for damaging others? Explain your choice.
3. Which quotation, for you, offers the greatest insight? Why?

Class Acts: America's Changing Middle Class

RALPH WHITEHEAD, JR.

Beginning his career as a journalist in Chicago, Ralph Whitehead became a professor of journalism at the University of Massachusetts in 1973. He is the author of many articles on social structures and public opinion and has been a consultant to political and labor groups and to the U.S. Department of Labor. His study of the changing social/economic hierarchy in American society was first published in the Jan./Feb. 1990 issue of the *Utne Reader*.

Questions to Guide Your Reading and Reflection
1. What does Whitehead mean by his use of "collar," as in "bright collar" and "new collar"? What does "collar" stand for?
2. Into what social class would you place yourself? On what basis?

1   As we enter the 1990s, American society exhibits a vastly different social and economic makeup from the one that we grew accustomed to in the thirty years that followed World War II. The gap between the top and bottom is far greater now, of course, but the economic position of people in the middle is changing, too. This new social ladder is seen most vividly in the lives of our younger generations, the baby boom and the later baby bust. Because the new ladder is so much steeper than the old one, it's creating an alarming new degree of polarization in American life.

2   As it held sway for roughly the first three decades after World War II, the old social ladder was shaped largely by the continuing expansion of the middle class. For the first time, many people could afford to buy a house, a car (or two), a washer and dryer, an outdoor grill, adequate health coverage, maybe a motor boat, and possibly college for the kids. And for the first time, a growing number of blacks and Hispanics could enter the middle class.

3   Within this expanding middle class, there were a couple of fairly well-defined ways of life: white-collar life and blue-collar life. White-collar life was typified by TV characters like Ward and June Cleaver and later Mike and Carol Brady. Blue-collar life was typified by characters like Ralph and Alice Kramden and later Archie and Edith Bunker.

4   At the top of the old social ladder stood a small number of rich people. A larger but declining number of poor people stood at the bottom, and the rest of the ladder was taken up by the middle-class. The old social ladder looked roughly like this:

THE RICH

THE EXPANDING MIDDLE CLASS:
White collar
Blue collar

THE POOR

The new social ladder is markedly different. Within the baby ⁵ boom and baby bust generations, the middle class is no longer expanding. Therefore the new social ladder is shaped by—and at the same time is helping to shape—a new polarization between the haves and the have-nots. The social ladder of the 1990s looks roughly like this:

UPSCALE AMERICA:
The Rich
The Overclass

THE DIVERGING MIDDLE CLASS:
Bright collar
New collar
Blue collar

DOWNSCALE AMERICA:
The Poor
The Underclass

The rich are still on top, of course. But the new generation of rich people is typified by Donald Trump, the billionaire developer of luxury buildings for the newly rich, rather than by someone like his father, Fred Trump, a developer who made millions building modestly priced postwar homes and apartments for the expanding middle class—the kinds of homes in which the Kramdens and Bunkers lived.

The poor are still with us, of course, but they're no longer at ⁶ the bottom. It's not because they've risen to the middle class but rather because some of them have fallen into the underclass. Because definitions of the underclass vary, so do estimates of its size. However, it does include at least two million people who lead lives that aren't typified in America's popular culture. To belong to the underclass is to be without a face and without a voice.

Just as an underclass has emerged, so has an overclass, ⁷ which occupies the rung just below the rich. Located chiefly in a dozen metropolises and heavily concentrated in lucrative management and professional jobs, the overclass is roughly the same size as the underclass. Its significance lies not in its numbers, however, but in its immense power throughout American society. The overclass holds the highest level positions in the fields of entertainment, media, marketing, advertising, real estate, finance, and politics. It's pursued for its consumption dollars and cajoled for its investment dollars. It is crudely typified by the media stereotype of the yuppie.

8   What clearly stood out on the old social ladder that shaped American society during the fifties and sixties was the dominant presence of an expanding middle class. What is noticeable about the new social ladder is the unmistakable emergence of distinct upper and lower rungs, and the vast social, economic, and psychological distance between them. Together, the rich and the overclass form Upscale America. Together, the underclass and the poor form Downscale America.

9   The expanding middle class, with its white and blue collars, has given way in the baby boom and baby bust generations to a diverging middle class. It consists largely of three kinds of workers:

10   • **Bright collars.** Within the ranks of managerial and professional workers a new category of job has emerged. The white-collar worker is receding and the bright-collar worker is advancing. The bright collars are the 20 million knowledge workers born since 1945: lawyers and teachers, architects and social workers, accountants and budget analysts, engineers and consultants, rising executives and midlevel administrators. They earn their living by taking intellectual initiatives. They face the luxury and the necessity of making their own decisions on the job and in their personal lives.

11   Bright-collar people lack the touchstones that guided white-collar workers like Ward Cleaver in the 1950s and 1960s. The white collars believed in institutions; bright collars are skeptical of them. The corporate chain of command, a strong force in white-collar life then, is far weaker for bright collars today. They place a premium on individuality, on standing out rather than fitting in. Although the older white collars knew the rules and played by them, bright collars can't be sure what the rules are and must think up their own. The white collars were organization men and women (mostly men); bright collars are entrepreneurs interested in building careers for themselves outside big corporations.

12   Three quarters of the managers and professionals of the 1950s were men. Today half are women. Seven percent are black or Hispanic or Asian. Bright collars make up a third of the baby boom work force. They're typified by figures like *L.A. Law's* attorneys.

13   • **Blue Collars.** Within the manufacturing workplace, blue-collar work endures, but on a much smaller scale. Thirty years ago almost 40 percent of the adult work force did blue-collar work.

Today, after the relative decline of American heavy industry, it's done by less than 25 percent of baby boom workers. During the fifties and sixties, blue-collar wages rose steadily, thus helping fuel the expansion of the middle class. In the past 15 years these wages have been relatively flat. Young blue collars often must live near the economic margins.

The blue-collar world is still a man's world. Roughly three quar-   14
ters of today's younger blue collars are men—the same percentage as in the 1950s. Twelve percent are black, Hispanic, or Asian. Within a growing number of innovative manufacturing workplaces, new models of blue-collar work have begun to emerge, but they haven't yet advanced enough to trigger a new category of American worker. In the popular culture the new generation of blue collars finds a voice in Bruce Springsteen, but it still hasn't found a face.

• **New Collars.** These people aren't managers and professionals, and   15
they don't do physical labor. Their jobs fall between those two worlds. They're secretaries, clerks, telephone operators, key-punch operators, inside salespeople, police officers. They often avoid the grime and regimentation of blue-collar work. Two thirds of the new collars are women. More than 15 percent are black, Hispanic, or Asian. The new collars make up at least 35 percent of the baby boom work force.

Federal Express truck drivers are typical new-collar workers.   16
They design pickup and delivery routes, explain the company's services and fees, provide mailing supplies, and handle relatively sophisticated information technology in their trucks. They aren't traditional truck drivers so much as sales clerks in offices on wheels.

The rise of the new social ladder has helped to drive a num-   17
ber of changes in American life, but one of them, already evident, should be underscored: the dramatic shift of power within both the middle class and the society as a whole.

As members of the expanding middle class of the postwar   18
years, blue collars once held considerable leverage. In the electorate, for every vote cast by the white collars in 1960, the blue collars cast two. In the workplace, they acted through powerful unions. In the marketplace, they were valued as consumers. As a result, blue collars dealt with white collars as equals. In the fifties and sixties, whatever class lines still divided the two groups seemed to be dissolving.

Within the diverging middle class today, the balance of   19
power is much different. In the electorate, for every vote cast by younger blue collars in 1988, bright collars cast two. In the

workplace, younger blue-collar workers are losing union power, while bright collars exert the power of their knowledge and privilege of their status. In the marketplace, blue-collar consumers are written off as too downscale, while the bright-collar consumer is courted as an aspiring member of the over-class. Deep divisions have sprung up between bright collars and blue collars. They look a lot like class lines.

20   The rise of an overclass throws the decline of blue-collar life into sharper relief, and vice versa. Upscale yuppie haunts spring up: the health club, the gourmet takeout shop, the pricy boutique, the atrium building. Downscale blue-collar haunts wither: the union hall, the lodge, the beauty parlor, the mill. The guys with red suspenders began showing up in the beer commercials right about the time the loggers and guys with air hammers began to disappear. The overclass's stock portfolios began to get fat just as blue-collar families were losing their pensions and health insurance. Condo prices were climbing in Atlanta just as bungalow prices fell in Buffalo. It seems that there's a battle here, a zero-sum game, whereby the rise of one comes at the expense of the other.

21   The contrast between the rich and the underclass is sharper than ever. If you look at the new social ladder in New York, you see Donald Trump in his penthouse and the homeless people in the subways.

22   This situation intensifies the shift of power in society as a whole. With the middle class divided, the center cannot hold. The dominant forces in society become Upscale America and Downscale America—or, more precisely, Upscale America versus Downscale America. Upscale America uses its power to secure privileges such as proposed cuts in the capital gains tax. Downscale America strikes back blindly through rising rates of crime. Through the old social ladder, the expanding middle class acted as the nation's glue. With the new social ladder, the diverging middle class is merely caught in the crossfire.

Expanding Vocabulary

Study the definitions for any of the following words that you do not know. Then select five words and use each one in a separate sentence. The number in parentheses is the number of the paragraph in which the word appears.

polarization (1)
lucrative (7)
cajoled (7)
yuppie (7)
entrepreneurs (11)

innovative (10)
sophisticated (16)
leverage (18)
zero-sum (20)

Understanding Content

1. In the social ladder that existed for thirty years after World War II, what was happening to the middle class?
2. What were the four categories on the older social ladder?
3. What two important changes are taking place in the middle class?
4. What are the characteristics of the underclass?
5. Who makes up the new overclass?
6. What are the characteristics of the three new categories of workers in the new middle class?
7. How has power changed in the new bright collar and blue collar classes?

Drawing Inferences about Thesis and Purpose

1. What is Whitehead's purpose in writing? Does he have more than one? State his thesis.
2. What does Whitehead mean when he writes of a "zero-sum game" played between upscale and downscale America (paragraph 20)?
3. What implications for America do we find in the final paragraph?

Analyzing Strategies and Style

1. What does the author gain by the visual presentation of both the former and the current class categories?
2. Whitehead uses several TV characters as examples. How are they effective? What do they imply about his expected audience?
3. The author uses contrast within his classification structure. Find several nicely balanced contrast sentences and consider why they are effective.

Thinking Critically

1. Does Whitehead's classification of contemporary American class structure seem on target? Why or why not?

2. Many Americans like to believe that we are a "classless" society; everybody is the same. Whitehead doesn't do anything to address, or counter, this attitude. What might this tell us about his expected audience?
3. Do you agree with Whitehead that the diverging middle class and the conflict between upscale and downscale America pose serious social problems for the United States? Why or why not?

STUDENT ESSAY—DIVISION AND CLASSIFICATION

BUYING TIME
Garrett Berger

Chances are you own at least one wristwatch. Watches allow us immediate access to the correct time. They are indispensable items in our modern world, where, as the saying goes, time is money. Today the primary function of a wristwatch does not necessarily guide its design; like clothes, houses, and cars, watches have become fashion statements and a way to flaunt one's wealth.

Introduction connects to reader.

To learn how watches are being sold, I surveyed all of the full-page ads from the November issues of four magazines. The first two, GQ and Vogue, are well-known fashion magazines. The Robb Report is a rather new magazine that caters to the overclass. Forbes is of course a well-known financial magazine. I was rather surprised at the number of advertisements

Student explains his methodology of collecting ads. Paragraph concludes with his thesis.

I found. After surveying 86 ads, marketing 59 brands, I have concluded that today
watches are being sold through five main
strategies: DESIGN/BRAND appeal, CRAFTS-
MANSHIP, ASSOCIATION, FASHION appeal, and
EMOTIONAL appeal.

In most DESIGN/BRAND appeal ads, only
a picture and the brand name are used. A
subset of this category uses the same
basic strategy with a slogan or phrases
to emphasize something about the brand or
product. A Mont Blanc ad shows a watch
profile with a contorted metal link band,
asking the question, "Is that you?" The
reputation of the name and the appeal of
the design sell the watch. Rolex, perhaps the best-known name in high-end
watches, advertises, in <u>Vogue</u>, its "Oys-
ter Perpetual Lady-Date Pearlmaster." A
close-up of the watch face showcases the
white, mother-of-pearl dial, sapphire
bezel, and diamond-set band. A smaller,
more complete picture crouches under-
neath, showing the watch on its side. The
model name is displayed along a gray band
that runs near the bottom. The Rolex
crest anchors the bottom of the page.
Forty-five ads marketing 29 brands use
the DESIGN/BRAND strategy. A large picture of the product centered on a solid
background is the norm.

*Discussion of
first category.*

CRAFTSMANSHIP, the second strategy, focuses on the maker, the horologer, and the technical sides of form and function. Brand heritage and a unique, hand-crafted design are major selling points. All of these ads are targeted at men, appearing in every magazine except <u>Vogue</u>. Collector pieces and limited editions were commonly sold using this strategy. The focus is on accuracy and technical excellence. Pictures of the inner works and cutaways, technical information, and explanations of movements and features are popular. Quality and exclusivity are all-important.

Discussion of second category.

A Cronoswiss ad from <u>The Robb Report</u> is a good example. The top third pictures a horologer, identified as "Gerard Lange, master watchmaker and founder of Cronoswiss in Munich," directly below. The middle third of the ad shows a watch, white-faced with a black leather band. The logo and slogan appear next to the watch. The bottom third contains copy beginning with the words: "My watches are a hundred years behind the times." The rest explains what that statement means. Mr. Lange apparently believes that technical perfection in horology has already been attained. He also offers his book, <u>The Fascination of Mechanics</u>, free of charge along with the

Detailed examples to illustrate second category.

"sole distributor for North America" at the bottom. A "Daniel Roth" ad from the same magazine displays the name across the top of a white page; towards the top, left-hand corner a gold buckle and black band lead your eye to the center, where a gold watch with a transparent face displays its inner works exquisitely. Above and to the right, copy explains the exclusive and unique design accomplished by inverting the movement, allowing it to be viewed from above.

The third strategy is to sell the watch by establishing an ASSOCIATION with an object, experience, or person, implying that its value and quality are beyond question. In the six ads I found using this approach, watches are associated with violins, pilots, astronauts, hot air balloons, and a hero of the free world. This is similar to the first strategy, but relies on a reputation other than that of the maker. The watch is presented as being desirable for the connections created in the ad.

Discussion of third category.

Parmigiani ran an ad in <u>The Robb Report</u> featuring a gold watch with a black face and band illuminated by some unseen source. A blue-tinted violin rises in the background; the rest of the page is black. The brief copy reads: "For those who think a Stradivarius is only a violin. The Parmigiani Toric Chronograph is only a wristwatch." "The Moon Watch" proclaims an Omega ad from G̲Q̲. Inset on a white background is a picture of an astronaut on the moon saluting the American flag. The silver watch with a black face lies across the lower part of the page. The caption reads: "Speedmaster Professional. The first and only watch worn on the moon." Omega's logo appears at the bottom.

The fourth strategy is to present the watch simply as a FASHION statement. In this line of attack, the ads appeal to our need to be current, accepted, to fit in and be like everyone else, or to make a statement, setting us apart from others as hip and cool. The product is presented as a necessary part of our wardrobes. The watch is fashionable and will send the "right" message. Design and style are the foremost concerns; "the look" sells the watch.

Discussion of fourth category.

Techno Marine has an ad in G̲Q̲ which shows a large close-up of a watch running down the entire length of the left side of the page. Two alternate color schemes are pictured on the right, separating small bits of copy. At the bottom on the right are the name and logo. The first words at the top read: "Keeping time—you keep your closet up to the minute, why not your wrist? The latest addition to your watch wardrobe should be the AlphaSport." Longines uses a similar strategy in <u>Vogue</u>. Its ad is divided in half lengthwise. On the left is a black-and-white picture of Audrey Hepburn. The right side is white with the Longines' logo at the top and two ladies' watches in the center. Near the bottom is the phrase, "Elegance is an Attitude." Retailers appear at the bottom. The same ad ran in <u>GQ</u>, but with a man's watch and a picture of Humphrey Bogart. A kind of association is made, but quality and value aren't the overriding concerns. The point is to have an elegant attitude like these fashionable stars did, one that these watches can provide and enhance.

The fifth and final strategy is that of EMOTIONAL appeal. The ads using this approach strive to influence our emotional responses and allege to influence the emotions of others towards us. Their power and appeal are exerted through the feelings they evoke in us. Nine out of ten ads rely on a picture as the main device to trigger an emotional

Discussion of fifth category.

link between the product and the viewer. Copy is scant; words are used mainly to guide the viewer to the advertiser's desired conclusions.

A Frederique Constant ad pictures a man, wearing a watch, mulling over a chess game. Above his head are the words "Inner Passion." The man's gaze is odd; he is looking at something on the right side of the page, but a large picture of a watch superimposed over the picture hides whatever it is that he is looking at. So we are led to the watch. The bottom third is white and contains the maker's logo and the slogan "Live your Passion." An ad in GQ shows a man holding a woman. He leans against a rock; she reclines in his arms. Their eyes are closed, and both have peaceful, smiling expressions. He is wearing a Tommy Hilfiger watch. The ad spans two pages; a close-up of the watch is presented on the right half of the second page. The only words are the ones in the logo. This is perhaps one of those pictures that are worth a thousand words. The message is he got the girl because he's got the watch.

Even more than selling a particular watch, all of these ads focus on building the brand's image. I found many of the ads extremely effective at conveying

their messages. Many of the better-known
brands favor the comparatively simple DE-
SIGN/BRAND appeal strategy, to reach a
broader audience. Lesser-known, high-end
makers contribute many of the more specialized strategies. We all count and
mark the passing hours and minutes. And
society places great importance on time,
valuing punctuality. But these ads strive
to convince us that having "the right
time" means so much more than "the time."

*Strong
conclusion;
the effect of
watch ads.*

MAKING CONNECTIONS

1. The writers in this chapter have examined many ways in
   which humans connect to one another. Sometimes the connections are good ones (using manners, serene ex-smokers); sometimes the connections are less than ideal
   (intruding on someone's space). What can you learn from
   these writers about human needs in relationships? What
   do we need to feel good? What missing needs lead to conflicts in human relationships?

2. Review the questions about advertising at the beginning of
   Chapter 5. Then think about what human needs are ap-
   pealed to in the advertising of various products. How, for
   example, are perfumes (or cars) sold to us? To what specific
   needs do perfume (or car) ads appeal? You may want to do
   some reading on this subject, beginning with Maslow's hierarchy of needs—which you can read about online.

3. Which writer in this chapter offers the greatest insight into
   human connections? To answer this question, you will
   need to define *greatest*. The term could mean most profound, or most useful to readers, or most original or startling. You may want to classify the writers into these three
   categories—or others of your own—before deciding whom
   to select as having the greatest insight. Your initial analysis
   then becomes the basis for the defense of your choice.

4. Often conflicts in human relationships result from people with different personalities not understanding each other's ways of seeing the world or making decisions. Some of these conflicts can be avoided if we know ourselves better and can recognize specific traits in others we interact with. One strategy is to take the Myers/Briggs personality test to know yourself better and to understand elements of personality. At some colleges, students can arrange to take this test and have a counselor "score" it and discuss the results with the student. You can learn more about Myers/Briggs online and see if you are interested in following through on this approach to learning about yourself. A good site to explore is: *www.teamtechnology.co.uk/ad.html.*

TOPICS FOR WRITING

1. Look over your Getting Started exercise—your classification of recent reading, movies, or television shows. Do you think your reading (or viewing) habits are fairly typical of someone in your situation? Or are your reading (or viewing) habits unusual, reflecting, perhaps, a hobby or special interest? If you see some point—a thesis—that your classification of reading (or viewing) can support, then you have an essay topic.

2. Reflect on the parents, teachers, or coaches you have known. Can they be divided into categories based on their ways of using discipline? Select one group (parents, teachers, or coaches), and then classify that group according to their strategies for disciplining. (You might want to give each type or category a label, as Zimring labels ex-smokers.)

3. Along the same lines as in topic 2, reflect on a particular group of people you know well—teachers, students, dates, workers in a particular field, athletes, and so on. Select one group and classify it according to the different types within that group. Try to make your classification complete. You are saying to your reader that these are the types of dates—or teachers—that one could conceivably know. Make your divisions clear by labeling each type, and then define and il-

lustrate each type. One possible thesis could be your view of the best and worst types in the group you are writing about.

4. Watch (and perhaps tape so that you can review) at least six evenings of the ABC, NBC, or CBS evening news. Analyze the news programs according to the types of news stories and determine the amount of time given to each type of story, to commercials, and to "what's coming" segments. What have you learned? How much serious news do we get in a half hour? How much time (in minutes or seconds) is devoted to each type of story? Report the results of your study in an essay. Introduce your topic in paragraph 1, explain how you conducted your analysis in paragraph 2, and then report on the results of your study. Illustrate your categories with specific examples from the programs you watched. (For example, if one type of story that appears regularly is what can be called "national news," then what news stories from the shows you watched fit into that category? You might explain and illustrate the category with several stories about the president or Congress.)

5. What are some of the "games" that people play in their relationships with one another? That is, what strategies are used by people to get along or get ahead? In what situations are they likely to use particular games? If you have been a careful observer of human behavior or if you have watched people behaving in one particular situation, you potentially have an essay on this topic. Take one of two approaches. (1) Write on the games people play, classifying game playing as fully as you can. Explain and illustrate each game with examples. Remember that you can use hypothetical (made-up) examples as well as those drawn from your experience. (2) Write on the ways that people behave in a particular situation you know well. That is, how can people be classified by their behavior in the classroom, at the doctor's (or dentist's) office, in the library, at the beach, while driving, or at the movies. This second approach can be serious or humorous.

6. Think of one job category you know well (such as small business, farming, the medical profession, teaching, or banking). Then, within that one category, think of all the various workers and classify them according to White-

head's new class divisions. Your point will be to show that not everyone in a job category is in the same class, although you may discover that not all categories are represented. For example, would anyone in teaching be placed in the underclass?

A CHECKLIST FOR DIVISION AND CLASSIFICATION ESSAYS

Invention

☐ Have I selected a topic consistent with the instructor's guidelines for this assignment?

☐ Have I chosen among the possible topics one that fits my knowledge and experience?

☐ Have I reflected on the topic to write a tentative thesis that establishes the use of division and classification?

☐ Have I thought through the categories I need to best organize my subject matter?

☐ Is my classification plan complete, providing a category for all elements of the subject?

☐ Have I thought about the most effective order for my categories?

Drafting

☐ Have I succeeded in completing a first draft at one sitting so that I can "see" the whole?

☐ Do I have enough—enough to meet assignment demands and enough to develop and support my thesis? If not, do I need new paragraphs or more examples or details or more reflection within some paragraphs?

☐ Have I clearly explained the differences among my categories and justified my classification strategy? If not, do I need to rethink my classification system?

☐ Do I have good examples and details to illustrate each category?

☐ Does the order work? If not, what needs to be moved—and where?

☐ Am I satisfied with the way I have expressed the insights to be gained? Have I been too heavy-handed with a message?

Revision

- ☐ Have I made any needed additions, deletions, or changes in order based on answering the questions about my draft?
- ☐ Have I revised my draft to produce coherent paragraphs, using transition and connecting words that reveal my classification system?
- ☐ Have I eliminated wordiness and clichés?
- ☐ Have I avoided or removed any discriminatory language?
- ☐ Have I used my word processor's spell check and proofread a printed copy with great care?
- ☐ Do I have an appropriate and interesting title?

8

Using Definition
Understanding Ideas and Values

"Define your terms!" someone shouts in the middle of a heated debate. Although yelling may not be the best strategy, the advice is sound. Quite frequently the basis for a disagreement turns out to be a key word used differently by those whose discussion can now best be defined as an argument. We cannot let words mean whatever we want them to and still communicate, but, as you know from your study of vocabulary, many words have more than one dictionary definition (*denotation*). If we add to those meanings a word's *connotation* (associations and emotional suggestions), it is no wonder that we disagree over a word's meaning. To some, civil disobedience is illegal behavior; to others it is an example of patriotism. When we don't disagree over a word's generally understood meaning, we can still disagree over its connotation.

When to Use Definition

When do you need to define terms to avoid confusion? First, define words that most readers are not likely to know. If you need to use a technical term in an essay directed to nonspecialists, then you should provide a brief definition. Textbooks are, as you know, filled with definitions as the authors guide students through the vocabulary of a new subject. Second, define any word that you are using in a special way or in one of its special meanings. If you were to write: "We need to teach discrimination at an early age," you probably should add: "By discrimination I do not mean prejudice; I mean discernment, the ability to see differences." (*Sesame Street* has been teaching children this good kind of discrimination for years.)

A third occasion for using definition occurs when a writer chooses to develop a detailed explanation of the meaning of a complex, abstract, frequently debated, or emotion-laden term. Words such as *freedom, happiness, wisdom,* and *honesty* need to be reexamined, debated, and clarified in discussions that go beyond a dictionary's brief entry. We use the term *extended definition* to refer to the essay that has, as its primary purpose, the examination of a word's meaning. Sometimes the writer's purpose is to clarify our thinking: what does it mean to be *happy*? Sometimes a writer wants to reclaim a word from its current negative (or positive) connotations. This is what Robert Miller does when he argues that *discrimination* can have—and should be used with—a positive connotation.

How to Develop an Extended Definition

Extended definition describes a writing purpose. It does not suggest a particular organizational strategy. To develop an extended definition, you need to use some of the writing strategies that you have already been practicing. Suppose three Martians landed in your backyard, saw your Burmese cat, and asked, "What is that?" They are curious to know more than just the name of your pet. You could begin to answer their question with a dictionary-styled definition: a cat is a domesticated mammal (placing the object in a class) with retractable claws (distinguishing it from other members of the class—such as dogs). Your Martian friends, possibly interested in taking some cats home, want more information, so you continue with *descriptive details:* soft fur, usually long tails, padded feet, agile climbers (onto furniture, trees, and rooftops), rumbling sounds when contented. Developing your definition further, you can *contrast* cats with dogs: cats are more independent, can be trained to a box, will clean themselves. You can continue by providing *examples:* there are Siamese cats, Persian cats, tabby cats, and so on.

"This is all very interesting," the Martians respond, "but what do cats do, what are cats for?" You answer by explaining *use* or *function:* cats are pets, friends and companions, fun to play with and cuddle. Some people have even worshipped cats as gods, you add, providing *history.* A variation of providing history is to explain *word origin* or *etymology.* Often we get clues about a word's meaning by studying its origin and the changes in meaning over time. This information can be found in dictionaries that specialize in etymology, the *Oxford English Dictionary (OED),* for example. (Your library will have the *OED,* probably both in a print format and online.)

The previous two paragraphs list and illustrate a number of strategies for developing an extended definition:

descriptive details	comparison/contrast
examples	use or function
etymology	

To write a definition essay, you need to select those strategies that best suit your word and your particular purpose in defining that word. Remembering that effective writing is concrete writing, you want to include plenty of details and examples. Also give thought to the most effective organization of specifics so that the result is a unified essay, not a vocabulary exercise. Keep in mind that one of the most important strategies is contrast, for your purpose in defining is to discriminate, to explain subtle differences among words. (For example, what is the difference between wisdom and knowledge? Can one be wise without having knowledge? Or, how do self-esteem and self-respect differ? Is one better than the other?) Keep in mind that one kind of comparison, the metaphor, is especially useful because metaphors help make the abstract concrete. The Getting Started exercise below shows you how one writer used metaphors to define the concept *democracy.*

WRITING FOCUS:
USING METAPHORS, AVOIDING CLICHÉS

Just as there are colorless words—vague, general words such as *nice* and *thing*—so there are colorless expressions. These are metaphors that once had freshness but now are dulled by overuse. "In the twinkling of an eye" we become "starry-eyed" and are on "pins and needles" awaiting our true love's call. Or, in today's "fast-paced world" we have trouble avoiding "the rat race." To these expressions, called clichés, readers stop listening because they have heard them too many times before. So, when you are about to write that your friend was "as hungry as a bear," stop, ask yourself if this is *your* expression of an idea or a pat phrase you've pulled out of the air, and then erase all tuneless clichés.

Fresh metaphors, on the other hand, both delight readers and give them insight into a writer's thoughts and feelings. Here are some metaphors you will find in this chapter's essays.

> Andrew Vachss writes that a "veil of secrecy and protection then descends."
> Margaret Mead and Rhoda Metraux write that a friend is someone "with whom you sparkle."
> John Ciardi writes that the concept of happiness "will not sit still for easy definition."
> David Fischer writes that the words *freedom* and *liberty* have an "old tension betwen them" that "persists like a coiled spring in our culture."

Find your own clever metaphors when you can. When you can't, write simply and directly, avoiding the pat phrases that so easily come to mind.

Getting Started: Reflections on E. B. White's Ideas of Democracy

E. B. White, author of "Education" (see pp. 131–34), once defined democracy largely through a series of metaphors. Three of his metaphors are

1. Democracy is "the line that forms on the right"
2. Democracy is "the hole in the stuffed shirt through which the sawdust slowly trickles"
3. Democracy is "the score at the beginning of the ninth"

First, analyze each metaphor. For each one, explain what the concrete situation is to which democracy is being compared. Ask yourself, how is that situation democratic? That is, what is White saying about democracy through the comparison? Then select the metaphor you like best and expand the idea that it suggests into a paragraph of your own on democracy. Try to include at least one metaphor of your own in your paragraph.

On Friendship

MARGARET MEAD AND RHODA METRAUX

Margaret Mead (1901–1978) may be the most famous anthropologist of our time. She revolutionized the field with the publication of her field work: *Coming of Age in Samoa* and *Growing Up in New Guinea*. Curator at the American Museum of Natural History and adjunct professor at Columbia University for many years, in later life Mead wrote and spoke often on issues in modern culture. Rhoda Metraux, also an anthropologist attached to the American Museum in New York City and coauthor with Mead of *Themes in French Culture*, did her field work in several Caribbean and South American countries. Mead and Metraux wrote a series of articles for *Redbook* magazine that were collected in *A Way of Seeing* in 1970. Their definition of friendship, from the *Redbook* series, reveals the cross-cultural approach of anthropology.

Questions to Guide Your Reading and Reflection

 1. Why do American friendships confuse many Europeans?
 2. What do you expect from a friendship?

1   Few Americans stay put for a lifetime. We move from town to city to suburb, from high school to college in a different state, from a job in one region to a better job elsewhere, from the home where we raise our children to the home where we plan to live in retirement. With each move we are forever making new friends, who become part of our new life at that time.

2   For many of us the summer is a special time for forming new friendships. Today millions of Americans vacation abroad, and they go not only to see new sights but also—in those places where they do not feel too strange—with the hope of meeting new people. No one really expects a vacation trip to produce a

close friend. But surely the beginning of a friendship is possible? Surely in every country people value friendship?

They do. The difficulty when strangers from two countries 3
meet is not a lack of appreciation of friendship, but different expectations about what constitutes friendship and how it comes into being. In those European countries that Americans are most likely to visit, friendship is quite sharply distinguished from other, more casual relations, and is differently related to family life. For a Frenchman, a German or an Englishman friendship is usually more particularized and carries a heavier burden of commitment.

But as we use the word, "friend" can be applied to a wide 4
range of relationships—to someone one has known for a few weeks in a new place, to a close business associate, to a childhood playmate, to a man or woman, to a trusted confidant. There are real differences among these relations for Americans—a friendship may be superficial, casual, situational or deep and enduring. But to a European, who sees only our surface behavior, the differences are not clear.

As they see it, people known and accepted temporarily, ca- 5
sually, flow in and out of Americans' homes with little ceremony and often with little personal commitment. They may be parents of the children's friends, house guests of neighbors, members of a committee, business associates from another town or even another country. Coming as a guest into an American home, the European visitor finds no visible landmarks. The atmosphere is relaxed. Most people, old and young, are called by first names.

Who, then, is a friend? 6

Even simple translation from one language to another is dif- 7
ficult. "You see," a Frenchman explains, "if I were to say to you in France, 'This is my good friend,' that person would not be as close to me as someone about whom I said only, 'This is my friend.' Anyone about whom I have to say *more* is really less."

In France, as in many European countries, friends generally 8
are of the same sex, and friendship is seen as basically a relationship between men. Frenchwomen laugh at the idea that "women can't be friends," but they also admit sometimes that for women "it's a different thing." And many French people doubt the possibility of a friendship between a man and a

woman. There is also the kind of relationship within a group—
men and women who have worked together for a long time,
who may be very close, sharing great loyalty and warmth of
feeling. They may call one another *copains*—a word that in English becomes "friends" but has more the feeling of "pals" or
"buddies." In French eyes this is not friendship, although two
members of such a group may well be friends.

9   For the French, friendship is a one-to-one relationship that
demands a keen awareness of the other person's intellect, tem-
perament and particular interests. A friend is someone who
draws out your own best qualities, with whom you sparkle
and become more of whatever the friendship draws upon.
Your political philosophy assumes more depth, appreciation of
a play becomes sharper, taste in food or wine is accentuated,
enjoyment of a sport is intensified.

10   And French friendships are compartmentalized. A man may
play chess with a friend for thirty years without knowing his
political opinion, or he may talk politics with him for as long a
time without knowing about his personal life. Different friends
fill different niches in each person's life. These friendships are
not made part of family life. A friend is not expected to spend
evenings being nice to children or courteous to a deaf grandmother. These duties, also serious and enjoined, are primarily
for relatives. Men who are friends may meet in a café. Intellectual friends may meet in larger groups for evenings of conversation. Working people may meet in the little *bistro* where they
drink and talk, far from the family. Marriage does not affect
such friendships; wives do not have to be taken into account.

11   In the past in France, friendships of this kind seldom were
open to any but intellectual women. Since most women's lives
centered on their homes, their warmest relations with other
women often went back to their girlhood. The special relationship of friendship is based on what the French value most—on
the mind, on compatibility of outlook, on vivid awareness of
some chosen area of life.

12   Friendship heightens the sense of each person's individuality. Other relationships commanding as great loyalty and devotion have a different meaning. In World War II the first
resistance groups formed in Paris were built on the foundation
of *les copains*. But significantly, as time went on these little
groups, whose lives rested in one another's hands, called them-

selves "families." Where each had a total responsibility for all, it was kinship ties that provided the model. And even today such ties, crossing every line of class and personal interest, remain binding on the survivors of these small, secret bands.

In Germany, in contrast with France, friendship is much 13 more articulately a matter of feeling. Adolescents, boys and girls, form deeply sentimental attachments, walk and talk together—not so much to polish their wits as to share their hopes and fears and dreams, to form a common front against the world of schools and family and to join in a kind of mutual discovery of each other's and their own inner life. Within the family, the closest relationship over a lifetime is between brothers and sisters. Outside the family, men and women find in their closest friends of the same sex the devotion of a sister, the loyalty of a brother. Appropriately, in Germany friends usually are brought into the family. Children call their father's and their mother's friends "uncle" and "aunt." Between French friends, who have chosen each other for the congeniality of their point of view, lively disagreement and sharpness of argument are the breath of life. But for Germans, whose friendships are based on mutuality of feeling, deep disagreement on any subject that matters to both is regarded as a tragedy. Like ties of kinship, ties of friendship are meant to be irrevocably binding. Young Germans who come to the United States have a great difficulty in establishing such friendships with Americans. We view friendship more tentatively, subject to changes in intensity as people move, change their jobs, marry, or discover new interests.

English friendships follow still a different pattern. Their 14 basis is shared activity. Activities at different stages of life may be of very different kinds—discovering a common interest in school, serving together in the armed forces, taking part in a foreign mission, staying in the same country house during a crisis. In the midst of the activity, whatever it may be, people fall into step—sometimes two men or two women, sometimes two couples, sometimes three people—and find that they walk or play a game or tell stories or serve on a tiresome and exacting committee with the same easy anticipation of what each will do day by day or in some critical situation. Americans who have made English friends comment that, even years later, "you can take up just where you left off." Meeting after a long interval, friends are like a couple who begin to dance again when the orchestra strikes up after a pause. English friendships are formed outside the family circle, but they are not, as in Germany, contrapuntal to the family nor are they, as in France, separated from the family. And a break in an English friendship comes not necessarily as a result of some irreconcilable difference of viewpoint or feeling but instead as a result of misjudgment, where one friend seriously misjudges how the other will think or feel or act, so that suddenly they are out of step.

15   What, then, is friendship? Looking at these different styles, including our own, each of which is related to a whole way of life, are there common elements? There is the recognition that friendship, in contrast with kinship, invokes freedom of choice. A friend is someone who chooses and is chosen. Related to this is the sense each friend gives the other of being a special individual, on whatever grounds this recognition is based. And between friends there is inevitably a kind of equality of give and take. These similarities make the bridge between societies possible, and the American's characteristic openness to different styles of relationships makes it possible for him to find new friends abroad with whom he feels at home.

Expanding Vocabulary

Mead and Metraux do not use complex terms from the social sciences, but they do use words that frequently appear in discussions of human relationships. Thus the following words are ones you want to know and use. Study their use in the essay, look up their definitions if necessary, and then use eight of the words in separate sentences of your own. The number in parentheses is the number of the paragraph in which the word appears.

particularized (3)	mutuality (13)
commitment (3)	irrevocably (13)
confidant (4)	exacting (14)
superficial (4)	kinship (12)
landmarks (5)	articulately (13)
accentuated (9)	congeniality (13)
compartmentalized (10)	contrapuntal (14)
niches (10)	invokes (15)
enjoined (10)	

Understanding Content

1. In general, how do the friendships of French, German, and English people differ from many American friendships?
2. What are the specific characteristics of friendship for the French? What sort of friendship do they think unlikely? What other term do the French use for people whom they would not consider close friends?
3. What lies at the core of friendships for Germans? How are friendships related to families? What can destroy a German friendship?
4. What is the basis for English friendships? What image best characterizes English friendships? How does this make possible a renewal of friendship after a time? What will lead to a break in friendships among the English?
5. After examining American and some European concepts of friendship, what do the authors conclude about the characteristics of friendship that extend over cultural differences?

Drawing Inferences about Thesis and Purpose

1. Do the authors make any judgments about friendships in the four countries?
2. What is their thesis? Is it stated or implied?

Analyzing Strategies and Style

1. Analyze the essay's organization. What paragraphs compose the introduction? The body of the essay? The conclusion?
2. What question indicates the shift from introduction to body? From body to conclusion?
3. Look at the use of transitions. What phrases guide readers through the paragraphs on French friendships? How is the shift to German friendship indicated? How is the shift to English friendship indicated?
4. Examine the authors' lengthy introduction. How do paragraphs 1 and 2 provide an attention-getter? How does the attention-getter lead into the authors' cross-cultural approach?

Thinking Critically

1. Do you think that the authors accurately describe American attitudes toward friendship? Why or why not?
2. Had it occurred to you that friendship might be understood somewhat differently in different cultures? Does it make sense?

Do you know of other lifestyle differences between Americans and the French, Germans, English, or those of another culture? If so, be prepared to discuss these differences in class.

3. Is at least part of the difference in ideas of friendship a carelessness with words on the part of Americans? That is, do we use the word *friend* to refer to relationships that could be more accurately described by a different word? What are some other words that we could use? Should we use these more often than we do? Why or why not?

4. Do you agree with the key definition of friendship offered in the essay's final paragraph? If not, why not? Are there points you would add? If so, what?

Is Everybody Happy?

JOHN CIARDI

A graduate of Tufts and the University of Michigan, John Ciardi (1916–1986) was a lecturer, critic, and, primarily, a poet. Ciardi had many collections of poetry published, including some delightful poems for children. His major critical study is *On Poetry and the Poetic Process* (1971). Ciardi was also for many years poetry editor of *Saturday Review*. In the following essay, from *Saturday Review* (May 14, 1964), Ciardi defines happiness as never perfectly attainable and requiring effort.

Questions to Guide Your Reading and Reflection

1. What seems to be the American concept of happiness?
2. How would you define happiness?

1   The right to pursue happiness is issued to Americans with their birth certificates, but no one seems quite sure which way it ran. It may be we are issued a hunting license but offered no game. Jonathan Swift[1] seemed to think so when he attacked the idea of happiness as "the possession of being well-deceived," the felicity of being "a fool among knaves." For Swift saw society as Vanity Fair, the land of false goals.

[1]Irish-born English clergyman and satiric writer, 1667–1745.—Ed.

It is, of course, un-American to think in terms of fools and   2
knaves. We do, however, seem to be dedicated to the idea of
buying our way to happiness. We shall all have made it to
Heaven when we possess enough.

And at the same time the forces of American commercialism   3
are hugely dedicated to making us deliberately unhappy. Advertising is one of our major industries, and advertising exists
not to satisfy desires but to create them—and to create them
faster than any man's budget can satisfy them. For that matter,
our whole economy is based on a dedicated insatiability. We are
taught that to possess is to be happy, and then we are made to
want. We are even told it is our duty to want. It was only a few
years ago, to cite a single example, that car dealers across the
country were flying banners that read "You Auto Buy Now."
They were calling upon Americans, as an act approaching patriotism, to buy at once, with money they did not have, automo-
biles they did not really need, and which they would be required
to grow tired of by the time next year's models were released.

Or look at any of the women's magazines. There, as Bernard   4
DeVoto[2] once pointed out, advertising begins as poetry in the
front pages and ends as pharmacopoeia and therapy in the
back pages. The poetry of the front matter is the dream of perfect beauty. This is the baby skin that must be hers. These, the
flawless teeth. This, the perfumed breath she must exhale. This,
the sixteen-year-old figure she must display at forty, at fifty, at
sixty, and forever.

Once past the vaguely uplifting fiction and feature articles, the   5
reader finds the other face of the dream in the back matter. This
is the harness into which Mother must strap herself in order to
display that perfect figure. These, the chin straps she must sleep
in. This is the salve that restores all, this is her laxative, these are
the tablets that melt away fat, these are the hormones of perpetual youth, these are the stockings that hide varicose veins.

Obviously no half-sane person can be completely persuaded   6
either by such poetry or by such pharmacopoeia and orthope-
dics. Yet someone is obviously trying to buy the dream as offered and spending billions every year in the attempt. Clearly
the happiness-market is not running out of customers, but
what is it trying to buy?

[2]American novelist and critic, 1897–1955.—Ed.

7   The idea "happiness," to be sure, will not sit still for easy definition: the best one can do is try to set some extremes to the idea and then work in toward the middle. To think of happiness as acquisitive and competitive will do to set the materialistic extreme. To think of it as the idea one senses in, say, a holy man of India will do to set the spiritual extreme. That holy man's idea of happiness is in needing nothing from outside himself. In wanting nothing, he lacks nothing. He sits immobile, rapt in contemplation, free even of his own body. Or nearly free of it. If devout admirers bring him food he eats it; if not, he starves indifferently. Why be concerned? What is physical is an illusion to him. Contemplation is his joy and he achieves it through a fantastically demanding discipline, the accomplishment of which is itself a joy within him.

8   Is he a happy man? Perhaps his happiness is only another sort of illusion. But who can take it from him? And who will dare say it is more illusory than happiness on the installment plan?

9   But, perhaps because I am Western, I doubt such catatonic happiness, as I doubt the dreams of the happiness-market. What is certain is that his way of happiness would be torture to almost any Western man. Yet these extremes will still serve to frame the area within which all of us must find some sort of balance. Thoreau[3]—a creature of both Eastern and Western thought—had his own firm sense of that balance. His aim was to save on the low levels in order to spend on the high.

10   Possession for its own sake or in competition with the rest of the neighborhood would have been Thoreau's idea of the low levels. The active discipline of heightening one's perception of what is enduring in nature would have been his idea of the high. What he saved from the low was time and effort he could spend on the high. Thoreau certainly disapproved of starvation, but he would put into feeding himself only as much effort as would keep him functioning for more important efforts.

11   Effort is the gist of it. There is no happiness except as we take on life-engaging difficulties. Short of the impossible, as Yeats[4] put it, the satisfactions we get from a lifetime depend on how high we choose our difficulties. Robert Frost[5] was thinking in

---

[3]American author and naturalist, 1817–62.—Ed.
[4]Irish essayist, dramatist, and poet, 1865–1939.—Ed.
[5]American poet, 1874–1963.—Ed.

something like the same terms when he spoke of "The pleasure of taking pains." The mortal flaw in the advertised version of happiness is in the fact that it purports to be effortless.

We demand difficulty even in our games. We demand it because without difficulty there can be no game. A game is a way   12
of making something hard for the fun of it. The rules of the game are an arbitrary imposition of difficulty. When the spoilsport ruins the fun, he always does so by refusing to play by the rules. It is easier to win at chess if you are free, at your pleasure, to change the wholly arbitrary rules, but the fun is in winning within the rules. No difficulty, no fun.

The buyers and sellers at the happiness-market seem too often to have lost their sense of pleasure of difficulty. Heaven   13
knows what they are playing, but it seems a dull game. And the Indian holy man seems dull to us, I suppose, because he seems to be refusing to play anything at all. The Western weakness may be in the illusion that happiness can be bought. Perhaps the Eastern weakness is in the idea that there is such a thing as perfect (and therefore static) happiness.

Happiness is never more than partial. There are no pure states of mankind. Whatever else happiness may be, it is nei-   14
ther in having nor in being, but in becoming. What the Founding Fathers declared for us as an inherent right, we should do well to remember, was not happiness but the *pursuit* of happiness. What they might have underlined, could they have foreseen the happiness-market, is the cardinal fact that happiness is in the pursuit itself, in the meaningful pursuit of what is life-engaging and life-revealing, which is to say, in the idea of *becoming*. A nation is not measured by what it possesses or wants to possess, but by what it wants to become.

By all means let the happiness-market sell us minor satisfactions and even minor follies so long as we keep them in scale   15
and buy them out of spiritual change. I am no customer for either puritanism or asceticism. But drop any real spiritual capital at those bazaars, and what you come home to will be your own poorhouse.

Expanding Vocabulary

Match each word in column A with its definition in column B. When in doubt, first find the word in the essay and look for context clues to aid your understanding of the word's meaning. Then, if necessary, use your dictionary to complete the matching exercise. The number in parentheses is the number of the paragraph in which the word appears.

Column A	Column B
insatiability (3)	ointment that soothes or heals
pharmacopoeia (4)	beliefs of Puritans who regarded pleasure as sinful
therapy (4)	
salve (5)	medical specialty dealing with injuries to the skeleton
varicose (5)	
orthopedics (6)	in a stupor, with rigid body
acquisitive (7)	stock of drugs
catatonic (9)	professes to be
purports (11)	treatment of illness
inherent (14)	intrinsic, essential characteristic
puritanism (15)	belief in life of austerity
asceticism (15)	eager to possess, grasping
	abnormally swollen or knotted
	state of not being satisfied

Understanding Content

1. How would Jonathan Swift have described people who thought they were happy?
2. Why does Ciardi reject both extremes of happiness?
3. How do the extremes help to define happiness? What must we find to begin to achieve happiness?
4. What else is essential to happiness? What role does this ingredient play in our games? Why is the advertised version of happiness flawed? Why is the Eastern version flawed?
5. Ciardi says that "happiness is never more than partial." What is another characteristic of happiness?

Drawing Inferences about Thesis and Purpose

1. What are the ingredients for happiness that Ciardi presents? State, in your own words, the key elements of his definition.
2. Examine Ciardi's discussion of American advertising in paragraphs 3 through 5. What is his attitude toward advertising? How do you know?

Analyzing Strategies and Style

1. In developing his definition, Ciardi refers to five writers. What do these references tell you about the author? What do they suggest about Ciardi's anticipated audience?

2. Ciardi begins and ends his essay with metaphors. Explain the metaphor in his first two sentences and the metaphor in his last two sentences. What points about happiness does each metaphor suggest?
3. List all the strategies that Ciardi uses to develop his definition, giving an example of each one.

Thinking Critically

1. Ciardi thinks that happiness is a difficult term to define. Do you agree? Would you agree that it is the sort of concept that we think we understand until we are pressed to define it?
2. Ciardi asserts that "there is no happiness except as we take on life-engaging difficulties." Do you agree? Why or why not?
3. Ciardi does not think that happiness can be found in "getting the most toys," to use a modern expression. What is the relationship between money and happiness? Can some money help? Does having money make happiness more difficult to obtain? Be prepared to explain and defend your views.

Discrimination Is a Virtue

ROBERT KEITH MILLER

Holding a Ph.D. from Columbia University, Robert Keith Miller is a professor of English at St. Thomas University. He has published scholarly articles and books on such writers as Mark Twain, Oscar Wilde, and Willa Cather and has written for popular magazines and newspapers as well. In the following essay, which appeared in *Newsweek*'s "My Turn" column in 1980, Miller seeks to rescue the word *discrimination* from its misuse in our time.

Questions to Guide Your Reading and Reflection

1. What does *discrimination* mean, as Miller defines it?
2. How do most Americans use this word today?

When I was a child, my grandmother used to tell me a story   1
about a king who had three daughters and decided to test their
love. He asked each of them "How much do you love me?" The
first replied that she loved him as much as all the diamonds

and pearls in the world. The second said that she loved him more than life itself. The third replied "I love you as fresh meat loves salt."

2   This answer enraged the king; he was convinced that his youngest daughter was making fun of him. So he banished her from his realm and left all of his property to her elder sisters.

3   As the story unfolded it became clear, even to a 6-year-old, that the king had made a terrible mistake. The two older girls were hypocrites, and as soon as they had profited from their father's generosity, they began to treat him very badly. A wiser man would have realized that the youngest daughter was the truest. Without attempting to flatter, she had said, in effect, "We go together naturally; we are a perfect team."

4   Years later, when I came to read Shakespeare, I realized that my grandmother's story was loosely based upon the story of King Lear, who put his daughters to a similar test and did not know how to judge the results. Attempting to save the king from the consequences of his foolishness, a loyal friend pleads, "Come sir, arise, away! I'll teach you differences." Unfortunately, the lesson comes too late. Because Lear could not tell the difference between true love and false, he loses his kingdom and eventually his life.

5   We have a word in English which means "the ability to tell differences." That word is *discrimination*. But within the last twenty years, this word has been so frequently misused that an entire generation has grown up believing that "discrimination" means "racism." People are always proclaiming that "discrimination" is something that should be done away with. Should that ever happen, it would prove to be our undoing.

6   Discrimination means discernment; it means the ability to perceive the truth, to use good judgment and to profit accordingly. The *Oxford English Dictionary* traces this understanding of the word back to 1648 and demonstrates that, for the next 300 years, "discrimination" was a virtue, not a vice. Thus, when a character in a nineteenth-century novel makes a happy marriage, Dickens has another character remark, "It does credit to your discrimination that you should have found such a very excellent young woman."

7   Of course, "the ability to tell differences" assumes that differences exist, and this is unsettling for a culture obsessed with the notion of equality. The contemporary belief that discrimi-

nation is a vice stems from the compound "discriminate against." What we need to remember, however, is that some things deserve to be judged harshly: we should not leave our kingdoms to the selfish and the wicked.

Discrimination is wrong only when someone or something   8
is discriminated against because of prejudice. But to use the word in this sense, as so many people do, is to destroy its true meaning. If you discriminate against something because of general preconceptions rather than particular insights, then you are not discriminating—bias has clouded the clarity of vision which discrimination demands.

One of the great ironies of American life is that we man-   9
age to discriminate in the practical decisions of daily life, but usually fail to discriminate when we make public policies. Most people are very discriminating when it comes to buying a car, for example, because they realize that cars have differences. Similarly, an increasing number of people have learned to discriminate in what they eat. Some foods are better than others—and indiscriminate eating can undermine one's health.

Yet in public affairs, good judgment is depressingly rare. In   10
many areas which involve the common good, we see a failure to tell differences.

Consider, for example, some of the thinking behind modern   11
education. On the one hand, there is a refreshing realization that there are differences among children, and some children— be they gifted or handicapped—require special education. On the other hand, we are politically unable to accept the consequences of this perception. The trend in recent years has been to group together students of radically different ability. We call this process "mainstreaming," and it strikes me as a characteristically American response to the discovery of differences: we try to pretend that differences do not matter.

Similarly, we try to pretend that there is little difference be-   12
tween the sane and the insane. A fashionable line of argument has it that "everybody is a little mad" and that few mental patients deserve long-term hospitalization. As a consequence of such reasoning, thousands of seriously ill men and women have been evicted from their hospital beds and returned to what is euphemistically called "the community"—which often means being left to sleep on city streets, where confused and helpless

people now live out of paper bags as the direct result of our refusal to discriminate.

13   Or to choose a final example from a different area: how many recent elections reflect thoughtful consideration of the genuine differences among candidates? Benumbed by television commercials that market aspiring officeholders as if they were a new brand of toothpaste or hair spray, too many Americans vote with only a fuzzy understanding of the issues in question. Like Lear, we seem too eager to leave the responsibility of government to others and too ready to trust those who tell us whatever we want to hear.

14   So as we look around us, we should recognize that "discrimination" is a virtue which we desperately need. We must try to avoid making unfair and arbitrary distinctions, but we must not go to the other extreme and pretend that there are no distinctions to be made. The ability to make intelligent judgments is essential both for the success of one's personal life and for the functioning of society as a whole. Let us be open-minded by all means, but not so open-minded that our brains fall out.

Expanding Vocabulary

Examine the following words in their contexts in the essay and then write a brief definition or synonym for each one. (Do not use a dictionary; try to guess the word's meanings from its context.) The number in parentheses is the number of the paragraph in which the word appears

banished (2)	undermine (9)
realm (2)	evicted (12)
hypocrites (3)	euphemistically (12)
discernment (6)	benumbed (13)
preconceptions (8)	

Understanding Content

1. Currently, how is the word *discrimination* being used? How does the current use of the word change its connotation? (See the Glossary, if necessary, for the definition of *connotation*.)
2. When is discrimination wrong? When it is wrong, what should it be called? What has actually happened to one's ability to discriminate?

3. Under what circumstances do people usually discriminate? In what area of life do we often fail to discriminate?

Drawing Inferences about Thesis and Purpose

1. What is Miller's purpose in defining *discrimination*? What point does he want to make about the word?
2. State Miller's thesis.

Analyzing Strategies and Style

1. What opening strategy does Miller use? How does it lead into his subject?
2. What are Miller's examples of public policy failures in discrimination? Are they effective examples, showing a range of public policy problems?
3. Examine Miller's closing paragraph. Is it effective in its balanced language? What makes the final sentence clever?

Thinking Critically

1. Is the definition of *discrimination* that Miller wants to highlight familiar to you, or do you know the word only as it means to show prejudice? Do you see how the two meanings could develop in the same word?
2. Do you agree with Miller that we are "benumbed by television commercials" and "vote with only a fuzzy understanding of the issues"? Have you voted with a good knowledge of the candidates and the issues? (Have you voted? If not, why not?)
3. Is the American focus on equality keeping us from learning to discern differences? Explain.
4. Should differences in ability be ignored in education in favor of "mainstreaming"? Why or why not?

Doubts About Doublespeak

WILLIAM LUTZ

William Lutz is a name almost synonymous with the defense of plain language. He is a professor of English at Rutgers University and is also a member of the Pennsylvania Bar. For 14 years he was the editor of the *Quarterly Review of Doublespeak*.

A consultant to corporations seeking help in plain language, Lutz is the author of many books and articles on language, including *The New Doublespeak: Why No One Knows What Anyone's Saying Anymore* (1996) and *Doublespeak Defined* (1999). The following essay was published in the July 1993 issue of *State Government News.*

Questions to Guide Your Reading and Reflection

1. Why should doublespeak not be confused with careless writing?
2. What examples of doublespeak can you recall—or make up?

---

1   During the past year, we learned that we can shop at a "unique retail biosphere" instead of a farmers' market, where we can buy items made of "synthetic glass" instead of plastic, or purchase a "high velocity, multipurpose air circulator," or electric fan. A "wastewater conveyance facility" may "exceed the odor threshold" from time to time due to the presence of "regulated human nutrients," but that is not to be confused with a sewage plant that stinks up the neighborhood with sewage sludge. Nor should we confuse a "resource development park" with a dump. Thus does doublespeak continue to spread.

2   Doublespeak is language which pretends to communicate but doesn't. It is language which makes the bad seem good, the negative seem positive, the unpleasant seem attractive, or at least tolerable. It is language which avoids, shifts or denies responsibility; language which is at variance with real or purported meaning. It is language which conceals or prevents thought.

3   Doublespeak is all around us. We are asked to check our packages at the desk "for our convenience" when it's not for our convenience at all but for someone else's convenience. We see advertisements for "preowned," "experienced" or "previously distinguished" cars, not used cars and for "genuine imitation leather," "virgin vinyl" or "real counterfeit diamonds." Television offers not reruns but "encore telecasts." There are no slums or ghettos just the "inner city" or "substandard housing" where the "disadvantaged" or "economically nonaffluent" live and where there might be a problem with "substance abuse." Nonprofit organizations don't make a profit, they have

"negative deficits" or experience "revenue excesses." With doublespeak it's not dying but "terminal living" or "negative patient care outcome."

There are four kinds of doublespeak. The first kind is the eu-   4
phemism, a word or phrase designed to avoid a harsh or distasteful reality. Used to mislead or deceive, the euphemism becomes doublespeak. In 1984 the U.S. State Department's annual reports on the status of human rights around the world ceased using the word "killing". Instead the State Department used the phrase "unlawful or arbitrary deprivation of life," thus avoiding the embarrassing situation of government-sanctioned killing in countries supported by the United States.

A second kind of doublespeak is jargon, the specialized lan-   5
guage of a trade, profession or similar group, such as doctors, lawyers, plumbers or car mechanics. Legitimately used, jargon allows members of a group to communicate with each other clearly, efficiently and quickly. Lawyers and tax accountants speak to each other of an "involuntary conversion" of property, a legal term that means the loss or destruction of property through theft, accident or condemnation. But when lawyers or tax accountants use unfamiliar terms to speak to others, then the jargon becomes doublespeak.

In 1978 a commercial 727 crashed on takeoff, killing three   6
passengers, injuring 21 others and destroying the airplane. The insured value of the airplane was greater than its book value, so the airline made a profit of $1.7 million, creating two problems: the airline didn't want to talk about one of its airplanes crashing, yet it had to account for that $1.7 million profit in its annual report to its stockholders. The airline solved both problems by inserting a footnote in its annual report which explained that the $1.7 million was due to "the involuntary conversion of a 727."

A third kind of doublespeak is gobbledygook or bureau-   7
cratese. Such doublespeak is simply a matter of overwhelming the audience with words—the more the better. Alan Greenspan, a polished practitioner of bureaucratese, once testified before a Senate committee that "it is a tricky problem to find the particular calibration in timing that would be appropriate to stem the acceleration in risk premiums created by falling incomes without permanently aborting the decline in the inflation-generated risk premiums."

8   The fourth kind of doublespeak is inflated language, which is designed to make the ordinary seem extraordinary, to make everyday things seem impressive, to give an air or importance to people or situations, to make the simple seem complex. Thus do car mechanics become "automotive internists," elevator operators become "members of the vertical transportation corps," grocery store checkout clerks become "career associate scanning professionals," and smelling something becomes "organoleptic analysis."

9   Doublespeak is not the product of careless language or sloppy thinking. Quite the opposite. Doublespeak is language carefully designed and constructed to appear to communicate when in fact it doesn't. It is language designed not to lead but to mislead. Thus, it is not a tax increase but a "revenue enhancement" or "tax-base broadening." So how can you complain about higher taxes? Those aren't useless, billion dollar pork barrel projects; they're really "congressional projects of national significance," so don't complain about wasteful government spending. That isn't the mafia in Atlantic City; those are just "members of a career-offender cartel," so don't worry about the influence of organized crime in the city.

10   New doublespeak is created every day. The Environmental Protection Agency once called acid rain "poorly-buffered precipitation" then dropped that term in favor of "atmospheric deposition of anthropogenically-derived acidic substances," but recently decided that acid rain should be called "wet deposition." The Pentagon, which has in the past given us such classic doublespeak as "hexiform rotatable surface compression unit" for steel nut, just published a pamphlet warning soldiers that exposure to nerve gas will lead to "immediate permanent incapacitation." That's almost as good as the Pentagon's official term "servicing the target," meaning to kill the enemy. Meanwhile, the Department of Energy wants to establish a "monitored retrievable storage site," a place once known as a dump for spent nuclear fuel.

11   Bad economic times give rise to lots of new doublespeak designed to avoid some very unpleasant economic realities. As the "contained depression" continues so does the corporate policy of making up even more new terms to avoid the simple, and easily understandable, term "layoff." So it is that corporations "reposition," "restructure," "reshape" or "realign" the

company and "reduce duplication" through "release of resources" that involves a "permanent downsizing" or a "payroll adjustment" that results in a number of employees being "involuntarily terminated."

Other countries regularly contribute to doublespeak. In 12 Japan, where baldness is called "hair disadvantaged," the economy is undergoing a "severe adjustment process," while in Canada there is an "involuntary downward development" of the work force. For some government agencies in Canada, wastepaper baskets have become "user friendly, space effective, flexible, deskside sanitation units." Politicians in Canada may engage in "reality augmentation," but they never lie. As part of their new freedom, the people of Moscow can visit "intimacy salons," or sex shops as they're known in other countries. When dealing with the bureaucracy in Russia, people know that they should show officials "normal gratitude," or give them a bribe.

The worst doublespeak is the doublespeak of death. It is the 13 language, wrote George Orwell in 1946, that is "largely the defense of the indefensible . . . designed to make lies sound truthful and murder respectable, and to give an appearance of solidity to pure wind." In the doublespeak of death, Orwell continued, "defenseless villages are bombarded from the air, the inhabitants driven out into the countryside, the cattle machine-gunned, the huts set on fire with incendiary bullets. This is called pacification. Millions of peasants are robbed of their farms and sent trudging along the roads with no more than they can carry. This is called transfer of population or rectification of frontiers," Today, in a country once called Yugoslavia, this is called "ethnic cleansing."

It's easy to laugh off doublespeak. After all, we all know 14 what's going on, so what's the harm? But we don't always know what's going on, and when that happens doublespeak accomplishes its ends. It alters our perception of reality. It deprives us of the tools we need to develop, advance and preserve our society, our culture, our civilization. It breeds suspicion, cynicism, distrust and, ultimately, hostility. It delivers us into the hands of those who do not have our interests at heart. As Samuel Johnson noted in 18th century England, even the devils in hell do not lie to one another, since the society of hell could not subsist without the truth, any more than any other society.

Expanding Vocabulary

Study the definitions for any of the following words you do not know. Then use each one in a separate sentence. The number in parentheses is the number of the paragraph in which the word appears.

variance (2)	cynicism (14)
deprives (14)	subsist (14)

Understanding Content

1. What is doublespeak? Define it in your own words.
2. What are the four kinds of doublespeak? Explain each one.
3. What is the purpose of doublespeak?
4. What kinds of times invite new doublespeak?
5. What is the worst kind of doublespeak?
6. What is the problem with doublespeak? Why do we need to take it seriously?

Drawing Inferences about Thesis and Purpose

1. What is Lutz's purpose in writing?
2. How does Lutz feel about doublespeak? How do you know?
3. Write a thesis for the essay.

Analyzing Strategies and Style

1. Lutz opens with examples of doublespeak. What does he gain by this strategy?
2. List the specific strategies the author uses to develop his definition.
3. In your view, what two or three examples are the best in illustrating doublespeak? Why?

Thinking Critically

1. Lutz asserts that doublespeak "alters our perception of reality." How can this be? What role does language play in our understanding of reality?
2. Are you bothered by doublespeak? Why or why not?
3. Why do ordinary people resort to doublespeak? What might be some of the motivation?
4. Why do governments resort to doublespeak?

The Difference Between "Sick" and "Evil"

ANDREW VACHSS

A lawyer whose only clients are children, Andrew Vachss is also the author of more than a dozen novels. More information about Mr. Vachss, and more articles written by him, can be found at *www.vachss.com*. In response to the news coverage of Roman Catholic priests accused of child abuse, Vachss has written the following essay, which appeared in *Parade* magazine July 14, 2002.

Questions to Guide Your Reading and Reflection

1. What is the context in which the author raises the question of the difference between sick and evil?
2. What should the Roman Catholic Church do about pedophile priests?

The shock waves caused by the recent exposures of so-called 1
"pedophile priests" have reverberated throughout America. But beneath our anger and revulsion, a fundamental question pulsates: Are those who abuse positions of trust to prey upon children—a category certainly not limited to those in religious orders—sick . . . or are they evil?

We need the answer to that fundamental question. Because, 2
without the truth, we cannot act. And until we act, nothing will change.

My job is protecting children. It has taken me from big cities 3
to rural outposts, from ghettos to penthouses and from courtrooms to genocidal battlefields. But whatever the venue, the truth remains constant: Some humans intentionally hurt children. They commit unspeakable acts—for their pleasure, their profit, or both.

Many people who hear of my cases against humans who 4
rape, torture and package children for sale or rent immediately respond with, "That's sick!" Crimes against children seem so grotesquely abnormal that the most obvious explanation is that

the perpetrator must be mentally ill—helpless in the grip of a force beyond his or her control.

5   But that very natural reaction has, inadvertently, created a special category of "blameless predator." That confusion of "sick" with "sickening" is the single greatest barrier to our primary biological and ethical mandate: the protection of our children.

6   The difference between sick and evil cannot be dismissed with facile eye-of-the-beholder rhetoric. There are specific criteria we can employ to give us the answers in every case, every time.

7   Some of those answers are self-evident and beyond dispute: A mother who puts her baby in the oven because she hears voices commanding her to bake the devil out of the child's spirit is sick; and a mother who sells or rents her baby to child pornographers is evil. But most cases of child sexual abuse—especially those whose "nonviolent" perpetrators come from within the child's circle of trust—seem, on their surface, to be far more complex.

8   That complexity is an illusion. The truth is as simple as it is terrifying:

9   Sickness is a condition.

10   Evil is a behavior.

11   Evil is always a matter of choice. Evil is not thought; it is conduct. And that conduct is always volitional.

12   And just as evil is always a choice, sickness is always the absence of choice. Sickness happens. Evil is inflicted.

13   Until we perceive the difference clearly, we will continue to give aid and comfort to our most pernicious enemies. We, as a society, decide whether something is sick or evil. Either decision confers an obligation upon us. Sickness should be treated. Evil must be fought.

14   If a person has desires or fantasies about sexually exploiting children, that individual may be sick. (Indeed, if such desires are disturbing, as opposed to gratifying to the individual, there may even be a "cure.") But if the individual chooses to act upon those feelings, that conduct is evil. People are not what they think; they are what they do.

15   Our society distrusts the term "evil." It has an almost biblical ring to it—something we believe in (or not) but never actually understand. We prefer scientific-sounding terms, such

as "sociopath." But sociopathy is not a mental condition; it is a specific cluster of behaviors. The diagnosis is only made from actual criminal conduct.

No reputable psychiatrist claims to be able to cure a so- 16 ciopath—or, for that matter, a predatory pedophile. Even the most optimistic professionals do not aim to change such a person's thoughts and feelings. What they hope is that the predator can learn self-control, leading to a change in behavior.

Such hopes ignore the inescapable fact that the overwhelm- 17 ing majority of those who prey upon children don't want to change their behavior—they want only to minimize the consequences of being caught at it.

In the animal kingdom, there is a food chain—predators and 18 prey. But among humans, there is no such natural order. Among our species, predators select themselves for that role.

Psychology has given us many insights of great value. But it 19 also has clouded our vision with euphemisms. To say a person suffers from the "disease" of pedophilia is to absolve the predator of responsibility for his behavior.

Imagine if an attorney, defending someone accused of com- 20 mitting a dozen holdups, told the jury his poor client was suffering from "armed-robberia." That jury would decide that the only crazy person in the courtroom was the lawyer.

When a perpetrator claims to be sick, the *timing* of that claim 21 is critical to discovering the truth. Predatory pedophiles carefully insinuate themselves into positions of trust. They select their prey and approach cautiously. Gradually, sometimes over a period of years, they gain greater control over their victims. Eventually, they leave dozens of permanently damaged children in their wake.

But only when they are caught do predatory pedophiles de- 22 clare themselves to be sick. And the higher the victim count, the sicker (and therefore less responsible) they claim to be.

In too many cases, a veil of secrecy and protection then de- 23 scends. The predator's own organization appoints itself judge and jury. The perpetrator is deemed sick and sent off for inhouse "treatment." The truth is never made public. And when some secret tribunal decides that a cure has been achieved, the perpetrator's rights and privileges are restored, and he or she is given a new assignment.

24   In fact, such privileged predators actually are assisted. They enter new communities with the blessing of their own organization, their history and propensities kept secret. As a direct result, unsuspecting parents entrust their children to them. Inevitably, the predator eventually resumes his or her conduct and preys upon children again. And when that conduct comes to light, the claim of "sickness" re-emerges as well.

25   Too often, our society contorts itself to excuse such predators. We are so eager to call those who sexually abuse children "sick," so quick to understand their demons. Why? Because sickness not only offers the possibility of finding a cure but also assures us that the predator didn't really mean it. After all, it is human nature to try to understand inhuman conduct.

26   Conversely, the concept of evil terrifies us. The idea that some humans *choose* to prey upon our children is frightening, and their demonstrated skill at camouflage only heightens this fear.

27   For some, the question, "Does evil exist?" is philosophical. But for those who have confronted or been victimized by predatory pedophiles, there is no question at all. We are what we do.

28   Just as conduct is a choice, so is our present helplessness. We may be powerless to change the arrogance of those who believe they alone should have the authority to decide whether predatory pedophiles are "sick" or when they are "cured." But, as with the perpetrators themselves, we do have the power to change their behavior.

29   In every state, laws designate certain professions that regularly come into contact with children—such as teachers, doctors, social workers and day-care employees—as "mandated reporters." Such personnel are required to report reasonable suspicion of child abuse when it comes to their attention. Failure to do so is a crime.

30   Until now, we have exempted religious organizations from mandated-reporter laws. Recent events have proved the catastrophic consequences of this exemption. We must demand— now—that our legislators close this pathway to evil.

31   A predatory pedophile who is recycled into an unsuspecting community enters it cloaked with a protection no other sex offender enjoys. If members of religious orders were mandated reporters, we would not have to rely on their good-faith belief that a predator is cured. We could make our own informed decisions on this most vital issue.

Modifying the law in this way would not interfere with   32
priest-penitent privileges: When child victims or their parents
disclose abuse, they are not confessing, they are crying for help.
Neither confidentiality nor religious freedom would in any
way be compromised by mandatory reporting.

Changing the laws so that religious orders join the ranks of   33
mandated reporters is the right thing to do. And the time is
right now.

Expanding Vocabulary

Match each word in column A with its definition in column B. When
in doubt, first find the word in the essay and look for context clues
to aid your understanding of the word's meaning. Then, if necessary, use your dictionary to complete the matching exercise. The
number in parentheses is the number of the paragraph in which the
word appears.

Column A	*Column B*
pedophile (1)	vibrates
reverberated (1)	one who is guilty of, responsible for
revulsion (1)	site, place
pulsates (1)	psychopath with aggressive, antisocial
genocidal (3)	behavior
venue (3)	conscious choice
grotesquely (4)	destructive, cruel, evil
perpetrator (4)	select, specify
mandate (5)	echoed repeatedly, resounded
facile (6)	inoffensive terms used for offensive ones
volitional (11)	imposed on
inflicted (12)	cleverly place
pernicious (13)	hiding
sociopath (15)	command
euphemisms (19)	natural inclinations
insinuate (21)	binds and twists out of shape
tribunal (23)	one who has a preference for children
propensities (24)	freed from obligation
contorts (25)	distortedly, bizarrely
camouflage (26)	simple, easy
designate (29)	disgust, loathing
exempted (30)	court or committee giving a legal
	decision
	engaged in planned killing of a
	particular group

Understanding Content

1. Is Vachss writing only about pedophile priests? How do you know?
2. What, according to the author, is our primary mandate? In what sense is it our primary biological mandate?
3. What is the difference between *sick* and *evil?*
4. What should be our response to sickness? To evil?
5. Why do we have problems with the word *evil?*
6. How have some child abusers avoided punishment?
7. What does Vachss want to see changed? How does he think this will improve the situation—that is, help protect more children?

Drawing Inferences about Thesis and Purpose

1. What is Vachss's thesis? You may need to use more than one sentence to give a definition of evil and to connect that to the author's call for action.
2. Vachss says that psychology "has clouded our vision with euphemisms." Explain his meaning.

Analyzing Strategies and Style

1. How would you describe the author's tone? You may need to use more than one word, for example, "outrageously silly" or "deeply caring."
2. Generally, Vachss's paragraphs are short, but paragraphs 8 through 12 are especially brief. Why? What does he gain by short sentences and paragraphs in this part of his essay?

Thinking Critically

1. Do you agree with Vachss's definitions of *sick* and *evil?* Why or why not?
2. Do you agree that, today, we have trouble with the term *evil?* Why or why not?
3. Should religious organizations be covered under the mandated-reporter law? Why or why not?
4. Is our society doing an adequate job of caring for and protecting our children? Explain your views.

Freedom's Not Just Another Word

DAVID HACKETT FISCHER

Holding a Ph.D. from Johns Hopkins, Dr. Fischer is a professor of history at Brandeis University and the author of many articles and books on American history, including *Bound Away: Virginia and the Westward Movement* (2000) and *Liberty and Freedom: A Visual History of America's Founding Ideas* (2004). His *New York Times* essay on the terms *liberty* and *freedom* appeared on February 7, 2005.

Questions to Guide Your Reading and Reflection

1. What is the relationship of these terms' meanings and history and culture?
2. Do you see a distinction between the terms *liberty* and *freedom*?

In Baghdad's Fardus Square, where Iraqi civilians and 1
American marines so famously pulled down the statue of Saddam Hussein in the spring of 2003, Iraqi artists have raised a new sculpture on the same pedestal. It is a monument to liberty and freedom, and unlike any other in the world.

In Europe and America, the favorite symbols of liberty and 2
freedom are individual figures like Marianne or the Statue of Liberty. This Iraqi statue is a family group: mother, father and child so close together that they become one being. Above them are a crescent moon and sun, emblems of Islamic faith and Sumerian culture. One of its creators remarked that both civilizations "have called for love, peace and freedom."

The Baghdad monument was the work of a group of Iraqi 3
artists called Najeen, or the Survivors. After the Persian Gulf war in 1991, they worked underground to keep alive the spirit of liberty and freedom. Their monument has a message about that. "Freedom is not a gift from people with tanks," Basim Hassad, a Najeen member, told a BBC reporter. "What we see in our country could be the first signs of freedom. What remains is a history that we will make together with the Najeen group at its heart."

4 Foreigners who opposed the Iraqi war were not impressed. "On top of the marble column where Saddam's statue stood, someone put up the most hideous monstrosity I've ever seen," one wrote contemptuously,"A green statue with a face that's not recognizable as anything human. It's supposed to be some kind of 'goddess of liberty,' but it looks like nothing in any of the worlds."

5 The writer missed the meaning of the monument, which in fact has much to teach us about liberty and freedom. These ideas are growing and changing rapidly today, and their long history is more dynamic and diverse than our thoughts about it. There is no one true definition of liberty and freedom in the world, though many people to the left and right believe that they have found it. And, yet, there is one great historical process in which liberty and freedom have developed, often in unexpected ways.

6 The words themselves have a surprising history. The oldest known word with such a meaning comes to us from ancient Iraq. The Sumerian "ama-ar-gi," found on tablets in the ruins of the city-state of Lagash, which flourished four millenniums ago, derived from the verb "ama-gi," which literally meant "going home to mother." It described the condition of emancipated servants who returned to their own free families—an interesting link to the monument in Baghdad. (In contemporary America, the ancient characters for "ama-ar-gi" have become the logos of some libertarian organizations, as well as tattoos among members of politically conservative motorcycle gangs, who may not know that the inscriptions on their biceps mean heading home to mom.)

7 Equally surprising are the origins of our English words liberty and, especially, freedom. They have very different roots. The Latin *libertas* and Greek *eleutheria* both indicated a condition of independence, unlike a slave. (In science, *eleutherodactylic* means separate fingers or toes.) Freedom, however, comes from the same root as friend, an Indo-European word that meant "dear" or "beloved." It meant a connection to other free people by bonds of kinship or affection, also unlike a slave. Liberty and freedom both meant "unlike a slave." But liberty meant privileges of independence; freedom referred to rights of belonging.

We English-speakers are possibly unique in having both   8
"liberty" and "freedom" in our ordinary speech. The two
words have blurred together in modern usage, but the old tension between them persists like a coiled spring in our culture.
It has inspired an astonishing fertility of thought. Americans
have invented many ideas of liberty and freedom. Some are
close to independence, others to rights of belonging. Most are
highly creative combinations. For most people they are not academic abstractions or political ideologies, but inherited ideas
that we hold as what Tocqueville called "habits of the heart."
They tend to be entire visions of a free society, and we see them
in our mind's eye through symbols and emblems, much as Najeen envisions symbols in Iraq.

I have counted more than 500 such literal symbols of liberty   9
and freedom in America alone. In the American Revolution
they included New England's Liberty Tree with its collective
sense of town-born rights, Philadelphia's great Quaker Bell
ringing for all humanity, Virginia's hierarchical Liberty Goddess, South Carolina's Liberty Crescent, and the rattlesnake of
individual independence, with its motto, "Don't Tread on Me."
Other emblems were invented by German immigrants, African
slaves, trans-Atlantic artisans and Loyalist elites. All were different combinations of liberty and freedom.

The Civil War, of course, was a conflict between visions of   10
liberty, freedom, union and rights of belonging on one side;
and ideas of states' rights, separation and liberty to keep a
slave on the other. Many competing images of liberty and freedom appeared in the Progressive Era, and again in the 1930's
when President Franklin D. Roosevelt's "broader definition of
liberty" and "greater freedom, greater security" were fiercely
opposed by the conservative Liberty League. It happened
again in the 1950's and 60's, with the Rev. Dr. Martin Luther
King Jr.'s dream of freedom as rights of belonging, and Barry
Goldwater's impassioned idea of liberty as independence from
intrusive government. But perhaps the most fertile period of
invention was the late 20th century. Through 16 generations,
American ideas of liberty and freedom have grown larger,
deeper, more diverse and yet more inclusive in these collisions
of contested visions.

11   One can observe this growth not only in America as a whole, but also in the thought of individual Americans. An example, of course, is George W. Bush. His speeches before 2001 centered on a particular idea of personal liberty, private property, individual responsibility and minimal government. By his second inaugural last month, that vision had grown larger. It preserved the idea of individual liberty, but also quoted Franklin Roosevelt's "broader definition of liberty" and "greater freedom from want and fear." It embraced Dr. King's "freedom now," and adopted the universal Quaker vision of "liberty throughout all the land," even enlarging it to "liberty throughout all the world."

12   How these words will be defined by acts in Mr. Bush's second term remains to be seen. His first administration was very careless of civil liberties for others, and little interested in civil rights; he spoke often of the rights of the unborn but enacted fiscal policies that betrayed the rights of generations to come. One hopes that the larger spirit of the second inaugural address will appear in political acts to come.

13   I found it most striking that Mr. Bush also explicitly recognized that liberty and freedom take different forms throughout the world, where "others find their own voice, attain their own freedom, and make their own way." His phrasing would seem to recognize that this is a global process that is broader than the American experience of liberty and freedom, and yet preserves the same dynamics.

14   In India, for example, leaders of the Congress Party have combined Western ideas with Hindu and Buddhist beliefs to create old-new visions of liberty and freedom that are unique to that republic. In Beijing, the students who constructed the Goddess of Tiananmen Square in 1989 created a new symbol that combined American liberty and freedom, Russian socialism and Chinese culture, a radical new vision of a free world. The people of Eastern Europe have invented their own visions from traditions like Poland's collective memory of its "golden freedom" during the 17th century. The same thing is happening in Ukraine and the Balkans, Latin America and Africa, Southeast Asia and the Pacific.

15   Most of all it is happening in Islam today. We find it in the Baghdad monument that links liberty and freedom to the faith

of Islam and the history of Mesopotamia. We see it in the ink-stained fingers of millions of Iraqis, held upright in a new symbol of courage against tyranny, pride in an ancient past, and hope for the future of a free world.

The catch, of course, is that people become more truly free 16
only when the central ideas are respected: liberty as the rights of individual independence, freedom in the rights of collective belonging. Many on the right and left continue to call for one idea without the other, but the strongest ground is in the center, where they come together.

People across the globe will continue to create new combi- 17
nations of liberty and freedom, with an inexhaustible fertility of invention. These visions are profoundly different from one another, but they are all part of one great historical process that is more open and free than any one idea of liberty or freedom has ever been, or even wished to be.

Expanding Vocabulary

Study the definitions for any of the following words that you do not know. Then select four of the words and use each one in a separate sentence. The number in parentheses is the number of the paragraph in which the word appears.

crescent (2)	ideologies (8)
Sumerian (2)	hierarchical (9)
contemptuously (4)	intrusive (10)
emancipated (6)	

Understanding Content

1. What is the oldest source of a word for *liberty* or *freedom*? What does the word mean?
2. What do the origins of the English words *liberty* and *freedom* have in common? How do their original definitions differ?
3. What has been the relationship of the two words in America's history?
4. How should Americans see their meanings of the words in relationship to other cultures?
5. When did Iraqis hold up ink-stained fingers as a new symbol of hope for freedom?

Drawing Inferences about Thesis and Purpose

1. Fischer writes that the words *freedom* and *liberty* exist in a "tension" "like a coiled spring." What does he suggest with this metaphor?
2. How does Fischer want the terms to connect? Write a thesis for his essay.

Analyzing Strategies and Style

1. Fischer's rather lengthy introduction discusses a new statue in Baghdad's Fardus Square. What does the statue mean to Iraqis? How does the opening connect to Fischer's topic?
2. List all the strategies the author uses to develop his definition.

Thinking Critically

1. Fischer refers to a number of symbols of liberty. Why do we have so many symbols for this term?
2. The author connects the meanings of *liberty* and *freedom* to history and to culture. Why is it important to recognize that there is not one, unchanging definition of these terms?
3. How do the differing definitions of these terms in American culture help us to understand conflicts between Republicans and Democrats?

Curiosity

ALASTAIR REID

A Scotsman who prefers to live in Spain, Alastair Reid is a poet, translator, essayist, writer of children's books, and lecturer. Holding a master's degree from Scotland's St. Andrews University, Reid has lectured at schools in England, Spain, and the United States. He has had several books of poems published, has translated much of the poetry of Latin American poet Pablo Neruda, and has been a staff writer for *The New Yorker*. "Curiosity" appeared first in *The New Yorker* and was then included in the collection *Weathering* (1959).

Curiosity

may have killed the cat. More likely,
the cat was just unlucky, or else curious
to see what death was like, having no cause
to go on licking paws, or fathering
litter on litter of kittens, predictably.   5

Nevertheless, to be curious
is dangerous enough. To distrust
what is always said, what seems,
to ask odd questions, interfere in dreams,
smell rats, leave home, have hunches,   10
does not endear cats to those doggy circles
where well-smelt baskets, suitable wives, good lunches
are the order of things, and where prevails
much wagging of incurious heads and tails.

Face it. Curiosity   15
will not cause us to die—
only lack of it will.
Never to want to see
the other side of the hill
or that improbable country   20
where living is an idyll
(although a probable hell)
would kill us all.
Only the curious
have if they live a tale   25
worth telling at all.
Dogs say cats love too much, are irresponsible,
are dangerous, marry too many wives,
desert their children, chill all dinner tables
with tales of their nine lives.   30

Well, they are lucky. Let them be
nine-lived and contradictory,
curious enough to change, prepared to pay
the cat-price, which is to die
and die again and again,   35
each time with no less pain.

A cat-minority of one
is all that can be counted on
to tell the truth; and what cats have to tell
40 on each return from hell
is this: that dying is what the living do,
that dying is what the loving do,
and that dead dogs are those who never know
that dying is what, to live, each has to do.

Understanding Content and Strategies

1. What is more likely than curiosity to have killed the cat?
2. Why is being curious "dangerous enough"?
3. What kind of people belong to "doggy circles"?
4. What do dogs say about cats? What traits do they ascribe to them? Are we to agree with the dogs' view of cats? How do you know?
5. What are the characteristics of the curious life? Given the rather negative-sounding elements of this life, why should we be like the curious cat rather than the incurious dog?
6. Notice that the title runs into the first line. How does Reid's use of punctuation (to stop us) or no punctuation (to keep us reading) parallel what he is observing about curiosity or the lack of it?
7. What is the term for poems that have the pattern—or lack of pattern—that you find in "Curiosity"?

Drawing Inferences about Theme

1. When the poet writes that "dying is what, to live, each has to do," what does he mean? The statement seems contradictory. What is the term for this strategy for gaining emphasis? For the statement to make sense, how do you have to take the word *dying?*
2. State the poem's meaning or theme. What does Reid want us to understand about the role of curiosity in life?

Thinking Critically

1. Do you find the use of cats and dogs an effective one? For the most part, do the personalities of cats and dogs seem to fit the distinction Reid wants to make?
2. Is curiosity an important trait? Why or why not? What are its virtues? What are its dangers?
3. Are most children more like cats or dogs? If they are like cats, then why are some adults so incurious? If they are like dogs, what are some ways they can be encouraged to develop curiosity?

STUDENT ESSAY—DEFINITION

PARAGON OR PARASITE?
Laura Mullins

Do you recognize this creature? He is low maintenance and often unnoticeable, a favorite companion of many. Requiring no special attention, he grows from the soil of pride and rejection, feeding regularly on a diet of ignorance and insecurity, scavenging for hurt feelings and defensiveness, gobbling up dainty morsels of lust and scandal. Like a cult leader clothed in a gay veneer, disguising himself as blameless, he wields power. Bewitching unsuspecting but devoted groupies, distracting them from honest self-examination, deceiving them into believing illusions of grandeur or, on the other extreme, unredeemable worthlessness, he breeds jealousy, hate, and fear; thus, he thrives. He is Gossip.

Attention-getting introduction

Clever extended metaphor

Subject introduced

One of my dearest friends is a gossip. She is an educated, honorable, compassionate, loving woman whose character and judgment I deeply admire and respect. After sacrificially raising six children, she went on to study medicine and become a doctor who graciously volunteers her expertise. How, you may be wondering, could a gossip deserve such praise?

Then you do not understand the word. My friend is my daughter's godmother; she is my gossip, or *god-sib*, meaning sister-in-god. Derived from Middle English words *god,* meaning spiritual, and *sip/sib/syp,* meaning kinsman, this term was used to refer to a familiar acquaintance, close family friend, or intimate relation, according to the *Oxford English Dictionary*. As a male, he would have joined in fellowship and celebration with the father of the newly born; if a female, she would have been a trusted friend, a birth-attendant or midwife to the mother of the baby. The term grew to include references to the type of easy, unrestrained conversation shared by these folks.

Etymology of gossip and early meanings

As is often the case with words, the term's meaning has certainly evolved, maybe eroded from its original idea. Is it harmless, idle chat, innocuous sharing of others' personal news, or back-biting, rumor-spreading, and manipulation? Is it a beneficial activity worthy of pursuit, or a deplorable danger to be avoided?

Current meanings

In her article "Evolution, Alienation, and Gossip" (for the Social Issues Research Centre in Oxford, England), Kate Fox writes that "gossip is not a trivial

Good use of sources to develop definition

pastime; it is essential to human social, psychological, and even physical well-being." Many echo her view that gossip is a worthy activity, claiming that engaging in gossip produces endorphins, reduces stress, and aids in building intimate relationships. Gossip, seen at worst as a harmless outlet, is encouraged in the workplace. Since much of its content is not inherently critical or malicious, it is viewed as a positive activity. However, this view does nothing to encourage those speaking or listening to evaluate or examine motive or purpose; instead, it seems to reflect the "anything goes" thinking so prevalent today.

Conversely, writer and high school English and geography teacher Lennox V. Farrell of Toronto, Canada, in his essay titled "Gossip: An Urban Form of Sorcery," presents gossip as a kind of "witchcraft . . . based on using unsubstantiated accusations by those who make them, and on uncritically accepting these by those enticed into listening." Farrell uses gossip in its more widely understood definition, encompassing the breaking of confidences, inappropriate sharing of indiscretions, destructive tale-bearing, and malicious slander.

What, then, is gossip? We no longer use the term to refer to our children's godparents. Its current definition usually comes with derogatory implications. Imagine a backyard garden: you see a variety of greenery, recognizing at a glance that you are looking at different kinds of plants. Taking a closer look, you will find the gossip vine; inconspicuously blending in, it doesn't appear threatening, but ultimately it destroys. If left in the garden it will choke and then suck out life from its host. Zoom in on the garden scene and follow the creeping vine up trees and along a fence where two neighbors visit. You can overhear one woman saying to the other, "I know I should be the last to tell you, but your husband is being unfaithful to me." (Caption from a cartoon by Alan De la Nougerede!)

Good use of metaphor to depict gossip as negative

The current popular movement to legitimize gossip seems an excuse to condone the human tendency to puff-up oneself. Compared in legal terms, gossip is to conversation as hearsay is to eyewitness testimony; it's not credible. Various religious doctrines abhor the idea and practice of gossip. An old Turkish proverb says, "He who gossips to you will

Conclusion states view that gossip is to be avoided—the writer's thesis.

gossip of you." From the Babylonian Talmud, which calls gossip the three-pronged tongue, destroying the one talking, the one listening, and the one being spoken of, to the Upanishads, to the Bible, we can conclude that no good fruit is born from gossip. Let's tend our gardens and check our motives when we have the urge to gossip. Surely we can find more noble pursuits than the self-aggrandisement we have come to know as gossip.

MAKING CONNECTIONS

---

1. John Ciardi says that happiness is difficult to define—and to obtain. Is happiness possible without the ability to discriminate, as Robert Miller defines the term? How would each author answer this question? How would you answer the question?
2. Is happiness possible without curiosity? How would John Ciardi and Alastair Reid each answer the question? How would you answer the question?
3. John Ciardi stresses that true happiness takes effort. Andrew Vachss suggests that we shy away from distinguishing between sick and evil because it is a difficult philosophical problem. Are we getting tired? Or lazy? As a society? Individually? Examine the essays and then prepare your answer to these questions.
4. Robert Miller deplores our feeling that we can no longer use the word *discrimination* in its important meaning of discerning differences. Andrew Vachss is bothered by our unwillingness to call specific actions evil, to use such a strong word. William Lutz examines euphemisms as one form of doublespeak. Have we become hemmed in by political correctness or the attitudes of the social sciences such that we

are unwilling to use precise language? Has this become an age of indirection and "softness" in language use? If so, is this a good or a bad situation? Think about how the authors would answer these questions, and think about how you would answer them.

5. Select one of the words defined in this chapter to study in the *Oxford English Dictionary,* either in its print or online version. Prepare a one to two page discussion of the word based on your study in the *OED.*

TOPICS FOR WRITING

---

1. In this chapter you can find definitions of *friendship, happiness,* even *curiosity.* If you have disagreed at least in part with one of the definitions presented in the chapter, write your own definition of that term. Include in your essay at least one reference to the writer with whom you disagree, discussing his or her views and contrasting them with your own. Make your purpose your own definition, but use the ideas with which you disagree as one way to develop your definition.

2. In an essay develop a definition of one of the terms below. Use at least three of the specific strategies for developing a definition discussed in the chapter's introduction. Try to make one of those strategies the metaphor, including several in your essay. And use contrast as one of your strategies, contrasting the word you select with its contrasting term in parentheses.

   patriotism (chauvinism)   wisdom (knowledge)
   courtesy (manners)   ghetto (neighborhood)
   leader (elected official)   hero (star)
   community (subdivision)   gossip (conversation)

3. In "Curiosity," Alastair Reid plays paradoxically with the terms *living* and *dying.* In an essay, define either *work* or *play,* developing your definition in part by reflecting on the word's relationship with its apparent opposite. In what situations, under what conditions, can play become work? Or, in what situations, under what conditions, can work be play? We use these terms frequently to suggest

opposite activities. In your definition of one of these words, show that there are some contexts in which its "opposite" is not really opposite.

4. Define a term that is currently used to label people with particular traits and values. Possibilities include: *nerd, yuppie, freak, jock, redneck, bimbo, wimp*. Reflect, before selecting this topic, on why you want to explain the meaning of the word you have chosen. One purpose might be to explain the term to someone from a different culture. Another purpose might be to defend people who are labeled negatively by one of these terms; that is, your goal is to show why the term should not have a negative connotation.

5. Select a word that you believe is currently misused. The word can be misused because it has taken on a negative (or positive) connotation that it did not once have, or because it has changed meaning and has lost something in the change. A few suggestions include *awful, fabulous, exceptional* (in education), *awesome, propaganda*.

6. If you are familiar with a culture other than American culture, define either *liberty* or *freedom* as the term is used in that culture.

7. William Lutz points to government and business as sources of doublespeak. Check out some government Websites and/or company Webpages to see what examples you can find. Your essay will be a study of the extent and kinds of doublespeak found on government or company Websites.

A CHECKLIST FOR DEFINITION ESSAYS

Invention

- ☐ Have I selected a topic consistent with the instructor's guidelines for this assignment?
- ☐ Have I chosen among the possible topics one that fits my knowledge and experience?
- ☐ Have I reflected on my topic to understand why I want to define my chosen term?
- ☐ Have I reflected on my topic to write a tentative thesis that establishes my purpose of definition?

☐ Have I considered all the possible strategies I can use to develop an extended definition: word origin, history of usage, descriptive details, examples, comparison and contrast, function or use, metaphors?

☐ Have I selected several strategies that are best suited to defining my term and fulfilling my purpose in defining?

☐ Have I generated specifics from the strategies I selected?

☐ Have I thought about the most effective order for the specifics?

Drafting

☐ Have I succeeded in completing a first draft at one sitting so that I can "see" the whole?

☐ Do I have enough—enough to meet assignment demands and enough to develop and support my thesis—my definition?

☐ Do I have good specifics to make my definition clear and concrete? If not, do I need to use other strategies or do I need more specifics within strategies I have used? (For example, do I need to add an explanation of word origin or do I need more examples?)

☐ Does the order work? If not, what needs to be moved—and where?

Revision

☐ Have I made any needed additions, deletions, or changes in order based on answering the questions about my draft?

☐ Have I revised my draft to produce coherent paragraphs, using transitions and connecting words that reveal my classification system?

☐ Have I eliminated wordiness and clichés?

☐ Have I avoided or removed any discriminatory language?

☐ Have I used my word processor's spell check and proofread a printed copy with great care?

☐ Do I have an appropriate and interesting title?

9

Using Causal Analysis

Examining Family and Community Issues

You may know the old—and very bad—joke that asks why the chicken crossed the road. When we give up and ask for the answer, the jokester, laughing merrily at trapping us in such silliness, says: "to get to the other side." The joke isn't in the answer but on us because we expect a more profound explanation of cause. Human beings characteristically ask why things happen. The four-year-old who asks her mother why there are stars in the sky may grow up to be the astrophysicist who continues, in a more sophisticated manner, to probe the same question.

When to Use Causal Analysis

We want to know what produced past events (why did the Roman Empire collapse?), what is causing current situations (why is there an increased fear of violence in our society?), and what will happen if we act in a particular way (will inflation be avoided if the Federal Reserve lowers interest rates?). Whether the questions are about the past, the present, or the future, we are seeking a causal explanation. We usually make a distinction between a study of *causes* (what produced A) and a study of *effects* (what has happened or will happen as a result of B), but actually the distinction is more one of wording than of approach or way of thinking. If, for example, we think that inflation can be avoided (effect) by raising interest rates (cause), we are saying that low interest rates can cause inflation. So, when we want to know why, we need to explore cause, whether we approach the "connection" from the causal end or the effects end.

How to Use Causal Analysis

In the study of causes and effects, we need to stress the key word *analysis*. In Chapter 6, you learned that process analysis answers the question *how* something is done or was accomplished by determining the steps, in proper time sequence, to complete the activity. When we examine cause, we also need to analyze the situation, both present and past, to make certain that we recognize all contributing elements and that we sort out the more important from the less important. Fortunately, there are some terms for distinguishing among different kinds of causes that can help us examine cause in a thoughtful and thorough way.

Thinking about Cause

First, events do not occur in a vacuum. There are *conditions* that surround an event, making the finding of only one cause unlikely. Suppose you have decided to become a veterinarian, and you want to understand why you have made that career choice. The conditions of your family life and upbringing probably affected your decision. You grew up with a dog you loved and cared for; your parents tolerated all the frogs and wounded birds you brought home and taught you to value living things. Second, there are more specific *influences* that contribute to an event. Perhaps the family vet let you help when your dog needed shots or bandaging and by example influenced your career plans.

In addition to conditions and influences, there are the more *immediate causes* that shape an event, leading up to the *precipitating cause,* the triggering event. In your choice to become a veterinarian, these events may include your good grades in and enjoyment of high school chemistry and biology, a recognition that you like working with your hands and that you want to be your own boss, and two summers of working at an animal hospital. In short, going off to college and having to declare a major did not cause you to choose veterinary medicine. The search for cause is a search for deeper, more fundamental answers than the college's requirement that you state a major field of study.

In our need, as humans, to have explanations for what happens, we can sometimes fool ourselves into thinking that we understand events, and we can be comforted by "finding" simple explanations for complex situations. But the desire to settle for simplistic explanations or for explanations for which there is no clear evidence of a causal connection must be resisted, both in thinking about life and in writing about cause. Two all-too-common ways of generating illogical causal explanations are to mistake a *time relationship* for a causal one and a *correlation* between two events for a causal relationship. For example, you went out to dinner last night and awoke with an upset stomach this morning. Can you conclude that something you ate last night caused the stomach upset? Certainly not without further evidence. Perhaps you already had a stomach virus before you went to dinner. To understand the difference between a correlation and a cause, consider the relationship between IQ scores and college grades. Students who have high IQ scores generally get good grades in college, but scores on an IQ test do not *cause* the good grades. (Whatever skills or knowledge produce high IQ scores are certainly one cause, though, of good grades. On the other hand, IQ tests do not measure motivation or good study habits.)

Evidence and Thesis

Writing a causal analysis challenges both thinking and writing skills. Remember that readers will evaluate your logic and evidence. After all, your purpose in writing is to show readers that your analysis of cause is sound and therefore useful to them. So, resist simplistic thinking and consider the kinds of evidence needed to illustrate and support your analysis. In addition to drawing on your own experience, you may need, depending on your topic, to obtain some evidence from reading. You will discover, for example, that many writers in this chapter include statistical evidence drawn from their reading. If you plan to emphasize one cause of a situation because you believe others have overlooked that cause or have failed to understand its importance, be certain that readers understand this limited and focused purpose.

Organization

Several organizational strategies are appropriate, depending on your topic and purpose. If you are examining a series of causes, beginning with background conditions and early influences, then your basic plan will be time sequence. Use appropriate terms for types of causes you discuss and transitional words to guide your reader through the sequence of events. If you want to examine an overlooked cause, you could begin by briefly discussing the causes that are usually stressed and then go on to introduce and explain the cause you want to emphasize. If your goal is to demonstrate that the same cause has operated in several different circumstances, then you need to show how that cause is the single common denominator in each circumstance. Whatever your overall strategy, remember to illustrate your points and to explain how your examples serve as evidence in support of your thesis.

WRITING FOCUS:
REFERENCES TO AUTHORS, WORKS, AND THE WORDS OF OTHERS

Readers expect writers to follow the standard conventions for referring to authors and titles of works and for indicating when words belong to someone other than the writer. For you to be an effective writer, you need to follow these conventions both in the academic community and the workplace.

References to People

- In the first reference give the person's full name: *Amitai Etzioni, Linda J. Waite.* In all other references to that person, use the last name (surname): *Etzioni, Waite.*
- Do not use Mr., Mrs., or Ms. Special titles such as President, Chief Justice, or Doctor may be used in the first reference with the person's full name.
- Never refer to an author by his or her first name. Write *Waite,* not *Linda.*

References to Titles

- Always write titles as titles. This involves proper capitalizing of words in the title and then using either quotation marks or underlining (italics in print) depending on the work.
- Capitalizing: The first and last words are capitalized. The first word of a subtitle is capitalized. All other words are capitalized except:
  Articles (*a, an, the*)
  Coordinating conjunctions (*and, or, but, for, nor, yet, so*)
  Prepositions of five or fewer letters. Longer prepositions are capitalized.
- Titles requiring quotation marks: All works published within other works, including essays ("Duty: The Forgotten Virtue"), short stories, poems ("Dream Deferred"), chapter titles, lectures.
- Titles requiring underlining (italics in print): Works that are separate publications, including newspapers (<u>New York Times</u>), magazines (<u>Newsweek</u>), novels (<u>The Old Man and the Sea</u>), textbooks (<u>Patterns of Reflection</u>), films (<u>The Wizard of Oz</u>).

Quotations

- Put *all* words taken from a source within quotation marks. Never change any of the words within the quotation marks.
- Do not leave out any words in the quoted passage unless you use ellipses (three spaced dots: . . .). If you have to add words to make the passage clear, place them in square brackets ([]), not parentheses.
- Always provide the source of the quoted passage, preferably *before* the quoted passage.
- When working a quoted passage into your sentence, place commas and periods within the final quotation mark—even when you quote only one word: Etzioni asserts that one reason for our loss of a sense of duty is too much "me-ism."
- Place semicolons and colons outside the end quotation mark. Do not quote punctuation at the end of

a quoted passage; use only the punctuation you need for your sentence.

- Use single quotation marks (the apostrophe key on your keyboard) to identify quoted material within quoted material: Barnett and Rivers point out that "'family-friendly' corporate policies reduce burnout." *Note: There is no comma before the beginning of the quoted passage; it is smoothly worked into the sentence.*

- When a quoted passage runs to more than three lines of type, use a block style: indent quoted lines ten spaces from the left margin; go to the right margin; continue to double space throughout the block quotation; do not use quotation marks—the indenting indicates a direct quotation.

- Remember your reader! Keep direct quoting to a minimum; keep quoted passages brief. You probably would not use a block quotation in a short essay, although you might use one in a research essay.

Getting Started: Reflections on Why You Are in College

Why are you in college? List the main reasons for your decision to attend college. Then reflect on some of the sources of those reasons. What people (parents, teachers, friends) and what experiences helped shape your decision? What, in other words, were the conditions and influences, as well as the more immediate causes, that led to your decision? Write in your journal on these questions or prepare responses for class discussion.

Duty: The Forgotten Virtue

AMITAI ETZIONI

Amitai Etzioni is an internationally renowned sociologist. Born in Germany, he earned his Ph.D. at the University of California. He has been University Professor at George Washington University and director of the Center for Policy Research. He is the author of many books, including *From Empire to Community: A New Approach to International Relations* (2004) and *An Immodest Agenda: Rebuilding America Before the Twenty-First Century* (1983) in which he calls for an increased sense of community and decreased focus on the self. Similar ideas are expressed in his article on duty, published in 1986 in the *Washington Post*.

Questions to Guide Your Reading and Reflection

1. What is Etzioni's attitude toward duty? What is his thesis?
2. Do you think that you have a duty to society?

Air accidents can be viewed as random tests of the extent to   1
which those responsible for keeping airplanes flying are doing their duty.

For example, the crew of an American Airlines plane re-   2
cently tried to land it three times, in low visibility, with 124 people aboard, in Harlingen, Texas. On the third pass, they hit two sets of runway approach lights four feet off the ground. The collision was severe enough to deploy some oxygen masks in the passenger cabin and knock ceiling panels loose. Yet after the plane regained altitude and landed safely in San Antonio, other crews took it to Dallas-Fort Worth and then on to Denver where damage to the exterior of the plane was discovered and the plane taken out of service.

One may view this as nothing more than an isolated incidence   3
of questionable judgment, but there is some evidence to suggest that Americans—always ambivalent about their duties—have been particularly loath to live up to their responsibilities in recent years.

A survey of young Americans found that most rank trial by   4
jury high among their rights. However, few indicated a willingness to serve on a jury.

Patriotism is reported to be in vogue. However, Americans   5
would rather pay volunteers to serve in the military than support a draft in which all would share the burden.

A survey conducted by H & R Block shows that Americans   6
favor a flat tax. However, that support is offered on one troubling condition: that the respondent's favorite loophole not be closed.

7   These observations led me to ask my class at The George
Washington University what the term "duty" brought to their
mind. They responded uneasily. They felt that people ought to
be free to do what *they* believe in. Duties are imposed, alien, authoritarian—what the principal, the curriculum committee, the
society, "they," want you to do.

8   I responded with a little impassioned address about the
common good: If everyone goes to the forest and fells a tree,
soon the hillsides will be denuded. We cannot rely on the fact
that once we are out of trees, people will recognize the need to
plant new ones; it takes years for trees to grow. Hence, we
must, I explained, expect members of society to plant some
trees now, invest in the infrastructure, trim the deficit, etc., so
that the next generation will have a forest, a thriving economy,
a future. We must balance the desire to focus on one's own interests with some obligation to the commons. True, duties are
not fun, *otherwise there would be no need to impose them.* But a civil
society cannot do without them.

9   Well, the students reflected aloud; they understood where I
was coming from. Okay, they said, maybe there was room for
duty, but—compliance ought to be voluntary, they insisted. I
felt I had failed them; I never got the point across.

10   Americans have never been very duty-bound. The country
was created by people who escaped duties imposed by authoritarian monarchies and dogmatic churches. And the ethos
of the pioneers was of striking out on one's own—even if, as a
matter of fact, settlement was carried out by groups very much
dependent on one another.

11   But over the last decades the need for duty to the commons
has grown as the supply diminished. Consider:

12   *Demand Side.* Practically no one expects that America can do
without *some* defense. The problem is that defense requires a
continuous willingness to dedicate resources to national security that might otherwise be used to enhance one's standard of
living. As obvious as this may seem, the fact is that Americans
have found it very difficult to sustain such a commitment. The
defense budget typically reflects cycles of neglect followed by
hysterical reactions to some real or alleged crisis. There is no
well-grounded commitment.

On the domestic front, voluntarism is now supposed to re- 13
place many government services. Anyone who points to the
limits of such an approach is immediately suspect of being an
old-time liberal, a champion of big government. But this sim-
ple-minded dichotomy—do things privately *or* via the government—conceals the real issue: What duties to the commons
should the government impose?

Most would include, aside from defense, support for basic 14
and medical research, some environmental protection, public
education and services for the deserving poor. But today these
obligations to the commons are left without a moral underpin-
ning. Most do not subscribe to a social philosophy which en-
dorses these commitments. Instead, we celebrate *laissez faire*
and a generation rich in Me-ism.

Supply Side. Americans are hardly enamored with the no- 15
tion that they have duties to the social weal. They find escape
in an odd concoction: a misapplication of Adam Smith mixed
with surging libertarianism, pop psychology and a dash of
liberation theory.

Americans have been brought up on a highly simplified no- 16
tion of the invisible hand: Everybody goes out and tries to
"maximize" himself—and the economy thrives for all. There is
no need to curb self-interest, even greed; it is the propellant
that fires up economies.

Now the reach of the invisible hand has been extended to 17
wholly new spheres. Antismoking campaigns, pro-seatbelt
moves, Social Security, environmental protection and employee safety are said to work best without "coercion"—if people are left to their own devices.

In this rejection of any sense that we have duties to each 18
other, we gloss over the consequences to innocent bystanders
of such a free-for-all, it's-up-to-you-Jack attitude. These
range from the effect on children of those who choose not to
buy insurance, to the neglect of "public goods"—goods we
all need but no one is individually entrusted with procuring
(e.g., highways).

Pop psychology is still with us. It argues that everyone 19
ought to focus on his or her own growth. Society and its duties
are viewed as standing in the way of self-fulfillment.

20   Pollster Daniel Yankelovich estimated that in the late 1970s, 17 percent of Americans were deeply committed to a philosophy of self-fulfillment and another 63 percent subscribed to it in varying degrees. These people said they "spend a great deal of time thinking about myself" and "satisfactions come from shaping oneself rather than from home and family life." They had a strong need for excitement and sensation and tended to feel free to look, live and act however they wanted, even if this violated others' concepts of what is proper.

21   The significance of this is that the escape from duty reaches beyond neglect of the community's needs to the neglect of one's immediate family.

22   Last but not least are the interest groups which elevate Me-ism to a group level. True, lobbies have been around since the founding of the Republic. But in recent years their power has increased sharply. And the consequence is that service to each interest group is easily put above a concern for the general welfare.

23   How do we redress the balance between the "I" and the "We"—so that we enhance the sense of duty?

24   There obviously are no simple solutions, but schools could help. They could change their civics courses from teaching that the government has three branches and the Supreme Court nine members (and so on), and instead promote civility. However, since most schools are overworked and underfunded, they are unlikely to do much.

25   More may be achieved if the issue is put on the agenda of the nationwide town-hall meetings we are, in effect, constantly conducting. The subjects vary, from civil rights to environmental protection to deficit reduction. However, the process is the same: triggered by a leading book (such as *Silent Spring*), a series of reports in leading newspapers or on television (e.g., on Vietnam), or by commissions (on education), we turn our collective attention to an issue. We debate it at length.

26   At first it seems nothing happens, but gradually a new consensus arises that affects people's behavior. We agree to pollute less or drink less; we exercise more; we become more sensitive to the rights of minorities or women.

27   The issue of our social obligations as Americans—our duties—is overdue for such a treatment. Meanwhile, we each ought to examine ourselves: What have you done for your community lately?

Expanding Vocabulary

Etzioni's essay provides a good opportunity for expanding your knowledge of terms and concepts used in discussing social and political issues.

1. In a sentence or two, explain each of the following terms or references, using an online dictionary, such as dictionary.com, if necessary. The number in parentheses is the number of the paragraph in which the word appears.

   loophole (6)
   infrastructure (8)
   deficit (8)
   ethos (10)
   laissez faire (14)
   Me-ism (14)
   Adam Smith (15)

   libertarianism (15)
   pop psychology (15)
   liberation theory (15)
   invisible hand (16)
   civics (24)
   civility (24)
   Silent Spring (25)

2. Be able to define each of the following words. Then, select five words and use each one in a separate sentence.

   deploy (2)
   ambivalent (3)
   loath (3)
   denuded (8)
   dogmatic (10)

   alleged (12)
   dichotomy (13)
   enamored (15)
   concoction (15)
   consensus (26)

Understanding Content

1. When Etzioni asked his students about the concept of duty, what was their response? Where does duty come from? Should it be imposed or voluntary?
2. In the author's view, what is the dominant value affecting the behavior of Americans?
3. What three solutions does Etzioni offer to "enhance the sense of duty"?

Drawing Inferences about Thesis and Purpose

1. The author uses two economic terms—*Demand Side* and *Supply Side*—as subheadings. How is he using these terms in this essay? What is being "demanded"? What is being "supplied"?
2. How did Etzioni feel about his students' views on duty?
3. Etzioni offers three solutions. How have his own actions shown his attempt to act on each one of them—to take his own advice?

Analyzing Strategies and Style

1. Look at the first six paragraphs. What do they provide?
2. One could say that paragraphs 7 through 9 are also part of the introduction. What does the author present in these paragraphs?
3. What is effective about Etzioni's use of specifics and his own students as an introductory strategy? Why might long introductions filled with specifics be effective openings for controversial topics?
4. The author uses a popular three-part organization for discussing a problem: (1) statement of the problem, (2) causes of the problem, (3) solutions to the problem. Analyze the essay according to this pattern, indicating the paragraphs that make up each of the three parts.
5. Now that you have marked the essay's parts, can you find sentences that signal the beginning of the second and third parts? Which sentence sums up the point of the first part?

Thinking Critically

1. If you had been in Etzioni's class, would you have responded much as his students did? If not, how would your response have differed?
2. Do you agree that most Americans are motived by the desire for self-fulfillment? Why or why not? What evidence can you offer to support your view?
3. Etzioni suggests that special-interest groups are really a form of "Me-ism." Is this a helpful way to understand these groups?
4. Is Etzioni suggesting that participating in groups is only a self-centered act, not a sign of commitment to others? What are the characteristics of the politically active groups Etzioni has in mind?
5. What is your answer to the essay's final question? Are you satisfied with your answer? Why or why not?

When Parents Are Toxic to Children

KEITH ABLOW

Keith Ablow, a graduate of the Johns Hopkins University Medical School, is a writer and psychiatrist who practices in the Boston area. He has published several nonfiction books, including *With Mercy* (1996), *Compulsion* (2006), and several novels. In the following article, which appeared in the *Washington Post's* Health Section in May 1996, Ablow examines the effects of bad parenting and argues for change.

Questions to Guide Your Reading and Reflection

1. Reflect on Ablow's title. What is the key word in his title? What point is he making?
2. What would you list as the worst ways parents abuse children?

I sat with a 15-year-old girl in the interview room where I   1
meet psychiatric inpatients for the first time, watching her as she gazed through her long black hair at her forearm. She gingerly traced the superficial cuts she had made with a razor the night before when she had flirted with suicide.

Her chart indicated that since the age of 11 she had suffered   2
repeated bouts of severe depression that antidepressant medication didn't touch. At times she was intermittently paranoid, believing that someone was out to steal her mind or even to take her life.

"I'm not going back there," she finally said, looking up at   3
me. "I'll kill myself, if they make me live with my parents."

"What happens there?" I asked.   4

"Constant fighting. Screaming. Swearing. Hitting. It's been   5
like that my whole life."

"Do they hit you?" I asked.   6

"They used to. A lot. They don't anymore. They hit my   7
brothers, though. And they keep telling me I'm ugly . . . and stupid. Worthless." She looked at her arm. "I don't care where I get sent. I'll go anywhere but home."

I was certain she would return home. Social service agencies   8
had been involved in her case for years. No doubt there would be another family meeting during her hospitalization, perhaps more frequent home visits by a social worker afterward. But the mental health system's prejudice in favor of keeping families intact, as well as a perennial shortage of acceptable foster parents, would likely keep my young patient with her own parents and in peril.

I have repeatedly treated teenagers like this girl whose bio-   9
logical parents have inflicted irreparable psychological harm

on their children. Some are the victims of sexual abuse, others of pervasive neglect. They end up in my office with symptoms that include panic attacks, severe depression and psychosis. Many are addicted to drugs before they even begin high school. Some see suicide as a reasonable way to end their pain. I prescribe them a variety of antidepressant, anti-anxiety and sometimes antipsychotic medications, hoping that their symptoms of mental illness are temporary, but worried that the damage they have suffered may be permanent. Worst of all I know that these are preventable illnesses.

10   Nor does the damage end with them. These teenage patients are tomorrow's parents. And experience has repeatedly demonstrated that many of them are likely to reenact the same destructive scenarios with their own children. Most people who harbor rage from their childhood don't expect it to surface after they become parents. Many fail to see the traumas they survived as sources of great risk for a new generation.

11   If we are to make a serious attempt to prevent some forms of serious mental illness, parenting must no longer be seen as an inalienable right, but as a privilege that can—and will—be revoked for abuse or neglect. Society must be much less tolerant of harm to children and also must be willing to devote considerably more resources to providing alternative living situations for children and adolescents who are in danger.

12   Only in the most egregious cases of physical violence or emotional neglect have I seen the state terminate parental rights. It seems that damage to children must reach the level of near catastrophe to justify cleaving a parent-child relationship that has been anything but loving.

13   Parents need to get a new message. If you do a lousy job parenting, you lose your job. In cases involving child custody, blood ties must be given less weight not only by the mental health system, but by the government and the court system. At the federal, state and local levels, keeping children with their parents can no longer be considered more important than keeping them safe.

14   Another young woman I treated had been repeatedly beaten by her older brothers for years. As a girl she had been raped by her mother's boyfriend. Her moods had become erratic, and her temper unpredictable. She had turned to marijuana for relief and had been expelled from school for fighting. Yet she con-

tinued to live at home, with the blessing of the state Department of Social Services.

"She's got to get off these damn drugs," her mother com- 15
plained in my office. "That [stuff] has got her all screwed . . . "

"I'm not gonna listen to you," the girl interrupted. She 16
turned to me. "This is the woman who let me get beat on for
about 10 years and let her boyfriend sneak into my bedroom,
without her saying two words. How am I supposed to live as
a normal human being with a mother like her?"

Privately I agreed with her. I felt hopeless about the situation 17
myself. I could see that this girl was trapped in a family that was
eroding her emotional resiliency, leaving her increasingly vulnerable to severe psychiatric illness. And society had no plan to
rescue her from this situation. In fact, it tacitly endorsed it.

One of the difficulties of working as a therapist with ado- 18
lescents is that they often clearly perceive the psychological
dangers confronting them, but are powerless to deal with
them. It's no wonder then that such experiences lay the
groundwork for panic attacks, post-traumatic stress disorder,
depression and paranoia that seem to come "out of the blue"
later in life. The coping mechanisms of some of the teenagers I
treat have short-circuited already. These patients "dissociate":
They unpredictably enter altered states of consciousness in
which they lose touch with reality.

One 17-year-old whom I treated for depression asked me 19
plainly: "If you were me, what would you do to make sure
your parents didn't get you even sicker during the next year? I
mean, if I can get to 18, I can leave home, maybe join the Army
or something, and they won't be able to do anything about it."

I told him that he needed to be less confrontational in the 20
face of his parents' unreasonable demands for strict obedience, if only to conserve his emotional energy, not to mention
avoid his father's belt. "Prisoners of war don't get in beefs
every day with their captors," I told him. "They lay low until
they can escape."

Like most of the abusive parents I have met, this young 21
man's father, for example, made it clear to me that he too had
faced traumas as a young person, including horrific beatings.
He tried to do his best for his son despite severe depression and
alcoholism that limited his ability to function. Doing his best,
however, was not nearly good enough.

22   This is why a social policy that would raise expectations for healthy parenting and more frequently and quickly impose the loss of parental rights should include a vigorous attempt to educate parents on how to avoid harming their children. The loss of parental rights is a tragedy we should attempt to avoid.

23   Another key requirement is to recruit good foster families. Too often such families have not proven to be much better for kids than the homes they have left; sometimes they are even worse. It makes no sense to take the admittedly drastic step of removing children from bad biological parents only to place them with bad foster parents.

24   One 19-year-old woman I met recently had spent a decade living in a foster family. She had been beaten and neglected for the years prior to her placement and, even with obviously concerned and empathic foster parents, had required years of psychotherapy to cope with her traumatic past.

25   With the support of a new family, however, she had achieved in school, shunned drugs and made close and lasting friendships. She hoped to save money to attend college. While she considered leaving her biological parents as one of the major stresses in her life, she made it clear that she would have been much worse staying with them. "I'm one of the lucky ones," she said. "I got out."

26   The tragedy is that too few children do.

Expanding Vocabulary

Match each word in column A with its definition in column B. When in doubt, first find the word in the essay and look for context clues to aid your understanding of the word's meaning. Then, if necessary, use your dictionary to complete the matching exercise. The number in parentheses is the number of the paragraph in which the word appears.

Column A	*Column B*
bouts (2)	dividing, separating
paranoid (2)	impossible to repair or fix
perennial (8)	quietly, implied rather than stated
irreparable (9)	outlines of possible future events
psychosis (9)	serious emotional shocks that may
scenarios (10)	result in lasting damage
traumas (10)	notably offensive
inalienable (11)	contests, matches

egregious (12)	destroying, eating away at
cleaving (12)	one with a disorder characterized by
eroding (17)	delusions of persecution or grandeur
resiliency (17)	ability to recover from serious problems
tacitly (17)	lasting through many years
	what cannot be transferred to another
	mental disorder marked by disconnection
	with reality and social dysfunction

Understanding Content

1. For what two reasons are abused children kept with the parents who are abusing them?
2. What problems do the abused teenagers experience; what are the effects of their situation? How does Ablow treat them?
3. How do abused adolescents view their situation?

Drawing Inferences about Thesis and Purpose

1. What is Ablow's thesis? What change in policy does he want to see? Where does he state his thesis?
2. What specific actions are needed to improve the health of abused children?

Analyzing Strategies and Style

1. The author provides several examples of abused teenagers; how do the examples help to advance his argument? Ablow begins and ends with extended examples that include dialogue. What makes these effective ways to begin and end?
2. What, in your view, is the most telling example, detail, or argument in the essay? Why?

Thinking Critically

1. Have you known any abused teens? If so, have you seen any good solutions to their problems, such as foster care or therapy? Do you know adolescents who need help? If so, what can you do?
2. Should bad parents lose their children? Why or why not?
3. Would you favor more resources to help abused children? Why or why not?
4. How can we improve education for prospective parents so that they will be prepared for good parenting? What suggestions do you have?

Social Science Finds: "Marriage Matters"

LINDA J. WAITE

A former senior sociologist at the Rand Corporation, Linda Waite is currently a professor at the University of Chicago. She has several books including *The Ties That Bind: Perspectives on Marriage and Cohabitation* (2000) and *Aging, Health, and Public Policy: Demographic and Economic Perspectives* (2004) In this article, published in *The Responsive Community* in 1996, Waite examines various studies of marriage to determine the effects that marriage has on those who are married.

Questions to Guide Your Reading and Reflection

1. What groups of people are the healthiest and live the longest?
2. Do the benefits of marriage extend to cohabitation?

1   As we are all too aware, the last few decades have witnessed a decline in the popularity of marriage. This trend has not escaped the notice of politicians and pundits. But when critics point to the high social costs and taxpayer burden imposed by disintegrating "family values," they overlook the fact that individuals do not simply make the decisions that lead to unwed parenthood, marriage, or divorce on the basis of what is good for society. Individuals weigh the costs and benefits of each of these choices to themselves—and sometimes their children. But how much is truly known about these costs and benefits, either by the individuals making the choices or demographers like myself who study them? Put differently, what are the implications, for individuals, of the current increases in nonmarriage? If we think of marriage as an insurance policy—which it is, in some respects—does it matter if more people are uninsured, or are insured with a term rather than a whole-life policy? I shall argue that it does matter, because marriage typically provides important and substantial benefits, benefits not enjoyed by those who live alone or cohabit.

2   A quick look at marriage patterns today compared to, say, 1950 shows the extent of recent changes. Figures from the Cen-

sus Bureau show that in 1950, at the height of the baby boom, about a third of white men and women were not married. Some were waiting to marry for the first time, some were divorced or widowed and not remarried. But virtually everyone married at least once at some point in their lives, generally in their early twenties.

In 1950 the proportion of black men and women not married   3
was approximately equal to the proportion unmarried among whites, but since that time the marriage behavior of blacks and whites has diverged dramatically. By 1993, 61 percent of black women and 58 percent of black men were not married, compared to 38 percent of white men and 41 percent of white women. So, in contrast to 1950 when only a little over one black adult in three was not married, now a majority of black adults are unmarried. Insofar as marriage "matters," black men and women are much less likely than whites to share in the benefits, and much less likely today than they were a generation ago.

The decline in marriage is directly connected to the rise in   4
cohabitation—living with someone in a sexual relationship without being married. Although Americans are less likely to be married today than they were several decades ago, if we count both marriage and cohabitation, they are about as likely to be "coupled." If cohabitation provides the same benefits to individuals as marriage does, then we do not need to be concerned about this shift. But we may be replacing a valuable social institution with one that demands and offers less.

Perhaps the most disturbing change in marriage appears in   5
its relationship to parenthood. Today a third of all births occur to women who are not married, with huge but shrinking differences between blacks and whites in this behavior. One in five births to white mothers and two-thirds of births to black mothers currently take place outside marriage. Although about a quarter of the white unmarried mothers are living with someone when they give birth, so that their children are born into two-parent—if unmarried—families, very few black children born to unmarried mothers live with fathers too.

I believe that these changes in marriage behavior are a cause   6
for concern, because in a number of important ways married men and women do better than those who are unmarried. And I believe that the evidence suggests that they do better because they are married.

Marriage and Health

7   The case for marriage is quite strong. Consider the issues of longevity and health. With economist Lee Lillard, I used a large national survey to follow men and women over a 20-year period. We watched them get married, get divorced, and remarry. We observed the death of spouses and of the individuals themselves. And we compared deaths of married men and women to those who were not married. We found that once we took other factors into account, married men and women faced lower risks of dying at any point than those who have never married or whose previous marriage has ended. Widowed women were much better off than divorced women or those who had never married, although they were still disadvantaged when compared with married women. But all men who were not currently married faced significantly higher risks of dying than married men, regardless of their marital history. Other scholars have found disadvantages in death rates for unmarried adults in a number of countries besides the United States.

8   How does marriage lengthen life? First, marriage appears to reduce risky and unhealthy behaviors. For example, according to University of Texas sociologist Debra Umberson, married men show much lower rates of problem drinking than unmarried men. Umberson also found that both married men and women are less likely to take risks that could lead to injury than are the unmarried. Second, as we will see below, marriage increases material well-being—income, assets, and wealth. These can be used to purchase better medical care, better diet, and safer surroundings, which lengthen life. This material improvement seems to be especially important for women.

9   Third, marriage provides individuals—especially men— with someone who monitors their health and health-related behaviors and who encourages them to drink and smoke less, to eat a healthier diet, to get enough sleep and to generally take care of their health. In addition, husbands and wives offer each other moral support that helps in dealing with stressful situations. Married men especially seem to be motivated to avoid risky behaviors and to take care of their health by the sense of meaning that marriage gives to their lives and the sense of obligation to others that it brings.

More Wealth, Better Wages—For Most

Married individuals also seem to fare better when it comes to   10
wealth. One comprehensive measure of financial well-being—
household wealth—includes pension and Social Security wealth,
real and financial assets, and the value of the primary residence.
According to economist James Smith, in 1992 married men and
women ages 51–60 had median wealth of about $66,000 per
spouse, compared to $42,000 for the widowed, $35,000 for those
who had never married, $34,000 among those who were di-
vorced, and only $7,600 for those who were separated. Although
married couples have higher incomes than others, this fact accounts for only about a quarter of their greater wealth.

How does marriage increase wealth? Married couples can   11
share many household goods and services, such as a TV and
heat, so the cost to each individual is lower than if each one
purchased and used the same items individually. So the married spend less than the same individuals would for the same
style of life if they lived separately. Second, married people
produce more than the same individuals would if single. Each
spouse can develop some skills and neglect others, because
each can count on the other to take responsibility for some of
the household work. The resulting specialization increases ef-
ficiency. We see below that this specialization leads to higher
wages for men. Married couples also seem to save more at the
same level of income than do single people.

The impact of marriage is again beneficial—although in this   12
case not for all involved—when one looks at labor market outcomes. According to recent research by economist Kermit
Daniel, both black and white men receive a wage premium if
they are married: 4.5 percent for black men and 6.3 percent for
white men. Black women receive a marriage premium of almost 3 percent. White women, however, pay a marriage
penalty, in hourly wages, of over 4 percent. In addition, men
appear to receive some of the benefit of marriage if they cohabit, but women do not.

Why should marriage increase men's wages? Some re-   13
searchers think that marriage makes men more productive at
work, leading to higher wages. Wives may assist husbands directly with their work, offer advice or support, or take over
household tasks, freeing husbands' time and energy for work.

Also, as I mentioned earlier, being married reduces drinking, substance abuse, and other unhealthy behaviors that may affect men's job performance. Finally, marriage increases men's incentives to perform well at work, in order to meet obligations to family members.

14   For women, Daniel finds that marriage and presence of children together seem to affect wages, and the effects depend on the woman's race. Childless black women earn substantially more money if they are married but the "marriage premium" drops with each child they have. Among white women only the childless receive a marriage premium. Once white women become mothers, marriage decreases their earnings compared to remaining single (with children), with very large negative effects of marriage on women's earnings for those with two children or more. White married women often choose to reduce hours of work when they have children. They also make less per hour than either unmarried mothers or childless wives.

15   Up to this point, all the consequences of marriage for the individuals involved have been unambiguously positive—better health, longer life, more wealth, and higher earnings. But the effects of marriage and children on white women's wages are mixed, at best. Marriage and cohabitation increase women's time spent on housework; married motherhood reduces their time in the labor force and lowers their wages. Although the family as a whole might be better off with this allocation of women's time, women generally share their husbands' market earnings only when they are married. Financial well-being declines dramatically for women and their children after divorce and widowhood; women whose marriages have ended are often quite disadvantaged financially by their investment in their husbands and children rather than in their own earning power. Recent changes in divorce law—the rise in no-fault divorce and the move away from alimony—seem to have exacerbated this situation, even while increases in women's education and work experience have moderated it.

Improved Intimacy

16   Another benefit of married life is an improved sex life. Married men and women report very active sex lives—as do those who are cohabiting. But the married appear to be more satis-

fied with sex than others. More married men say that they find sex with their wives to be extremely physically pleasurable than do cohabiting men or single men say the same about sex with their partners. The high levels of married men's physical satisfaction with their sex lives contradicts the popular view that sexual novelty or variety improves sex for men. Physical satisfaction with sex is about the same for married women, cohabiting women, and single women with sex partners.

In addition to reporting more active and more physically 17 fulfilling sex lives than the unmarried, married men and women say that they are more emotionally satisfied with their sex lives than do those who are single or cohabiting. Although cohabitants report levels of sexual activity as high as the married, both cohabiting men and women report lower levels of emotional satisfaction with their sex lives. And those who are sexually active but single report the lowest emotional satisfaction with it.

How does marriage improve one's sex life? Marriage and 18 cohabitation provide individuals with a readily available sexual partner with whom they have an established, ongoing sexual relationship. This reduces the costs—in some sense—of any particular sexual contact, and leads to higher levels of sexual activity. Since married couples expect to carry on their sex lives for many years, and since the vast majority of married couples are monogamous, husbands and wives have strong incentives to learn what pleases their partner in bed and to become good at it. But I would argue that more than "skills" are at issue here. The long-term contract implicit in marriage—which is not implicit in cohabitation—facilitates emotional investment in the relationship, which should affect both frequency of and satisfaction with sex. So the wife or husband who knows what the spouse wants is also highly motivated to provide it, both because sexual satisfaction in one's partner brings similar rewards to oneself and because the emotional commitment to the partner makes satisfying him or her important in itself.

To this point we have focused on the consequences of mar- 19 riage for adults—the men and women who choose to marry (and stay married) or not. But such choices have consequences for the children born to these adults. Sociologists Sara McLanahan and Gary Sandefur compare children raised in intact, two-parent families with those raised in one-parent families, which could result either from disruption of a marriage or from unmarried childbearing. They find that approximately twice as many children raised in one-parent families than children from two-parent families drop out of high school without finishing. Children raised in one-parent families are also more likely to have a birth themselves while teenagers, and to be "idle"—both out of school and out of the labor force—as young adults.

20   Not surprisingly, children living outside an intact marriage are also more likely to be poor. McLanahan and Sandefur calculated poverty rates for children in two-parent families—including stepfamilies—and for single-parent families. They found very high rates of poverty for single-parent families, especially among blacks. Donald Hernandez, chief of marriage and family statistics at the Census Bureau, claims that the rise in mother-only families since 1959 is an important cause of increases in poverty among children.

21   Clearly poverty, in and of itself, is a bad outcome for children. In addition, however, McLanahan and Sandefur estimate that the lower incomes of single-parent families account for only half of the negative impact for children in these families. The other half comes from children's access—or lack of access—to the time and attention of two adults in two-parent families. Children in one-parent families spend less time with their fathers (this is not surprising given that they do not live with them), but they also spend less time with their mothers than children in two-parent families. Single-parent families and stepfamilies also move much more frequently than two-parent families, disrupting children's social and academic environments. Finally, children who spend part of their childhood in a single-parent family report substantially lower quality relationships with their parents as adults and have less frequent contact with them, according to demographer Diane Lye.

Correlation Versus Causality

22   The obvious question, when one looks at all these "benefits" of marriage, is whether marriage is responsible for these dif-

ferences. If all, or almost all, of the benefits of marriage arise because those who enjoy better health, live longer lives, or earn higher wages anyway are more likely to marry, then marriage is not "causing" any changes in these outcomes. In such a case, we as a society and we as individuals could remain neutral about each person's decision to marry or not, to divorce or remain married. But scholars from many fields who have examined the issues have come to the opposite conclusion. Daniel found that only half of the higher wages that married men enjoy could be explained by selectivity; he thus concluded that the other half is causal. In the area of mental health, social psychologist Catherine Ross—summarizing her own research and that of other social scientists—wrote, "The positive effect of marriage on well-being is strong and consistent, and the selection of the psychologically healthy into marriage or the psychologically unhealthy out of marriage cannot explain the effect." Thus marriage itself can be assumed to have independent positive effects on its participants.

So, we must ask, what is it about marriage that causes these 23 benefits? I think that four factors are key. First, the institution of marriage involves a long-term contract—" 'til death do us part." This contract allows the partners to make choices that carry immediate costs but eventually bring benefits. The time horizon implied by marriage makes it sensible—a rational choice is at work here—for individuals to develop some skills and to neglect others because they count on their spouse to fill in where they are weak. The institution of marriage helps individuals honor this long-term contract by providing social support for the couple as a couple and by imposing social and economic costs on those who dissolve their union.

Second, marriage assumes a sharing of economic and social 24 resources and what we can think of as co-insurance. Spouses act as a sort of small insurance pool against life's uncertainties, reducing their need to protect themselves—by themselves— from unexpected events.

Third, married couples benefit—as do cohabiting couples— 25 from economies of scale.

Fourth, marriage connects people to other individuals, to their 26 social groups (such as in-laws), and to other social institutions (such as churches and synagogues) which are themselves a source of benefits. These connections provide individuals with a sense of obligation to others, which gives life meaning beyond oneself.

27   Cohabitation has some but not all of the characteristics of marriage and so carries some but not all of the benefits. Cohabitation does not generally imply a lifetime commitment to stay together; a significant number of cohabiting couples disagree on the future of their relationship. Frances Goldscheider and Gail Kaufman believe that the shift to cohabitation from marriage signals "declining commitment within unions, of men and women to each other and to their relationship as an enduring unit, in exchange for more freedom, primarily for men." Perhaps, as a result, many view cohabitation as an especially poor bargain for women.

28   The uncertainty that accompanies cohabitation makes both investment in the relationship and specialization with this partner much riskier than in marriage and so reduces them. Cohabitants are much less likely than married couples to pool financial resources and more likely to assume that each partner is responsible for supporting himself or herself financially. And whereas marriage connects individuals to other important social institutions, cohabitation seems to distance them from these institutions.

29   Of course, all these observations concern only the average benefits of marriage. Clearly, some marriages produce substantially higher benefits for those involved. Some marriages produce no benefits and even cause harm to the men, women, and children involved. That fact needs to be recognized.

Reversing the Trend

30   Having stated this qualification, we must still ask, if the average marriage produces all of these benefits for individuals, why has it declined? Although this issue remains a subject of much research and speculation, a number of factors have been mentioned as contributing. For one, because of increases in women's employment, there is less specialization by spouses now than in the past; this reduces the benefits of marriage. Clearly, employed wives have less time and energy to focus on their husbands, and are less financially and emotionally dependent on marriage than wives who work only in the home. In addition, high divorce rates decrease people's certainty about the long-run stability of their marriage, and this may re-

duce their willingness to invest in it, which in turn increases the chance they divorce—a sort of self-fulfilling prophecy. Also, changes in divorce laws have shifted much of the financial burden for the breakup of the marriage to women, making investment within the marriage (such as supporting a husband in medical school) a riskier proposition for them.

Men, in turn, may find marriage and parenthood a less attrac- 31 tive option when they know that divorce is common, because they may face the loss of contact with their children if their marriage dissolves. Further, women's increased earnings and young men's declining financial well-being may have made women less dependent on men's financial support and made young men less able to provide it. Finally, public policies that support single mothers and changing attitudes toward sex outside of marriage, toward unmarried childbearing, and toward divorce have all been implicated in the decline in marriage. This brief list does not exhaust the possibilities, but merely mentions some of them.

So how can this trend be reversed? First, as evidence accu- 32 mulates and is communicated to individuals, some people will change their behavior as a result. Some will do so simply because of their new understanding of the costs and benefits, to them, of the choices involved. In addition, we have seen that attitudes frequently change toward behaviors that have been shown to have negative consequences. The attitude change then raises the social cost of the newly stigmatized behavior.

In addition, though, we as a society can pull some policy 33 levers to encourage or discourage behaviors. Public policies that include asset tests (Medicaid is a good example) act to exclude the married, as do AFDC programs and most states. The "marriage penalty" in the tax code is another example. These and other policies reinforce or undermine the institution of marriage. If, as I have argued, marriage produces individuals who drink less, smoke less, abuse substances less, live longer, earn more, are wealthier, and have children who do better, we need to give more thought and effort to supporting this valuable social institution.

Expanding Vocabulary

After studying definitions of the following words, select five and use each one in a separate sentence. The number in parentheses is the number of the paragraph in which the word appears.

pundits (1)	exacerbated (15)
demographers (1)	monogamous (18)
cohabit (1)	implicit (18)
diverged (3)	disruption (19)
unambiguously (15)	stigmatized (32)

Understanding Content

1. Waite argues that most people weigh the advantages and disadvantages of marriage based on what?
2. Although marriage has declined, what has taken its place?
3. What percentage of births occur to women who are not married? What percentage of white mothers are living with someone? What percentage of black mothers are living with someone?
4. Which arrangement type has the greatest income? Which type has the least?
5. In what ways can marriage increase wealth? Who, when married, loses in hourly wages?
6. What may be causes for increased productivity for married men?
7. Which living arrangement reports having the most physical and emotional satisfaction from sex?
8. What situations increase poverty for children?
9. What are some effects of single-parent families on children?
10. Does Waite conclude that marriage itself is a cause of the improved lives of most married people? In general, who benefits the least from marriage?

Drawing Inferences about Thesis and Purpose

1. Why, if marriage has benefits, are fewer people getting married and more getting divorced?
2. What does Waite think should be done to change the movement away from marriage?

Analyzing Strategies and Style

1. This is a longish essay. What does Waite do to help readers follow her discussion?
2. What kind of evidence, primarily, does the author provide? How is this consistent with your expectations, based on your knowledge of the author?

Thinking Critically

1. Which statistic most surprises you? Why?

2. Do you think that the evidence Waite provides should encourage people to choose marriage over divorce, cohabitation, or the single life? If so, why? If not, why not?
3. What can be done to increase marriage benefits for women, the ones who have least benefited by marriage?

The Overlooked Victims of AIDS

JUDITH D. AUERBACH

A sociologist and former college professor, Judith Auerbach is now vice president for public policy of the American Foundation for AIDS Research. Auerbach has published and presented in a variety of areas of research interest, including AIDS, health research, and family policy and gender. The following column, published in the *Washington Post* during the last presidential campaign (Oct. 14, 2004), deplores our lack of awareness of who is suffering from AIDS.

Questions to Guide Your Reading and Reflection

1. Who, now, is most often becoming infected with HIV-AIDS?
2. Do you know how most women become infected with AIDS?

In last week's vice presidential debate, moderator Gwen Ifill 1
talked about the disproportionate impact of HIV-AIDS on African American women and asked what role the government should play in slowing the growth of this domestic epidemic. Both candidates displayed an alarming ignorance of the reality of the crisis in the United States, choosing instead to focus their comments on AIDS in Africa, which Ifill had explicitly asked them not to do.

What is inexcusable among the nation's top policymakers is 2
a persistent problem in the general public as well: a failure to recognize that AIDS now disproportionately affects women.

According to the Centers for Disease Control and Preven- 3
tion, the proportion of all AIDS cases reported among adolescent and adult women in the United States has more than tripled since 1986. AIDS is the fourth-leading cause of death among women in this country between the ages of 25 and 44,

and is the *leading* cause of death among African American women ages 25 to 34. Black women represent about two-thirds of all new HIV infections among adult and adolescent females.

4   Globally, about half of the 12,000 people ages 15 to 49 infected every day are women. Sixty-two percent of those ages 15 to 24 living with HIV-AIDS are girls and women. In South Africa, that figure climbs to 77 percent. Most women worldwide, including in the United States, acquire HIV infection through heterosexual intercourse.

5   Why is this "feminization of AIDS" occurring? The answer lies in the complex ways that sex and gender intersect, conferring increased vulnerability to HIV infection on women and girls. Biological, sociological and political factors interact differently for women and men, leaving women more susceptible to viral transmission, more distant from prevention and care services, farther away from accurate information, and far more vulnerable to human rights violations. Here are some of the specifics:

6   • Women are more vulnerable to HIV infection than men. The physiology of the female genital tract makes women twice as likely to acquire HIV from men as vice versa. Among adolescent girls, this effect is even more pronounced.

7   • Poverty is correlated with higher rates of HIV infection all over the world. Globally, more than half of the people living in poverty are women. In the United States, nearly 30 percent are African American women.

8   • Lack of education is associated with higher HIV infection rates. Girls in developing countries are less likely to complete secondary education than boys, and almost twice as likely to be illiterate.

9   • Early marriage is a significant risk factor for HIV among women and girls. In developing countries, a majority of sexually active girls ages 15 to 19 are married. Married adolescent girls tend to have higher HIV infection rates than their sexually active unmarried peers.

10   • A significant risk factor for HIV infection is violence, to which women are more susceptible in virtually all societies. In a South African study, for example, women who were beaten or dominated by their partners were 48 percent more likely to become infected than women who lived in nonviolent households.

11   • Rape of women has been used as a tool for subjugation and so-called ethnic cleansing in war and conflict situations. Of the 250,000 women raped during the Rwandan genocide, about 70 percent of the survivors are HIV-positive.

The experience of women and girls in the HIV-AIDS epi-   12
demic in the United States and around the world highlights
how social arrangements, cultural norms, laws, policies and institutions contribute to the unequal status of women in society
and to the spread of disease. Together they undermine the capacity of women and girls to exercise power over their own
lives and to control the circumstances that increase their vulnerability to HIV infection, particularly in the context of sexual
relationships. For African American women, gender inequali-
ties are exacerbated by persistent racism.

It is only when this unhealthy mix is acknowledged and ad-   13
dressed—particularly by the highest levels of government—
that we will be able to stem the alarming increase of HIV-AIDS
among more than half the world's population.

Expanding Vocabulary

Match each word in column A with its definition in column B. When
in doubt, first find the word in the essay and look for context clues
to aid your understanding of the word's meaning. Then, if necessary, use a dictionary to complete the matching exercise. The number in parentheses is the number of the paragraph in which the
word appears.

Column A	*Column B*
disproportionate (1)	brought into a parallel relationship
intersect (5)	easily attacked or hurt
vulnerability (5)	under control of
correlated (7)	increased in difficulty or harshness
subjugation (11)	lacking proper balance
genocide (11)	cross through, interact
exacerbated (12)	planned killing of a specific group of people

Understanding Content

1. What do politicians, and Americans generally, seem not to know
   about AIDS?
2. How do most women become infected?
3. For what group of Americans is AIDS the leading cause of death?
4. What are six specifics about women's experiences that make them
   more vulnerable to HIV infection? Explain in your own words.

Drawing Inferences about Thesis and Purpose

1. What is Auerbach's purpose in writing? How does she want to affect her readers?
2. What is the author's thesis?

Analyzing Strategies and Style

1. How would you describe Auerbach's style—her sentence structures and word choice?
2. Is her style effective for her subject and purpose? Explain.
3. What is effective about the use of bullets in this essay?

Thinking Critically

1. Were you aware of the "feminization of AIDS"? Does this surprise? Shock? Make you wonder how this shift in infected group has happened?
2. Which statistic in the essay is most shocking to you? Why?
3. Which one of the six experiences correlating with increased risk for AIDS is most surprising to you? Why?
4. What should be done to address this serious world health problem? If you were the president's "AIDS czar," what specific programs would you seek to put into place in this country? Explain your cause and effect reasoning.

Not Much Sense in Those Census Stories

STEPHANIE COONTZ

A professor of history at Evergreen State College in Olympia, Washington, Stephanie Coontz is the author of numerous articles and books, including *The Way We Never Were: American Families and the Nostalgia Trap* (1992), *The Way We Really Are* (1997), and *Marriage, A History: How Love Conquered Marriage* (2005). Coontz is also national cochair of the Council on Contemporary Families (*www.contemporaryfamilies.org*); it is in this capacity that she is frequently contacted by media personnel working on stories about families. The following article was published July 15, 2001, in the *Washington Post*.

Questions to Guide Your Reading and Reflection

1. What has led the Census Bureau to assert an increase in children living in *traditional* family homes?
2. What are some of the reasons why the media get stories about families wrong?

Nearly every week, the U.S. Census Bureau releases a new   1
set of figures on American families and the living arrangements they have been creating in the past decade. And each
time, as the media liaison for a national association of family
researchers, I'm bombarded with telephone calls from radio
and television producers seeking a talking head to confirm the
wildly differing—and usually wrong—conclusions they've
jumped to about what those figures say about the evolving nature of family life in America.

In April, for example, Census officials announced that 56   2
percent of American children were living in "traditional" nuclear families in 1996, up from 51 percent in 1991. Several prime
time television shows excitedly reported this "good news"
about the American family, and I heard one radio commentator declare that young couples were finally rejecting the "divorce culture" of their parents' generation.

But this supposedly dramatic reversal of a 30-year trend   3
was based on a peculiarly narrow definition of a traditional
family: a two-parent household with children under 18 and no
other relatives in the home. If a grandchild, grandparent or
other relative were living in the house, the family was "non-
traditional." (There's an obvious irony here, given that nothing is quite so traditional as an extended nuclear family that
includes a grandparent!)

Evidently, the definition itself was largely responsible for this   4
"trend": Enough such relatives moved to separate households
during the first half of the 1990s to increase the proportion of
"traditional families," even though the percentage of children
living with both biological parents had stayed steady at about 62
percent, and the percentage of married couples had continued
its 30-year slide. In other words, the initial reports of a resur-
gence in traditional families were the result of wishful thinking
and a misunderstanding of the terms being used by the census.

5   But hope springs eternal among talk show producers desperate for a new angle. In mid-May, expanding on its earlier
study, the Census Bureau reported that the absolute numbers
of married couples with children at home had grown in 2000
after falling in two previous head counts (although the proportion of such families in the total population was still shrinking). TV producers jumped on the story, apparently ready to
trumpet the return of the "Ozzie and Harriet" family of the
'50s. I soon heard from several talk show hosts in the West who,
state-by-state printouts in hand, were agog about the exceptionally large increase of such families in *their* regions. They
wanted me to find them an expert to comment on the heaten-
ing return to traditional values.

6   Their enthusiasm dimmed, however, when I told them that
this regional increase in married-couple households with children was due largely to the well-reported influx of Asian and
Hispanic immigrants. Their interest evaporated entirely when
I reminded them that, as immigrants assimilate, their family
patterns tend to match those of the preexisting population.

7   A week later, the Census Bureau reported that the number of
unmarried women with children had increased by 25 percent,
dwarfing the 7 percent growth in married-couple families. This
time we moved into the "bad news" cycle: Media pundits called
to confirm their worst fears, looking for more figures to prove
that the explosion of single motherhood was creating an ever-
deepening social and cultural crisis in the land.

8   In fact, most of the growth in "single" motherhood during
the 1990s was due to an increase in births to women who, while
not married, were living with the child's father. So, much of the
recent increase in single motherhood simply reflected the 71
percent increase in cohabitation between 1990 and 2000. But
the fact that many "single mother" families actually had fathers present didn't faze the talk show hosts who called seeking confirmation that the sky was falling because of the
"collapse of marriage." This time around, they weren't the least
bit interested in any good news—such as the figures, also released in May, that showed a 20 percent drop in births to
teenagers over the decade.

9   Then, last month, the Census Bureau reported that the number of households headed by single fathers had increased five-

fold, from 393,000 in 1970 to 2 million in 2000. I got two calls from TV producers that day, each rushing to air a show on this new trend. One asked me to explain how this reflected the increasing equality of men and women in their commitment to parenting, while the other wanted someone to tell her viewers why it represented a backlash against working mothers, who were obviously losing custody to unwed and divorced fathers.

Both producers were crushed when I told them our re- 10 searchers couldn't confirm either claim, and that we have no way of even knowing how many of these so-called single fathers are in fact living with the mother of their child outside of marriage, and how many are divorced dads who simply happened to have their children with them for the weekend on the day they filled out the form. When I called a Census Bureau researcher to see if he could help straighten this out, he said my guess was as good as his.

It's not that the census researchers are doing a bad job. The 11 problem is that they're asked to compress America's increasingly fluid family arrangements into one-dimensional categories that were established at a time when most single-parent households were created by death rather than by divorce, and when most people made things easy for data collectors by lying rather than admitting to "living in sin."

People's new candor about their lifestyles, combined with 12 the undeniable changes in family arrangements that have occurred over the past 40 years, makes it increasingly hard to capture new family realities in old census categories. And using such categories to talk about families has consequences.

Labeling people single parents, for example, when they may 13 in fact be coparenting—either with an unmarried other parent in the home or with an exspouse in a joint custody situation—stigmatizes their children as the products of "single parenthood" and makes the uncounted parent invisible to society. This can lead teachers, school officials, neighbors and other family members to exclude the uncounted parents from activities and interactions into which they might otherwise be drawn. In fear of such marginalization, some separated parents find it hard to agree on a custody arrangement that's in the best interests of the child, because each wants to be the socially recognized parent.

14   In the past, many "intact" families had fathers who were AWOL from their children's lives. Today, conversely, many "broken" families have fathers who remain active parents. Harvard fellow Constance Ahrons, who has conducted a 20-year study of post-divorce families and their children, has certainly seen plenty of cases where the nonresident parent, usually the father, stops doing any parenting. But she has found many instances where nonresidential fathers became *more* active in their children's lives after divorce than they were during the marriage. These men need to be recognized for their support, rather than relegated to the same state of nonbeing as the deadbeat dad.

15   It's not only parents who are marginalized by outdated household categories. When I speak on work-family issues to audiences around the country, some of the biggest complaints I hear come from individuals who are described by the census as living in "non-family households." They resent the fact that their family responsibilities literally don't "count," either for society or for their employers. There is no category, for instance, for individuals who spend several days a week caring for an aging parent in the parent's separate residence. Yet one in four households in America today is providing substantial time and care to an aging relative, and more than half of all households say they expect to do so within the next 10 years.

16   It's time for our discussion of family trends to better reflect the complexities of today's family commitments. Perhaps, as Larry McCallum, a therapist who directs the family life program at Augustana College in Rock Island, Ill., suggests, we should do for parents what we have begun to do with racial categories in the census—provide several alternative ways for people to express their overlapping identities. At the very least, we need to drop the idea that we can predict how a family functions solely by its form.

17   The place where we keep our clothes isn't always the only place where we keep our commitments.

Expanding Vocabulary

Match each word in column A with its definition in column B. When in doubt, first find the word in the essay and look for context clues to aid your understanding of the word's meaning. Then, if necessary, use

a dictionary to complete the matching exercise. The number in paren-   16
theses is the number of the paragraph in which the word appears.

Column A	Column B
liaison (1)	authorities
resurgence (4)	bother, concern
agog (5)	frankness, honesty
pundits (7)	full of eager excitement
cohabitation (8)	brands; labels in a negative way
faze (8)	one who maintains communication
candor (12)	between groups 17
stigmatizes (13)	placing on the edge of the scene;
marginalization (13)	making one less important
deadbeat (14)	one who does not pay his or her debts
	renewal or revival
	living together

Understanding Content

1. Why does the author get calls from media people asking for explanations of recent Census figures on families?
2. Why does Coontz find the Census Bureau's definition of traditional family "ironic"?
3. What number continues a 30-year decline? That is, what important change in American families continues?
4. Why did western states show an increase in "married-with-children" households?
5. What accounts for most of the growth in "single" motherhood?
6. What are the several consequences of using the old Census categories to describe today's families?

Drawing Inferences about Thesis and Purpose

1. What attitude toward the media does Coontz have—and invite readers to have? How do you know?
2. What is the author's thesis? You may need more than one sentence to present several interconnected key ideas.

Analyzing Strategies and Style

1. In paragraph 2, Coontz puts "traditional" and "good news" in quotation marks. Why? What does she want to communicate with the quotation marks?
2. The author's final paragraph is one sentence. What makes it effective? What key words are connected by sound?

Thinking Critically

1. While showing the problems in using the Census Bureau's old categories, Coontz also provides readers with some interesting statistics. What data are most surprising to you? Why?
2. Have you thought about the consequences of stigmatizing and marginalizing the nonlegal father or the divorced parent without primary custody, as Coontz suggests we do with the old categories? Does this make sense to you? Do you see this as a problem we need to address?
3. Are you accepting of the various living arrangements of families today? What makes a family? Do we need to broaden our definition? Reflect on these questions.

What Really Scares Us

DAVID ROPEIK

A journalist with a Master's Degree from the Northwestern University School of Journalism, David Ropeik is currently director of risk communication at the Harvard Center for Risk Analysis. Ropeik also teaches risk communication at the Harvard School of Public Health and is coauthor of *Risk: A Practical Guide for Deciding What's Really Safe and What's Really Dangerous in the World Around You* (2002). The following article, published in 2003 in *Parade* magazine, explores the causes of our often groundless fears.

Questions to Guide Your Reading and Reflection

1. What are the causes of many of our fears?
2. What are your five greatest fears?

1   The list of things to be afraid of seems to grow daily: Terrorism. Snipers. Child abductions. West Nile virus. According to a number of public-opinion surveys, many people think it's more dangerous to be living now than it ever has been.

2   But those fears fly in the face of evidence that, in many ways, things are better than they've ever been. The average American life expectancy in 1900 was about 47 years. Now it's nearing 80.

Diseases that plagued us—polio, smallpox, tuberculosis—have been all but eradicated in the U.S. In 1960, out of every 1000 babies born, 26 did not survive their first year. That number is now down to seven.

So why this disconnect between the facts and our fears? 3 Well, it turns out that when it comes to the perception of risks, facts are only part of how we decide what to be afraid of and how afraid to be. Another huge factor—sometimes the most important factor—is our emotions.

Why do humans perceive risks this way if our highly ad- 4 vanced brain gives us the power to reason? It's because our brains are biologically built to fear first and think second. Which, in the end, is a pretty good strategy for our survival.

Say you're walking through the woods and see a line on the 5 ground, and you're not sure if it's a snake or a stick. The visual information goes to two parts of the brain. One is called the prefrontal cortex, behind your forehead. That's the area where we do a lot of our reasoning and thinking. The other area is called the amygdala, which is the brain's key emotion center.

Because of the way the brain is constructed, the information 6 gets to the amygdala before it gets to the prefrontal cortex. So, before the reasoning part of the brain has had a chance to consider the facts, the fear center is saying, "Jump back, you dummy! It *could* be a snake!"

But how does the brain turn raw sensory information into 7 fear? Apparently our brains have built-in patterns for interpreting sensory information that help us subconsciously filter incoming messages, making us more afraid of some things than others. Psychologists have identified many of the specific emotional characteristics of risks that are likely to make us more, or less, afraid.

Emotional Factors That Determine Our Fears

Control. Imagine that you're driving down the highway, 8 feeling pretty safe because you're behind the wheel. Now switch seats with your passenger. You're probably a little more nervous, maybe even turning into a full-fledged backseat driver. Not because the risk has gone up—the annual odds of being killed in a motor vehicle crash are 1 in 6,700—but because you are no longer in control.

9   **Trust.** We trust certain sources more than others. We're less afraid when a trusted doctor or scientist, such as the head of the Centers for Disease Control and Prevention, explains anthrax than when a politician explains it.

10   **Newness.** When a risk first shows up, we treat it more like a snake until we've lived with it for a while and our experience lets us put the risk in perspective. We are more afraid of West Nile virus when it first shows up in our area than after it has been around for a few years. (Odds of dying from West Nile virus: 1 in 1,000,000.)

11   **Choice.** We're more afraid of risks that are imposed on us than risks we take by choice. Imagine that you're driving along, talking on your cell phone. In the next lane, some other guy is driving and using *his* cell phone. Though both of you are in danger, the risk from the motorist next to you feels greater, because it is being imposed on you.

12   **Dread.** Things that can kill us in really awful ways seem riskier. We're more afraid of being eaten alive by a shark (odds, 1 in 281,000,000) or dying in a plane crash (1 in 9,000,000) than of dying from heart disease (1 in 300).

13   **Me or Them.** If the risk is to you, it's worse than if that same risk only threatens somebody else. We're *all* worried about terrorism, now that we know it can happen here too, to us. A one in a million risk is too high if we think *we* could be that "one."

14   **Is it hard to understand?** The more complicated a risk is, the less we can understand it—and the more we treat it like a snake, just to be safe. For example, we're concerned about ionizing (nuclear) radiation, but we're not worried about infrared radiation, which we know simply as heat.

15   **Natural or manmade?** If it's natural, we're less afraid than if it's manmade. We're more frightened of nuclear power accidents (odds, 1 in 200,000) than of solar radiation. Yet sun exposure caused an estimated 1.3 million new cases of skin cancer in America per year, 7,800 of which are fatal.

16   Several of these factors are often at work on the same risk at the same time, some making us more afraid and some less. The effect of these factors changes over time. Also, individual fears vary based on individual circumstances. For instance, women fear breast cancer more than men, while men fear prostate cancer more than women.

While it's understandable that we perceive risks this way, it 17 can also be dangerous. Some people, afraid to fly because they lack control or because the risk of terrorism is new and feels high, choose instead to drive—a much bigger risk. It may make them *feel* safer, but overreacting this way raises their risks.

Underreacting can be dangerous too. People who aren't con- 18 cerned about the risk of the sun—because it's natural and because of that nice glowing tan—raise their risk of cancer by not taking the danger of sun exposure seriously enough to slap on sunscreen or wear a hat.

FACTS CAN HELP YOU FEEL SAFER

Here are your chances of dying in a given year due to . . .

Child Kidnapping	1 in 1,300,000
Dog Bite	1 in 19,000,000
Cell Phone Radiation	0
Flood	1 in 6,900,000
Flu	1 in 130,000
Lightning	1 in 3,000,000
Guns	1 in 28,000
Snake/Lizard/Spider	1 in 56,000,000

(Facts provided by the author, based on data from private and U.S. government agencies. Odds are for the average American. Individual risk may vary.)

In the end, the best way to reduce the danger of any given 19 risk is to arm yourself with some basic facts from a reliable, neutral source, so the rational side of your perceptions can hold its own in the contest against your natural emotions. The better you can do at keeping your perceptions of risks closer in line with what the risks actually are, the happier *and* safer you'll be.

Expanding Vocabulary

Examine the following words in their contexts in the essay and then write a brief definition or synonym for each one. (Do not use a dictionary; try to guess the word's meaning from its context.)

plagued (2)
eradicated (2)
disconnect (3)
dread (9)

Understanding Content

1. Why do we ignore facts and fail to use reason and thereby become fearful?
2. What are the specific factors that contribute to our fears?
3. What can be the consequences of the ways we react emotionally to perceived risks?
4. What is the best way to reduce actual risks—and our fears?

Drawing Inferences about Thesis and Purpose

1. Ropeik opens with some statistics. What is his purpose? What does he want to illustrate at the beginning of his essay?
2. Write a thesis for the essay.

Analyzing Strategies and Style

1. The author lists seven emotional factors that determine fear. How does he present and explain each one? What makes this strategy effective?
2. How would you describe the tone of the essay? Why is Ropeik's tone important in this essay?

Thinking Critically

1. Were you aware of the brain functioning that Ropeik describes? Does it seem logical to you that perceptions affect the emotional center of the brain before the reasoning center? Why?
2. Are you surprised by any of the items in the list of emotional factors? On reflection, do the factors that surprise you seem logical as influences on our fears? Explain.
3. From your experience, do some of the emotional factors seem to be more powerful influences than others? If so, which ones? If not, why not?
4. Do you know people who think life is scarier today than in the past? If so, what are their reasons for their fears? Do you think you will be able to change their thinking after reading Ropeik's essay? Explain.

Dream Deferred

LANGSTON HUGHES

Like many American writers, Langston Hughes (1902–1967) came from the Middle West to New York City, lived in Europe, and then returned to the United States to a career of writing. He was a journalist, fiction writer, and poet, and author of more than sixty books. Hughes was also the first African American to support himself as a professional writer. Known as "the bard of Harlem," Hughes became an important public figure and voice for black writers. "Dream Deferred," one of Hughes's best-loved poems, which comes from *The Panther and the Lash: Poems of Our Time* (1951), illustrates the effective use of metaphor to convey the poet's attitudes and emotions.

What happens to a dream deferred?

Does it dry up
like a raisin in the sun?
Or fester like a sore—
And then run?   5
Does it stink like rotten meat?
Or crust and sugar over—
like a syrupy sweet?

Maybe it just sags
like a heavy load.   10

Or does it explode?

Understanding Content and Strategies

1. How is the poem structured; that is, what is it a series of?
2. The "answers" to the poem's first question are all similes except one. Which line is a metaphor? Explain the metaphor. Why is the one metaphor an effective strategy?
3. What does Hughes mean by a "deferred" dream?
4. Explain each simile. How does each one present a response to, or the effect of, a deferred dream?
5. What do the similes and metaphor have in common?

Drawing Inferences about Theme

1. What, then, is Hughes's attitude toward his subject? What does he want us to understand about deferred dreams?
2. Might the poem also be making a social comment? If so, what?

Thinking Critically

1. Which simile do you find most effective? Why?
2. Has Hughes included most of the responses to deferred dreams? Is there any response you would add? If so, can you state it as a simile?

MAKING CONNECTIONS

---

1. Amatai Etzioni sees today's obsession with self-fulfillment as a major cause of social problems. Could one describe the breakdown of family as a loss of a sense of duty? Compare Etzioni's views with Linda Waite's. Will an obsession with the self bring happiness? Consider what Ciardi (see Chapter 8) has to say about happiness.
2. Linda Waite thinks that, generally, people's lives are improved by marriage. Keith Ablow is concerned with the deviance of parents that leads to abused children. Apparently not all marriages result in happier adults and children. Should we encourage marriage for everyone? Should there be testing of some kind leading to a marriage license? A parenting license?
3. Have we, in this society, chosen the search for affluence over family commitments and family joys? Does this search divide us by gender or class? Does it affect our compassion for those less fortunate? If the answer is yes to these questions, should we be concerned? Are these problems for society? If so, what can we do to change?
4. Perhaps one indicator of how successfully families today are coping is the rate and types of crimes committed by juveniles. Go online to gather some statistics on juvenile crime. You can look for trends (the last ten years, for example) or look at arrest figures for one type of crime. There are many Websites with statistical information on juvenile crime. Pick a search engine and type in "juvenile crime statistics."

5. AIDS is not a gay problem; it is a family problem and a global scourge. Go online for the latest facts. What groups are most at risk? In what countries is HIV-AIDS spreading the most?

6. We are now living in what seems a scarier world. We read about terrorism, war, the spread of AIDS, the abuse of children by parents, teachers, priests. What are we most at risk for? Find some data on the risks associated with these problems. Be prepared to discuss your findings.

TOPICS FOR WRITING

1. In your prereading exercise, you reflected on your decision to attend college. Now reflect on your reasons for selecting the particular college you are attending. In an essay, explain the causes for your choice of school. You can organize according to the decision process you went through, or you can organize from least to most important causes. You might think of writing this essay as a feature article in your college newspaper.

2. Have you ever done something that you did not think you ought to do? If so, why did you do it? And what were the consequences of your actions? In an essay, examine the causes and effects of your action. Be sure that you have a point to make. You might want to show that you should have listened to the warning voice inside you, or you might want to show that one effect of such a situation is that we do learn something about ourselves.

3. Are you "addicted" to something? To chocolate or beer or cigarettes? To television soaps, video games, bridge, or something else? If so, reflect on why you and others like you are addicted to whatever it is that absorbs you. Drawing on your personal experience, your knowledge of others, and perhaps some reading on the topic, develop an analysis of the causes of your addiction. If you use ideas from your reading, give proper credit by stating author and title.

4. Linda Waite and Stephanie Coontz both bring up some of the problems we face with today's redefining and redesigning of the family. Drawing on your reading and your

own experiences, develop an essay on one (or two related) problems that many face because of changes in family structures or lifestyles today. Give appropriate credit to any of the authors from whose essays you draw material. You may want to focus only on explaining the problems, or you may want to conclude with one or more possible solutions to the problem.

5. Do you get along well (or poorly) with a parent? If so, reflect on why you have a good (or bad) relationship with that parent. What are the causes? Are your experiences similar to those of friends? What do some of the experts say about parent/children relationships? Drawing on your personal situation, your knowledge of others, and perhaps some reading, develop an analysis of the causes for good (or bad) parent/child relationships. If you use ideas from your reading, give proper credit.

6. Have you experienced divorce either as a once-married person or as a child of divorced parents? If so, reflect on the effects of divorce. Drawing on your own experience, your knowledge of the experiences of others, and perhaps some reading, develop an analysis of the effects of divorce on divorced persons or their children. Follow the guidelines for crediting your reading given in topic 4.

7. Amitai Etzioni feels strongly about the decline of a sense of duty in our society, and this has led him to write on the subject. Is there a current social or political problem that you are especially interested in? If so, think about the causes and effects of this problem. Then write an essay on the problem. Focus on the causes of the problem, the effects of the problem, or both causes and effects. You might want to conclude with one or more proposed solutions to the problem.

A CHECKLIST FOR CAUSAL ANALYSIS ESSAYS

Invention

☐ Have I selected a topic consistent with the instructor's guidelines for this assignment?

☐ Have I chosen among the possible topics one that fits my knowledge and experience?

☐ Have I reflected on my topic to sort through the various influences and causes that are necessary to my analysis?

☐ Have I reflected on my topic to write a tentative thesis that makes clear my purpose to analyze cause?

☐ Have I "tested" my initial analysis of cause against experience and logic?

☐ Have I generated specifics from my thinking and, if appropriate, reading to illustrate and support my analysis?

☐ Have I thought about the most effective organization?

Drafting

☐ Have I succeeded in completing a first draft at one sitting so that I can "see" the whole?

☐ Do I have enough—enough to meet assignment demands and enough to explain and support my causal analysis?

☐ Does the order work?

Revision

☐ Have I made any needed additions, deletions, or changes in order based on answering the questions about my draft?

☐ Have I revised my draft to produce coherent paragraphs, using transitions and connecting words that reveal my causal analysis?

☐ Have I eliminated wordiness and clichés?

☐ Have I avoided or removed any discriminatory language?

☐ Have I used my word processor's spell check and proofread a printed copy with great care?

☐ Do I have an appropriate and interesting title?

10

Using Argument and Persuasion

Preserving a Safe and Sane World

Losing patience with two friends, you finally moan, "Will you two *please* stop arguing! You've been bickering all evening; you're ruining the party." How often many of us have said, or wanted to say, something similar to parents, children, colleagues, or friends who seem unable to stop yelling or name calling, or quibbling over some insignificant point. In this context, the term *argument* has a negative connotation. In a classroom debate, a courtroom, a business conference, or writing, however, a sound argument is highly valued.

The Characteristics of Argument

Understanding the characteristics of good argument will help you to think critically about the arguments of others and to write better arguments of your own. Some of these characteristics may surprise you, so read thoughtfully and reflect on the following points.

- *An argument makes a point.* Sound reasons and relevant evidence are presented to support a claim, a main idea that the arguer keeps in focus. Collecting data on a particular topic may produce an interesting report, but unless the specifics support a point, there is no argument.
- *Argument assumes an audience.* The purpose of argument is not just to provide information but to change the way listeners or readers think about an issue, to move them to agree with you. Once you ac-

cept that argument implies an audience, you have to accept the possibility of counterarguments, of listeners or readers who will not agree with you and will challenge your thinking. You have not defended your argument by simply asserting that it is *your opinion.* If you have not based your opinion on good evidence and reasons, your opinion will be challenged, and you will lose the respect of your audience.

- *Good argument is based on a recognition of the complexities of most issues and the reality of opposing views.* One of the greatest dangers to good argument lies in oversimplifying complex issues, or in oversimplifying reality by assuming that our claim is "clearly right" and that therefore everyone agrees with us.

- *Good argument makes clear the values and beliefs that we consider relevant to the issue.* Argument is not just an intellectual game. We need to recognize the values that are a part of our reasoning, our way of approaching a particular issue. For example, if you argue that abortion is wrong because it is murder, you *believe* that the fetus is a human being at the moment of conception. Your argument is convincing only to those who share your *belief.* Wanting no uncertainty about the values upon which his claim was founded, Thomas Jefferson wrote: "We hold these truths to be self-evident" and then listed such values as "all men are created equal" and "governments are instituted among men."

- *In argument, we present evidence to support a claim on the assumption that there is a valid or logical connection between evidence and claim,* what British philosopher Stephen Toulmin calls a *warrant.* When you argue that abortion is wrong because it is murder, you assume or warrant that the fetus is a human being who can be murdered. Arguments can be challenged not only on the evidence or stated reasons but also on the assumptions or warrants that support the argument's structure. Therefore, you must know what your assumptions are because you may need to defend them as part of the support for your argument.

- *Argument includes the use of persuasive strategies.* When you write an argumentative essay, you want to convince readers to share your views, or at least to reconsider theirs in the light of your discussion. Of course you are involved in your topic and want to affect readers. Indeed, you will write more persuasively if you write about issues that concern you. In good argument, however, emotions are tempered by logic and channeled into the energy needed to think through the topic, to gather evidence, to consider audience, and to plan the paper. Remember that one of the best *persuasive* strategies is to present yourself to readers as a reasonable person who has done your homework on the topic and who wants to find some common ground with those who disagree.

How to Use Argument and Persuasion

How can you put together a good argumentative essay? Accepting that writing an effective argument is a challenging task, you may want to give appropriate time and thought to *preparing to write* before you actually draft your essay. Use the following guidelines to aid your writing.

1. **Think about audience and purpose.** Unless you are writing about a most unusual topic, expect your readers to be aware of the issue. This does not mean that you can skip an appropriate introduction or necessary background information. It does mean that you can expect readers to know (and perhaps be a part of) the opposition, so be prepared to challenge counterarguments and consider the advantages of pointing out common ground. Also define your purpose in writing; that is, recognize the *type* of argument you are planning. Are you presenting the results of a study, perhaps the results of a questionnaire you prepared? (For example, you could do a survey of attitudes toward campus security, or proposals to eliminate the school newspaper.) Are you writing to state your position on a value-laden issue, such as euthanasia or capital punishment? Are you writing on a public-policy issue, such as whether to restrict smoking in all restaurants? Each of these types of arguments needs somewhat different support and development, so as you work on your argument's thesis or claim, think about the type of argument as well.

2. **Brainstorm about your topic to develop a tentative thesis and think about the kinds of support your thesis (claim) will need.** If you have done an investigation, you need to study your evidence to see what appropriate conclusions can be drawn. (For example, if 51 percent of the students you polled want more security on campus at night, you could say that a majority of students think that increased security is needed. But, it is more accurate to say that about half of the students polled expressed that view.) If you are

writing an argument based primarily on values rather than facts, decide on your position and then begin to list your reasons. Suppose you support euthanasia. What, exactly, are you in favor of? Physician-assisted suicide? A patient's right to refuse all life-support systems? A family-member's right to make that decision? Be sure that you state your claim so that it clearly represents your position, a position you believe you can support. Then consider why: To eliminate unnecessary suffering? To give individuals control over their deaths? If you are examining a problem in education or arguing for restricting smoking in restaurants, you may need to do some reading to locate appropriate facts and statistics. You may also need to consider the feasibility of putting your proposal into place. Will it cost money? Where will the money come from? Who may be hurt or inconvenienced? How can you bring these people to your side?

3. **Plan the organization of your essay.** Remember that any plan is just a guide so that you can get started. As you draft or when you revise, you may find that you want to switch parts around or add new ideas and examples that have come to you while writing. But remember as well that usually some plan is better than no plan. If you are writing an argument based on values, consider these steps:

a. **Begin with an introduction to get your reader's attention.** If you are writing on euthanasia, you can mention the news coverage of Dr. Kevorkian.

b. **Decide where to place your thesis.** Although typically a thesis or claim comes early in the essay, you may want to experiment with placing it at the end, after you have presented support for that claim.

c. **Organize reasons in a purposeful way.** One strategy is to move from less important to most important reasons. Another approach is to organize around counterarguments, explaining why each of the opposition's arguments does not hold up. (In this chapter, Molly Ivins uses the arguments of the gun lobby as an organizing strategy in her argument for gun control.) Consider using some of the methods of development discussed throughout this text.

Draw on your reading for statistical details, on your own experience for examples.

d. **Provide support for each reason.** You have not written an effective argument just by stating your reasons. You need to argue for them, to show why they are reasonable, or better than the opposition's reasons, or have the support of good evidence.

e. **Conclude by effectively stating or restating your claim.** As a part of your conclusion, you may want to explain to readers how this issue affects them, how they could benefit from embracing your position or your proposal for change.

4. **Revise, revise, revise.** After completing a first draft based on your tentative plan, study the draft carefully both for readability and effective argument. Examine reasons and support to be sure you have avoided logical fallacies. See where you may need to qualify statements or control your language. Be certain that you have maintained an appropriate level of seriousness so that you retain the respect of readers. As the writers in this chapter illustrate, you want to write movingly about issues that concern you without forsaking good sense and relevant evidence.

WRITING FOCUS:
LOGICAL FALLACIES

When you ignore the complexities of issues or choose emotional appeals over logic, you risk producing an essay filled with *logical fallacies.* Many arguments that could be won are ruined by those who leave reasoned debate for emotional appeals or who oversimplify the issues. Here are some frequent fallacies to avoid in your writing and to watch out for in the arguments of others.

- *ad hominem* Attacking the opponents instead of defending your position is not an effective strategy with intelligent readers. You have not supported an anti-abortion position, for example, by calling pro-choice advocates "murderers" or labeling them "proabortion."

- **Straw Man** The straw man fallacy seeks to defend one's position by accusing opponents of holding a position that is easier to attack but is not actually what the opponents believe. To "argue" that those seeking gun registration just want to take guns away from good people and leave them in the hands of criminals is a good example. Those who want gun registration certainly do not want criminals to have guns.

- **Bandwagon** Another substitute for good argument is the appeal to join in, or join the majority, often without providing evidence that a majority holds the view of the arguer or, even more important, that the view is a sound one. Appeals to national interest or the good of the country often contain the bandwagon fallacy. For example: All good Americans want respect shown for the flag, so we need a law banning flag burning. Some "good Americans" also value free speech and see flag burning as an example of free speech.

- **Common Practice** Similar to the bandwagon fallacy, the appeal to common practice is the false logic that "everyone is doing it, so it must be a good thing." However, cheating on tests or on one's income taxes, for example, cannot be logically defended by "arguing" that everybody does it. First, it is not true that everybody does it, and second, even if that were true, it would not make cheating right.

- **Hasty Generalization or Overstatement** When drawing on your own experiences for evidence, you need to judge if your experiences are representative. For example, you may be having difficulty in calculus, but it would be illogical to conclude that the instructor is inept or that the course is too hard. These could be explanations, but they are not the only possible ones. How are other students doing in the course is a key question to ask. Even when you gather extensive evidence from reading, be cautious about generalizing. It is not true that all people on welfare are lazy or that lawyers only want to make piles of money. Qualify assertions; avoid such words as *always, never, everybody,* and *none.* (These words entice readers to find the one exception that will disprove your sweeping generalization.)

- **False Dilemma** The false dilemma is often called either/or thinking. It is the illogic of asserting that only two possibilities are available when there may be several. The effectiveness of this strategy (if you have readers who are not thinking critically) is that you can make one possibility seem a terrible choice, thereby making your choice sound good by contrast. For example: Either we pay more taxes or we will have to cut educational programs. Now these are clearly not the only two possibilities. First, there are other programs that could be cut. Second, we could find ways to save money in the running of government. Third, we can have a growing economy that brings in more government revenues without increasing taxes. Those are just three additional possibilities; there are probably others.

- **Slippery Slope** The slippery slope fallacy makes the argument that we cannot allow A to take place because if we do, then we will head down a slope all the way to Z, a place where no one wants to be. The strategy here is to make Z so awful that readers will agree with you that we should not do A. The error in logic is the unsupported assumption that if A takes place, Z will follow. For example: If the government is allowed to register guns, then before you know it they will ban handguns and then take away all guns, even hunting rifles. Unfortunately, for those who want to scare people with this illogic, there is no evidence that registration will lead to confiscation. We register cars and planes and boats; the government has not confiscated any of these items.

Getting Started: Reflections on the Challenges Facing Ourselves, Our Society, Our World

What do you consider the greatest challenge facing you in your personal life? Is it completing school? Giving up cigarettes or junk food? Reestablishing a relationship with a parent or friend? What do you consider the greatest challenge facing society? Is it reestablishing a sense of community? Improving schools? Improving race relations? Finding deterrents to crime? What do you consider the greatest challenge facing the world? Is it saving the environment? Establishing world peace? Eliminating hunger and injustice? Decide on the challenge, in one of the categories, that most troubles you and brainstorm about the reasons for the problem and possible solutions to the problem. Be prepared to discuss your reasons and proposed solutions with classmates.

Ban the Things. Ban Them All.

MOLLY IVINS

Molly Ivins, a graduate of Smith College and Columbia University, began her career as a reporter. She has been a columnist since 1980 and is currently with the *Fort Worth Star-Telegram*. Ivins is also a contributor to magazines such as the *Nation* and *Ms.*, and she has a collection of essays published under the title *Molly Ivins Can't Say That, Can She?* An insightful political commentator, Ivins is also known for her wit and irreverent style, traits shown in the following column published March 16, 1993.

Questions to Guide Your Reading and Reflection

1. Where does Ivins first state her thesis?
2. Ivins is not timid about expressing her views. As you read, note words that reveal her attitude through their negative meanings and connotations.

AUSTIN—Guns. Everywhere guns.   1

Let me start this discussion by pointing out that I am not   2
anti-gun. I'm pro-knife. Consider the merits of the knife.

3   In the first place, you have to catch up with someone to stab him. A general substitution of knives for guns would promote physical fitness. We'd turn into a whole nation of great runners. Plus, knives don't ricochet. And people are seldom killed while cleaning their knives.

4   As a civil libertarian, I of course support the Second Amendment. And I believe it means exactly what it says: "A well-regulated militia being necessary to the security of a free state, the right of the people to keep and bear arms shall not be infringed." Fourteen-year-old boys are not part of a well-regulated militia. Members of wacky religious cults are not part of a well-regulated militia. Permitting unregulated citizens to have guns is destroying the security of this free state.

5   I am intrigued by the arguments of those who claim to follow the judicial doctrine of original intent. How do they know it was the dearest wish of Thomas Jefferson's heart that teenage drug dealers should cruise the cities of this nation perforating their fellow citizens with assault rifles? Channeling?

6   There is more hooey spread about the Second Amendment. It says quite clearly that guns are for those who form part of a well-regulated militia, i.e., the armed forces including the National Guard. The reasons for keeping them away from everyone else get clearer by the day.

7   The comparison most often used is that of the automobile, another lethal object that is regularly used to wreak great carnage. Obviously, this society is full of people who haven't got enough common sense to use an automobile properly. But we haven't outlawed cars yet.

8   We do, however, license them and their owners, restrict their use to presumably sane and sober adults and keep track of who sells them to whom. At a minimum, we should do the same with guns.

9   In truth, there is no rational argument for guns in this society. This is no longer a frontier nation in which people hunt their own food. It is a crowded, overwhelmingly urban country in which letting people have access to guns is a continuing disaster. Those who want guns—whether for target shooting, hunting or potting rattlesnakes (get a hoe)—should be subject to the same restrictions placed on gun owners in England—a nation in which liberty has survived nicely without an armed populace.

10   The argument that "guns don't kill people" is patent nonsense. Anyone who has ever worked in a cop shop knows how

many family arguments end in murder because there was a gun in the house. Did the gun kill someone? No. But if there had been no gun, no one would have died. At least not without a good footrace first. Guns do kill. Unlike cars, that is all they do.

Michael Crichton makes an interesting argument about technology in his thriller *Jurassic Park*. He points out that power without discipline is making this society into a wreckage. By the time someone who studies the martial arts becomes a master—literally able to kill with bare hands—that person has also undergone years of training and discipline. But any fool can pick up a gun and kill with it.   11

"A well-regulated militia" surely implies both long training and long discipline. That is the least, the very least, that should be required of those who are permitted to have guns, because a gun is literally the power to kill. For years, I used to enjoy taunting my gun-nut friends about their psychosexual hangups—always in a spirit of good cheer, you understand. But letting the noisy minority in the National Rifle Association force us to allow this carnage to continue is just plain insane.   12

I do think gun nuts have a power hangup. I don't know what is missing in their psyches that they need to feel they have the power to kill. But no sane society would allow this to continue.   13

Ban the damn things. Ban them all.   14

You want protection? Get a dog.   15

Expanding Vocabulary

Study definitions of the following words and then use each of them in separate sentences. The number in parentheses is the number of the paragraph in which the word appears.

ricochet (3)	lethal (7)
wacky (4)	carnage (7)
intrigued (5)	taunting (12)
perforating (5)	psyches (13)
hooey (6)	

Understanding Content

1. What, according to Ivins, does the Second Amendment mean? How does she cleverly turn the pro-gun group's use of the Second Amendment to her advantage in this paragraph?

2. What reason does Ivins give to support the assertion that "there is no rational argument for guns in this society"? What restrictions does she want this country to adopt?
3. Why, in the author's view, is the pro-gun argument that guns don't kill people "patent nonsense"?
4. What psychological explanation does Ivins offer to account for "gun nuts"?

Drawing Inferences about Thesis and Purpose

1. When Ivins writes, in paragraph 2, that she is "not anti-gun," how do you know that she does not mean this?
2. When the author writes, in paragraph 2, "I'm pro-knife," she introduces an idea that she develops through an entire paragraph and returns to later in her essay. In what sense do knives have "merit"? In what way is she being serious? What else is she doing; that is, what does she accomplish through her discussion of the merits of the knife?

Analyzing Strategies and Style

1. Characterize Ivins's style. Consider her word choice and sentence patterns.
2. Look especially at her first two and last two paragraphs; what tone is created by her style?
3. When Ivins writes that she used to taunt friends "in a spirit of good cheer," does she mean what she says? What technique does she use in this passage?
4. How does Ivins organize her discussion of gun control? To what points is she responding as a way to develop her argument? What type of argument is this?

Thinking Critically

1. Does the author effectively challenge the "Second Amendment argument" of the gun lobby? The argument that licensing will lead to outlawing guns? The "guns don't kill" argument? Do you think that her refutation of one argument is more convincing than another? Explain and defend your evaluation of her argument.
2. What audience is likely to be offended by this column? What does your answer tell you about the audience to which her essay is targeted? Which audience do you fit into? Does that explain, at least in part, the way you responded to the first set of questions?
3. How might Ivins justify her approach of "grabbing the reader by the shoulders and shaking him or her"? Why does she think this approach is necessary?

Why Guns Matter

NED ANDREWS

A graduate of Yale University, Ned Andrews was a member of the Yale Conservative Party and author of articles for both the *Yale Daily News* and *Yale Herald* while at Yale. As part of a summer internship at the *American Enterprise* magazine, Andrews posted a longer version of his article on gun control issues online. The shorter version, which follows, appeared in the September 2002 issue of the magazine.

Questions to Guide Your Reading and Reflection

1. Which color represents "Gore" states and which represents "Bush" states?
2. To which "state" do you belong? Why?

During the tense weeks that followed Election Night 2000, many Americans became familiar with the color-coded map dividing their country into patches of red and blue. Many publications, including *TAE* (see March 2002), have described the cultural differences between the primarily coastal pockets that supported Gore and the expanses of Bush territory in between. But if column inches and word counts are any indicator, few commentators have investigated the underlying philosophical difference between Blue and Red America. They might start by examining the debate over gun control.

Gun-control advocates frequently argue that the Second Amendment is "obsolete," that in our era the government can fulfill all our law-enforcement needs. So, how well does the government take care of Blue America? According to the FBI, Gore-leaning states reported one crime for every 27 residents in 2000. The situation is on the mend, but there are still plenty of holes in the Left's security blanket.

Blue America's overconfidence exemplifies the elitism and insularity that characterize its culture in general. Blue America forgets that not everyone lives in cities with beat cops or in suburbs with ample law-enforcement budgets. From my east Tennessee home, the nearest police station is a good 20-minute drive away. Add the time it takes to process a 911 call and locate the offender, and it becomes evident that if my family did not own guns, criminals could wreak havoc with impunity. Apparently my situation is not unique: In Red America, those 1-in-27 odds rise to 1 in 22. Out here, the arm of the law just isn't long enough, and even liberals such as Mississippi's Mike Espy know that big government can't "go it alone" against criminals who will respect new anti-gun statutes no more than the laws they break already.

4   Blue America holds not only that the government is a competent agent on our behalf, but also that in forming that government we alienated our own right to fend for ourselves. Since the government is capable of defending us, it does no wrong by disarming the public. Such reasoning ignores the fact that the right to bear arms helps ensure not only our current safety but our future liberty as well.

5   Legal scholars disagree on whether the Second Amendment merely permits states to maintain defense forces or also allows individuals to arm themselves. Yet no matter which position is correct, the goal is the same: to check the law's enforcers as well as its violators.

6   This is why Red America values the Second Amendment so highly. Red America still evaluates the political sphere from a moral perspective: Ultimately, the role of government is not to create law but to obey it. And when government deviates from its ethical mandate, citizens have a duty to restore it to its rightful place. Red America realizes that a disarmed citizenry will be unable to stand up for what is right when its government does wrong.

7   Blue America has abandoned this moral point of view, instead evaluating conflicts in terms of "interests." It further relinquishes critical evaluation of those interests, assuming that all are equally worthy of satisfaction. Blue America views government not as an enforcer of duties and rights but as a facilitator of individuals' personal ends, appealing for justification not to any categorical moral code but to entirely pragmatic concerns.

8   This is why the Second Amendment is so bothersome to Blue America. The right to bear arms is the right to take a stand, to act on the belief that you are right and someone else is wrong, and as such it is a threat to the amoral collectivism that the New Left embodies. For it is our guarantee—our only guarantee—that we may transform our moral beliefs into action.

Expanding Vocabulary

Match each word in column A with its definition in column B. When is doubt, first find the word in the essay and look for context clues to aid your understanding of the word's meaning. Then, if necessary, use your dictionary to complete the matching exercise. The number in parentheses is the number of the paragraph in which the word appears.

Column A	*Column B*
exemplifies (3)	inflict widespread destruction
elitism (3)	those who compel obedience
insularity (3)	abandons, gives up
wreak havoc (3)	belief that certain persons or groups
impunity (3)	deserve favored treatment
enforcers (5)	one who assists to make things easier
deviates (6)	without punishment
relinquishes (7)	not caring about moral issues
facilitator (7)	reveals by example
amoral (8)	differs from the usual way
	narrow-mindedness, closed off
	from others

Understanding Content

1. In the discussions following the 2000 elections, what did the commentators *not* examine, in the author's view?
2. What issue will reveal differences between "Blue" and "Red" America?
3. What was the crime rate in 2000 in Blue America? What was the crime rate in Red America?
4. With what attitudes does Andrews charge Blue America?
5. Andrews argues that Red America values the Second Amendment for what two reasons?
6. By rejecting the Second Amendment, Blue America shows that it holds what beliefs about government, according to the author?

Drawing Inferences about Thesis and Purpose

1. What is Andrews's position on gun control?
2. What is his thesis?
3. What can you infer to be his political affiliation?

Analyzing Strategies and Style

1. Andrews organizes his discussion around a color-coded map revealing election results. What does he gain by this strategy? What does he expect his audience to know?
2. What word choice in paragraph 1 seems to reveal the author's political leanings?

Thinking Critically

1. Examine Andrews's argument. Has he demonstrated that those who favor gun control are elitists? That they have forgotten that not everyone lives in cities or the suburbs?

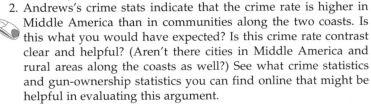

2. Andrews's crime stats indicate that the crime rate is higher in Middle America than in communities along the two coasts. Is this what you would have expected? Is this crime rate contrast clear and helpful? (Aren't there cities in Middle America and rural areas along the coasts as well?) See what crime statistics and gun-ownership statistics you can find online that might be helpful in evaluating this argument.
3. What, if any, logical fallacies do you find in this argument?

Adult Crime, Adult Time

LINDA J. COLLIER

An attorney, Linda J. Collier is currently dean of public services and social sciences at Delaware County Community College in Pennsylvania. She has been the director of student legal services at Penn State University and special assistant for legal affairs to two college presidents in addition to teaching courses in sociology and criminal justice. The following essay, published in the *Washington Post* in 1998, is written in response to the case of a 12-year-old and a 14-year-old shooting four students and a teacher at their school in Jonesboro, Arkansas that same year.

Questions to Guide Your Reading and Reflection

1. What is the trend in juvenile crime?
2. Why do you think we have a juvenile court system?

When prosecutor Brent Davis said he wasn't sure if he could   1
charge 11-year-old Andrew Golden and 13-year-old Mitchell
Johnson as adults after Tuesday afternoon's slaughter in Jonesboro, Ark., I cringed. But not for the reasons you might think.

I knew he was formulating a judgment based on laws that   2
have not had a major overhaul for more than 100 years. I knew
his hands were tied by the longstanding creed that juvenile offenders, generally defined as those under the age of 18, are to be
treated rather than punished. I knew he would have to do legal
cartwheels to get the case out of the juvenile system. But most of
all, I cringed because today's juvenile suspects—even those who
are accused of committing the most violent crimes—are still regarded by the law as children first and criminals second.

As astonishing as the Jonesboro events were, this is hardly   3
the first time that children with access to guns and other
weapons have brought tragedy to a school. Only weeks before
the Jonesboro shootings, three girls in Paducah, Ky., were
killed in their school lobby when a 14-year-old classmate allegedly opened fire on them. Authorities said he had several
guns with him, and the alleged murder weapon was one of
seven stolen from a neighbor's garage. And the day after the
Jonesboro shootings, a 14-year-old in Daly City, Calif., was
charged as a juvenile after he allegedly fired at his middle-
school principal with a semiautomatic handgun.

It's not a new or unusual phenomenon for children to com-   4
mit violent crimes at younger and younger ages, but it often
takes a shocking incident to draw our attention to a trend already in progress. According to the U.S. Department of Justice,
crimes committed by juveniles have increased by 60 percent
since 1984. Where juvenile delinquency was once limited to
truancy or vandalism, juveniles now are more likely to be the
perpetrators of serious and deadly crimes such as arson, aggravated assault, rape and murder. And these violent offenders increasingly include those as young as the Jonesboro
suspects. Since 1965, the number of 12-year-olds arrested for
violent crimes has doubled and the number of 13- and 14-year-
olds has tripled, according to government statistics.

Those statistics are a major reason why we need to revamp our   5
antiquated juvenile justice system. Nearly every state, including
Arkansas, has laws that send most youthful violent offenders to

the juvenile courts, where they can only be found "delinquent" and confined in a juvenile facility (typically not past age 21). In recent years, many states have enacted changes in their juvenile crime laws, and some have lowered the age at which a juvenile can be tried as an adult for certain violent crimes. Virginia, for example, has reduced its minimum age to 14, and suspects accused of murder and aggravated malicious wounding are automatically waived to adult court. Illinois is now sending some 13-year-olds to adult court after a hearing in juvenile court. In Kansas, a 1996 law allows juveniles as young as 10 to be prosecuted as adults in some cases. These are steps in the right direction, but too many states still treat violent offenders under 16 as juveniles who belong in the juvenile system.

6   My views are not those of a frustrated prosecutor. I have represented children as a court-appointed guardian *ad litem*, or temporary guardian, in the Philadelphia juvenile justice system. Loosely defined, a guardian *ad litem* is responsible for looking after the best interest of a neglected or rebellious child who has come into the juvenile courts. It is often a humbling experience as I try to help children whose lives have gone awry, sometimes because of circumstances beyond their control.

7   My experience has made me believe that the system is doing a poor job at treatment as well as punishment. One of my "girls," a chronic truant, was a foster child who longed to be adopted. She often talked of how she wanted a pink room, a frilly bunk bed and sisters with whom she could share her dreams. She languished in foster care from ages 2 to 13 because her drug-ravaged mother would not relinquish her parental rights. Initially, the girl refused to tolerate the half-life that the state had maintained was in her best interest. But as it became clear that we would never convince her mother to give up her rights, the girl became a frequent runaway. Eventually she ended up pregnant, wandering from place to place and committing adult crimes to survive. No longer a child, not quite a woman, she is the kind of teenage offender for whom the juvenile system has little or nothing to offer.

8   A brief history: Proceedings in juvenile justice began in 1890 in Chicago, where the original mandate was to save wayward children and protect them from the ravages of society. The system called for children to be processed through an appendage of the family court. By design, juveniles were to be kept away

from the court's criminal side, the district attorney and adult correctional institutions.

Typically, initial procedures are informal, non-threatening   9
and not open to public scrutiny. A juvenile suspect is inter-
viewed by an "intake" officer who determines the child's fate.
The intake officer may issue a warning, lecture and release; he
may detain the suspect; or, he may decide to file a petition, sub-
jecting the child to juvenile "adjudication" proceedings. If the
law allows, the intake officer may make a recommendation that
the juvenile be transferred to adult criminal court.

An adjudication is similar to a hearing, rather than a trial, al-   10
though the juvenile may be represented by counsel and a juvenile prosecutor will represent the interests of the community. It
is important to note that throughout the proceedings, no matter which side of the fence the parties are on, the operating
principle is that everyone is working in the best interests of the
child. Juvenile court judges do not issue findings of guilt, but
decide whether a child is delinquent. If delinquency is found,
the judge must decide the child's fate. Should the child be sent
back to the family—assuming there is one? Declare him or her
"in need of supervision," which brings in the intense help of
social services? Remove the child from the family and place
him or her in foster care? Confine the child to a state institution
for juvenile offenders?

This system was developed with truants, vandals and   11
petty thieves in mind. But this model is not appropriate for
the violent juvenile offender of today. Detaining a rapist or
murderer in a juvenile facility until the age of 18 or 21 isn't
even a slap on the hand. If a juvenile is accused of murdering,
raping or assaulting someone with a deadly weapon, the suspect should automatically be sent to adult criminal court.
What's to ponder?

With violent crime becoming more prevalent among the ju-   12
nior set, it's a mystery why there hasn't been a major overhaul
of juvenile justice laws long before now. Will the Jonesboro
shootings be the incident that makes us take a hard look at the
current system? When it became evident that the early release of
Jesse Timmendequas—whose murder of 7-year-old Megan
Kanka in New Jersey sparked national outrage—had caused un-
warranted tragedy, legislative action was swift. Now New Jersey has Megan's Law, which requires the advance notification of

a sexual predator's release into a neighborhood. Other states have followed suit.

13   It is unequivocally clear that the same type of mandate is needed to establish a uniform minimum age for trying juveniles as adults. As it stands now, there is no consistency in state laws governing waivers to adult court. One reason for this lack of uniformity is the absence of direction from the federal government or Congress. The Bureau of Justice Statistics reports that adjacent states such as New York and Pennsylvania respond differently to 16-year-old criminals, with New York tending to treat offenders of that age as adults and Pennsylvania handling them in the juvenile justice system.

14   Federal prosecution of juveniles is not totally unheard of, but it is uncommon. The Bureau of Justice Statistics estimates that during 1994, at least 65 juveniles were referred to the attorney general for transfer to adult status. In such cases, the U.S. attorney's office must certify a substantial federal interest in the case and show that one of the following is true: The state does not have jurisdiction; the state refuses to assume jurisdiction or the state does not have adequate services for juvenile offenders; the offense is a violent felony, drug trafficking or firearm offense as defined by the U.S. Code.

15   Exacting hurdles, but not insurmountable. In the Jonesboro case, prosecutor Davis has been exploring ways to enlist the federal court's jurisdiction. Whatever happens, federal prosecutions of young offenders are clearly not the long-term answer. The states must act. So as far as I can see, the next step is clear: Children who knowingly engage in adult conduct and adult crimes should automatically be subject to adult rules and adult prison time.

Expanding Vocabulary

Match each word in column A with its definition in column B. When in doubt, first find the word in the essay and look for context clues to aid your understanding of the word's meaning. Then, if necessary, use your dictionary to complete the matching exercise. The number in parentheses is the number of the paragraph in which the word appears.

Column A	*Column B*
cringed (1)	occurrence
formulating (2)	those who are responsible for what
allegedly (3)	has happened

phenomenon (4)
truancy (4)
perpetrators (4)
revamp (5)
antiquated (5)
malicious (5)
waived (5)
awry (6)
languished (7)
relinquish (7)
ravages (8)
scrutiny (9)
adjudication (9)
unequivocally (13)

obsolete, outdated
revise, make over
existed in miserable conditions
claim or right given up
damages
preparing in an organized way
hear a judicial proceeding
give up
clear examination
pulled back in fear
absence without permission
clearly, without question
presumably, unproven
amiss, wrong
desire to hurt someone

Understanding Content

1. Summarize the author's examples of recent violent juvenile crime.
2. What are some of the problems with current state laws governing juvenile crimes?
3. Briefly summarize the author's history of the juvenile justice system.
4. In addition to failing to punish properly, in the author's view, what else do juvenile court systems fail to do?
5. Where does Collier look for help in correcting the juvenile justice system?

Drawing Inferences about Thesis and Purpose

1. What is Collier's thesis? Where does she state it?
2. In paragraph 11, when she writes "What's to ponder?" what response does she want from readers?

Analyzing Strategies and Style

1. Although Collier is writing in response to the Jonesboro murders, she refers to other juvenile murders in paragraph 3. What does she seek to gain by this?
2. Collier asserts that she is not writing as a "frustrated prosecutor" and describes her experience as a court-appointed guardian. What does she gain by her discussion in paragraphs 6 and 7?

Thinking Critically

1. What are the main points of Collier's argument? Make a list of the key steps in her argument and then evaluate the argument. Has she supported her thesis convincingly?

2. Could the example of one of Collier's court-appointed "girls" be used to argue *for*, rather than against, the juvenile justice system? Explain your answer.

3. Do you think that juveniles should be tried as adults? If so, in what situations?

Kids Who Kill Are Still Kids

RICHARD COHEN

Richard Cohen, a *Washington Post* columnist who has been syndicated since 1976, writes about both political issues and contemporary culture. The following column appeared in newspapers on August 3, 2001.

Questions to Guide Your Reading and Reflection

1. How many juveniles have been tried as adults in U.S. courts?
2. What assumption is contained in Cohen's title?

1   When I was about 12, I heaved a cinder block over my neighbor's fence and nearly killed her. I didn't know she was there. When I was about the same age, I started a small fire in a nearby field that spread until it threatened some nearby houses. I didn't mean to do it. When I was even younger, I climbed on top of a toolshed, threw a brick in the general direction of my sister and sent her, bleeding profusely and crying so that I can still hear her, to the hospital. I didn't mean to do that, either.

2   I tell these stories to remind us all that kids are kids and to suggest that even the worst of them—even the ones who commit murder—are still kids. I would be lying if I said that I knew what to do with them—how long they should be jailed and where—but I do know that something awful has come over this country. It seems the more incomprehensible the crime, the more likely it is that a child will be treated as an adult.

3   This is what happened to Nathaniel Brazill, 14, who was recently sentenced to 28 years in prison for the murder of a teacher, Barry Grunow. Brazill was only 13 when he shot the teacher on the final day of school. Grunow, a much-beloved teacher, had

stopped Brazill from talking to two girls and disrupting the class. Earlier in the day, the boy had been suspended for throwing water balloons. He had gone home, gotten a gun and returned to school. Grunow was Brazill's favorite teacher.

I always feel in columns of this sort the necessity to say   4
something about the victim and how his life was taken from him. I feel a particular need to do so in this case because Grunow seemed to be an exceptional teacher, a good person. Anyway—and this is only me talking—I feel a certain awe, a humility, toward people who dedicate their lives to teaching kids instead of, say, peddling tech stocks or mouthing off on television about Gary Condit.[1]

But Grunow is gone and nothing can be done to bring him   5
back. That is not merely a cliché but also an important point. Because always in these cases when it comes time to justify why a minor was treated as an adult, someone says something about sending a message to other kids. This is absurd.

Consider what Brazill did. He shot his teacher before oodles   6
of witnesses. He shot a man he liked. He shot someone without any chance of his getting away. He shot someone for almost no reason at all. He shot someone not in the course of a robbery or a sex crime or because he put a move on his girlfriend but because he is a screwed-up kid, damaged, full of anger and with not much self-control. He shot someone without fully comprehending the consequences. He shot someone because, among other things, he was just 13 years old.

And yet, he was prosecuted—and sentenced to three years   7
more than the mandatory minimum—as an adult. If there is one thing he is not, it is an adult. But Brazill and, earlier, 13-year-old Lionel Tate were sentenced as if they were button men for some crime family. Tate was given life without parole for the killing of a 6-year-old girl he maintained died in a wrestling accident. These boys were tried as adults but, I'd guess, their ability to participate in their own defense would be labeled juvenile.

Amnesty International says about 200,000 children have   8
been tried as adults by American courts. Florida alone reports that 3,300 kids were prosecuted as adults in fiscal 1999–2000. This sends a message—but it's to the adult community: We're

[1]Former Californian member of Congress—Ed.

getting tough. Kids, however, are unlikely to get the message. I mean, you know how kids are.

9   Where is the deterrence in this policy? Will other 13-year-olds now hesitate before killing their teacher? Hardly. Who is being punished? The child at first, but later the adult he becomes.

10   Brazill will be over 40 when he gets out of jail. When he's, say, 35, will he have anything in common with the child who pulled the trigger? No more, I'd say, than I do with the jerk who nearly killed Richie Miller's mother with a cinder block. I didn't set out to hurt anyone, it's true. But neither did Brazill, he says. He just pulled the trigger and the man, somehow, died. It is, when you think about it, a childish explanation.

Expanding Vocabulary

Study definitions of each of the following words and then use each one in a separate sentence. The number in parentheses is the number of the paragraph in which the word appears.

> heaved (1)
> profusely (1)
> incomprehensible (2)
> prosecuted (7)
> deterrence (9)

Understanding Content

1. What is Cohen's primary example?
2. What was Brazill's sentence?
3. What is Cohen's explanation for Brazill's behavior?
4. When we try juveniles as adults, who, in Cohen's view, is being sent a message?

Drawing Inferences about Thesis and Purpose

1. Why does Cohen doubt that punishing children as adults acts as a deterrent to crime?
2. What is Cohen's thesis?

Analyzing Strategies and Style

1. Cohen begins by recounting stories of his childhood. Why? What point does he want to make?
2. Look at the author's concluding paragraph. What makes it effective? What is clever about the last sentence?

Thinking Critically

1. When you were young, did you do anything that could have resulted in a court case? If so, what were the consequences and how do you feel about the incident now?
2. Evaluate Cohen's argument. Are his reasons and evidence convincing? Why or why not?
3. How should the two boys used as examples by Cohen have been tried and sentenced? Take a stand.

An Elastic Institution

JOHN BORNEMAN AND LAURIE KAIN HART

The two authors are both anthropologists. John Borneman is professor of anthropology at Princeton University and the author of books and articles, including *Settling Accounts: Violence, Justice, and Accountability in Postsocialist Europe* (1997). Laurie Kain Hart is chair of the anthropology department at Haverford College and author of *Time, Religion, and Social Experience in Rural Greece* (1992). Their discussion of marriage, from a historical and sociological perspective, was originally published April 14, 2004, in the *Washington Post*.

Questions to Guide Your Reading and Reflection

1. What do the authors suggest about marriage in their title?
2. What do you know about marriage from a historical and cross-cultural perspective?

Since its origins in the late 19th century, anthropology— 1 more than any other field of knowledge—has made the understanding of marriage across human societies one of its central tasks. Today the question arises: Can a scientific understanding inform current debates about the meaning of marriage? Would homosexual marriage destroy the principle of marriage as a social institution?

In the 1860s New York lawyer and anthropologist Louis 2 Henry Morgan attempted a systematic cross-cultural study of the institution of marriage. Morgan's data were imperfect, but he was able to demonstrate that the record of human societies showed a startling diversity of socially approved forms of marriage. All societies had some form of regularized partnership, but no single standard human form could be identified. Generally, even within a society, there was a certain elasticity of marriage forms.

3   The most famous of these unions were the ones most foreign to Western Victorian society: marriage between a woman and several men; marriage between a man and several women; forms of "visiting" marriage, whereby a man might visit his wife but not live with her. As anthropologists assembled more reliable data, they found it difficult to produce a definition of human marriage that would hold true for all its socially legitimate forms.

4   Marriage generally functioned to provide a "legitimate" identity to children—a kind of "last name." Yet, the structure of these arrangements was extraordinarily diverse: Biological paternity was not universally the basis of identity—as, indeed, it is not in the case of adoption in America. In many cases, the biological father (the Latin term is genitor) was distinct from the legal father (pater) produced by the marriage contract and ceremony. Alternatively, it could be the mother's family and not the father that bestowed identity on a child.

5   As for sex, rarely if ever has marriage been able to restrict its varied practice to the relation of man and wife. In most cases, anthropologists agreed, what counted was that some socially approved form of marriage provided a secure place for the child in the social order.

6   But marriage has not been solely about children. In most societies known to us, everyone marries; it is an expected rite of passage and part of the normal life course of all adults. Only in post-classical Western societies do we find high numbers of unmarried people. Unlike other peoples, we consider marriage—however desirable or undesirable—optional.

7   Claude Levi-Strauss, the father of French structural anthropology, argued that it is only the "division of labor between the sexes that makes marriage indispensable." It follows that if men and women are granted equal access to jobs of similar worth—as is often the case today—the meaning of marriage will change.

8   The cult of romantic love in a companionate marriage is a recent innovation in the history of marriage. While romantic pas-

sion has existed in all societies, only in a few has this unstable emotion been elaborated and intensified culturally and con- sidered the basis for the social institution of marriage. Indeed, marriage has traditionally been more concerned with—and successful in—regulating property relations and determining lineage or inheritance rights than with confining passion and sexual behavior.

Marriage, in other words, is not only diverse across cultures   9 but also dynamic and changing in America's own history. We live in a pluralist society, where marriage is not the only form of union or of mutual care in our society. When individuals and groups can, under certain conditions, choose their patterns of self-expression—their intimacy, child-care arrangements, sex- ual practices, place of residence, partnership forms—there will be increased variability. The meaning of marriage—and the value of marriage—changes when it becomes one of several options in a society of self-determining individuals.

This said, it is not the case that "anything goes." Every soci-   10 ety favors forms of union that conform to its ethical standards and its needs.

Our society no longer approves of treating women as in-   11 competent minors and the wards of their husbands within the structure of a patriarchal union. We do not approve, generally, of plural marriages—the basis of our disapproval being that they abrogate the rights of women and especially of young girls. We no longer generally feel that the sole function of women in society is to produce children and serve men as do- mestic labor. In other words, when we censure certain types of marriage, the basis on which we do so is our defense of indi- vidual human rights. This is our ethical standard.

Marriage is, then, foundational because it provides a recog-   12 nized form of identity and security for children in society. Its function is not universally to produce children but to provide legitimate forms for their care. And marriage's primary ac- complishment is not to regulate sex (as a quick glance at Amer- ican society would tell us). The institution survives despite infidelity, and sex does not by itself create marriage.

In addition, it is a system of exchange whereby families   13 "give up" their own offspring to make new alliances with oth- ers, and to enter into broad networks of relationships, including and especially with one's "enemies." Without such arrangements, we would have a world of isolated, incestuous, biological clans—and endemic warfare.

14   What, then, about restriction of the legal bond of marriage to a man and a woman? Does marriage have to be heterosexual? The human record tells us otherwise. While the model of marriage is arguably heterosexual, the practice of marriage is not. In a broad spectrum of societies in Africa, for example, when a woman's husband dies, she may take on his legal role in the family, and acquire a legal "wife" to help manage the domestic establishment. This role of wife is above all social, and not contingent on her sexual relations. These societies, which practice heterosexuality, take this woman-woman marriage as commonsensical; they recognize that above all marriage functions socially to extend and stabilize the network of care.

15   As for marriage as a legal institution, the ethnographic record makes clear that law expresses the dominant ethics of the group. Our history reflects the evolution of our values, and we as Americans are most proud of our deepening tradition of civil rights. To deny marriage to same-sex couples, as President Bush proposes, expresses a rejection of this civil rights tradition and a regression to a politics of exclusion.

Expanding Vocabulary

Match each word in column A with its definition in column B. When in doubt, first find the word in the essay and look for context clues to aid your understanding of the word's meaning. Then, if necessary, use your dictionary to complete the matching exercise. The number in parentheses is the number of the paragraph in which the word appears.

Column A	*Column B*
diverse (4)	dependent on
paternity (4)	rebuke, official disapproval
lineage (8)	having distinct groups coexisting within a society
pluralist (9)	
patriarchal (11)	a system in which the father is head of the family
abrogate (11)	
censure (11)	close, formal associations
alliances (13)	constant, widespread
endemic (13)	having variety, differences
contingent (14)	abolish

ethnographic (15)   study comparing human cultures
                           direct descent from a particular ancestor
                           fatherhood

Understanding Content

1. What did Morgan's 1860s study of marriage reveal?
2. Why is it difficult to define marriage?
3. What has been the primary, traditional function of marriage? What has marriage not been able to restrict or control?
4. How has the thinking about marriage changed today in Western societies?
5. By what ethical standard do we object to some attitudes and practices within marriages in the past in our culture?
6. By the same ethics, what position on same-sex marriage follows, in the authors' view?

Drawing Inferences about Thesis and Purpose

1. What is the authors' purpose in writing? Do they have more than one purpose?
2. What is their thesis? Where is it stated?

Analyzing Structures and Style

1. What approach do the authors take to their topic? Think about the essay as an argument. What is the nature of their evidence to support their claim?
2. How would you describe the tone of the essay? How is this an important element in their argument?

Thinking Critically

1. Were you aware that only in contemporary Western societies has marriage now become just one option for structuring one's social life? What is your reaction to this reality? What may be the causes for this change?
2. The authors largely dismiss romantic love as having much influence on marriage as a social institution. Does this surprise you? If so, why? On reflection, do the authors make sense to you on this point?
3. Evaluate the argument.

Abolish Marriage

MICHAEL KINSLEY

A member of the bar with a law degree from Harvard, Michael Kinsley is a former editor of both *Harper's* and *The New Republic*. He is the founding editor (in 1996) of *Slate*, the online magazine, has been a co-host of CNN's *Crossfire*, and currently writes a weekly column for the *Washington Post*. The following column appeared in the *Post* July 3, 2003.

Questions to Guide Your Reading and Reflection

1. What are gay marriage proponents seeking? What are social conservatives seeking?
2. Should state governments control marriages?

1   Critics and enthusiasts of *Lawrence v. Texas*, last week's Supreme Court decision invalidating state anti-sodomy laws, agree on one thing: The next argument is going to be about gay marriage. As Justice Scalia noted in his tart dissent, it follows from the logic of *Lawrence*. Mutually consenting sex with the person of your choice in the privacy of your own home is now a basic right of American citizenship under the Constitution. This does not mean that the government must supply it or guarantee it. But the government cannot forbid it, and the government also should not discriminate against you for choosing to exercise a basic right of citizenship. Offering an institution as important as marriage to male-female couples only is exactly this kind of discrimination. Or so the gay rights movement will now argue. Persuasively, I think.

2   Opponents of gay rights will resist mightily, although they have been in retreat for a couple of decades. General anti-gay sentiments are now considered a serious breach of civic etiquette, even in anti-gay circles. The current line of defense, which probably won't hold either, is between social toleration of homosexuals and social approval of homosexuality. Or between accepting the reality that people are gay, even accepting that gays are people, and endorsing something called "the gay agenda." Gay marriage, the opponents will argue, would cross

this line. It would make homosexuality respectable and, worse, normal. Gays are welcome to exist all they want, and to do their inexplicable thing if they must, but they shouldn't expect a government stamp of approval.

It's going to get ugly. And then it's going to get boring. So, we have two options here. We can add gay marriage to the short list of controversies—abortion, affirmative action, the death penalty—that are so frozen and ritualistic that debates about them are more like Kabuki performances than intellectual exercises. Or we can think outside the box. There is a solution that ought to satisfy both camps and may not be a bad idea even apart from the gay-marriage controversy. [3]

That solution is to end the institution of marriage. Or rather (he hastens to clarify, Dear) the solution is to end the institution of government-sanctioned marriage. Or, framed to appeal to conservatives: End the government monopoly on marriage. Wait, I've got it: Privatize marriage. These slogans all mean the same thing. Let churches and other religious institutions continue to offer marriage ceremonies. Let department stores and casinos get into the act if they want. Let each organization decide for itself what kinds of couples it wants to offer marriage to. Let couples celebrate their union in any way they choose and consider themselves married whenever they want. Let others be free to consider them not married, under rules these others may prefer. And, yes, if three people want to get married, or one person wants to marry herself, and someone else wants to conduct a ceremony and declare them married, let'em. If you and your government aren't implicated, what do you care? [4]

In fact, there is nothing to stop any of this from happening now. And a lot of it does happen. But only certain marriages get certified by the government. So, in the United States we are about to find ourselves in a strange situation where the principal demand of a liberation movement is to be included in the red tape of a government bureaucracy. Having just gotten state governments out of their bedrooms, gays now want these governments back in. Meanwhile, social-conservative anti-gays, many of them Southerners, are calling on the government in Washington to trample states' rights and nationalize the rules of marriage, if necessary, to prevent gays from getting what they want. The Senate Majority Leader, Bill Frist of Tennessee, responded to [5] the Supreme Court's *Lawrence* decision by endorsing a constitutional amendment, no less, against gay marriage.

6   If marriage were an entirely private affair, all the disputes over gay marriage would become irrelevant. Gay marriage would not have the official sanction of government, but neither would straight marriage. There would be official equality between the two, which is the essence of what gays want and are entitled to. And if the other side is sincere in saying that its concern is not what people do in private, but government endorsement of a gay "lifestyle" or "agenda," that problem goes away, too.

7   Yes, yes, marriage is about more than sleeping arrangements. There are children, there are finances, there are spousal job benefits like health insurance and pensions. In all these areas, marriage is used as a substitute for other factors that are harder to measure, such as financial dependence or devotion to offspring. It would be possible to write rules that measure the real factors at stake and leave marriage out of the matter. Regarding children and finances, people can set their own rules, as many already do. None of this would be easy. Marriage functions as what lawyers call a "bright line," which saves the trouble of trying to measure a lot of amorphous factors. You're either married or you're not. Once marriage itself becomes amorphous, who-gets-the-kids and who-gets-health-care become trickier questions.

8   So, sure, there are some legitimate objections to the idea of privatizing marriage. But they don't add up to a fatal objection. Especially when you consider that the alternative is arguing about gay marriage until death do us part.

Expanding Vocabulary

Write a definition for each of the following words. Then select five of the words and use each one of those in a separate sentence of your own. The number in parentheses is the number of the paragraph in which the word appears.

tart (1)	government-sanctioned (4)
breach (2)	implicated (4)
ritualistic (3)	trample (5)
Kabuki (3)	amorphous (7)

Understanding Content

1. What has just happened that is the occasion for Kinsley's column? What argument does he think the event will lead to?
2. Who will win the argument, in Kinsley's view?
3. What is the author's solution to end the argument?
4. What is ironic about gays fighting for the right to marry? What is ironic about conservatives seeking a constitutional amendment against gay marriage?
5. What problems would we have if governments stopped sanctioning marriage? Can the problems be solved?

Drawing Inferences about Thesis and Purpose

1. When Kinsley writes that the argument over gay marriage will "get boring," what does he mean? How does his comparison to Kabuki performances or to debates over abortion illustrate his point?
2. What is the author's thesis, the claim of his argument? Where does he state it?

Analyzing Strategies and Style

1. What is clever about the last sentence of the essay?
2. When Kinsley writes "Or rather (he hastens to clarify, Dear) . . . " who is the "Dear" in this sentence? What makes this line amusing?
3. Analyze the essay's tone. How serious is Kinsley in presenting his solution to the argument over gay marriage? If he is not entirely serious, why is he proposing his solution? What seems to be his purpose in writing?

Thinking Critically

1. Do you agree with Kinsley—whether you like it or not—that gay marriage will be sanctioned? If you disagree, what evidence do you have to support your view?
2. What is your reaction to Kinsley's proposal?
3. Is there any hope of finding common ground on this issue, or are we doomed to live with another issue that generates only ritualistic "debates"? Do you have any new suggestions for thinking outside the box on any social issues that are currently divisive?

The Case For Compromise on Abortion

ANDREW SULLIVAN

A native of England with a Ph.D. in political science from Harvard, Andrew Sullivan is editor of *Andrewsullivan.com*, an online source of commentary on current issues, a *Time* magazine essayist, and a columnist for the Sunday *Times* of London. He lectures widely and appears frequently on both radio and television programs. The following is a *Time* essay from March 7, 2005.

Questions to Guide Your Reading and Reflection

1. What principle regarding abortion can we all agree on?
2. Can you imagine a compromise position on the abortion issue?

1   Something very unusual is happening to some Democrats and pro-choice abortion activists in the U.S. They're getting smarter about their strategy. For years, they've harped on and on about a woman's right to choose, while failing to capture in any meaningful way the moral qualms so many of us have about abortion itself. So they often seemed strident, ideological and morally obtuse. They talked about abortion as if it were as morally trivial as a tooth extraction—not a profound moral choice that no woman would ever want to make if she could avoid it.

2   But that obtuseness seems—finally and mercifully—to be changing. Senator Hillary Clinton led the way in a recent speech to abortion-rights activists. She said something so obvious and so right it's amazing it has taken this long for it to be uttered: whatever side you're on in the pro-choice vs. pro-life debate, we surely all want to lower the number of abortions. Whether you believe that an abortion is a difficult medical procedure for a woman or whether, like me, you believe that all abortions are an immoral taking of human life, we can all agree on a third principle: we would be better off with fewer of them. And the happy truth is, abortions have been declining in numbers. According to the most recent data from the Centers for Disease Control in Atlanta, since 1990 the number of reported

legal abortions in the States dropped from 1.4 million a year to 853,000 in 2001. The number of abortions for every 1,000 live births dropped from 344 to 246.

How did this happen? No one is quite sure. It could be re-   3
lated to less access to abortion providers, but more likely it is a function of declining teenage pregnancies, more widespread use of contraception, abstinence programs and cultural shifts toward sexual restraint among young women. None of these strategies separately is a panacea, but each has a part to play. So what's the new pro-choice line? Let's keep up the progress. Let's defend the right to an abortion while doing all we can to ensure that fewer and fewer women exercise it. Leave the contentious issue of *Roe v. Wade* for one minute, quit the ideological bickering about when life begins for a while, take down the barricades, and craft a strategy that assumes abortion will be legal for the foreseeable future, but try to reduce it.

Both sides have something to contribute. Sure, U.S. taxpay-   4
ers should fund abstinence programs, as many pro-lifers argue. They can work for some women. But so too does expanded access to contraception. The pro-life Senate minority leader, Harry Reid, has a bill called the Prevention First Act that would expand access to birth control. Or Americans can focus on expanding adoption as an alternative to abortion (which means adoption by gays as well as straights). NARAL Pro-Choice America, formerly known as the National Abortion Rights Action League, actually took out an ad in the conservative *Weekly Standard* last month, appealing to pro-life groups to join in the antiabortion crusade—not by making it illegal but by increasing access to contraception.

What's the downside? I cannot see any. Both sides can still   5
fight to keep abortion legal or illegal. But both can also work hard to reduce the moral and human toll of abortion itself. Why shouldn't a future Democratic candidate commit to an actual goal of reducing abortions nationally by, say, one-fifth in a four-year term? Alas, the pro-life side is leery. A key part of their coalition is made up of conservative Catholics who oppose any kind of birth-control devices; others are hostile to any adoption rights for gay couples. Still others may fear that if the number of abortions drops significantly, their argument for making it completely illegal may become less salient.

6   But none of those arguments makes sense on its own terms. If abortion really is the evil that pro-lifers believe it is, they should stop at nothing to reduce its prevalence—now. Is it really better that someone should have an abortion rather than be on the pill? Is it really preferable for an unborn life to be snuffed out than to allow him to have loving gay parents? Those are the questions that pro-choicers should be posing to pro-lifers. Saving human life is the priority. Why are you so reluctant to do it? Call this position the pro-choice, pro-life compromise. If America's Democrats want to regain credibility on moral issues, it's a great way to start. And if Republicans want to prevent abortions rather than use the issue as a political tool, they can get on board. Americans have nothing to lose but trauma and pain and politics and death. And they have something far more precious to gain: life itself.

Expanding Vocabulary

Examine the following words in their contexts in the essay and then write a brief definition or synonym of each one. Avoid using a dictionary; try to guess each word's meaning from its context. The number in parentheses is the number of the paragraph in which the word appears.

qualms (1)	contentious (3)
strident (1)	leery (5)
ideological (1)	coalition (5)
obtuse (1)	salient (5)
abstinence (3)	prevalence (6)
panacea (3)	

Understanding Content

1. How did pro-choice activists used to talk?
2. Who has changed the language?
3. What is the common ground being offered?
4. What has changed since 1990? What are possible reasons for this change?
5. Why is it difficult for pro-life groups to commit to a common ground position? What do they have to support to work toward common ground?

Drawing Inferences about Thesis and Purpose

1. Is Sullivan liberal or conservative? Pro-life or pro-choice? How do you know?
2. What is his purpose in writing? What change would he like to see?
3. Write a thesis for the essay.

Analyzing Strategies and Style

1. Explain Sullivan's simile in paragraph 1. Is it effective in making his point?
2. Examine the last sentence in paragraph 3. What gives the sentence its power?
3. In paragraph 6, Sullivan poses questions that he says pro-choicers should be asking. How does he think the questions should be answered?

Thinking Critically

1. Sullivan asserts that there is no downside to both sides working toward the common ground of fewer abortions. Do you think that those who oppose abortion rights will all agree with him? Why or why not?
2. Sullivan shrewdly raises the point of Republicans possibly wanting to keep the fight against abortions as "a political tool." Has this issue become a political tool for Republicans? What is your assessment of its importance to this party?
3. What are some other issues that could use some compromising but remain divisive issues used by each of the parties? List several. Then select one and think about how you might argue for common ground.

No Safer and Less Free

LAURA W. MURPHY

A graduate of Wellesley College, Laura Murphy served as director of the Washington Legislative Office of the ACLU from 1993 to 2005. Prior to holding this position as the American Civil Liberties Union's leading lobbyist, she has worked in other positions for the ACLU and has been a legislative assistant for two members of Congress. Murphy is the first woman and first

African American to be the ACLU's Washington office director. Her commentary on national ID cards was published December 13, 2004, in *USA Today.*

Questions to Guide Your Reading and Reflection

1. What legislation did Congress approve regarding national ID cards?
2. Do you think we need a national ID card?

1   "Show me your papers" is a phrase most Americans would never expect to hear in their everyday lives, but with the intelligence bill passed by Congress last week, that's the type of Big-Brother society we're becoming. The de facto national ID that lawmakers approved won't make us any safer, but it will make us much less free.

2   Most people already use a driver's license—to cash checks, vote and travel—so what's wrong with standardizing and consolidating data?

3   A national ID is an identity thief's dream come true. Under new federal guidelines, state IDs must include personal information, plus a digital photograph, and they must be "machine readable." Businesses might soon be able to swipe your ID to track what you bought, and when and where you bought it. They could be able to use that information themselves or sell it to others.

4   Since 9/11, Americans have had to weigh tradeoffs between privacy and security. A national ID, though, protects neither. Of the 25 countries most affected by terrorist attacks—including Israel—80% already have national IDs. A national ID hasn't made these nations any safer.

5   A convincing case has not been made that this system would have stopped 9/11 or the Oklahoma City bombing, because a national ID cannot reveal malicious intentions. For example, some of the 9/11 hijackers obtained identification documents legally, and were in the country legally.

6   It takes good, old-fashioned police work to follow up on leads and separate the Mohamed Attas and Timothy McVeighs from law-abiding people.

7   A national ID wouldn't have stopped those with fake IDs, either. An ID is only as secure as the "source documents" it

requires. Someone who used a fake birth certificate and fake Social Security card to get an ID will still be able to do so under the new law; the same people who manufacture fake driver's licenses today will be manufacturing fake national IDs tomorrow.

Our privacy isn't the only price we'll pay for this system. En- 8 acting this legislation will cost billions of dollars—money better spent on real security measures that will keep us both safe and free.

Expanding Vocabulary

Study the context in which the following words are used, or study their definitions in your dictionary, and then use each word in a separate sentence. The number in parentheses is the number of the paragraph in which the word appears.

de facto (1)
malicious (5)

Understanding Content

1. What will the new guidelines require our driver's licenses to contain? Why is this a problem, in the author's view?
2. What is Murphy's argument point in paragraph 5? Does she make a convincing argument for her side? Explain.
3. What is the author's view of the problem of fake IDs?

Drawing Inferences about Thesis and Purpose

1. What is Murphy's claim? Where does she state it?
2. Do we know that Israel is no safer with national ID cards? Is it not possible that more terrorist attacks may have occurred if there were no IDs to check? Can we necessarily draw the inference that Murphy draws?

Analyzing Strategies and Style

1. When we read the question in paragraph 2, what can we expect to follow in the rest of the essay?
2. What does the author mean by the expression, in paragraph 1, that we are becoming a "Big-Brother society"? What is the emotional impact of this image?

Thinking Critically

1. What are the specific arguments in support of the author's claim? Evaluate each one. Are some more convincing than others? Explain.

2. Murphy asserts, at the end of her essay, that the requirement of national IDs will be very expensive. Why will it cost money? Is there evidence that it will cost billions? See what you can learn online about the possible costs of making driver's licenses national ID cards.

Try National ID Card—You Might Like It

ROBERT KUTTNER

Robert Kuttner is founder and coeditor of *The American Prospect*, a monthly magazine of liberal ideas with an online version, too. He is the author of six books, most recently *Everything for Sale: The Virtues and Limits of the Markets* (1997). The following article, published December 4, 2004, is one of Kuttner's regularly appearing *Boston Globe* columns.

Questions to Guide Your Reading and Reflection

1. What is the greatest concern about adopting a national ID card?

2. Do you think that we should have national ID cards?

1   As a card-carrying member of the American Civil Liberties Union, I'd like to have one more card in my wallet. The card I want, contrary to the views of most civil liberties activists, is a national ID card.

2   Privacy advocates have always resisted this idea, for fear of government snooping on citizens. But that cat is out of the bag. Nearly all of us have driver's licenses, Social Security cards, passports. And corporations, credit agencies, and HMOs keep dossiers, too—often more extensive than what government maintains.

3   For civil libertarians, the real issue is not whether government and business collect databases on citizens, but whether there are adequate protections against abuses.

Those protections have come under particular assault in the   4
era of George W. Bush and the USA Patriot Act. But we will not
solve the privacy problem by pretending that we are back in a
pre-computer era. For that matter, Hitler did not need computers to abuse citizens.

There are several good reasons to support a national ID card.   5
The first has to do with voter registration and democracy.

Tens of millions of Americans don't vote because we make   6
voters go through a two-step process of registering and then
voting. As we saw in the elections of 2000 and 2004, the registration process is an invitation to endless political mischief.

In fact, registration was introduced in the late 19th century   7
precisely to hold down the numbers of votes, from former
slaves and from recent immigrants. It still functions to hold
down voting today.

In most countries, the national ID card certifies your identity,   8
age, and citizenship. That's it. You present the card, and you vote.

In America, millions of volunteer hours and hundreds of   9
millions of dollars go into the needless process of registering
voters—time and money that could go toward political ac-
tivism and education. So a national ID card, with proper safe-
guards, would make America more democratic, not less.

The second big reason involves immigration and labor   10
rights. We try to control our borders, but millions of foreigners
overstay tourist or student visas or slip in illegally, in order to
work. They are able to take jobs because business wants them
here to work for low wages and be conveniently frightened of
exercising their labor rights.

Our immigration laws require workers to have proof of law-   11
ful status, but employers are not punished if the papers turn
out to be forgeries, which are easy to obtain. It's much harder
to forge a passport-quality national ID card.

So let's decide just what level of immigration we want, make   12
it possible for those immigrants currently working in the country to regularize their status, and then use a national ID card to
make clear who is able to work—and to freely exercise rights
as workers without fear of being deported.

In an era where there is justifiable fear of terrorism, a na-   13
tional ID card would also help law enforcement. Identity theft
would also be much harder if there were a single, government
issued ID card.

14   A national ID card could help government pursue valuable record keeping, for instance to make sure that all children are immunized, and to pursue epidemiological research that is now difficult or impossible. A single government ID card would dramatically reduce underage drinking. Frail elderly people would cease having to renew drivers licenses solely for the purpose of ID. But libertarians are absolutely right to worry about potential and actual abuses. So the other side of the bargain is a much tougher set of laws protecting against improper invasions of privacy and snooping, both by government and by corporations.

15   There should be tougher penalties if an HMO sells confidential medical records. We need stronger measures against unwanted telemarketing, and against abuse of credit records.

16   The so-called USA Patriot Act has outrageous provisions, such as warrant-less snooping and "sneak and peak" searches in which the subject of the search is never informed that his or her privacy has been violated. These need to be repealed and replaced with far narrower search and seizure provisions that are not broad fishing licenses.

17   Right now, we liberty-loving Americans have the worst of both worlds. Far too many databases keep far too much information on us, with too few controls on its misuse. Yet we don't take advantage of the most basic uses of ID, such as making clear who is properly in the country and making it easier for citizens to vote.

Expanding Vocabulary

Examine the following words in their contexts in the essay and then write a brief definition or synonym for each one. (Do not use a dictionary; try to guess the word's meanings from its context.) The number in parentheses is the number of the paragraph in which the word appears.

advocates (2)	epidemiological (14)
dossiers (2)	forgeries (11)
immunized (14)	

Understanding Content

1. What are the concerns of civil libertarians? How should their concerns be understood? Why are their concerns not really related to national IDs?
2. What is Kuttner's first reason for supporting a national ID card?

3. What is the author's second reason for supporting a national ID card?
4. What are additional advantages of a national ID card?
5. What needs to happen to control potential abuses of privacy?

Drawing Inferences about Thesis and Purpose

1. When we read Kuttner's second sentence, what do we conclude to be the claim of his argument?
2. Is Kuttner proposing a national ID card in order to identify and deport illegal immigrants? How do you know?

Analyzing Strategies and Style

1. The author opens by telling readers that he is a member of the ACLU. What does he gain by this opening?
2. What transition words and phrases does Kuttner use to guide readers through his argument? List all of them.

Thinking Critically

1. Kuttner concludes by identifying with and appealing to "liberty-loving Americans." What can we infer about those who are most likely to oppose national ID cards? What group is Kuttner especially interested in influencing on this issue?
2. Evaluate the author's argument: Are his reasons convincing?
3. Compare Kuttner's argument to Murphy's: Who has, in your view, the stronger argument? Why?

STUDENT ESSAY—REFUTATION

BLAME IT ON THE MEDIA AND OTHER WAYS TO DRESS A WOLF IN SHEEP'S CLOTHING
David M. Ouellette

If an activity is legal, then people should be free to engage in that activity without fear of defamation. But smokers are being defamed, even persecuted, by a biased media bent on casting smoking as an unmitigated evil. This is Robert J. Samuelson's assertion in his September 24, 1997, <u>Newsweek</u> article "Do Smokers Have Rights." He says the media distort research on passive smoking's effects, demonize tobacco companies into teen-targeting drug pushers, and use these ill-founded claims as justification for punitive cigarette taxes. The result, Samuelson says, is that we "deny, ignore or minimize" the right of smokers to do something that is perfectly legal. He is mistaken on all counts.

When it comes to the effects of passive smoking, Samuelson does not want to accept what researchers have to say. He cites a ten-year study of non-smoking nurses that reported 25 to 30 percent of their heart attacks were caused by passive smoking. No matter how you look at the figure, it clearly states that passive smoking is dangerous. He says, "the practical significance of this is negligible." Ask any one of those people whose heart attacks were caused by someone else's smoking if what happened to them was "negligible." The practical impact is that if smoking were eliminated, heart attacks among nonsmokers would drop by 25 to 30 percent, according to this study.

Introduction includes author, title, publication place, and date of work to be refuted.

Attention-getter

Thesis

Student blends summary and direct quotation to present author's position.

The media, contrary to Samuelson, are not the ones who have painted tobacco companies as purveyors of addiction to teenagers. The tobacco industry has demonized itself. Samuelson himself admits that "the tobacco industry no doubt targets teens," but he excuses this by saying, "the ads may affect brand choices more than the decision to smoke." However, advertising for a brand of cigarettes is, necessarily, at the same time advertising for smoking. If a brand is made to look attractive, then that also means smoking itself is made to look attractive, for you cannot have one without the other.

Student analyzes the author's logic.

Finally, Samuelson argues that heavy cigarette taxes actually hurt smokers more than help them. In reality, the taxes are intended to deter people from smoking by raising the price. The people who would most likely be deterred are teenagers and the poor, both of whom smoke more than any other age group or economic class. "Sin taxes," such as cigarette taxes, attempt to limit or discourage legal behavior. A high price is not tantamount to unlegislated prohibition; it is society's way of dissuading people from destructive behavior. Samuelson asks whether we have a right to limit legal behaviors, or is this infringing on individuals' rights. There is a middle ground between prohibition and unlimited right. Alcohol consumption is just such an example, a behavior so dangerous that its use is controlled yet still legal. Clearly, society has a right to prohibit or control dangerous behavior. Not only is it society's right to control the danger to which its citizens are exposed, it is its responsibility.

Student uses a comparison with alcohol to challenge the author's argument.

Samuelson's claim that the media are besmirching smokers and tobacco companies with misleading reports is false. It is the media's responsibility to report news, such as the health threat of passive smoking, and how tobacco companies target teenagers. As for the right to smoke, smoking's dangers—both to smokers and nonsmokers alike—demand its control. Conceding fist-pounding demands for unlimited rights, regardless of who gets hurt or what other rights get infringed, would be an abdication of our responsibility to protect the health and welfare of the nation.

Student concludes by restating his thesis and defending it as the responsible one.

MAKING CONNECTIONS

---

1. Examine the arguments in this chapter for the various strategies that the authors use. Then decide: (a) What particular strategy works consistently well from one essay to

the next? And (b) What particular essay is the best argument, overall? Be prepared to defend your decisions.

2. Select one of the pairs of arguments and study the pair for any common ground that you can find. You may find something stated directly in the essays, or you may have to infer some common ground based on what the authors have written in general. Think about how you would explain to the two authors that they do share some common ground in spite of their differences.

3. Select one of the issues debated in this chapter, perhaps the one you know the least about, and get some facts relevant to the issue. For example: What are the statistics regarding gun deaths per year in the U.S.? In other countries? By state or region of the country? By type of crime—murder of someone known, suicide, armed robbery, gang killing, etc.? Be prepared to discuss how this information may influence the way your classmates should read the relevant essay(s) in the chapter.

TOPICS FOR WRITING

---

1. Did any one of the writers change your way of thinking on his or her issue? If so, write an essay in which you explain how that writer's argument convinced you to rethink your position and why the writer's argument should convince other readers. Do not assume that your audience knows the essay, so provide the author, title, and publication information in your essay.

2. Select a personal problem that concerns you, perhaps because you have a friend or family member with that problem. In an essay, present and defend your view on this issue. You can write to a general audience or directly to the person involved in a letter format and tone. Possible topics include staying in school, quitting smoking or using drugs or abusing alcohol, controlling starving or binge eating, maintaining relationships with parents, selecting a career, eliminating abusive language, or other bad habits.

3. Select any writer in this chapter whose position you disagree with and prepare a refutation of the writer's argument. Do

not assume that your reader has read the article you are re-
futing. As shown in the student essay, begin by giving author, title, publication information, and the author's
position. Then present and support your position. Your argument may be developed in part by showing weaknesses
in the opposing view.

4. Reflect on educational issues and problems to select a topic
   from this area that interests and concerns you. There are
   many possible topics, including censorship of books in
   high school libraries, control of high school and college
   newspapers, discrimination in sororities and fraternities,
   academic freedom, plagiarism, grading systems, admis-
   sions policies, and others. Definitions may play an important role in developing your argument. Be sure that you
   understand the arguments on both sides, acknowledge
   whatever common ground you share with opponents, and
   write in a restrained, conciliatory manner.

5. Many serious problems face our society—from drugs to
   taxes (and the deficit) to illegal aliens to homelessness to insider trading and other business and banking crimes to
   AIDS to ethical concerns such as abortion, euthanasia, and
   genetic engineering. Select a problem that concerns you and
   write an argumentative essay that presents and defends
   your proposed solutions to the problems. Part of your development will probably include challenging other proposed solutions with which you disagree. You may want to
   do some reading so that you have current facts about the
   problem. (If you use sources, including Internet sources, be
   sure to credit them properly.)

6. Serious problems also face our world, for example, deple-
   tion of the ozone layer, acid rain, deforestation, polluted
   water, global warming, and possibly overpopulation. Select a problem that concerns you and prepare an argumentative essay according to the guidelines discussed in topic
   5. Give thought to how you can narrow your topic to a
   manageable length. For example, instead of examining the
   problem of water pollution, write about the pollution of a
   lake or river or bay near where you live.

A CHECKLIST FOR ARGUMENT ESSAYS

Invention

☐ Have I selected a topic consistent with the instructor's guidelines for this assignment?

☐ Have I chosen among possible topics one that fits my knowledge and experience?

☐ Have I thought about reasons and evidence that can be used to support my topic?

☐ Have I reflected on my topic and support to write a tentative thesis, a clear claim for my argument?

☐ Have I "tested" my initial brainstorming of reasons and evidence against experience and logic?

☐ Have I thought about an effective organization, based on my support and the type of argument I am preparing—for example, presenting solutions to a problem, challenging someone else's argument?

Drafting

☐ Have I succeeded in completing a first draft at one sitting so that I can "see" the whole?

☐ Do I have enough—enough to meet assignment demands and enough to provide convincing support for my claim?

☐ Does the order work?

☐ Have I avoided logical fallacies?

Revision

☐ Have I made any needed additions, deletions, or changes in order based on answering questions about my draft?

☐ Have I revised my draft to produce coherent paragraphs, using transitions and connecting words that emphasize my logic and evidence?

☐ Have I eliminated wordiness and clichés?

☐ Have I avoided or removed any discriminatory language?

☐ Have I used my word processor's spell check and proofread a printed copy with great care?

☐ Do I have an appropriate and interesting title?

11

Works for Further Reading and Analysis

The works in this chapter demonstrate the use of a number of the strategies discussed and illustrated in previous chapters, including narration, description, definition, contrast, and argument. They also provide opportunities for exciting and challenging reading and critical thinking.

Declaration of Sentiments

ELIZABETH CADY STANTON

Elizabeth Cady Stanton (1815–1902) was one of the most important leaders of the women's rights movement. Educated at a local academy and then the Emma Willard Seminary in Troy, NY, Stanton studied law with her father before her marriage. An active reformer in the abolition and temperance movements, she later focused her attention on women's issues. At the Seneca Falls Convention in 1848, Stanton gave the opening speech and read her "Declaration of Sentiments." She founded and became president of the National Women's Suffrage Association in 1869. "The Declaration of Sentiments," patterned after the Declaration of Independence, lists the grievances of women suffering under the tyranny of men.

Keep the Declaration of Independence in mind as you read Stanton's version and use the following questions to guide your analysis.

    1. What do women demand? How will they achieve their goals?

2. How have women been restricted in education, in work, if married, and psychologically?
3. What charges made by Stanton continue to be legitimate complaints, in whole or in part?
4. Consider: Do we need a new declaration of sentiments for women? If so, what specific changes would you list? Do we need a new declaration of sentiments for other groups? If so, who? For what reasons?

When, in the course of human events, it becomes necessary 1
for one portion of the family of man to assume among the people of the earth a position different from that which they have hitherto occupied, but one to which the laws of nature and of nature's God entitle them, a decent respect to the opinions of mankind requires that they should declare the causes that impel them to such a course.

We hold these truths to be self-evident: that all men and 2
women are created equal; that they are endowed by their Creator with certain inalienable rights; that among these are life, liberty, and the pursuit of happiness; that to secure these rights governments are instituted, deriving their just powers from the consent of the governed. Whenever any form of government becomes destructive of these ends, it is the right of those who suffer from it to refuse allegiance to it, and to insist upon the institution of a new government, laying its foundation on such principles, and organizing its powers in such form, as to them shall seem most likely to effect their safety and happiness. Prudence, indeed, will dictate that governments long established should not be changed for light and transient causes; and accordingly all experience hath shown that mankind are more disposed to suffer, while evils are sufferable, than to right themselves by abolishing the forms to which they were accustomed. But when a long train of abuses and usurpations, pursuing invariably the same object evinces a design to reduce them under absolute despotism, it is their duty to throw off such government, and to provide new guards for their future security. Such has been the patient sufferance of the women under this government, and such is now the necessity which constrains them to demand the equal station to which they are entitled.

3   The history of mankind is a history of repeated injuries and usurpations on the part of man toward woman, having in direct object the establishment of an absolute tyranny over her. To prove this, let facts be submitted to a candid world.

4   He has never permitted her to exercise her inalienable right to the elective franchise.

5   He has compelled her to submit to laws, in the formation of which she had no voice.

6   He has withheld from her rights which are given to the most ignorant and degraded men—both natives and foreigners.

7   Having deprived her of this first right of a citizen, the elective franchise, thereby leaving her without representation in the halls of legislation, he has oppressed her on all sides.

8   He has made her, if married, in the eye of the law, civilly dead.

9   He has taken from her all right in property, even to the wages she earns.

10   He has made her, morally, an irresponsible being, as she can commit many crimes with impunity, provided they be done in the presence of her husband. In the covenant of marriage, she is compelled to promise obedience to her husband, he becoming, to all intents and purposes, her master—the law giving him power to deprive her of her liberty, and to administer chastisement.

11   He has so framed the laws of divorce, as to what shall be the proper causes, and in case of separation, to whom the guardianship of the children shall be given, as to be wholly regardless of the happiness of women—the law, in all cases, going upon a false supposition of the supremacy of man, and giving all power into his hands.

12   After depriving her of all rights as a married woman, if single, and the owner of property, he has taxed her to support a government which recognizes her only when her property can be made profitable to it.

13   He has monopolized nearly all the profitable employments, and from those she is permitted to follow, she receives but a scanty remuneration. He closes against her all the avenues to wealth and distinction which he considers most honorable to himself. As a teacher of theology, medicine, or law, she is not known.

He has denied her the facilities for obtaining a thorough ed- 14
ucation, all colleges being closed against her.

He allows her in Church, as well as State, but a subordinate 15
position, claiming Apostolic authority for her exclusion from
the ministry, and, with some exceptions, from any public par-
ticipation in the affairs of the Church.

He has created a false public sentiment by giving the world 16
a different code of morals for men and women, by which moral
delinquencies which exclude women from society, are not only
tolerated, but deemed of little account in man.

He has usurped the prerogative of Jehovah himself, claim- 17
ing it as his right to assign for her a sphere of action, when that
belongs to her conscience and to her God.

He has endeavored, in every way that he could, to destroy 18
her confidence in her own powers, to lessen her self-respect,
and to make her willing to lead a dependent and abject life. 19

Now, in view of this entire disfranchisement of one-half the
people of this country, their social and religious degradation—
in view of the unjust laws above mentioned, and because
women do feel themselves aggrieved, oppressed, and fraudu-
lently deprived of their most sacred rights, we insist that they
have immediate admission to all the rights and privileges
which belong to them as citizens of the United States.

In entering upon the great work before us, we anticipate no 20
small amount of misconception, misrepresentation, and
ridicule; but we shall use every instrumentality within our
power to effect our object. We shall employ agents, circulate
tracts, petition the State and National legislatures, and en-
deavor to enlist the pulpit and the press in our behalf. We hope
this Convention will be followed by a series of Conventions embracing every part of the country.

The Story of an Hour

KATE CHOPIN

Now a highly acclaimed fiction writer, Kate Chopin (1851–1904) enjoyed a decade of popularity from 1890 to 1900, and then experienced

critical condemnation followed by sixty years of neglect. Chopin began her career after her husband's death, having returned to her home in St. Louis with her six children. She saw two collections of her stories published—*Bayou Folk* in 1894 and *A Night in Acadie* in 1897—before losing her popularity with the publication of her short novel *The Awakening* in 1899, the story of a woman struggling to free herself from years of repression and subservience. "The Story of an Hour" depicts another character's struggle.

After reading, you will want to be able to summarize the story and analyze elements of the story to respond fully to it. Use these questions to aid your analysis:

1. What do the details of the scene outside Mrs. Mallard's window have in common? How do they help us understand what she experiences in her room?
2. How does Mrs. Mallard change as a result of her reflections in her room?
3. Are we to agree with the doctor's explanation for Mrs. Mallard's death? Explain the story's conclusion. What term describes the story's ending?

---

1   Knowing that Mrs. Mallard was afflicted with a heart trouble, great care was taken to break to her as gently as possible the news of her husband's death.

2   It was her sister Josephine who told her, in broken sentences; veiled hints that revealed in half concealing. Her husband's friend Richards was there, too, near her. It was he who had been in the newspaper office when intelligence of the railroad disaster was received, with Brently Mallard's name leading the list of "killed." He had only taken the time to assure himself of its truth by a second telegram, and had hastened to forestall any less careful, less tender friend in bearing the sad message.

3   She did not hear the story as many women have heard the same, with a paralyzed inability to accept its significance. She wept at once, with sudden, wild abandonment, in her sister's arms. When the storm of grief had spent itself she went away to her room alone. She would have no one follow her.

4   There stood, facing the open window, a comfortable, roomy armchair. Into this she sank, pressed down by a physical exhaustion that haunted her body and seemed to reach into her soul.

She could see in the open square before her house the tops of   5
trees that were all aquiver with the new spring life. The deli-
cious breath of rain was in the air. In the street below a peddler
was crying his wares. The notes of a distant song which someone was singing reached her faintly, and countless sparrows
were twittering in the eaves.

There were patches of blue sky showing here and there   6
through the clouds that had met and piled one above the other
in the west facing her window.

She sat with her head thrown back upon the cushion of the   7
chair, quite motionless, except when a sob came up into her
throat and shook her, as a child who has cried itself to sleep
continues to sob in its dreams.

She was young, with a fair, calm face, whose lines bespoke   8
repression and even a certain strength. But now there was a dull
stare in her eyes, whose gaze was fixed away off yonder on one
of those patches of blue sky. It was not a glance of reflection, but
rather indicated a suspension of intelligent thought.

There was something coming to her and she was waiting for   9
it, fearfully. What was it? She did not know; it was too subtle
and elusive to name. But she felt it, creeping out of the sky,
reaching toward her through the sounds, the scents, the color
that filled the air.

Now her bosom rose and fell tumultuously. She was begin-   10
ning to recognize this thing that was approaching to possess
her, and she was striving to beat it back with her will—as powerless as her two white slender hands would have been.

When she abandoned herself a little whispered word es-   11
caped her slightly parted lips. She said it over and over under
her breath: "free, free, free!" The vacant stare and the look of
terror that had followed it went from her eyes. They stayed
keen and bright. Her pulses beat fast, and the coursing blood
warmed and relaxed every inch of her body.

She did not stop to ask if it were or were not a monstrous joy   12
that held her. A clear and exalted perception enabled her to
dismiss the suggestion as trivial.

She knew that she would weep again when she saw the   13
kind, tender hands folded in death; the face that had never
looked save with love upon her, fixed and gray and dead. But
she saw beyond that bitter moment a long procession of years

to come that would belong to her absolutely. And she opened and spread her arms out to them in welcome.

14   There would be no one to live for her during those coming years; she would live for herself. There would be no powerful will bending hers in that blind persistence with which men and women believe they have a right to impose a private will upon a fellow-creature. A kind intention or a cruel intention made the act seem no less a crime as she looked upon it in that brief moment of illumination.

15   And yet she had loved him—sometimes. Often she had not. What did it matter! What could love, the unsolved mystery, count for in face of this possession of self-assertion which she suddenly recognized as the strongest impulse of her being!

16   "Free! Body and soul free!" she kept whispering.

17   Josephine was kneeling before the closed door with her lips to the keyhole, imploring for admission. "Louise, open the door! I beg; open the door—you will make yourself ill. What are you doing, Louise? For heaven's sake open the door."

18   "Go away. I am not making myself ill." No; she was drinking in a very elixir of life through that open window.

19   Her fancy was running riot along those days ahead of her. Spring days, and summer days, and all sorts of days that would be her own. She breathed a quick prayer that life might be long. It was only yesterday she had thought with a shudder that life might be long.

20   She arose at length and opened the door to her sister's importunities. There was a feverish triumph in her eyes, and she carried herself unwittingly like a goddess of Victory. She clasped her sister's waist, and together they descended the stairs. Richards stood waiting for them at the bottom.

21   Someone was opening the front door with a latchkey. It was Brently Mallard who entered, a little travel-stained, composedly carrying his grip-sack and umbrella. He had been far from the scene of the accident, and did not even know there had been one. He stood amazed at Josephine's piercing cry; at Richards' quick motion to screen him from the view of his wife.

But Richards was too late. 22

When the doctors came they said she had died of heart dis- 23
ease—of joy that kills.

TAXI

AMY LOWELL

Educated at private schools and widely traveled, Amy Lowell
(1874–1925) was a poet and critic. Her most important critical
work is a study of the British poet John Keats. Lowell frequently
read her poetry and lectured on poetic techniques, defending
her free verse and the work of other modern poets.

As you study "Taxi," use the following questions as guides.

1. Explain the metaphor in lines 2–3. What emotional state
   does it communicate?
2. What do the words "jutted," "ridges," "wedge," "prick,"
   and "sharp" have in common?
3. Explain the metaphor in lines 11–12.
4. What tone is created by the poem's metaphors?
5. What is the speaker's attitude toward leaving?

When I go away from you
The world beats dead
Like a slackened drum.
I call out for you against the jutted stars
And shout into the ridges of the wind. 5
Streets coming fast,
One after the other,
Wedge you away from me,
And the lamps of the city prick my eyes
So that I can no longer see your face. 10
Why should I leave you,
To wound myself upon the sharp edges of the night?

Border Hazards: An Obsession to Become Unhealthy

RICHARD RODRIGUEZ

Richard Rodriguez holds degrees in literature from Stanford and Columbia Universities and has studied at Berkeley and the Warburg Institute in London. He is an editor of Pacific News Service and an author of both articles and books, including *Days of Obligation: An Argument with My Mexican Father* (1992). He has won awards for his writing, and excerpts from his autobiography *Hunger of Memory* (1982) are frequently anthologized. In the following article, published September 20, 1998, Rodriguez examines the effects of migration to the United States and the changes in lifestyles occurring around the world.

Use these questions to guide your reading.

1. What, for Rodriguez, is ironic about the study findings by William Vega?
2. What ideas does America "sell," especially to young people?
3. In paragraph 18, the author lists specifics that American life offers. What is startling about this list? How does it help to develop Rodriguez's thesis?
4. Is America hazardous to our health?

1   Maybe we need to put a sign at the border and in our international airports. WARNING: AMERICA MAY BE DANGEROUS TO YOUR HEALTH.

2   It has never been easy to be an immigrant. Imagine what those 19th-century immigrants knew, leaving certainty behind, abandoning Ireland and Italy and Russia, to travel to America. (In those days, an ocean's separation from loved ones was permanent as death.) What bravery, what recklessness the journey to Ellis Island required. What a price there was to pay for leaving certain poverty.

3   A study, headed by Professor William Vega of UC Berkeley and published last week, has found that Mexican immigrants suffer increased mental stress the longer they stay in this country. Rates of mental illness and other social disorders, like drug use

and divorce, rise after immigration. Vega's team of researchers observed the breakdown of immigrant families within a generation, on a scale comparable to other Americans.

These findings are, at least, ironic. For generations, Ameri   4
cans have assumed moral superiority toward Latin America. Early this century, for example, citizens of San Diego traveled south, into Tijuana, whenever they wanted to sin. Just as today, Americans like to imagine that Mexican drug lords are contaminating our "innocent" youth.

The tables have turned. Four years ago, the Center for Sci   5
ence in the Public Interest in Washington warned Americans away from Mexican food. Eating a chile relleño is the equivalent of devouring a cube of butter! Now, U.S. professors warn immigrants away from burgers and fries.

A week before Vega's report, a panel of the National Re   6
search Council and the Institute of Medicine found that the longer an immigrant child lives in this country, the greater the chance of physical and psychological deterioration. The panel's chairman, Dr. Evan Charney of the University of Massachusetts Medical School, warned, "The longer you're in this country, the more you want to eat at McDonald's."

Immigrants. I see them all the time in California, their eyes   7
filled with terror and wonder. Their jogging shoes have transported them from villages in Mexico or Central America into the postmodern city of freeways and peroxide and neon. How will they find their way?

Vega and his team of researchers studied the problems of   8
Mexican immigrants in Fresno County. But the researchers would, I suspect, have come up with similar findings of social breakdown had they talked with young Mexicans in Tijuana. The poor are in movement, all over the world, from village to city, from tradition toward change.

Recently, in the boomtown of Monterrey, Mexico, I met   9
teenagers, poor alongside rich, who were busy consuming drugs. Cocaine was evidence of their modernity, a habit that made them just like the Americans on TV and the movies. Monterrey has not yet turned as violent as Mexico City. But the women in the new factories, on the outskirts of town, know divorce.

All over the world, from Andean villages to Southeast Asia,   10
America advertises the "I." You can drink America from a Coke bottle; you can dance America. America is seducing the

young all over the world with the idea of individual freedom. Change. Movement. Dollars.

11   On the line between Tijuana and San Diego tonight, you can meet kids waiting for dark to run into the United States. They say they do not want to become Americans. They do not speak of Thomas Jefferson or the Bill of Rights. There is, they say, a job waiting for them in Glendale or Fresno. A job in a pizza parlor or a job as a roofer that will keep them and their families from going hungry.

12   The U.S. professors fret. The panelists for the National Research Council advise against attempts "to push immigrant youth toward assimilation." But they might as well bemoan the jet engine or the bicycle.

13   Movement. America is not an easy country for either the native-born or the immigrant. Everything keeps changing. In small towns in Arkansas today, Mexican immigrants arrive to pluck dead chickens because no one else will do it. They paint their houses gaudy colors, speak Spanish at the post office. Native-born Americans bemoan the change. They become foreigners in their own town.

14   The kid from Oaxaca ends up making pizzas in Santa Monica. He learns English by hearing "Hold the pepperoni!" Day after day, he breathes America. America flows into his ears— California slang, the thump of rap. There is no resisting it.

15   Assimilation is more a biological process than a matter of choice. Immigrant kids end up breathing America, swallowing America. When you approach the counter at McDonald's, you buy more than a burger: You buy an American spirit of impatience. Immigrants end up walking like the native-born, assuming the same nervous slouch.

16   Drugs. Divorce. Anonymity. The religions of the world that are growing today are those religions that address the sadness of the migrating poor and their longing for the abandoned, lost village. Islam spreads through U.S. prisons. Evangelical Protestantism teaches children in Lima or in Los Angeles to be reborn and cleansed of the terrible city.

17   Immigrant parents turn pro-choice. They chose to leave Mexico, so they imagine their U.S.-born kids can choose to absent themselves from Los Angeles, "remain" Mexican despite the heaving and throbbing city around them. Papa is always grumbling that the kids are becoming disrespectful U.S.

teenagers. Mama is always saying that everyone was happier—poorer, yes, but happier—in the Mexican village.

America is a most remarkable country, the model of modernity 18 for people all over the world. It offers the world the possibility of individual life: the freeway onramp, the separate bedroom, the terrible loneliness, the range of choices on a TV remote.

The Mexican kid from Oaxaca will not go back. His dollars, 19 and maybe something more he cannot describe, will keep him making pizzas in Santa Monica. Yes, he will regret the disrespect of his U.S.-born children. Perhaps he will even send them back to Mexico during—that most American of seasons—adolescence.

But the village of Mexico is not, in truth, what it used to be. 20 It has changed. There are blond soap operas blaring from the television in the old family kitchen. Everyone in the village talks of jobs in Dallas and Guadalajara.

The guilt. The terrible guilt of becoming an American re- 21 mains. Every child of immigrant parents knows it. It is as old as America. The scorn of a grandmother: her black dress and her face at the window. Her mutterings in Yiddish or Chinese or Swedish. Her complaint: You are turning into a gringo, goy, a stranger to her.

Dear Nana. Forgive us! Forgive us our love of America, 22 this very strange country, the envy of the world. Look! Look at the fresh fruits at Ralphs. The meats and the cheeses, dear abuelita. Forgive us for transporting the 18th-century pronoun, the "I," all the way to Fresno. It has driven us mad. But it has gotten us a washer and dryer.

It has made your grandchildren so tall and so straight, like 23 movie stars. Look! Who would have guessed, dear Nana, you would have grandchildren so beautiful!

Neat People vs. Sloppy People

SUZANNE BRITT

Suzanne Britt graduated from Salem Academy, has a master's degree in English, and currently teaches at Meredith College in North Carolina. She is the author of several books and many poems and articles. In the following essay, from the collection of

her essays titled *Show and Tell,* Britt dishes up some kind and
some cruel comments about each type of person.

*As you read, think about her purpose in writing and use these
questions to aid your analysis.*

   1. What are the differences between neat and sloppy people?
   2. What is Britt's tone? Does she intend this to be funny? Does
      she also intend it to be serious in any way?
   3. How would you argue for the superiority of neat people
      over sloppy people?

1   I've finally figured out the difference between neat people
and sloppy people. The distinction is, as always, moral. Neat
people are lazier and meaner than sloppy people.

2   Sloppy people, you see, are not really sloppy. Their sloppi-
ness is merely the unfortunate consequence of their extreme
moral rectitude. Sloppy people carry in their mind's eye a
heavenly vision, a precise plan, that is so stupendous, so perfect, it can't be achieved in this world or the next.

3   Sloppy people live in Never-Never Land. Someday is their
métier. Someday they are planning to alphabetize all their
books and set up home catalogs. Someday they will go
through their wardrobes and mark certain items for tentative
mending and certain items for passing on to relatives of similar shape and size. Someday sloppy people will make family
scrapbooks into which they will put newspaper clippings,
postcards, locks of hair, and the dried corsage from their senior prom. Someday they will file everything on the surface of
their desks, including the cash receipts from coffee purchases
at the snack shop. Someday they will sit down and read all the
back issues of *The New Yorker.*

4   For all these noble reasons and more, sloppy people never
get neat. They aim too high and wide. They save everything,
planning someday to file, order, and straighten out the world.
But while these ambitious plans take clearer and clearer shape
in their heads, the books spill from the shelves onto the floor,
the clothes pile up in the hamper and closet, the family me-
mentos accumulate in every drawer, the surface of the desk is
buried under mounds of paper and the unread magazines
threaten to reach the ceiling.

Sloppy people can't bear to part with anything. They give 5
loving attention to every detail. When sloppy people say
they're going to tackle the surface of the desk, they really mean
it. Not a paper will go unturned; not a rubber band will go un-
boxed. Four hours or two weeks into the excavation, the desk
looks exactly the same, primarily because the sloppy person is
meticulously creating new piles of papers with new headings
and scrupulously stopping to read all the old book catalogs before he throws them away. A neat person would just bulldoze
the desk.

Neat people are bums and clods at heart. They have cavalier 6
attitudes toward possessions, including family heirlooms.
Everything is just another dustcatcher to them. If anything col-
lects dust, it's got to go and that's that. Neat people will toy
with the idea of throwing the children out of the house just to
cut down on the clutter.

Neat people don't care about process. They like results. 7
What they want to do is get the whole thing over with so they
can sit down and watch the rasslin' on TV. Neat people oper-
ate on two unvarying principles: Never handle any item twice,
and throw everything away.

The only thing messy in a neat person's house is the trash 8
can. The minute something comes to a neat person's hand, he
will look at it, try to decide if it has immediate use and, finding none, throw it in the trash.

Neat people are especially vicious with mail. They never go 9
through their mail unless they are standing directly over a
trash can. If the trash can is beside the mailbox, even better. All
ads, catalogs, pleas for charitable contributions, church bulletins and money-saving coupons go straight into the trash can
without being opened. All letters from home, postcards from
Europe, bills and paychecks are opened, immediately responded to, then dropped in the trash can. Neat people keep
their receipts only for tax purposes. That's it. No sentimental
salvaging of birthday cards or the last letter a dying relative
ever wrote. Into the trash it goes.

Neat people place neatness above everything, even economics. 10
They are incredibly wasteful. Neat people throw away several
toys every time they walk through the den. I knew a neat person
once who threw away a perfectly good dish drainer because it

had mold on it. The drainer was too much trouble to wash. And neat people sell their furniture when they move. They will sell a La-Z-Boy recliner while you are reclining in it.

11   Neat people are no good to borrow from. Neat people buy everything in expensive little single portions. They get their flour and sugar in two-pound bags. They wouldn't consider clipping a coupon, saving a leftover, reusing plastic nondairy whipped cream containers or rinsing off tin foil and draping it over the unmoldy dish drainer. You can never borrow a neat person's newspaper to see what's playing at the movies. Neat people have the paper all wadded up and in the trash by 7:05 A.M.

12   Neat people cut a clean swath through the organic as well as the inorganic world. People, animals, and things are all one to them. They are so insensitive. After they've finished with the pantry, the medicine cabinet, and the attic, they will throw out the red geranium (too many leaves), sell the dog (too many fleas), and send the children off to boarding school (too many scuffmarks on the hardwood floors).

A Date to Remember

LISA MUNDY

Lisa Mundy holds a master's degree in English literature from the University of Virginia and is a staff writer and columnist for the *Washington Post*, with a regular column in the paper's Sunday magazine. The following Sunday "Postmodern" column, appearing July 14, 2002, offers a thoughtful analysis of our times.

Use these questions to guide your reading of Mundy's essay.

1. How have we traditionally referred to important moments in our history?
2. What is different about our use of "9/11"?
3. How does the author explain the difference? How does 9/11 fit our times?
4. Is it troubling, in any way, to consider that a digital "shorthand" represents our era?

There's a Web site now that shows you how to fold the new   1
$20 bill to create a strange little origami construction that de-
picts, on one side, a scene that looks uncannily like the World
Trade Center on fire and, on the other, one that resembles the
Pentagon with flames coming out of the center. The site,
www.allbrevard.net, makes much of what it calls the "amazing
$20 bill 9/11 coincidence," and goes on to explore any number
of insane conspiracy theories, such as whether the U.S. government planned the attacks, whether it means anything that
you can also fold the $50 bill to depict a *plume of smoke,* etc. Pre-
dictably, responders to the site alternately glom onto these
nutty ideas or excoriate the site for using them to sell its own
Web-hosting service. Me, I was struck by something else: the
way "9/11" has entered our consciousness to the point where
even on a site clearly meant to appeal to the stupidest among
us, it needs no explanation. The numbers are there. Nine.
Eleven. We know instantly what they signify.

Up to now, there was no event in American history that we   2
designated digitally, if you will, by lining numerals up in a
row. Many people continue to say "September 11," it's true,
and somehow using the word, like that, seems more formal,

possibly more sad. But many others use the short form, without intending any disrespect. There are any number of Web sites and relief funds for the "victims of 9/11"; and just the other day Sen. Charles Schumer of New York used the short version in a Senate hearing, pointing out that "before 9/11, the FBI's computers were less sophisticated than the one I bought for my son for $1,400."

3   Up to now, the signal events of our history were known, more often than not, by place names. Pearl Harbor is the analogy everybody thought of when the attacks happened; the worst disaster the nation had known will be forever associated with a lyrically named spot in Hawaii, the very name of which conjures up images of horrified Americans hearing the news by radio, sailors tapping vainly on their ship's hull for days, it is said, before they died. It's synecdoche, the part standing for the whole, and it's how we have always remembered our major military events. Bunker Hill, Valley Forge, Gettysburg, Little Big Horn: Great and terrible moments have traditionally been evoked by the places where they happened, here and, often, around the world. Historically, battles are known by names like Hastings, Gallipoli, the Somme; treaties by names like Yalta; trials by names like Nuremberg; assassinations by names like Dallas, a word that connotes not only the shooting of a president but the end of a national innocence. Why did we not adopt, similarly, a place name for the national innocence that ended last fall? Was it because it happened in planes, in the air, everywhere and nowhere?

4   I think that's part of it. This was an assault with a strangely un-regional quality; despite the intensity with which the attacks were felt in New York and Washington, they were also experienced by those watching, live, on television. All of America was the target. The attack happened on a single day, a singular day, a day that shocked us not only with the attacks themselves but with the sudden recognition that the forces that caused them had been gathering, unknown to most of us, for a long time. In the same way, those relatively few historical events that are remembered by their dates—July 4th, Cinco de Mayo, Juneteenth—are days when something that had been coming for a long time happened; the social order had been changing, but now the change burst into the open. Nine-eleven is the

dark opposite of those celebratory occasions. It's the dark opposite of D-Day, too, another event we remember as just that, a day, its name evocative of the operational codes of World War II and the military determination of an era.

In the same way, the phrase "9/11" evokes something about 5 our own era. We would never refer to Independence Day as 7/4; that would seem anachronistic. But 9/11 fits. We are all digital thinkers now, accustomed to looking at our calendars, our watches, and seeing numerals. Granted, there is some especially odd thing about these numerals; it *is* weird that 911 is what people punched on their cell phones, often in vain, to seek help that day. There's significance in numbers, menace in numbers. It's a ridiculous stretch when one *allbrevard.net* link points out that $9 + 11 = 20$ ($20, get it?), but serious counterterrorism people have actually studied these numbers to see if there really is a pattern, a portent. Numbers involve ancient superstitions and modern habits. So do terrorists. Nine-eleven was a disaster born of an old evil, an old hatred, but one that could have happened only in the communication age, when terrorists can hook up using satellite phones and e-mail accounts and synchronized Casio watches. Funny how 9/11 exactly expresses all that: the menace, the placelessness, the precision of time. Like the event itself, our use of numbers to describe what happened signifies that something about us, and the way we think, has changed, possibly forever.

Glossary

Alliteration Repetition of initial consonant sound in two or more words. For example, the *first frost.*

Allusion Reference to lines or characters from literature or mythology or to figures or events from history. For example, if someone describes you as "an old *Scrooge,*" then, like the character in Charles Dickens's *A Christmas Carol,* you are not generous with money.

Analogy An extended comparison of two things that are essentially not alike with several points of similarity (or difference) established to support an idea or thesis.

Analysis The division of a work or a topic into its component parts. To analyze a writer's style is to examine the various elements that compose style, such as word choice, sentence structure, use of figurative language. (See also **Causal analysis.**)

Argumentation A form of thinking and writing in which reasons and evidence are presented to support a position on an issue. (See Chapter 10.)

Audience The readers of a piece of writing. Hence, as a writing concept, the expected or anticipated readers to whom a piece of writing is directed. A sense of audience should guide a writer's choice about approach, content, and tone for a piece of writing.

Brainstorm Prewriting strategy for generating material on a subject by jotting down all ideas and examples or details that come to mind.

Causal analysis The examination of a situation by division into and study of its several causes, or its pattern of conditions, influences, and remote and immediate causes. (See Chapter 9.)

Character Any person in narrative and dramatic works; also, the personality traits that together shape a person's "character."

Characterization The description of a person, either a real person or one from fiction or drama. A detailed characterization includes physical appearance, speech and behavior patterns, personality traits, and values.

Chronology   The arrangement of events in time sequence. A narrative or historical account organizes events in chronological order. A process analysis explains steps in their appropriate chronology.

Classification   A pattern of thinking and writing in which a subject is divided into logical categories, and then elements of the subject are grouped within those categories. (See Chapter 7.)

Cliché   Overused, worn-out expressions, often metaphors, that were once fresh and clever but should now be avoided in writing, except as examples or to reveal character. I'm *fit as a fiddle, hungry as a bear,* and *head over heels in love* are examples of clichés.

Coherence   A quality of good writing marked by a logical ordering of statements and by the use of words and phrases that guide readers through the material and show them how the writing hangs together. Some techniques for obtaining coherence include repetition of key words, use of pronouns, and use of transition words and phrases.

Colloquial language   Language used in conversation but usually avoided in writing, especially in academic and business writing, unless used purposely to create a particular effect.

Comparison   A pattern of writing in which similarities between two subjects (two schools, two jobs, two novels) are examined. (See Chapter 4.)

Complex sentence   Sentence containing at least one dependent or subordinate clause and one independent clause. For example, "When you come to a term about writing that you do not know, [dependent clause] you should look it up in the Glossary [independent clause]."

Compound sentence   Sentence containing at least two independent clauses. For example, "A comparison develops similarities between two like things [first independent clause], but [coordinating conjunction] a metaphor expresses a similarity between two unlike things [second independent clause].

Conclusion   The ending of a piece of writing; it gives the reader a sense of finish and completeness. Many strategies for concluding are available to writers, including restating and emphasizing the significance of the thesis, summarizing main points, and suggesting a course of action. Writing needs to conclude, not just stop.

Connotation   The suggestions and emotional overtones conveyed by a word. Selecting the word with the appropriate connotative significance allows writers to develop subtle shades of meaning and to convey their attitudes.

Context clues   The words or sentences surrounding a word that help readers to understand the meaning of that word.

Contrast   A pattern of writing in which differences between two subjects (e.g., two schools, two jobs, two novels) are examined. (See Chapter 4.)

Definition   Explanation of a word's meaning. It can be provided in a sentence or expanded into an essay. (See Chapter 8.)

Denotation   The meanings of a word, often referred to as a word's dictionary definitions. For example, a *house* is a building used primarily for private living. A *home*, however, also connotes family, love, and security.

Description   Details appealing to the five senses that help readers to "see" the writer's subject. (See Chapter 3.)

Details   Specific pieces of information that range from descriptions of people and places to statistical data and that are used by writers to illustrate and support ideas and general points.

Dialect   Variations in grammar, sentence patterns, and word choice that mark the particular use of a language by one group.

Dialogue   Exact words spoken by people introduced in essays or by characters in literature. The words are always set off by quotation marks, and a new paragraph is started to show a change of speaker.

Diction   A writer's choice of words. Levels of diction refer to the degree of formality or informality in word choice.

Division   A pattern of thinking and writing in which large and/or complicated subjects are separated into parts for clear and logical discussion. (See Chapter 7.)

Effects   The consequences or outcomes of events. Effects are often a part of causal analysis when writers examine both what has produced a given situation and what that situation will lead to. Writers also analyze only effects, explaining both immediate and long-term consequences. (See Chapter 9.)

E.g.   Abbreviation of the Latin words *exempli gratia,* meaning "for example."

Essay   A short prose work presenting the writer's views on a particular topic.

Evidence   Facts and examples used to support the thesis or proposition in an argument.

Example   A specific illustration used to develop a thesis or general idea. (See Chapter 5.)

Fable   A narrative written (or told) to teach a moral or lesson.

Fact   A statement that is verifiable by observation, measurement, experiment, or use of reliable reference sources such as encyclopedias, atlases, and almanacs.

Fiction   An imagined narrative; a story. "The Story of an Hour" by Kate Chopin is fiction. Essays are nonfiction.

Figurative language   Language containing figures of speech that extend meaning beyond the literal. A metaphor, for example, is a figure of speech.

Illustration   The use of examples to develop and support a thesis. (See Chapter 5.)

Image   The recreation in words of a sense experience. Vivid images enrich descriptive writing.

Imagery   All the images in a work. Also, a cluster of similar images creating a dominant impression in a work.

Introductions   The openings of essays; one or several paragraphs that seek to get the reader's attention and interest and to establish the writer's subject. Many strategies for good introductions are available, including using a startling statistic, stating the thesis, providing an interesting, relevant quotation, asking a question, and giving a brief anecdote or example. Introductions to avoid include sweeping generalizations that range beyond the paper's scope and purpose and statements such as "In this essay, I plan to discuss . . ."

Irony   In general, the expression of incongruity or discrepancy. *Verbal irony* expresses a discrepancy between what is said and what is meant. *Dramatic irony* expresses a discrepancy between what a character says or does and what readers understand to be true. *Irony of situation* develops a discrepancy between what we expect to happen and what actually happens.

Jargon   Specialized terms of a particular profession or subject area. Jargon often has a negative connotation, a reminder to writers that jargon should be avoided in essays written for general audiences who will be unfamiliar with the terms. Always define specialized terms that must be used.

Metaphor   A figure of speech in which a comparison is either stated or implied between two unalike things. (E.g., "this *bud* of *love*" or "*Life's* but a *walking shadow*.")

Narration   The account, usually in chronological order, of a historical event or a story (fiction). Also, a strategy for developing the main point of an essay. (See Chapter 2.)

Occasion   The situation or circumstances in which a writer produces a particular work. Writers are often motivated to write in response to an event or to their reading.

Order   The pattern in which the parts of an essay are arranged. This text explains many of the patterns available to writers.

Paradox   A statement that seems contradictory but can be understood to be true, usually by taking one part of the statement figuratively rather than literally. For example, "The more money I make, the less I have."

Part by part A structure for comparison or contrast that arranges by points of difference rather than by the subjects being compared.

Point of view The perspective or angle of vision from which a story is told. Sometimes the term is used to refer to the grammatical "person" used in essay writing, that is, the first person ("I," "we"), the second person ("you"), which is rarely used except when giving directions, or the third person ("he," "she," "they"). The fiction writer's choices are: *first person* (a character tells the story using "I"), *omniscient* (the all-knowing narrator), *limited omniscient* (through the eyes of one character but in the third person), or *objective* (reporting only what can be seen and heard, not what characters are thinking).

Process analysis A pattern of writing that takes the reader through the steps or stages necessary to complete a task, perform an activity, or accomplish a goal.

Purpose One's reason for writing. General purposes include to inform, to explain, and to persuade.

Refutation A form of argument in which the primary purpose is to counter, or show weaknesses in, another's argument. (See Chapter 10.)

Reporter's questions Traditionally the questions *who, what, where, when,* and *why* are considered those a journalist should answer about each story covered. Essay writers can also use these questions in planning a topic's development.

Rhetorical question A question raised by a writer when the writer believes that readers will see only one possible answer—the answer the writer would give.

Sarcasm Bitter or cutting expression, often ironic.

Satire Work that ridicules the vices and follies of humanity, often with the purpose of bringing about change.

Setting The physical locale of the work. Can be presented to create atmosphere as well.

Simile A comparison between two essentially unalike things that is stated explicitly by using connectors such as *like, as,* or *seems.* For example, "I wandered lonely *as* a cloud," written by William Wordsworth.

Simple sentence A sentence containing only one independent clause. For example, "A simple sentence contains only one independent clause."

Style A writer's selection and arrangement of language.

Summary A brief, objective restatement of the main ideas in a work.

Symbol An object, character, or action that suggests meanings, associations, and emotions beyond what is characteristic of its nature or function. A rose is a flower, but a rose symbolically represents love and beauty.

Theme The central idea (or ideas) that a work embodies.

Thesis The main idea of an essay. It is often but not always expressed in a *thesis sentence*.

Tone The expression of a writer's attitude (e.g., playful, bitter).

Transitions Words and phrases that show readers how ideas in a work are related or connected. For example, *in addition, for example, however.*

Unity A characteristic of good writing in which everything included relates to the work's main idea and contributes to its development.

Whole by whole A structure for comparison or contrast that organizes by the two subjects being compared rather than by their specific points of similarity or difference.

Credits

from *The Los Angeles Times*, September 20, 1998. Copyright 1998, *Los Angeles Times*. Reprinted by permission.

Suzanne Britt, "Neat People vs. Sloppy People," from *Show and Tell*. Reprinted by permission of the author.

Lisa Mundy, "A Date to Remember," from *The Washington Post*, July 14, 2002. Copyright © 2002 *The Washington Post*. Reprinted with permission.

Photo Credits

Page 74: © Mark Hemmings 2005.

Color Insert (following page 80):

Francisco de Goya y Lucientes, *Third of May, 1808*. Museo del Prado, Madrid, Spain. Copyright Scala/Art Resource, NY.

Edgar Degas, *The Dance Class*. Musée d'Orsay, Paris, France. Copyright Erich Lessing/Art Research, NY.

Vincent Van Gogh, *The Night Café*. Yale University Art Gallery, New Haven, Connecticut (bequest of Stephen Carlton Clark, B.A., 1903).

Pablo Picasso, *The Three Dancers*. Tate Gallery, London/Art Resource, NY. Copyright 2007 Estate of Pablo Picasso/Artists Rights Society (ARS), NY.

Salvador Dali, *The Persistence of Memory*. Digital Image copyright The Museum of Modern Art/Licensed by SCALA/Art Resource, NY. Copyright 2007 Salvador Dali, Gala-Salvador Dali Foundation/Artists Rights Society (ARS), NY.

Georgia O'Keeffe, *Jack-in-the-Pulpit No. IV*. National Gallery of Art, Washington. Alfred Stieglitz Collection, Bequest of Georgia O'Keeffe. Photo by Richard Carafelli.

Page 90: © 1991 Amy Tan.

Page 100: © Camazine/Photo Researchers.

Page 173: Fila advertisement reprinted by permission.

Page 174: "Got Milk?" advertisement reprinted by permission of Bozell Worldwide, Inc., as agent or the National Fluid Milk Processor Promotion Board.

Page 175: Biotechnology advertisement reprinted courtesy of the Council for Biotechnology Information.

Page 176: Expedia.com advertisement reprinted with permission. © Roy Zipstein.

Page 479: © Brian Noyes.

▆▆Index

Ablow, Keith, 380–85
"Abolish Marriage," 444–47
Ackerman, Diane, 98–101
"Adult Crime, Adult Time," 430–36
"Africa," 102–08
Aigner, John P., 228–33
"Always Running," 56–60
Analysis 11–15, 224–26, 369–72
Andrews, Ned, 427–30
Argument, 416–22
Auerbach, Judith D., 397–400

"Bad Raps: Music Rebels Revel in
    Their Thug Life," 207–11
Baker, Russell, 272–75
"Ban the Things. Ban Them All,"
    423–26
Barry, Dave, 211–14
Berger, Garrett, 310–17
"Blame It on the Media and Other
    Ways to Dress a Wolf in
    Sheep's Clothing," 457–60
Bonilla, Denisse, 159–64
"Border Hazards: An Obsession to
    Become Unhealthy," 472–75
Borneman, John, 439–43
"Boys and Girls: Anatomy and
    Destiny," 139–46
Britt, Suzanne, 475–78
"Buying Time," 310–17
"By Any Other Name," 46–53
Bzdek, Vincent P., 199–206

"Call Hating," 211–14
"Camping Out," 259–64

"Captivated," 72–76
"Case for Compromise on Abortion,
    The," 448–51
Chopin, Kate, 467–71
Ciardi, John, 332–37
"Class Acts: America's Changing
    Middle Class," 303–10
Classification, 268–71
Cliches, 324–25
Cohen, Richard, 436–39
Coherence, 124–25
Collier, Linda J., 430–36
Communicating, with instructors
    and peers, 38–39
Comparison, 121–24
Contrast, 121–24
"Conversational Ballgames,"
    126–31
Coontz, Stephanie, 400–06
Council for Biotechnology
    Information, ad, 175
"Curiosity," 358–60

Dali, Salvador, art insert
Dance Class, The, art insert
"Date to Remember, A," 478–81
"Death of an Officer," 60–68
"Declaration of Sentiments," 464–67
Definition, 322–24
Degas, Edgar, art insert
Description, 80–83
"Difference Between 'Sick' and
    'Evil,' The," 347–52
"Discrimination Is a Virtue," 337–41
Division and Classification, 268–71

"Doubts about Doublespeak,"
341–46
"Dream Deferred," 411–12
"Duty: The Forgotten Virtue,"
374–80

"Education," 131–35
"Elastic Institution, An," 439–43
Elgin, Suzette H., 234–44
"End of My Childhood, The," 53–56
Ehrlich, Gretel, 33–38
Ericsson, Stephanie, 293–303
Etzioni, Amitai, 374–80
Examples, 168–70
Expedia.com ad, 176
"Faded Stain, The," 159–64

Fallacies, 420–22
Fields, Suzanne, 207–11
Fila ad, 173
Fischer, David Hackett, 353–58
"Freedom's Not Just Another
Word," 353–58

Godwin, Gail, 18–22
Goodman, Ellen, 9–11
Got Milk? ad, 174
Goya, Francisco de, art insert
"Ground Zero," 109–13

Hart, Laurie Kain, 439–43
Hemingway, Ernest, 259–64
"Hot Boxes for Ex–Smokers,"
282–86
"How Mr. Dewey Decimal Saved
My Life," 68–72
"How to Get Unstuck Now!"
250–54
"How to Turn No into Yes!" 244–49
"How to Write with Style," 28–33
Hughes, Langston, 411–12
Hwang, Caroline, 244–49

"Improving Your Body Language
Skills," 234–44
"Is Everybody Happy?" 332–37

Ivins, Molly, 423–26

Jack–in–the–Pulpit, art insert

Kidder, Tracy, 84–89
"Kids Who Kill Are Still Kids,"
436–39
King, Colbert I., 154–57
King, Michael, 214–19
Kinsley, Michael, 444–47
Kingsolver, Barbara, 68–72
Krucoff, Carol, 255–58
Kuttner, Robert, 454–57

"Learning to Brake for Butterflies,"
9–11
"Let It Snow," 98–101
"Lost Lives of Women," 89–93
Lowell, Amy, 471
Lutz, William, 341–46

"Marks," 157–59
Martin, Judith, 275–82
McGarvey, Jack, 177–85
McMillan, Terry, 22–28
Mead, Margaret, 326–32
Mencimer, Stephanie, 191–99
Metaphor, 324–25
Metraux, Rhoda, 326–32
Miller, Robert Keith, 337–41
Momaday, N. Scott, 53–56
Mora, Pat, 93–98
"More Powerful Than . . . Ever:
On–Screen and Off,
Superheroes Are a Force to
Reckon With," 199–206
Morrow, Lance, 102–08
"Mrs. Zajac," 84–88
Mullins, Laura, 361–65
Mundy, Lisa, 478–81
Murphy, Laura W., 451–54
Narration, 42–44

"Neat People vs. Sloppy People,"
475–78
Night Café, art insert

"No Safer and Less Free," 451–54
"Not Much Sense in Those Census
    Stories," 401–06

"On Friendship," 326–32
"On Reading and Becoming a
    Writer," 22–28
Ouellette, David M., 457–60
"Overlooked Victims of AIDS,
    The," 397–400

"Paragon or Parasite?" 361–65
Pastan, Linda, 157–59
Persistence of Memory, The, art insert
Picasso, Pablo, art insert
"Plot Against People, The," 272–75
"Putting Your Job Interview into
    Rehearsal," 228–33

"Rap's Refusal of Injustice," 214–19
Rau, Santha Rama, 46–53
Reading
    responses to, 2–4
    steps to active, 4–11
Reid, Alastair, 358–60
"Remembering Lobo," 93–98
"Restoring Recess," 255–58
Ripley, Amanda, 146–53
Rodriguez, Luis J., 56–60
Rodriguez, Richard, 472–75
"Roles of Manners, The," 275–82
Ropeik, David, 406–10

Sakamoto, Nancy Masterson, 126–31
Saltz, Gail, 250–54
"Santa Rosa Island, 1998" (Journal),
    33–38
Schell, Jonathan, 109–13
"Science and Secrets of Personal
    Space, The," 287–93
Sentences
    punctuating, 226–28
    varying, 170–72
"Sex, Lies, and Advertising," 185–91
Skandar, Alexa, 113–16
Small, Meredith F., 72–76
"Social Science Finds: 'Marriage
    Matters,'" 386–97
Stanton, Elizabeth Cady, 464–67

Staples, Brent, 135–39
Steinem, Gloria, 185–91
"Story of an Hour, The," 467–71
Sullivan, Andrew, 448–51
Summary, 11–15
Suplee, Curt, 287–93
"Surveying the Damage on Campus
    USA," 154–57
Synthesis, 11–15

Tan, Amy, 89–93
"Taxi," 471
Third of May, 1898, The, art insert
Three Dancers, art insert
"Time's Trophy," 113–16
"To Be or Not to Be as Defined by
    TV," 177–85
Transitions, 123–25
'Try National ID Card—You Might
    Like It," 454–57

Vachss, Andrew, 347–52
Van Gogh, Vincent, art insert
"Violent Femmes," 191–99
Viorst, Judith, 139–46
Vonnegut, Kurt, 28–33

Wagner, Gaye, 60–68
Waite, Linda J., 386–97
"Watcher at the Gates, The," 18–22
"Ways We Lie, The," 293–303
"What Adolescents Miss When We
    Let Them Grow Up in
    Cyberspace," 135–39
"What Really Scares Us?" 406–10
"When Parents Are Toxic to
    Children," 380–85
White, E. B., 131–35
Whitehead, Ralph, Jr., 303–10
"Who Says a Woman Can't Be
    Einstein?" 146–53
"Why Guns Matter," 427–30
Wilbur, Richard, 16–17
"Writer, The," 16–17
Writing
    preparing manuscript, 44–45
    reasons for, 1–2

Zimring, Franklin E., 282–86